F.V.

**St. Louis Community
College**

Forest Park
Florissant Valley
Meramec

Instructional Resources
St. Louis, Missouri

Sociology

Sociology

Issues and Debates

Edited by
Steve Taylor

palgrave

First published 1999 by Macmillan Press Ltd

Published 2000 by
PALGRAVE
Houndmills, Basingstoke, Hampshire RG21 6XS and
175 Fifth Avenue, New York, N. Y. 10010
Companies and representatives throughout the world

PALGRAVE is the new global academic imprint of
St. Martin's Press LLC Scholarly and Reference Division and
Palgrave Publishers Ltd (formerly Macmillan Press Ltd).

Outside North America
ISBN 0–333–67619–X hardback
ISBN 0–333–67620–3 paperback

In North America
ISBN 0–312–23499–6 hardback

This book is printed on paper suitable for recycling and
made from fully managed and sustained forest sources.

A catalogue record for this book is available
from the British Library.

Library of Congress Cataloging-in-Publication Data
Sociology : issues and debates / edited by Steve Taylor.
      p. cm.
    Includes bibliographical references and index.
    ISBN 0–312–23499–6
     1. Sociology. I. Taylor, Steve (Steve D.)

    HM585 .S63 2000
    301—dc21

                                                      00–035256

10   9   8   7   6   5   4   3
09   08   07   06   05   04   03   02   01   00

Editing and origination by
Aardvark Editorial, Mendham, Suffolk

Printed in Great Britain by
Creative Print and Design (Wales), Ebbw Vale

Contents

List of Tables

List of Figures

Notes on Contributors

Robert Burgess is Vice-Chancellor of the University of Leicester and was formerly Pro-Vice-Chancellor, Director of CEDAR and Professor of Sociology at the University of Warwick. He has published widely on social research methodology and the sociology of education. His latest volume is entitled *Beyond the First Degree: Graduate Education, Lifelong Learning and Careers* (1997).

Rosemary Crompton is Professor of Sociology at City University, London. She has previously taught at the Universities of Leicester, Kent and East Anglia. She has researched widely in the sociology of work and women's employment. Her most recent books are *Women and Work in Modern Britain* (Oxford University Press), *Class and Stratification* (Polity Press) and *Restructuring Gender Relations and Employment* (Oxford University Press).

Grace Davie is Senior Lecturer in Sociology at the University of Exeter. She is author of *Religion in Britain Since 1945* (Blackwell, 1994) and is preparing a book on religion in modern Europe for Oxford University Press. She has written numerous articles on the sociology of religion. From 1994 to 1998 she was General Secretary of the International Society for the Study of Religion.

David Downes is Professor of Social Administration and Director of the Mannheim Centre for Criminology and Criminal Justice at the London School of Economics. His books include *The Delinquent Solution* (1966), *Understanding Deviance* (with Paul Rock, 1998) and *Contrasts in Tolerance: Postwar Penal Policy in the Netherlands and England and Wales* (1993). He was Editor of the *British Journal of Criminology* from 1985 to 1990.

Natalie Fenton is Lecturer in Communication and Media Studies and Women's Studies in the Department of Social Sciences at Loughborough University. Her books include *Nuclear Reactions* (with J. Corner and K. Richardson) and *Mediating Social Science* (with D. Deacon and A. Bryman). Her current research interests are the media and resistance, the voluntary sector and the media, alternative media and the popular presentation of public issues.

Christine Helliwell has taught both sociology and anthropology at several universities and is Senior Lecturer in Anthropology at the Australian National University in Canberra. She has carried out extensive ethnographic research in New Zealand and Borneo. Her primary research interests lie in social and cultural theory. Many of her publications are concerned with the difficulty of applying western analytic categories to the study of non-western societies. She is currently writing a book on the concept of culture.

Barry Hindess has worked in sociology and political science departments in universities in Great Britain and Australia. He is Professor of Political Science in the Research School of Social Sciences at the Australian National University in Canberra. He has published widely in the areas of social and political theory. His most recent books are *Discourses of Power: From Hobbes to Foucault* (Blackwell, 1996) and *Governing Australia: Studies in Contemporary Rationalities of Government* (edited with M. Dean, Cambridge University Press, 1998). He is writing a book on democracy.

Stevi Jackson is Professor of Women's Studies and Director of the Centre for Women's Studies at the University of York. She is the author of *Childhood and Sexuality* (Blackwell, 1982) and *Christine Delphy* (Sage, 1996). She has co-edited *Women's Studies: A Reader* (Harvester Wheatsheaf, 1993), *The Politics of Domestic Consumption: Critical Readings* (Prentice Hall/Harvester Wheatsheaf, 1995) and *Feminism and Sexuality* (Edinburgh University Press, 1996). She has also published a number of articles on romance, sexuality and family relationships and is currently researching the impact of risk and adult risk anxiety on the everyday world of children. Forthcoming books include *Concerning Heterosexuality* (Sage) and *Contemporary Feminist Theories* (Edinburgh University Press).

Mary Maynard is Professor in the Department of Social Policy and the Centre for Women's Studies at the University of York. Her work focuses on issues related to gender, 'race' and ethnicity, ageing, feminist and social theory, and feminist and social research methodology. Her most recent book is *Science and the Construction of Women* (University College London Press, 1997). She is finishing a book on feminist social research and initiating projects on women and ageing.

Robert Miles is Professor and Head of the Department of Sociology at the University of Glasgow. He has written widely on the theory and history of racism, on international migration and on the history of capitalist development. His recent publications include *Racism after 'Race Relations'* (Routledge, 1993) and (edited with D. Thranhardt) *Migration and European Integration* (Pinter, 1995).

Glenn Morgan is Senior Lecturer in Organizational Analysis at Warwick Business School, the University of Warwick. Previously, he worked at Manchester Business School. He has published a number of books and articles in the sphere of work and organizations, including *Organizations in Society* (Macmillan, 1990) and *Regulation and Deregulation in European Financial Services* (edited with D. Knights, Macmillan, 1997). His current research interests are primarily concerned with the impact of national and regional social institutions on organizational structures and strategies in an era of globalization.

Andrew Parker is Lecturer in Sociology/CEDAR at the University of Warwick. He was previously a Senior Lecturer in the School of Behavioural Studies at Nene University College, Northampton. He has written about the construction of masculinity in various educational and sporting locales.

Ray Pawson is a Reader in the School of Sociology and Social Policy at the University of Leeds. His main interest is research methodology and he has published widely on the principles and practice of research, covering methods – qualitative and quantitative, pure and applied, contemporaneous and historical. He is author of *A Measure for Measures: A Manifesto for Empirical Sociology* (Routledge, 1989) and (with N. Tilley) *Realistic Evaluation* (Sage, 1997). He is currently president of the Committee on Logic and Methodology of the International Sociological Association. He has recently served much time in prison (for research purposes), being the UK director of the International Forum on the Study of Education in Penal Systems.

Leslie Sklair is Reader in Sociology at the London School of Economics. He is on the Editorial Advisory Boards of the *Review of International Political Economy* and *Chinese Social Sciences Quarterly* and has served as a consultant to several United Nations bodies.

He has lectured at universities and at conferences all over the world. His publications include *Sociology of the Global System* (1995, translated into Portuguese, Japanese and Persian), *Assembling for Development: The Maquila Industry in Mexico and the United States* (1993) and he edited *Capitalism and Development* (1994). His paper, 'The transnational capitalist class and global capitalism: the case of the tobacco industry' appears in the journal *Political Power and Social Theory* (1998).

Stephen Small is Assistant Professor in the Department of African American Studies at the University of California, Berkeley. He is writing a book – *Black People of Mixed Origins in Jamaica and Georgia During Slavery: A Structural Analysis* – that entails an analysis of material inequalities, institutional practice and ideological articulations of 'race mixture'. His most recent book is *Racialised Barriers: The Black Experience in the United States and England in the 1980s* (Routledge, 1994).

Alan Swingewood is Senior Lecturer in Sociology at the London School of Economics. His main interests are sociological theory and the sociology of literature and culture. He has published widely in these areas and his books include *A Short History of Sociological Thought* (Macmillan, 1994) and *Cultural Theory and the Problem of Modernity* (Macmillan, 1998). His current research is a sociological and historical analysis of modern English culture focusing on music and modernist fiction.

Steve Taylor teaches medical sociology part time at the London School of Economics and Coventry University. He has undertaken research on suicide and self-harm, child care and medical law and his books include *Durkheim and the Study of Suicide* (Macmillan, 1982), *Suicide* (Longman, 1988), *Sociology of Health and Health Care* with D. Field (Blackwell, 1997) and *Sociological Perspectives on Health, Illness and Health Care*, edited with D. Field (Blackwell, 1998). He is a qualified lawyer and his current research is on the socio-legal aspects of changing attitudes to death. He is also the author of three sociology videos, the latest of which is on postmodernity.

Preface

The motivation for this book came a few years ago when, having taken on the first year sociology course at the LSE, I was wading through the available introductory sociology textbooks. I found there wasn't one I could recommend with any enthusiasm. Too many corners had been cut, too many tired old ideas recirculated and too many new ones omitted. Instead of being immersed in their topics, the writers often gave the impression that they were peering rather vaguely at them from a distance. In my view this was not the fault of the authors; indeed, it seemed to me most of them had done a pretty good job in the circumstances. It was just that 'the circumstances' seemed insurmountable. Sociology has become such a massive and diverse enterprise that the task of mastering the range of material now available is simply beyond a single author, or even a small team of authors.

Sociology: Issues and Debates is based on the very different idea of producing a *general* sociology text that makes use of *specialist* knowledge by having each chapter written by authors with established records of writing and research in the area. However, the contributors were chosen not only for their specific expertise, but also for their ability to write in a clear and accessible way and every effort has been made in this book to keep complex sociological terminology to a minimum. Terms of central importance, such as methodology, theory and the various dimensions of power, are all explained in the relevant chapters and a glossary of other key concepts is provided at the back of the book.

To try to ensure consistency, each chapter is structured around the origins, key ideas, development and current concerns of sociological work in the areas that have been examined. However, in a book with so many contributors, it is inevitable that there are some variations in style and emphasis. In my view, these variations are less a reflection of individual preferences and idiosyncrasies than of the different ways in which the specialist areas of sociology have developed. Two key differences can be identified in this context. First, while some areas in sociology have been driven primarily by theoretical developments, others, such as the sociology of health and medicine, are predominantly empirically orientated. Second, while some areas of research seem to be characterized by a sense of uncertainty, as if sociologists working within them recognize they are trying to construct a jigsaw puzzle where most of the pieces are missing, in other areas most sociologists do not seem greatly troubled by any sense of doubt, the picture is clear and sociology is about helping to right the wrongs it clearly reveals. My own position on this latter issue, for what it is worth, is that sociology sometimes has to be a little more robust in its assertion and defence of its capacity to provide specialist knowledge of human societies. However, at the same time, the exercise of justifying our claims to special knowledge lead us to recognize that the limitations of sociological theories and methods simply do not allow us to be *that* certain about anything. However, this book is not about my views, it is about how the key areas of sociology are seen by those with expert knowledge of them.

I would like to express my gratitude to all the contributors not only for their excellent work but also for their patience and co-operation with my various editorial requests. I should also like to thank Alf Barrett, David Field, Rosie Gosling, Tony Lawson, Andrew Pilkington, Jo Roberts, Keith Sharp and Nick Tilley for their help with various chapters; thanks also to Sue Taylor for her editorial help with all the chapters and, finally, to Catherine Gray of Macmillan for helpful and perceptive advice throughout this project.

STEVE TAYLOR

1

Introduction

Steve Taylor

Sociology is the most ambitious of all the social sciences. It is concerned with all that happens to people in terms of their relations with each other and the scope of its inquiries can range from things such as the mass movement of populations over centuries to two commuters catching each other's eye on the morning train to work. The key idea of sociology is that the lives of individuals cannot be understood apart from the social contexts in which they live. This chapter aims to introduce readers to the idea of 'sociological thinking', illustrate the importance of theory for all sociological research and outline the key areas of applied sociological research around which this book is organized. It should help you understand:

■ The key questions sociologists ask about human societies

■ Why all social research is theory dependent

■ What the central areas of applied sociological research are

■ The relationship of sociology to modernity

CONCEPTS

social order ▓ socialization ▓ objective knowledge
theory dependence ▓ social structure ▓ social action ▓ life chances
social institutions ▓ modernity ▓ postmodernism

What is Sociology?

The simplest definition of sociology is that it is the study of human societies. It stresses the *interdependence* of different parts of societies and attempts to go beyond the description of specific events by establishing *generalizations*. For example, we all know that there are hundreds of different occupations but rather than trying to classify them all, some sociologists have argued that groups of people who do much the same type of job and earn roughly the same amounts of money may be generalized as constituting distinct 'social classes'. Sociologists also attempt to be systematic in the ways they study societies. Rather than just snatching at 'facts' which happen to support a particular point of view, they try to collect evidence in a more consistent way. For example, sociologists interested in health and illness could look at rates of illness between different social classes and this may then allow them to make further generalizations about the relationship between health and society.

However, defining sociology as the systematic study of societies does not take us far enough, because there are other academic subjects – anthropology, economics, politics and psychology for example – which also attempt to make systematic generalizations about social behaviour. So, as sociology cannot be defined either in terms of *what* it studies (people living in families, going to work, getting ill and so on) or in terms of *how* it studies them (making generalizations, interpreting statistics, asking questions and so on), how is it distinguishable from the other social sciences? The answer to this is to be found in the *questions* that sociologists ask about social life. Sociology begins by asking how societies are possible. The fact that social life is a problem to be explained rather than a natural condition makes sociology *the* social science. It is first and foremost a particular way of thinking about societies. It involves being curious about the very fact of social order, about how it changes and, above all, about how our lives as individuals are shaped by the societies in which we live. I shall now consider each of these questions in a little more detail.

The Order of Social Life

Walk out into the street and just watch for a few minutes. There is social order all around you – people walking in an orderly way, queuing in line at bus stops, stopping their cars at red lights and so on. This is a taken for granted order and it is likely that the only time most people are aware of it is when someone breaks the rules, for example by moving straight to the front of the queue or not stopping the car at a red light. It seems as if there are sets of rules to social life which most people play by most of the time. Of course, we do not need sociologists to tell us that there are rules to social life. We know ourselves as members of society that we must not drive through red lights and that if we miss sociology classes and do not read the books, we will probably fail the course.

However, if we dig a little deeper we find more evidence of these regularities. For example, in a contemporary society roughly the same number of people are born each year, get married, get divorced, commit crimes or kill themselves. It seems as if there are other, underlying sets of rules by which people are unconsciously playing and which can, literally, affect their lives. For example, in developed societies, year in and year out, the death rates of people from the manual, or working, classes are consistently higher than those of the professional and managerial classes. Similarly, adults with few close social ties to other people have rates of illness which are more than double those with strong social ties.

Sociologists are interested in documenting and trying to explain these regularities of social life. They are interested in the unusual – things like mass suicides in religious cults, bizarre crimes and revolutions – but their starting point is a curiosity about the taken for granted world of order and regularity that is all around us. However, a problem for the sociologist is that, unlike the objects studied by most scientists, societies do not stand still, but are constantly changing.

Social Change and Narrative

Sociology began in nineteenth-century western Europe at a time of unprecedented and rapid social upheaval. There was a mass movement of population from the countryside to towns and cities, as an economic system based predominantly on agricultural production and craft industries gave way to a new industrial-capitalist economic order built around machine technology, organized labour and the systematic pursuit of profit. Localized personal authority, based on inheritance and aristocratic privilege, declined and political power became increasingly centralized in bureaucratic nation states. Culturally, traditional and customary ways of doing things were replaced by rational planning and bureaucratic regulations. Religious institutions increasingly lost power and authority, and religious interpretations of the world gave way to scientific and rational explanations. These changes are generally referred to as the transition from *traditional* to *modern* society.

The fact that societies could be transformed so dramatically and in such a comparatively short space of time led to an increasing curiosity about the nature of social order and social change. The subject that became sociology was born out of this curiosity. Some of the earliest sociologists such as Auguste Comte (1798–1857), who coined the term sociology, and Karl Marx (1818–93) tried to make sense of this new present by *comparing* it with what had come before. They tried to describe the main characteristics of this new industrial order and explain why western societies had developed this way. They also believed there was a purpose to these changes and that history was a progressive movement to 'higher' forms of social order. They were confident that careful application of scientific methods to the study of societies would reveal the sources of this change and that understanding the 'laws of historical progress' gave the power to anticipate and influence the future.

Today, most sociologists are much less optimistic about the societies they study and they talk about them changing rather than progressing. They are also rather less ambitious for sociology. Few believe that societies can be understood in the same way as the natural world; most of them talk about trends rather than laws and few attempt to predict the future. However, in some ways they are still like the early sociologists. They are trying to make sense of the present, but looking only at the present is a bit like coming into a film halfway through. To have any idea of what the film is about, you have to try to work out what has already happened. It is the same for sociologists. They can only make sense of the present by comparing it with what has just ceased to be. Sociology, then, involves a sense of narrative and a sense of history. As the chapters in the book will show, thinking sociologically means developing ideas which help us to understand societies, or aspects of them, as continually changing social processes.

The Individual and Society

Most people assume, and many social scientists argue, that as societies are clearly created by individuals, it is the study of the individual (through psychology and socio-biology for example) that provides the best way to understand societies. For example, in all human societies, most of which developed independently of each other, the fact that women have taken responsibility for things like nurturing the young and caring for the sick, while men have fought wars and run political institutions, could be explained in terms of the differences in 'natural' female and male instincts.

In questioning the idea that social behaviour can be reduced to the study of the individual, sociologists are not, as is sometimes claimed, rejecting the study of the individual in favour of the 'group'. Indeed, a great deal of sociological research involves talking to and observing individuals. It is rather that thinking sociologically involves seeing the relationship between the individual and society as a two-way, rather than a one-way, street. Individuals obviously create societies by their actions but, less obviously, individuals are also created by societies. But how can this happen?

As social life evolves from its most basic forms, certain types of behaviour and belief, such as religious practices or tribal customs, become reproduced by successive generations as 'accepted' ways of doing things. In sociological terms they become *institutionalized*. Language is a good example of a social institution. People learn their language and use it for their own purposes, but none of them created it and it will be there after they have gone. Many key areas in sociology, such as the family, education, work and religion, are defined around the study of distinct social institutions. The values and beliefs surrounding the institutional practices of a society or social group comprise its *culture*. The various ways in which this culture is transmitted to people, which begins from the time they are born and goes on throughout their lives, is called *socialization*. The pressures placed directly and indirectly on people to conform to the values and practices of a society is called *social control*. Of course, as people we are not simply passive recipients of socialization. We have various ways of responding to the expectations social institutions place on us: some may conform willingly, others reluctantly, while some may resist. However, even those who resist and try to behave in a very different way are still confronted by the pressure of social expectations. For example, if I refuse to speak in my native language and insist on speaking in some other way, I am still confronted by the institutional expectation to speak in a certain way. People may refuse, or find it impossible, to communicate with me; I may be refused work or perhaps treated as insane and locked up.

To return to the earlier example of differences in the behaviour of males and females. Sociologists, without necessarily rejecting biological explanations, have shown that there is still a tendency for different expectations to be placed on boys and girls. For example aggressive, boisterous behaviour is more acceptable in boys, while girls are expected to take on more domestic chores and help with younger siblings. Thus, to some extent, boys and girls learn to take on 'masculine' and 'feminine' roles: becoming a man or a woman is not simply a product of biology, it is also a process of socialization. These processes of socialization and social control are not confined to childhood. In Chapter 6 Mary Maynard shows how relations between women and men are structured and shaped by institutional practices, such as the sexual division of domestic labour, the law and the state, which act as sources of social control on women.

So far I have been looking at what sociology is in terms of the questions that sociologists ask about societies. However, to justify investment in sociological research, sociology departments in schools and universities (to say nothing of your investment in this book), sociology has to do rather more than ask interesting questions. It has to come up with a few answers. Furthermore, it has to validate these answers, that is, show that they are something more than opinion or common sense. To begin to understand how sociologists go about doing this and some of the problems they face, we have to know something about theory and method in sociology.

Theory and Method

It sometimes a source of annoyance to those involved in 'real' research that some of the most famous sociologists just write about theory. However, there are good reasons for sociologists' preoccupation with theory. Put simply, theory is unavoidable. First, all research findings are *dependent* on some form of theory. Second, it is only through theories that sociologists can hope to make sense of their data. Although these points are linked, I shall take each in turn.

Supposing I say that I am not interested in all this theorizing and that I just want to get on and do a piece of 'real' research, and uncover 'the facts' about the relationship between social class and illness. However, this ambition is just not tenable, because the very act of doing a piece of research *necessarily* involves making certain unproven – that is, *theoretical* – assumptions about the nature of the social world and how it is to be studied. Why is this so?

Before I can start my research I have to have a definition of social class and, as you will see in Chapter 5, sociologists have some very different ideas about what social class is. Thus I have to select, or construct for myself, what I think is the most appropriate idea of class. This is then a *theoretical* definition. Similarly, although it may seem obvious whether or not person is ill, I have to define what I mean by illness. For example, do I use a *subjective* definition of whether or not people *feel* ill and simply ask them, or do I use some more *objective* definition, such as whether or not a doctor has diagnosed them as ill? If I use the latter do I count all illnesses (in which case having a cold and having cancer would count in the same figure) or do I just count 'serious' illnesses and leave others out? The permutations are endless, but the point is that to do my research, I *have* to use theoretical notions of 'social class' and 'illness'. These ideas will then shape the 'facts' I come up with. Different theoretical ideas may well produce very different 'facts'. Research is thus dependent on theory. Rather than pretend otherwise, as sociologists are sometimes tempted to do when they are putting forward a favoured case, it is important to remember that data are not self-evident 'facts', but reflections of the theoretical ideas in terms of which they are collected. Thus, in assessing a piece of sociological research, it not just a question of what sociologists are telling us, but also a question of *how* they found out, how they can validate what they are telling us. This is where *methodology* comes in. It is the study of how sociologists find out.

In Chapter 2, Ray Pawson identifies the main principles of social research and illustrates some of the different strategies sociologists use to study the social world. Although there is considerable debate between the proponents of these different approaches all of them are confronted with the questions of how their research is validated. For many sociologists the aim of sociological research is to produce *objective* knowledge of societies – that is, knowledge which is free from bias and prejudice. They argue that the best way to achieve this is by following, as far as possible, the methods of the natural sciences, for example, by using clearly defined concepts that produce data that can be measured, compared and checked by other researchers. Other sociologists argue that the theory-dependent nature of research data and the fact that the same piece of data is open to different interpretations, means that sociology has to abandon its quest for objectivity. Sociological accounts are therefore validated not by any claims of scientific truth, but by the rich and authentic data they produce. However, if this view is taken it then becomes difficult to establish whether one account is better than any other. Sociology simply offers different interpretations and this view is called relativism.

In his chapter Pawson argues that for a long time discussion of methodology became trapped into a position of mutual hostility between these two approaches with the assumption that sociologists were obliged to choose one way or the other. However, contemporary thinking on methodology is moving on from this 'war'. For example, developing his position from more recent 'realist' philosophies of science and social science which attempt to reconcile the goal of objectivity with the theory-dependent nature of all data, Pawson argues that the purpose of empirical research is not to test whether a theory is 'true' or not, but rather to identify the competing theories and generate data which help the researcher to choose between them. This point of view means recognizing that, while sociological research can never be proved to be universally 'true', neither can we lapse into a relativism where one account is as good as any other. Research can show that one theory is better than another in given circumstances. Although complete objectivity is impossible in practice, it can still serve as a goal to which good research should aspire.

The second point is that theory is not just essential to the generation of data, it is also crucial to their interpretation and to the direction of further research. Suppose I have done my research on class and health. To try to make sense of this mass of data without theory would be rather like arriving late at night in a foreign city without a map. To pluck a statistic here, an interview extract there without the guidance of some theory would have no more purpose than wandering aimlessly from street to street with no idea where I was, where I had come from, or where I was going.

Of course, sociologists do not wander aimlessly through their data. Their research has a sense of direction and this comes from theory. For example, I might want to see if the relationship between health and class is influenced more by 'material' factors, such as type of housing, or lifestyle choices, such as diet. This would then guide me to construct research that might throw some light on this question. I might also want to relate my specific research on class and health to wider social contexts in which case I need some more general theory of how societies work and change. In short, theoretical ideas guide the research and give it a sense of purpose. They shape how it is structured, how the data are interpreted and how specific research data are related to other aspects of society.

Sociological theories, then, are kinds of 'sociological maps' that help researchers find their way around the mass of data available to them. Of course, just because we have a map does not solve all the problems. It is very easy to get lost! Sociological maps are always incomplete and are sometimes very sketchy. For some sociologists committed to a particular point of view they consist of little more than a single street. There is also the problem that sociologists working in the same area may be using very different maps! To understand where sociologists are taking us we need to know something about the maps they are using. This is where sociological theorists come in. They are the sociological cartographers. They examine the maps, compare them, identify in what ways they are different and where they are similar. They raise questions, such as whether the maps can be made clearer, extended, combined, updated and made relevant to new social developments.

Many of the earliest social theorists like Karl Marx and Emile Durkheim (1858–1917) developed theoretical maps which were rather like street plans of the whole city, looking at how the different parts were linked together. Theories which look at societies as a whole are called *structural* and the focus of research is on *macro-society;* that is, large-scale organizations and widespread social processes such as the distribution of resources within societies. However, Max Weber (1864–1920), another of the classical theorists, took a different approach. He argued that such large-scale maps tell us very little about the day-to-day lives of the people living in these streets. Individuals do not just react to social conditions but consciously act in certain directions. Thus, for Weber, sociological theory should be about what is called *social action*. It has to incorporate understanding of the meanings that individuals give to their action and what motivates them to act in certain ways. From this point of view, social research tends to focus on the *micro-dimensions* of social life, that is, detailed study of small-scale social processes.

The linking of macro- and micro-social processes is a major problem in sociology and it is the focal point of Alan Swingewood's chapter (3). He begins with the work of the classical sociologists and then examines the contribution of the major perspectives of 'modern' social theory, functionalism and interactionism. Structural functionalist theory, which tries to combine Durkheim's notion of structure with Weber's idea of action, starts with the idea of societies as systems into which individuals are socialized. Interactionism, in contrast, begins with the problem of how individuals make sense of the situations in which they find themselves and focuses on the importance of language in linking the micro with the macro. The final part of Swingewood's chapter looks at some of the more recent attempts in social theory to synthesize the macro- and micro-aspects of society, including those of three of the most famous theorists in contemporary sociology: Habermas, Giddens and Bourdieu.

Power is another central issue for sociological theory as the relations between individuals and institutions studied by sociologists necessarily involve questions of authority, control and actual (and potential) conflicts of interest. But what do sociologists mean by power and how is it used in sociological analysis? These questions are addressed in Chapter 4 by Christine Helliwell and Barry Hindess. They identify the three meanings of power most commonly used in sociology. The first of these is power as 'control or command over others', a capacity to get people to do what you want even if they do not want to. From this point of view, sociologists have been interested in identifying which social groups have power (and which do not) and the social conditions under which it is produced. For example, the famous American sociologist C. Wright Mills (1916–62) argued that political power in America was concentrated in a comparatively small 'élite', whose power stemmed from their control of the major institutions of industry, government and military.

The second meaning of power considered by Helliwell and Hindess is the legal ability or authority to act; for example, the legal right of governments to pass laws and collect taxes. While some sociologists, such as Weber, have merely concerned themselves with how legitimacy is established, most of them have taken a more *critical* stance and questioned whether or not such legitimacy is justified. For example, Mills argued that what he called the American 'power élite' were more concerned with their own interests rather than those of the majority of the population and, as they often used secret and 'undemocratic' means to pursue these ends, their authority was not legitimate as the people were not in a position to give true consent. However, as Helliwell and Hindess observe, the lack of any clear criteria for deciding whether or not true consent has been given, leads to sociologists passing judgement on the basis of their own preferences and commitments.

The third much more general meaning of power identified by Helliwell and Hindess is simply the ability to do or affect anything. From this point of view, power is not a 'resource' which some groups have more or less of, but simply an inevitable feature of everyday life. Contemporary social theory has become increasingly influenced by the development of this view in the work of the French social theorist, Michel Foucault (1926–84). Foucault's approach directs attention away from measuring power and debating its legitimacy towards trying to understand its effects. For example, Foucault and those influenced by him have shown how in modern societies government does not only come directly from the state (through laws and so on) but also indirectly from institutions such as education and medicine that also help to regulate citizens' conduct. For followers, the advantages of Foucault's approach is that sociology does not become trapped in intractable debates about who does or does not have power and whether or not it is legitimate.

Just as there can be no sociological research without theory, there is little point in developing theory for theory's sake in sociology. Theoretical ideas are only relevant to the extent that they inform research. Ideas have to be put into action to illuminate aspects of social life. The following section outlines the main areas of applied sociological research around which this book is organized.

Key Areas of Sociological Research

Social Divisions

Most sociologists are not concerned simply with how societies work and change, they are also interested in how they might be improved. A long-standing concern in this context has been with questions of various forms of social inequality. For many sociologists, the obvious inequalities of wealth, opportunity and status we see all around us are neither inevitable nor merely the result of differences of individual talent and effort. Rather, they are the consequence of institutional arrangements in societies that give rise to systematic differences in the 'life chances' of different social groups. From this point of view societies are not characterized by a consensus of common interests, but by conflicts of interest (acknowledged or not) between different social groups.

Of the classical sociologists, Marx was the most strident advocate of a conflict view. He argued that all societies were divided into a ruling class and subordinate classes. The ruling class owed its dominance to its ownership and control of the means of producing economic wealth. Modern industrial societies were dominated by the capitalist class which owned the factories and financial institutions. However, Marx did not see this inequality as permanent. He argued that class conflict in modern societies would lead to a new type of 'classless' socialist society, where the means of production would be collectively owned. Marx's predictions have not been realized, but the idea of social class – that is, a group of people sharing a similar economic position – continues to be seen by many sociologists as one of the most important, if not the most important, division in contemporary societies.

In Chapter 5 Rosemary Crompton begins by looking at the origins of the concept of social class in the classical sociology of Marx and Weber. She then looks at some of the key issues in the contemporary study of social class; the techniques of and problems involved in measuring class, the impact of recent social changes on class formation and the question of whether or not it still makes sense to talk of social classes in an increasingly fluid and individualized social world.

While the study of class has a long history, the sociological study of gender and gender relations is comparatively recent. As Mary Maynard observes in Chapter 6, there was little systematic study of gender and women prior to 1970. Maynard begins by illustrating how increased interest in gender has not only opened many new areas of study pertaining to women's experiences, but also led to new feminist ways of thinking sociologically. She then looks at the sexual division of labour in households, sexuality and violence and the law and state as examples of institutional arrangements which have functioned to reinforce existing patterns of gender relations and, in particular, the subordination of women to men. However, as Maynard notes, conventional ideas of gender and gender relations (like class relations) have recently been subjected to some critical scrutiny. In an increasingly diverse and rapidly changing world, it is becoming more difficult to conceptualize women and men as clearly identifiable social groups and some recent research has been concerned not simply with differences *between* women and men, but also with differences *within* these categories.

A third area of social division studied by sociologists focuses on 'racial' and ethnic inequalities. The word 'race' is invariably placed in quotation marks because it occupies an apparently paradoxical position in social research. While most sociologists (and scientists) reject the idea of naturally occurring 'racial' groups with fixed biological and mental attributes, they remain interested in the ways in which *ideas* of 'race' and 'race relations' contribute to discrimination and inequalities in societies.

Robert Miles and Stephen Small begin Chapter 7 with discussion of this problem, arguing that sociological explanations of 'racial' and ethnic inequalities have to be focused on economic, political and institutional processes that operate to create and sustain them. In this context, they put forward the key concept of *racialization*, which refers to processes whereby certain groups come to be *thought of* as constituting distinct biological races. Processes of racialization are independent of any specific physical attributes, such as skin colour. While in contemporary European societies most people are familiar with the racialization of diverse ethnic groups from Africa, the Caribbean and Asia, there have been many instances of the racialization of Europeans by other Europeans. For example, the Irish have been racialized by the British and the racialization of the Jews in Germany was a prelude to their mass slaughter by the Nazis. In the second part of the chapter Miles and Small compare the idea of racialization with more traditional sociological approaches based on the centrality of race, while the final section looks at patterns of racialized inequality in Britain.

Social Institutions

In spite of the rapidly changing nature of contemporary societies, most people living in them still grow up in families, spend many years in full-time education and the majority go to work in organizations of one sort or another. Sociologists have had a longstanding interest in the key social institutions of family, education and work; in particular, how they change, their relationship to each other and to other institutional processes, and how their organization and structure affects individuals' lives.

Traditionally, the sociology of 'the family' was primarily concerned with the relationship between different types of family life and wider society; for example, the changes to the family brought about by industrialization.

Sociologists tended to assume that experiences of family life were by and large positive and that problems were brought about by 'external' factors, such as poverty or war. However, as Stevi Jackson observes in Chapter 8, more recent research has tended to undermine these old sociological certainties about the family. First, the increasing instability and diversity of patterns of domestic life has led some sociologists to question whether it still makes any sociological sense to talk about the family. Second, many sociologists – and feminist sociologists in particular – have become increasingly sceptical about family life, arguing that families *themselves* can both reflect and reinforce patterns of inequality between women and men and adults and children.

Jackson argues that in spite of their increasing diversity, there remain regularities of family life which generate systematic economic and emotional inequalities between women and men; not only do women on average contribute more labour than men to the running of families, they also put in more emotional labour to child care and to the marriage itself. The chapter concludes by looking at relationships between adults and children and some of the current issues facing the sociology of the family.

Most of the early sociological work on education, like that on the family, was concerned with the macro-issue of the relationship of educational institutions (mainly schools) to wider institutional processes. For example, Durkheim argued that schools had an integrative function; first, by helping to socialize children into social values and second, by providing them with the opportunity to develop their skills and talents. An alternative macro-approach, developed more from Marxist ideas, argued that rather than creating equality of opportunity, education systems served to reproduce existing divisions of class and status. The extent to which education does, or does not, provide some form of equality of opportunity has been a recurring theme in educational studies and Robert Burgess and Andrew Parker begin Chapter 9 by looking at the evidence from Britain on education, social class and social mobility.

The second part of the chapter looks at sociological research within schools. From the 1960s there was a shift in emphasis in the sociology of education. Instead of just asking how schools fitted into society, sociologists became increasingly interested in finding out how teachers and pupils fitted into the school. There are obvious similarities here with the work of those sociologists who were trying to find out what was going on inside families. However, as family life is more or less impossible to observe directly, sociologists were largely dependent on what they were told second hand in interviews. Educational sociologists, in contrast, had the methodological advantage of being able to go into schools to observe what was going on for themselves. As Burgess and Parker observe, while questions of inequality (of gender and ethnicity as well as class) remained important, other issues general to education, such as the ways in which teachers established rules and how they were negotiated by teachers and pupils, were highlighted. The final part of the chapter examines educational policy and, in particular, the effects of reorientating education to the demands of an increasingly market-driven economy and the effects of greater accountability on teachers' working lives.

The study of work and organizations occupied a central place in the work of many of the classical sociologists who, as I observed earlier, were trying to make sense of the changes brought about in the nineteenth century by a transition from an agricultural to an industrial order. In the contemporary world, with new technologies and the development of a world economy bringing about another fundamental social transition, the sociology of work and organizations is back in the centre of the sociological stage. Glenn Morgan begins Chapter 10 by examining three key issues raised by classical sociologists' analysis of work and organizations in modern societies: an increasingly specialized division of labour, the emergence of new forms of power and inequality and the capacity of the free market to transform existing patterns of social order. The second part of the chapter looks at the development of these processes in the era of mass industrial production in developed societies, known as 'Fordism'. The following section looks at the disruption of this order since the 1970s with a new series of changes in work and organizations brought about by new forms of technology and the establishment of global markets. The chapter concludes by outlining a new economic sociology needed to make sense of these changes and their impact on people's daily lives.

Order, Deviance and Sickness

As I observed in the first section, in any society, or social situation, there are necessarily expectations as to how people should behave. Sociologists use the term *deviance* to describe behaviour which departs significantly from these expectations. Although criminal, delinquent and other forms of deviance are, by definition, breaking the rules of a society, they are not random acts but – like all forms of social action – have their own 'rules' and regularities which make them open to sociological explanation.

David Downes begins Chapter 11 by outlining some of these regularities, such as the fact that, in spite of the increasing prosperity of developed societies, crime rates continue to increase, some social groups consistently commit more crime than others and severity of punishment has little influence on crime. The second part of the chapter examines the four major theoretical explanations of crime: strain theories focus on social integration, interactionist theories are more concerned with the societal reaction to crime and its effects, radical theories relate crime to the political economy of capitalism and control theory, more pragmatically, focuses on the significance of various controls against deviance. The chapter concludes by outlining some of the current issues in the area.

The sociological study of health and illness has much in common with the study of deviance and some of its key ideas, such as labelling, illness and identity and illness career were adapted from the interactionist approach to deviance. Chapter 12 is structured around three distinct lines of sociological inquiry, each of which questions the dominant biological approach to health. First, sociologists have demonstrated that diseases have social as well as biological origins by documenting the relationship between health and social variables, such as class and integration. Second, sociological research has shown that becoming ill or disabled involves a series of social as well as biological changes, as people's experiences of illness are shaped by the reactions of others. Third, sociologists have explored the extent to which ideas about illnesses and their treatment are shaped by social and cultural influences.

A key distinction between crime and illness has long been that the former is intentional and usually results in punishment, while the latter is unintentional and results in treatment. However, in contemporary societies these boundaries are starting to become blurred. There are some doctors who now insist that many violent criminals should not be punished but treated, as they suffer from a genetic predisposition to violence, while other doctors are refusing some people treatment for their illness on the grounds that they are responsible for their condition by, for example, poor diet or smoking.

Culture and Globalization

Sociologists use the term *culture* to describe the beliefs, customs and way of life of a society or social group. Culture provides systems of meaning which people draw on to make sense of the world and for most of human history this has been provided by organized religion. But what exactly is religion and what part does it play in contemporary societies? These are the questions tackled by Grace Davie in Chapter 13. She begins by distinguishing between contrasting sociological definitions of religion which give rise to different questions. *Substantive* definitions focus on what religion is, while *functional* definitions focus on what it does. The second part of the chapter outlines the development of the sociology of religion from its classical origins, while the third section examines some of the major themes in the contemporary study of religion, such as the debate about whether or not organized religion is losing its influence, the rise of new religious movements and emergence of religious fundamentalism. The chapter concludes with a brief section on current dilemmas in the sociology of religion.

In the modern world cultural ideas are increasingly transmitted by the mass media, that is, means of communication such as radio, film and TV which reach mass audiences. Sociologists have very different interpretations of the role of the media. Some are pessimistic, arguing that the mass media are mechanisms by which the ideas and interests of the dominant groups are spread throughout societies. However, others are more optimistic, arguing that the media give people more access to information and help to promote social integration. However, as Natalie Fenton observes in Chapter 14, students of the media all believe that, in one way or another, the media have implications for freedom and control which are crucial to sociology's quest to understand societies.

Fenton begins by looking at the questions raised by the study of the mass media, especially the question of whether the media reflect or create cultural ideas. The second part of the chapter examines the sociology of media production, which covers both ownership and control and professional practices. The next two sections examine some of the ways in which sociologists study media content and how it is received by audiences; for example, are audiences relatively powerless or powerful consumers? The final section outlines some contemporary issues in media research, the most significant of which is the role of mass communications in helping to create a global culture in which western ideas, such as the ideology of consumerism, have spread across the world often supplementing, or replacing, local cultures. Some sociologists argue that the population of the world is now becoming bonded into a single, global society and new sociological ideas are required to understand it. The theme of globalization is the topic of the final chapter.

While most pieces of sociological research are restricted to one society, or comparisons between different societies, global theorists focus on processes – such as the activities of transnational corporations – which transcend national boundaries. So how have sociologists tried to explain these processes and what issues do they study? Leslie Sklair addresses these issues in Chapter 15. He begins by identifying four main theoretical approaches to globalization: world systems, global culture, world society and global capitalism models. He then examines some of the most important concrete issues studied by global theorists, such as environmental change, gender relations, global urbanization and the links between global and regional processes. The chapter then explores the relationship between globalization and everyday life, and some of the ways it has been resisted by new social movements. Although there is, as yet, no unified global theory and some sociologists remain sceptical of the idea, as Sklair observes, issues of globalization are now very much on the sociological agenda.

Modernity and Postmodernity

As I observed earlier, sociology emerged as an attempt to make sense of the transition from a 'traditional' to a 'modern' social order. However, this process of modernization was more than a series of economic and structural changes. It was also characterized by the consolidation of a distinctly modern way of thinking, the most important aspect of which was the replacement of faith in

God and divine Providence by a new faith in the power of human *reason* (manifested most clearly in the achievements of science) not only to understand how the world works but to improve it for the greater good of humanity. Sociology was a product of this modern way of thinking and it remains fundamentally 'modernist' today with the continuing ambition of most sociologists to explain how aspects of societies work and change in the hope of contributing, in some way or other, to their improvement.

However, in the last two decades in particular, there has been a mounting challenge – or, more precisely, series of challenges – to this 'modernist' way of thinking by a diverse group of writers loosely labelled 'postmodernists'. Postmodern ideas began in the arts and architecture, spread to the study of popular culture and were developed most fully in philosophy, but they are now becoming increasingly influential in the social sciences, particularly in sociology. Postmodernists argue first, that we are in another period of intense social change in which modernity is dissolving and being replaced by a new form of *post*-modern social order. Second, they reject the 'modernist' idea that it is possible (even in principle) to obtain some form of objective understanding of this world, which could then be used (in theory) for the betterment of the human condition.

A great deal of postmodern theory in sociology (and popular culture) is an attempt to come to terms with some of the effects of living in a media-saturated society. Postmodernists argue, contrary to some sociological theories, that a result of the 'information explosion' of the last two or three decades has been to offer people more choice and greater possibility of changing their lives. The postmodern condition has been described as a time of incessant choosing, where many established conventions and old certainties are called into question.

A consequence of this, postmodernists argue, is that the institutional orders sociologists call societies, or social structures, have become increasingly diverse and the 'divisions' between different social groups, such as class, gender and ethnic groupings, have fragmented. Thus the *generalizations* sociologists typically make about the relationship between social institutions and individual behaviour and the *comparisons* they make between different social groups have become increasingly difficult to sustain.

A second issue concerns the ideas sociologists use to try to understand this changing world. The discussion of methodology showed that sociologists differ about the best ways of trying to produce valid sociological knowledge. However, postmodernists would not be interested in such a debate because they reject what they see as the 'modernist' idea of valid social knowledge. They argue that in a fluid, fragmented social world, where even apparently hard scientific truths are called into question, there are no longer any clear criteria for determining whether one theory, or one piece of research, is any better than any other. For postmodernists, theories are evaluated not in terms of some abstract idea of 'truth', but simply in terms of their utility; how useful or helpful people find them. Postmodernists argue that sociologists have to recognize the diversity of the social world and develop their ideas accordingly. They are particularly critical of general sociological theories, such as Marxism and some feminisms, which they describe as grand narratives (big stories). What is called research in these theories is simply selectively accumulated data aimed only at convincing people of the 'truth' of the story.

Most sociologists are sceptical and even hostile to postmodernist ideas. First, critics have highlighted the inconsistencies in the postmodern position. They point out that, by suggesting that there has been a transition from one era to another and bringing in evidence to support their claims, postmodernists are exhibiting some strongly modernist tendencies.

Second, sociologists argue that postmodernist claims of a transition to a new social order are exaggerated as so many features of modernity – such as a tightly organized division of labour, rational calculation and the continuing dominance of science and technology – remain intact.

Nonetheless, postmodern theory should not be dismissed from the sociological agenda. It has made valuable contributions to the study of culture and media in particular and, by drawing attention to the increasingly diverse nature of contemporary societies, it has raised important questions for sociology and forced a re-examination of some key ideas. The chapters on methodology, theory, class, gender, education and media in this book, for example, all contain discussion of the postmodern point of view. Postmodern ideas also serve as a useful corrective for those sociologists, or schools of sociological thought, which tend to be intolerant of their key ideas being questioned. Postmodernism reminds us that there is no one right way of thinking about human societies. The diverse nature of social life and the precarious authority of sociological knowledge mean that sociologists can never be certain about any aspect of social life. If research discussed here, or in any other sociology book you read, seems to be preaching at you, giving you one point of view, then it is important to question it yourself and ask what other explanations are possible. Sociology offers interpretations of the world, not uncontested truths.

Further Reading

Bauman, Z. *Thinking Sociologically,* Oxford, Blackwell, 1990. A readable collection of essays from a leading sociologist using everyday examples to illustrate what it means to think sociologically.

Bourdieu, P. *Sociology in Question,* London, Sage, 1993. A collection of interviews, talks and question and answer sessions exploring some central issues in sociology.

Giddens, A. *Sociology: A Brief but Critical Introduction,* 2nd edn, Basingstoke, Macmillan, 1986. An accessible introduction to the origins of sociology and some of its key themes.

Mills, C. *The Sociological Imagination,* London, Penguin, 1959. One of the classic statements of sociology's quest to link the individual and the social.

Resources

Videos

Theory and Method in Sociology, a 45-minute video using case study examples and interview extracts from leading sociologists to explain the relationship between theories
of knowledge and sociological research.
Making Sense of Sociological Theory, a 60-minute video explaining the major theoretical
perspectives in sociology and linking them to case study examples.
Postmodernity, a 45-minute video examining modernity, the suggested transition to
postmodernity and the implications for sociology.
Videos available from Halo Vine Video, PO Box 104, Leicestershire LE10 2WW.

Journals

Sociology Review, a journal aimed at sociology students with articles of key areas of
sociological research, published four times a year.
Available from Philip Allan Publishers, Market Place, Deddington, Oxfordshire OX15
0SE.
S magazine, a quarterly magazine focusing on topical issues of sociological interest.
Available from Updates, PO Box 6, Denbeigh LL16 3WG.

2
Methodology

Ray Pawson

Methodology is the study of how sociological claims to specialized know-ledge of societies are validated. Methodological issues are thus funda-mental to all the areas of sociology covered in this book. The aim of this chapter is to examine and illustrate some of the major technical and theoretical issues involved in gathering and interpreting data. It should help you to understand and illustrate:

■ What is meant by methodology and the importance of epistemo-logical, ontological and technical questions in social research

■ The key strategies of social research and the myth of quantitative versus qualitative research

■ Why there is a discrepancy between the ideal and actual in the process of doing social research

■ The distinction between 'realism' and 'relativism'

CONCEPTS

epistemology ■ ontology ■ paradigms ■ positivism
phenomenology ■ hypothesis testing
interviews: structured and unstructured
realism ■ relativism

Introduction

The purpose of this chapter is to help the beginner reflect upon the justification for sociology's claim to specialist knowledge of human societies. The high ambitions of sociology need to be grounded in real substance. The fine words need to be matched with deeds. Sociologists know best, or at least like to think they do. But what is the basis for sociological knowledge? How do sociologists know that they are correct? How do they respond when challenged with alternative views? This chapter will attempt to chart some answers to these huge, age-old questions.

The great claim for sociological expertise goes by the name of *methodology*. As well as developing specialists in all the substantive areas covered in this book, such as gender relations, work, deviance and so on, sociology has always generated scholars (methodologists) whose task is to inspect and evaluate this research output in an attempt to improve the basic modes of investigation of the discipline. The assertion that sociological research provides an authoritative understanding of the workings of the social world is thus based on claims about the usage of some *special tools of inquiry*.

The Methodological Task: Principles and Practice

We have already achieved a pocket definition of 'methodology' as the 'tools of inquiry of a discipline'. As with any statement of such brevity, this is both helpful and misleading. Thinking about tools and toolboxes may lead one to ponder that carpenters use hammers, dentists use drills, scientists use microscopes and that, by extension, sociological methodology is thus about interviews, questionnaires and such like. This is true enough, but only *part* of the methodological story. We can get to the whole of the story by thinking about the tools of inquiry used in other disciplines like mathematics or philosophy. Mathematicians and philosophers, self-evidently, do research. But there are, self-evidently, no mathematical hammers, no philosophical drills, no algebraic microscopes, no metaphysical questionnaires to be seen. The tools of inquiry in such cases are thus not 'practical' skills but 'thinking' skills. Mathematical and philosophical inquiry are thus governed by the basic laws of number, arithmetic, proof, logic and reasoning. Inquiry, in such instances, is superintended by a set of 'agreed principles'.

Most disciplines, in fact, require a *blend* of thinking skills and practical skills. And thus sociological methodology can be said to have the task of *developing and amalgamating the principles and practice of social research*. A first attempt at describing these basic ingredients is made in Figure 2.1 in which a further important distinction is made. We expand the notion that 'methodology' = 'principles' + 'practice' by subdividing the middle term into two further categories drawn from the philosophical literature, namely 'epistemology' and 'ontology'.

> METHODOLOGY = EPISTEMOLOGY + ONTOLOGY + METHOD
>
> Epistemology = Guiding principles of inquiry
>
> Ontology = Essential nature of the (social) world
>
> Method = Practical techniques of research

Figure 2.1 The basic ingredients of research methodology

Epistemology establishes the guiding principles or rules of inquiry. 'An episte-mology is a theory of knowledge: it presents a view and a justification for what can be regarded as knowledge – what can be known, and what criteria knowledge must satisfy in order to be called knowledge rather than beliefs' (Blaikie, 1993: 7). For instance, of much concern for the epistemologist is the traditional question about whether sociology can be a *science* and thus follow the latter's methods of experimentation and measurement. This, in turn, generates other questions about whether sociology has *laws* in the same way that physics has laws, or whether the *causes* of social action can be understood in the same way as the causes of physical phenomenon. A quite different kind of epistemological question concerns the *subject/object* dilemma. People are the objects of sociological inquiry, but (until proof to contrary is available!) we assume that sociologists are people too. This has led to a debate about whether 'involvement' or 'detachment' is the best vantage point from which to understand the social world. Some epistemologists in the former camp, for instance, argue that to understand properly the 'subjugation of women' or the 'oppression of the working class', it is necessary to be a member of those groups. Others take the view that requiring every researcher to have a 'stand-point' will result in the total fragmentation of knowledge, so that only women will be said to understand women, only the working class will comprehend the working classes, only lesbians will follow lesbians, only Ford workers will fathom Ford workers and so on. No attempt is made to answer such *huge* questions here, my purpose here is simply to introduce the scope of episte-mology by noting the adjective.

Ontology establishes some first principles about the essential nature of the world we are studying. 'Ontology refers to the claims or assumptions... about the nature of social reality – claims about what exists, what it looks like, what units make it up and how these units interact with each other' (Blaikie, 1993: 6). More *huge* questions are on the agenda here. Given the consider-able scope of sociological explanation, there is a variety of claims made about what constitutes the core activities under study. These range from whole soci-eties and cultures and their histories to the actions, biographies, meanings and motivations of individuals. Not only is there debate about the 'stuff' of sociology, there are also ontological questions to be raised about how these basic components 'work'. For example, those favouring structural explanation perceive that human actions are shaped by institutions and ideologies, while those favouring 'human agency' stress the choice and reasoning lying behind our every action (see Chapter 3). The former camp has difficulty explaining why, if action is determined, people have changed history, and the latter has trouble with the fact that the exercise of free will appears to generate a world that is remarkably orderly.

'*Methods* of research are the actual techniques or procedures used to gather and analyse the data related to some research questions or hypothesis' (Blaikie, 1993: 7). There are dozens and dozens of techniques and procedures which make up the sociological toolbox. Some of these methods are extremely well known and used well beyond the sociological domain. Thanks to opinion polling and market research, most members of the general public will have a fair conception of what is involved in an 'interview' or 'question-naire', as well as some clue about what goes on and what can go wrong in 'sampling'. Next, but known more out of fear than familiarity, is the host of 'statistical' and 'computational' methods associated with data analysis. Beyond this there are methods of 'direct observation' and 'document analysis' imported from other disciplines such as social anthropology and history. Reaching still further, we come to the linguistic-based techniques where soci-ologists make detailed analysis of everyday conversations, and the methods of 'content analysis' used in media research (see Chapter 14). This list could go on and on, as can the permutation and combination of procedures, a situa-tion which has led to the analogy being made between research techniques and recipes, and thus the need for rather massive methods 'cookbooks' to demonstrate and teach them all (for example Babbie, 1989).

Clearly, there is much ground to cover in becoming a social researcher. There is a need to master both philosophy *and* craft. Social investigation is always a case of knowing *and* doing. The previous three paragraphs should be regarded as an 'invitation' to the daunting and complex territory of sociolog-ical methodology. Their purpose is simply to establish that, from the outset, researchers must have clear answers to some very basic questions:

- How do I know that my research provides answers which are valid?
- What is the nature of the social reality I have chosen to investigate?
- Why have I selected a particular technique as the best tool for the job?

The Scope of Sociological Research: Chalk and Cheese

Simply put questions like these often generate complex answers, and the first thing that I should make clear is that the methodological jury is still out, struggling to come to terms with these basic issues. There is, and never will be, complete agreement on the epistemological, ontological and technical foundations of the discipline as a whole. What I can report however is much localized progress and the fact that it is possible to distinguish several 'families' of social research which operate with close agreement on the hows, whats and whys of research methodology.

There is, then, a series of identifiable *research strategies* in sociology, each operating with a distinct *set* of interrelated epistemological, ontological and practical foundations. There are many reasons for this diversity of approach, the principal one being the 'life, universe, everything' explanatory ambitions of the discipline. If one is prepared to tackle questions such as 'why did capitalism follow feudalism in world history?' on one hand, and 'what does it feel like to be an assembly-line worker?' on the other, then it is hardly surprising that one formulates quite different strategies to answer them.

I shall return shortly to the pros and cons of having *rival* dynasties of research in the *same* discipline. For the present, I want to accomplish the three tasks of identifying the principal research strategies of sociology, showing how each blends together distinctive bodies of principle and practice, and providing a well-known exemplar of each approach in action. In Figure 2.2 and the paragraphs that follow, I distinguish *four* key families of social research. Let the reader beware – this is a textbook simplification! No one can say definitively whether there are two, three, four, seven, seventeen or 700 'types' of sociological research. The following typology will, therefore, do damage to some researchers' sensibilities about their own specialisms and it will ignore yet further permutations created by investigators who have attempted to combine facets of different approaches. The point, however, is simply to show that sociological researchers are not all the same.

Family I – The Ethnographers

These are also known as 'participant observers', 'field researchers', 'phenemenologists', 'qualitative researchers'. They are, incidentally, probably the biggest family active in empirical sociology in the UK at the present time. The family gets its identity from a crucial *ontological* belief that all social action is intentional. Understanding social behaviour is therefore a matter of deciphering the reasoning that underlies action. Social life revolves around shared meanings which are created in processes of social interaction. These fundamentals place immediate requirements on *method*. In order to understand how people behave, research has to imitate real life and become involved in those interactions which create the everyday meanings. Hence the basic research technique involves participating with the group under study over a length of time, observing and sharing their everyday activities, and asking them to explain their reasoning and choices. Analysis follows these same themes, thus the ethnographic report attempts to explain by reproducing the 'lived experience'

RESEARCH STRATEGY	EPISTEMOLOGY	ONTOLOGY	METHODS
Ethnography *a.k.a.* participant observation and field research	Reality is grounded in the beliefs and interpretations of particular groups. The primary task of social explanation is to 'reproduce' those meanings as accurately as possible.	The social world is a human creation. Social life is constituted in the reasoning and everyday meanings which people create in mundane, routine social interaction.	Methods imitate 'folk' reasoning:- fieldwork, participation, introspection, observation, narrative building, respondent validation and so on.
Survey research including measurement and statistical research	The primary task of social explanation is the discovery of societal regularities. Research is based on distinguishing the key variables and their interrelationship which express the social order.	The social world is ordered. While there is much local and immediate change in attitudes and behaviours, these actions underlie gross regularities and patterned outcomes at the societal level.	Variable analysis methods: sampling, questionnaires, measurement, indicator selection, coding, correlation and multivariate analysis and so on.
Comparative, historical and cross-cultural research	There is a pattern to societal evolution. The primary task of social explanation is to treat each nation as a case and to classify it according to patterns of similarities and differences.	The social world is an historical process. Societies evolve in the way that they do because they already possess configurations of properties which channel potential future possibilities.	Historical records are combed to identify countries with different configurational profiles. Data are created via a secondary analysis of existing historical reportage.
Applied, policy and evaluation research	The primary task of social explanation is to create experimental conditions so that the causes of change can be discerned. Research is thus based on manipulation, control and measurement of planned social change.	The social world is open to change via policies and programmes. Social reality is complex with other factors also producing change, making it difficult to discern whether a programme is the crucial agent of transformation.	Experimental and quasi-experimental designs. Random allocation of subjects to experimental and control groups. Pre- and post-programme measurement.

Figure 2.2 The principal research strategies of sociology

of the particular group. A narrative is produced which contains a series of crucial incidents and typical group behaviour in order to show how these are embedded in a common set of beliefs. The authenticity of the account is checked by such means as 'respondent validation' which involves putting the interpretations of the ethnographer back to the group for further comment and clarification. This devotion to the subject's point of view is further expressed in terms of an *epistemological* principle, known as Thomas' Dictum (1976), which posits that if 'people define situations as real they are real in their consequences'. Since the world is experienced as a reality by those who comprise it, participant observation is done on the basis that it gets closer to *the* lived reality of those being studied.

Example. For over twenty years, Willis' *Learning to Labour* (1977) has been cited as a major contribution to ethnography. The study followed twelve working-class boys in their final year at school. Willis attended their classes and career interviews, participated in their break-time conversations and after-school leisure activities, creating a mass of information by means of group discussions, tape recordings, diaries and self-reports. The study is saluted for its 'feel' of the thoughts, words and deeds of the 'lads'. These are reproduced in passage after passage of dialogue from the fieldwork, which for illustration's sake I boil down to a single utterance from 'Joey': 'I think... laffing is the most important thing in... everything.' To find out what makes Joey 'laff', you will need to go to page 29 of *Learning to Labour* and find his tale of 'coppin' it' in a fight which is told with a degree of realism yet to be achieved in a 1000 episodes of school-based soaps. Willis perceives the 'lads' laugh as a crucial symbol of their counter-school culture which centres on a loathing of 'pen-pushing' teachers and 'ear 'ole' conformist pupils. For Willis, the key aspect of the lads' culture is that it is born out of choice; they know that not everyone can succeed, they know that individual effort will not get them out of the pack, they know they are destined for manual work. Life is made more tolerable if it is laughed at in the face and this becomes their motto to prepare for life on the shopfloor.

Family II – The Surveyors

These are also known as 'quantitative researchers', 'variable analysts', and 'social statisticians' (and, by the unkind, as 'number crunchers'). There are family differences on, for instance, the best time-frame of the survey work and the particular techniques of statistical analysis to be preferred. What holds the dynasty together is the *epistemological* principle that explanation consists of uncovering the statistical 'regularities', 'tendencies', 'patterns', 'orderly outcomes' which constitute social life. For instance, inequalities of social condition (class, race, gender and so on) are common to most societies and remain in place over considerable time. This gives survey research the task of identifying the important regularities, specifying their scope (time and place), and explaining them. The *methods* of survey research consist of a well-rehearsed sequence of steps. The unit of analysis is established, usually at the 'societal' level, giving inquiry the task of establishing regularities which pertain across a whole nation or region or institution. A representative sample of that target population is obtained. Information is sought from them (usually by questionnaire) on a whole array of measures or 'variables'. Data analysis then takes place which seeks to establish regularities and patterns, known as 'correlations' between these variables (social group A does better than group B; the more of C one has, the more likely one is to have D; Es get X while Fs get Y). These patterns are further established by 'multivariate' analysis in which the relative influence of a number of variables (K, L, M, N, and so on) on a particular outcome (O) are deciphered. Theories are developed to explain the social processes which lead to these dominant patterns.

Example. Marshall *et al.*'s *Social Class in Modern Britain* (1988) provides a good example of survey research. Their task was to discover whether social class is still crucial in structuring economic, political and social life. They took a random sample of 1315 adults in the UK and asked questions to determine their social class and their attitudes and behaviour across a wide spectrum of other activities. The authors conclude that the influence of social class has not withered away and their data demonstrate a series of clear correlations between people's class position and how they vote, their housing tenure, their parent's class position, their membership of unions, and their support for a range of policies on such matters as 'taxation', 'wage restraint', 'positive discrimination' and so on. They show the quantitative tradition's concern for rigour in measurement by comparing the rival class definitions of Goldthorpe (1980) and Wright (1985) in order to discover which is better able to predict this range of behaviour (see Chapter 5). One of their particular interests is to engage with arguments suggesting that concerns other than class now lie at the root of political beliefs, as for instance the claim that housing tenure (owner-occupation or renting) is more significant than class position in determining voting patterns. They engage in multivariate analysis which shows that while the upper- and lower-class vote remains stable regardless of housing tenure, the vote of the intermediate classes changes significantly according to whether they own (Tory) or rent (Labour) their home.

Family III – The Comparative Researchers

These are also known as 'cross-cultural researchers' and, since the comparisons often feature very broad time-frames, strategies of 'historical sociology' are also kindred. We face a significant shift in scope here, for *whole nations* are often the unit of analysis and the strategy is aimed at explaining why nations have their particular characteristics (for example why did Britain industrialize early?) The crucial *ontological* principle is revealed in the way such a question is answered in terms of a *configuration* of other characteristics which give rise to the feature in question (for example Britain industrializes early because of technological advance, population pressure, weak aristocracy, emerging middle class, colonial empire to exploit and so on). It is the 'combination', the 'juxtaposition', the 'joining together' of all these other factors which is said to generate the crucial outcome. The big *epistemological* idea is that the crucial explanatory configurations are best uncovered by searching for *similarities and differences* between cases. The nation is thus treated as one of a number of *cases* featuring one outcome (say, early industrialization) and compared with cases with a different outcome (say, late industrialization). The *method* of comparative research is thus to search the historical records of different cases (nations) trying to find what is common in countries which have evolved the key characteristic in question and what differentiates those countries which have experienced an alternative development. The practical work of gathering information on what features are present and absent in each country's historical profile gets done in the form of *secondary analysis* of historical writing and other documents such as public records.

Example. Moore's *Social Origins of Dictatorship and Democracy* (1966) is a classic work of comparative historical sociology and is responsible for establishing much of the thinking behind the last strategy. He sought to explain the development of seven major agrarian states (England, France, the United States, Germany, Japan, China, Russia) and, in particular, why they had travelled along one of three roads – to democracy, fascist dictatorship or communist dictatorship. His answer involves studying each country with respect to the strength of the commercial middle classes in relation to landowners, the modes of agricultural commercialization, the rebellious potential and type of leadership of the peasantry, and the strength of the peasantry in relation to landlords. He argues, on the basis of available historical evidence, that it is the precise configuration of these factors which determines the path that will be followed. Each route contains two or three nations and Moore demonstrates that the nature and combination of these factors is highly similar *within* each pair or triple. For instance, in communist dictatorships (China and Russia), the commercializing tendencies are very weak, there is a rebellious peasant solidarity, and landowners have lacked absolute control over agricultural production. By contrast, substantial differences in these configurations are revealed as he makes comparisons *between* the growth of democratic, communist and fascist states.

Family IV – Evaluation Researchers

These researchers pursue a much more policy-orientated research task and their aim is to examine social programmes (educational schemes, crime-reduction initiatives, health-promotion interventions and so on) in order to see if they 'work'. The basic research strategy can be described as one of 'trial and error'. More formally, we can locate the *epistemological* loyalties in terms of experimental science notions of 'manipulation and control'. A laboratory scientist might apply heat (manipulation) to a metal rod, while keeping every other condition in the laboratory stable (control), and therefore be sure it is the heat which causes expansion. It is much more difficult to establish the link between social programmes and their effects because of the *ontological* reality that the complexity of the social world renders it much more difficult to control. For instance, if we introduce a neighbourhood watch scheme into a locality and find crime goes down, this may have been the result of other, unforeseen and uncontrolled activities, such as a change in police tactics, rather than the activities of the neighbours. This brings us to *method*, the primary task of which is to bring additional control to 'field settings'. The basic idea, as illustrated in Figure 2.3, is to split the recipients of a programme into two groups known as the 'experimental' and 'control' groups. Assignment to these groups is random, ensuring that the two groups are initially 'matched' or 'balanced' in their background characteristics. The programme (X) is then applied to the experimental group but not to the other. Changes are monitored by measuring the behaviour of both groups prior to (O_1) and after (O_2) the programme period. The explanatory logic is thus in place – being identical to begin with the only difference between the groups is the application of the programme, so if there is change, it must be the programme which is responsible.

Example. Because evaluation research is aimed at policy makers rather than an academic audience, there are no 'classics' of evaluation research in the same way as the other paradigms. I thus choose as illustration an example in which the programme may be well known, if not the research. *Sesame Street* played a key part in the US educational policy called 'head-start'. The guiding notion is that there is far more cognitive development going on in our heads between the ages of two and five than at any other interval in the lifespan. Educational disadvantage at this stage will thus prove harder to overcome. One fruit of such thinking was an educational television series, which was very serious about its playful approach to learning. Of particular note was the use of black and Hispanic presenters, a feature designed to attract members of those minority groups who were traditionally disadvantaged at school. Two types of field experiments were carried out – 'kindergarten' and 'at-home' evaluations (Bogatz and Ball, 1971). In the first, nursery classes in a particular area were randomly assigned to groups which were given facilities to view the programmes and those who were not. In the at-home version, households were randomly assigned to conditions in which the experimentees were canvassed, given publicity materials and visited by educational staff. The control groups received none of the material. 'Before and after' testing featured in both versions of the evaluation and took the form of simple reading and reasoning tests repeated at the obvious intervals. The results? As with so many other evaluations, these turned out to be complex and controversial (Pawson and Tilley, 1997). The very first trial with the scheme was pronounced a success, with the 'Sesame Street kids' significantly outperforming the controls in reading and reasoning by the end of the scheme. Successive follow-ups with the original groups, however, showed that these initial gains soon dissipated. Later trials in other localities resulted in smaller differences between experimentees and controls. Other data analysis also suggests that white, middle-class groups gained more advantage from the programmes than did blacks and Hispanics.

	Pre-test	Programme	Post-test
Experimental group	O_1	X	O_2
Control group	O_1		O_2

Figure 2.3   The basic experimental design

Paradigms: Heroes and Villains

I have introduced the diverse strategies of sociological research via the eminently sensible idea that one will need a different investigatory tack according to what it is one is investigating. At one level this is all perfectly satisfactory and straightforward. Most people would recognize this as the sheer commonsense notion of 'horses for courses'. Just as you hire a plumber to fix a leak and an electrician to mend the wiring, it is fairly obvious that the small-scale, unobtrusive, respondent-orientated style of ethnography suits the investigation of tight-knit, local communities, whereas skills in tracking documentary sources, cross-cultural sensitivity and experience in secondary analysis are the requirement for historical and comparative research. Not surprisingly, this idea that different-substantive-fields-of-enquiry-will-fetch-up-different-investigatory-strategies has pride of place in the canons of sociology research and has become known as the *principle of methodological pluralism*.

Alas, a notion which appears so balanced, uncontentious and fair minded, has, in fact, unleashed a torrent of bile, prejudice and polemic into the methodological literature. To understand why this has occurred, we need to go back to the original 'role' of methodology which was raised at the beginning of this discussion. For every social problem, there lurk scores of pundits and dogmatists waiting to express their own opinions and to deliver their own verdicts. Through its methodology, sociology aspires to go beyond spleen venting and axe grinding in order to deliver some expert and authenticated body of knowledge. Hence followed decades of careful and deliberate laying down of the basic principles and practice outlined in the previous section.

But what has been the result of these Herculean labours? Well, we have not seen the development of one unified and coherent set of sociological principles and practices. Neither have we seen a genteel, pluralist democracy in which epistemological chalk gives way gracefully to ontological cheese according to the research topic under study. Rather, according to many observers, the development of sociological methodology is a history of 'rift' and 'schism'. On this view, the research strategies depicted in the preceding section (and the summary in Figure 2.2) are not just 'different methodologies' but 'contradictory paradigms'. The term *paradigm* was introduced into the philosophical literature by Kuhn (1970) and by it, he intends to convey the idea that research gets organized not just through the rational adoption of particular strategies and methodologies, but rather that all the contributory ideas get wrapped up into an overall 'vision' or 'creed' or 'doctrine' about the correct way to do research. Thus methodology, Kuhn points out, can itself become a kind of dogmatism which *includes* by identifying good practice and thereby *excludes* by vilifying alternative approaches as misguided, wrong headed, dim witted and so on.

This rather combative language serves as my introduction to what have become known as *the paradigm wars*. What struck a whole generation of sociologists about the families of ontology-epistemology-method is that they are not only different but they, in fact, involve downright contradiction. Thus much methodological writing from the early 1960s to the early 1990s portrayed two camps of basically opposite persuasion gathering and glaring at each other in mutual hostility. And the name of that 30-year encounter was *Positivism versus Phenomenology*.

> Each of these schools of thought pays homage to a contrasting set of first principles. The positivists believe that social research can be accomplished according to the same set of guidelines which direct natural science inquiry. Consequently, they place their faith in the detached measurement and quantification of the subject's behaviour in carefully sampled and controlled conditions in the belief that social research will uncover a single reality revealing the laws of social order and organization. The phenomenologists are committed to a more humanist vision of the sociological enterprise born principally out of the belief that all social actions are intentional. Accordingly, they place their faith in close, empathetic relationships with their subjects in order to discover the processes of understanding and meaning which underlie social action in the belief that social research produces authentic qualitative descriptions of the multiple social realities which constitute social life. These two traditions are in a state of permanent warfare with positivist research instruments being accused of insensitivity in the face of the richness, mutability and adaptability of human thought and language, and phenomenological method being accused of unbridled subjectivity and thus reducing sociology to 1000 travellers' tales.

The whole of the above paragraph has been placed in a box, not for its wisdom but for its superficiality, and not because it is a methodological maxim but because it is a *methodological myth*. I occupy valuable space here in discussing a myth because *positivism versus phenomenology* and *qualitative versus quantitative* have been the standard formats of many introductory texts on methods. Exaggeration and simplification are inevitable features of all introductory treatments but I think in the case of methodology, this style has had the damaging consequence in that beginners, having sensed a battle, are keen to get on the winning side. Thus, perhaps inadvertently, perhaps surreptitiously, perhaps conspiratorially, a 'victor' has been allowed to emerge in many depictions of the paradigm wars. 'Since the sixties, a story has got about that no good sociologist should get his hands dirty with numbers... a generation of young researchers have been thrown out into a sceptical world with their heads full of the standard critiques of positivism but often empty of ideas about how to match exciting theories with rigorous research designs' (Silverman, 1985).

One purpose of this chapter is thus to insist that no good sociologist should get his or her hands dirty with the paradigm wars. I will make this case in detail in the following sections on data collection and data analysis, where I show that both qualitative and quantitative approaches face *identical* problems and need to adopt *common* solutions. In addition I can cite briefly three further problematics which also demonstrate that the war is over. The first is that so much of the sociological research agenda lies *outside* the 'positivism versus phenomenology' agenda. For instance, if one goes back to the domain of historical sociology and a typical task, for instance, of trying to compare the causes of the Russian and Chinese revolutions, it is not going to be a great deal of help to ponder a period of fieldwork and empathetic understanding, or to hit the research trail looking for samples, variables and correlations. Second is the fact that there exists so much social inquiry which has employed a *combination* of qualitative and quantitative methods – apparently without the researcher suffering signs of schizophrenia (Brannen, 1992). Third is the point that the bitterest methodological disputes are likely to occur, these days, *within* rather than between paradigms with, for instance, ethnographers being less sure whether their efforts end up 'reproducing' or 'constructing' reality. Recall that the original foundation for participant observation was the attempt to get closer to *the* lived reality of those being studied. Nowadays there is a family feud with many ethnographers conceding that there are *multiple* realities and their accounts are but one version among many (Hammersley, 1992). To be sure then, while we have not finished with methodological disputes, there is little more to said about 'that one'.

The Research Process: The Ideal and the Real

Having introduced some of the basic ingredients and strategies of methodology, it is time to press further into the tale and show how all the various parts are welded together into an activity which is known as the 'research process'. What I am describing here is the assembly line of sociological research, the actual process in which the sociological work gets done.

Research, of course, is always inspired by a 'problem'. The puzzles facing sociology, as I have already pointed out, are legion, and their variety is well represented by the issues tackled in the exemplars discussed earlier. It is questions such as these which start the production line of sociological knowledge. The first point of note about this particular assembly line is that it goes back and forth. This is illustrated in Figure 2.4a in which we see directional arrows leading to and fro between the sociologist's ideas (labelled 'theory') and the social behaviour of those under study (labelled 'subject'). In between comes 'method' and it is through method that sociological explanations get developed and refined. The figure illustrates a four-step process of inquiry which can be spelled out in a rather abstract way as follows. Research begins with a theory which is developed in the form of 'hypothesis making' which involves putting forward tentative ideas to solve the problem under study. These hypotheses suggest that particular forms of data on particular issues will shed light on the research problem and so 'data-collection' instruments are devised which extract the vital evidence from the appropriate people and places. There follows a phase of 'data analysis' in which all the material is collected together in order to see if the initial hunches of the researcher are borne out. This inspection of the data provides for 'hypothesis testing' – if the results of the investigation square with the researcher's initial ideas then the theory is said to be 'verified', and if these first hunches turn out to be wrong the theory is 'falsified'. There is little chance that the sociologist's initial stab at explanation will be correct first time and in all respects, and so the expectation is that the initial hypotheses may need a little refinement which will set in place a further sequence of hypotheses making, data collection, data analysis and testing. Further investigators join the fray and the process shunts back and forth between theory and evidence until the sociological community is satisfied that firm conclusions are being reached.

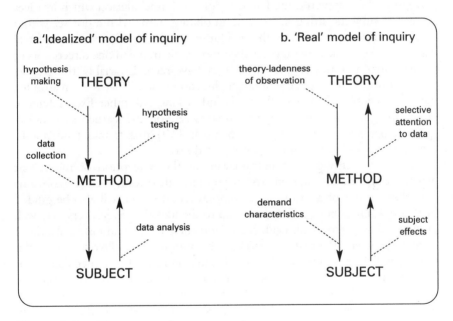

Figure 2.4   The research process

Figure 2.4a has labelled this process an 'ideal'. This is not simply a matter of the compression involved in my over-simple, single-paragraph, one-idea-at-a-time illustration. The 'real' picture is portrayed in Figure 2.4b. What this shows is that the move from theory to evidence is never straightforward and that all the processes of hypothesis making, data collection, data analysis and hypothesis testing are in fact *contested*. These problems and pitfalls are described in 2.4b using an alternative set of descriptors for the four legs of the journey. The overall dilemma being described here can be captured in the sentence – *evidence does not speak for itself*. What this means, as we observed in Chaper 1, is that we have to abandon the simplistic notion that social researchers are mere 'fact gatherers'. There is no such thing as 'raw data', 'out there', which we can observe 'directly' and use to 'prove' theories. Rather, it is the *process* of going back and forth between ideas and evidence which advances knowledge.

When encountered for the first time, such ideas can seem rather unsettling, particularly for those brought up on the notion that science *is* the business of gathering facts. It is necessary, therefore, to advance this alternative understanding of the nature of investigation by stages. The key idea is introduced by that mouthful of a phrase, the *theory-ladenness of observation*. This notion came to prominence with some famous experiments in the psychology of perception. Best known is the Dunker 'dot and frame' illusion which involves the use of subjects sitting in front of an oblong frame with a dot set within it. These objects are the only things illuminated in an otherwise completely darkened room. The experimenter then moves the frame in one direction (say, to the right) and asks subjects what they have seen. Invariably, they report that the dot has moved in the opposite direction (left). What is the reason for the misperception? Being in the dark and lacking any other fixed reference points for gauging movement, the subjects rely on the learned expectation (gained, perhaps, from watching too much TV!) that frames tend not to move, whereas objects within them might do so.

Now, if something as straightforward as the perception of movement depends on prior assumptions (or, if you like, 'theories'), then it is obvious that observations of a vastly more complex social world will also be guided by theories. From here, it is a short step to the idea that researchers may well pick and choose empirical evidence to suit their theoretical tastes. By this I refer to the likelihood that a researcher's commitment to a favoured idea (pet theory) will lead to the search for self-confirming evidence (pet data). For instance, in the sociology of religion, the 'secularization thesis' about the decline in religious belief in modern society is much debated. If the researcher is committed to this thesis, she might monitor the decline in church attendance over the decades in order to 'verify' it. If the researcher, however, is opposed the thesis, he might attempt to 'falsify' it by gathering evidence on the apparent rise in what is often called 'common religion', which refers to people's belief in magic, luck, superstition, cults, alternative lifestyles and so forth.

In Figure 2.4a, 'hypothesis making' is the prelude to 'hypothesis testing', and in Figure 2.4b the fact that 'all observation is theory-laden' has a counterpoint in the notion of 'selective attention to data'. This refers to the fact that evidence, once collected, does not speak for itself but will automatically enter a further round of interpretation and reinterpretation. For instance, let us consider one of the most famous bits of quantitative data in sociology, reproduced in almost every introductory textbook, showing that over the century there has been a steady decline in the proportion of the national wealth held by the richest one/five/ten per cent of the population. This is often taken at 'face value' to indicate that Marxian prediction about the increasing stranglehold of the capitalist class has proven woefully mistaken. Marxists, however, do not see it this way. They would ask, for instance: from whence does this evidence come? (answer – Inland Revenue Statistics based on death duties); who provides the initial information? (answer – accountants of the wealthy); in whose interests do these agents act? (answer – self-evident). The 'redistribution' of wealth, in this view, is thus seen as an accountancy ploy, and the 'real' evidence of the stranglehold of the capitalist class is sought elsewhere in terms of information on, say, 'interlocking' directorships and shareholdings in the major global conglomerates.

In utilizing these examples, I am not attempting to give succour to proponents or opponents of the secularization or polarization theses, merely to show that the very idea of 'proving' a theory is much more complex than the ideal model allows. I shall return to a more 'realistic' theory of theory testing later, but for now we turn to another mighty conundrum for the standard conception of the research process.

Figure 2.4a presents the idealized conceptualization of data collection and analysis. This is the point of interface between sociologists and their subjects. On the basis of their theoretical deliberations, researchers arrive at a body of information they require from respondents and this is translated into a range of questions, tests, scales and so on. Subjects attune themselves to these inquiries and return the requisite information to be processed in data analysis and provide a test of the original conjecture. So the story goes. Figure 2.4b presents the alternative picture. Its basic assumption is that human subjects are not passive respondents, so that retrieving information from the (wo)man on the street presents rather different problems from exploring the leaf on the tree or the specimen under the microscope.

Figure 2.4b thus describes the flow of information between the researcher and the researched with two different terms, *demand characteristics* and *subject effects*. The basic idea of the former is that the research act in sociology is invariably a meeting between people, and so is itself a social situation. In such a meeting, it is incredibly difficult to isolate the particular questions, variables and measures in which the sociologists are interested from the totality of other influences present. For instance, confront any normal living, breathing subject with a stranger asking questions and he or she will be thinking, 'who is this person?', 'why does she want to know this stuff?', 'what is she doing it for?', 'who is she doing it for?', 'why have I been selected?', 'am I getting anything out of this?', 'do I really want to tell her this?' and so on. In the face of all this, there is little wonder that the original intentions of the researcher may get distorted and the meaning of that apparently simple questionnaire item may get mangled. This *totality* of cues and concerns which confront the research subject are known as 'demand characteristics'.

The reverse side of the same coin consists of 'subject effects'. During the course of the research act, subjects will make up their mind in respect of some of their own anxieties and queries. Thus, what the researcher gets back from the subject are not mere 'responses' but a mixed bag of intuition, helpfulness, courtesy, curiosity, guesswork, vigilance, guardedness, pluck and bloody-mindedness. Subject effects are encountered in all research strategies. Picking out representative examples is difficult but probably the most (in)famous arise during the questionnaire and experimental approaches. According to the topics they raise, some questionnaire items can be seen by the subject as a 'threat'. Accordingly, a *social desirability effect* comes into play in which respondents are, for instance, likely to *over-report* 'voting', 'giving to charity', 'knowing the issues', 'participating in education', 'being employed' and so on, but *under-report* 'illness', 'disability', 'alcohol consumption', 'savings', 'being unemployed' and so on (Foddy, 1993: Ch. 9). Another admirable tendency in the majority of questionnaire respondents is *yea-saying*. Because most people are just so nice, they prefer on balance to 'acquiesce', and so answers labelled 'agree' rather than 'disagree', or 'satisfied' rather than 'dissatisfied' have a small but significant head-start when it comes to analysis (Foddy, 1993: Ch. 11). The grandfather of all subject effects is the *Hawthorne Effect* (Roethliberger and Dickson, 1939). This was one of the first examples of 'work study' which sought to discover the optimum conditions to maximize productivity at the Western Electric Works in Chicago. Researchers created workteams little and large, lighting levels subdued and bright, break patterns intermittent and absent, and to their surprise found productivity under the different conditions just kept on improving. Labour thus triumphs over logic, the scrupulous attention given to the workforce via the research being said to have been more significant that the actual work conditions.

Most researchers have their favourite example of subject effects and this is my opportunity to present mine. The research, conducted in a prison, was intended to evaluate whether a higher education course offered by the local university contributed towards rehabilitation. Recall that one of the standard ways to measure the effect of programme is to conduct some before-and-after measurement of attitudes, beliefs, behaviours, and so at the very start of the initiative, your intrepid researcher entered the prison classroom armed with a battery of questionnaires and attitude tests. There is a bit of prison folklore, which the reader should know and which I knew well enough at the time, that inmates like to retain control of the one thing they can control in an otherwise totally superintended world, namely – what goes on inside their own heads. The 'demand characteristic' thus loomed large that I was a Home Office spy, or (worse still) a psychologist, rather than a docile sociologist. I hoped to get by with charm, grace, humility, docility, and besides, the questionnaire was a compulsory part of the course! So how did it go?

Well, in fact all the questionnaires got completed, but in a way which led me directly back to the methodological drawing board. The expected grilling I received about the purpose of the questions including the unexpected thoughts of one prisoner, which you could actually see dawning on his face, 'you'll do these again at the end of the course to see if we have changed, eh?' The idea that subjects will try to figure out the ideas of the researcher is known as 'hypothesis-seeking behaviour' – this is a sophisticated example of 'methodology-seeking behaviour'. Another classic example of the subject effect is 'faking-good' and this tactic of sticking to socially desirable was also taken to new heights in the prison. One of the attitude tests used a fixed answer boxes for all items as follows:

Strongly agree	Generally agree	Somewhat agree	Somewhat disagree	Generally disagree	Strongly disagree
0	1	2	3	4	5

This was deliberately designed without a 'neutral point', but so keen was another of the respondents to appear as 'Mr Average', he went through and recorded most of the items as a 2½.

We return to the respondents-from-hell later in this chapter. Here, I simply affirm to newcomers to social inquiry the sheer significance of the quartet of ideas introduced in this section. The 'theory-ladenness of observation', 'selective attention to data', 'demand characteristics' and 'subject effects' constitute an immense battery of difficulties. It is not resorting to hyperbole to say that the battle for rigour in sociological research is the battle to confront these problems. It is of particular interest to note that this family of processes casts its uncertainties well beyond the particular cases I have illustrated and, in fact, afflicts all four strategies of research introduced in an earlier section. It is also true to say that it yields to no quick fix, indeed it is precisely these problems which have led some sociologists to wring their hands and declare that we should abandon the search for clear methodological principles and recognize that research is necessarily subjective and relativistic. Doughtier souls should, however, stay on board. While there is no instant dissolution of these problems, it is true to say that resolution begins with a proper recognition of the task in hand, and we now move on to describe some strategies developed with such a goal in mind.

Data Collection: Structured and Unstructured

The fact that 'talk is cheap' has propelled social researchers galore into using the interview as *the* tool for data collective. Yet, these artificial, unrehearsed encounters between strangers remain an enigma, leaving researchers at loggerheads on how to harness the flow of information that emerges from them. I refer, once again, to the paradigm wars and one particular battle which has developed during the conflict in respect of a preference for 'structured' versus 'unstructured' interviewing. My purpose here is to re-examine this old debate in order to transcend it. I want to show, first, that the investigatory goals of social research are so diverse that we need a variety of interview techniques at our disposal. Second, I want to show that these supposedly opposing methods have common failings and that all interviewing techniques share common priorities if they are to be improved.

Figure 2.5 represents the flow of information in the more formal, structured approaches to interviewing. The researcher begins with a theory which indicates the information (variables) required from the subject; these are then operationalized into set questions and fixed response categories; respondents answer by saying which of the categories applies to them; and finally responses are analysed to gain an overall picture of the population studied. The rationale is to provide a simple, neutral stimulus in order to tap the true 'responses' or true 'values' of individual subjects. Questions are asked in the simplest possible form which will nevertheless remain faithful to the conceptual intentions of the researcher. To these ends the major effort of this school can be summarized in the oft-stated goals that the interview schedule be clear, precise, unambiguous, intelligible and so on, yet *not* leading, hypothetical, embarrassing, memory defeating and so forth. Great care is also taken over question form, dealing with such matters as to whether to word questions negatively or positively, whether to include 'don't know' response categories, how to arrange the sequence of questions and so on. Since it is understood that 'who asks' can be as influential as 'what is asked', much effort is also made to neutralize and standardize personal factors which may influence the subjects. In short, the use of an identical stimulus and set responses categories with all subjects is said to allow for proper comparison to be made across the entire field of potential viewpoints.

Figure 2.6 represents the flow of information in the informal, unstructured interview. Since proponents of this view assume that the basis of all human action lies in the intelligibility of the social world to subjects, steps are taken to ensure that the research act is intelligible to them. There is thus no truck with question–response logic, it is assumed that even identical, plain words delivered by identical and plain interviewers can still mean different things to different people. There is no place for detachment and neutrality; what is required from the interviewer is 'involvement' and 'responsiveness'.

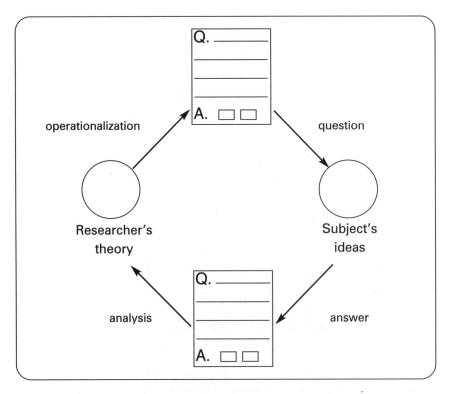

Figure 2.5   The structured interview

Data collection thus has the task of creating a conversational setting in which the information provided is faithful to the frame of reference of the respondent. The investigator offers minimal steerage of the research topics within broad areas of discussion as they seem appropriate to each respondent. The idea is that mutual understanding emerges via the in-depth exchange of ideas. The researcher then selects for report those extracts from the total dialogue which most thoroughly crystallize the perspective of the subject. Analysis then consists of a descriptive narrative, bringing together the key statements voiced by the respondents.

Readers will see at glance that there is little by the way of sweetness and light between these views and indeed there was a period when methodological writing on the interview was all bile and rancour. The classic contribution to this was Oakley's famous (1981) paper entitled, 'Interviewing women: a contradiction in terms'. She added a feminist twist to these antagonisms by advocating that the traditional textbook advice on the formal interview is written by powerful male academics who try to gain scientific respectability for their views by their stress on neutrality and objectivity. She makes her case

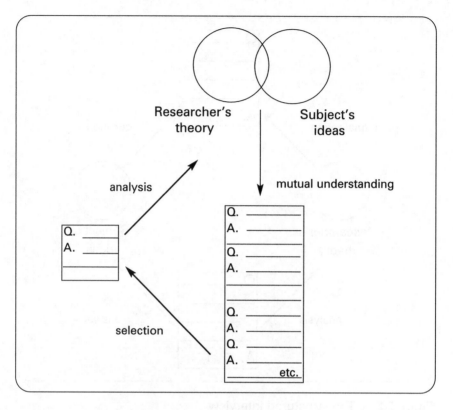

Figure 2.6   The unstructured interview

by quoting at length from some of the preposterous advice given to new researchers in some of the classic US 'methods' textbooks, with the following tips (on what the interviewer should do if the interviewee actually begins to speak up) taking the biscuit:

> Suppose the interviewee does answer the question but then asks for the opinion of the interviewer... In most cases the rule remains that he is there to obtain information, and to focus on the respondent not himself. Usually a few simple phrases will shift the emphasis back on the respondent. Some which have been fairly successful are 'I guess I haven't thought enough about it to give a good answer right now' [and] 'Well, right now, your answers are more important than mine'... Sometimes the diversion can be accompanied by a headshaking gesture which suggests 'That's a hard one!' while continuing with the interview. (Goode and Hatt, 1952)

At this point in my lectures on this topic, I usually stop and ask the students to try the 'head-shaking gesture'. For some reason, it usually seems to come out 'That's what it feels like to be a prat', rather than 'That's a hard one'. Meanwhile, back at the debate, Oakley continues to attempt to rip asunder the structured (male) model. She does this via an account of her own research on childbearing and motherhood which involved long periods of extensive interviews-cum-conversations. The argument is that the structured approach would just not work, and that before any genuine information of a worth- while nature would flow on the private experience of becoming a mother, there had to be a 'transition to friendship'. All of this is evoked in the famous, final sentence of her paper:

> The mythology of 'hygienic' research with its accompanying mystification of the researched and the researcher as objective instruments of data production [must] be replaced by a recognition that *personal involvement* is more than a dangerous bias – it is the condition under which people come to know each other and admit each other to their lives. (Oakley, 1981, my emphasis)

You will find no finer thumping of the tub in the literature – alas, it does not make for a honing of the methodology. An alternative picture is drawn by Malseed (1987) in a paper arguing that the conventional wisdom on inter- viewing, even in the ancient US cookbooks, does not really consist of the wooden detachment illustrated in the first quotation from Oakley. The basic ethos, according to Malseed, is a pluralist one – different research topics call for different interviewing styles. If, for instance, one was interviewing for the census or an opinion poll and the information sought was, 'how many toilets are there in your home?' or 'how will you vote in the next election?', it is tough to see the 'contradiction' involved which means that for half the sample a 'transition to friendship' would be required to extract the data. Conversely, if the researcher was involved in an in-depth inquiry into personal issues, he would indeed feel like a lemon, shaking his head to indicate 'that's a hard one', because it would have been he who was responsible for raising just that matter. Oakley, in short, can be said to have created a 'strawman' in her notion of the all-pervasive, all-powerful formal interview.

There is worse to come for die-hards of structured/unstructured battle. In their struggle over the *form* of the interview (neutrality versus detachment), both perspectives can be criticized for having a deficient understanding of the *role* of the interview (Pawson, 1996). In concentrating on their very different ways of posing questions, both can be accused of ignoring the issue of *why* questions are put. Both can be accused of forgetting the proper function of the interview in the production and testing of sociological explanation. Recall the basic idea of Figure 2.4a which shows that the task of data collection is to produce evidence which will help verify or falsify the researcher's theory. 'Hypotheses' rather than 'respondents' should be considered as the subject matter of research. In this light, both interviewing methods have been accused of common error, known as the *imposition problem*. Instead of being a test of the researcher's theory, that theory is said often to be 'invisible' to the respondent, being 'smuggled in' only in the wake of data collection. Let us follow this argument through in both interviewing styles.

In the formal style the researcher's conceptual system is *imposed* wholesale upon the flow of information. The researcher determines the range of questions to be asked and also the range of answers which are appropriate for each question. The subject's response is limited to ticking boxes, agreeing, disagreeing and so on. Set questions and predetermined response categories offer little opportunity to question, or even understand, the researcher's theoretical framework. The end result is that the evidence is necessarily couched in the concepts and variables chosen by the researcher, with the result that only a selection of the subject's own ideas may get across. For instance, recalling a previous example, Marshall *et al.* (1988) have been accused of the methodological 'imposition' of their view that social class remains a central feature of everyday experience via the use of a questionnaire which is dominated by items on social class (Emmison and Western, 1990).

The informal approach takes the form of a conversation and so its data are diverse and discursive and thus hard to compare from respondent to respondent. Researches are sometimes accused of *selecting* small fragments of the respondent's utterances into their own preferred explanatory framework. While the data are supposed to emerge in 'mutual' understanding, the researcher's theory may not be clearly on view to the subject, and only show its face after the event in the research report. The end result is that only a selection of the respondent's own ideas may get across. For instance, Oakley in her research on becoming a mother could be accused of 'imposition', by favouring those epidural-fearing, consultant-wary, control-seeking views which resemble her own.

In the face of this common problem, it might be that a rather different model of the interview is to be preferred. Rather than the interviewer only telling the researcher about themselves (through tick boxes or anecdotes), it may be preferable to think of the subject as an 'informant', passing judgement through their own eyes on the researcher's theory. I return to my respondents-with-attitude (or to be precise, 'with jail sentences') for an example. Recall that the research sought to discover whether education could play a significant role in their rehabilitation. I have already described how they reduced to tatters my first attempts to record their opinions through a formal, structured questionnaire. I should add that this was followed by several months of gathering informal tales about their lives and times, which taught me a lot about their lives and times, but little about whether education might change them.

What did the trick was actually a combination of the structured and unstructured approaches. I compiled a long list of formal statements, derived from the theoretical literature, about how education might be said to change a prisoner. These were asked in tick-box format to find out if the men strongly agreed, agreed, disagreed and so on with each item. Later each man was interviewed informally with the idea of getting them to explain the basis for each of their answers. These sessions brought forth a torrent of reflection about how the inmates were making use of their classroom experiences. Interestingly, the most acute observations often came in respect of initial questions which they deemed 'patronizing' or 'stupid'. These evoked important conceptual distinctions about how education had not change them directly but deepened their own *capacity* for change (for details, see Pawson, 1996). For the first time they talked about *their* world in *my* language. What we have here, in short, is not 'hygienic research', nor a 'transition to friendship', but a research relationship which allows respondents to think, 'well, that's your theory but in my experience it happens like this'. It is another important item for the interview toolkit.

Data Analysis: Qualitative and Quantitative

We now put the assembly line into reverse and follow through the issue of how to analyse the data in order to examine if the original hypotheses have been fruitful. Data arrive back at the social researcher's office in all shapes and sizes – from disks packed full of coded survey responses, to scratchy tapes of patchy conversations, to scribbled fieldnotes from frazzled fieldworkers, to unfileable heaps of newspaper clippings, to highlighted portions of illuminating manuscripts. Clearly, I am not about to work through the sometimes fearsome technical details of how all these materials get processed. I will tackle, instead, what is often considered to be the basic divide, that between the use of 'verbal' and 'numerical' data. Again, we are in the territory of the qualitative versus the quantitative and, once again, I want to attempt to break the mould and argue – same problem, same solution.

Numerical data

I take as my example the 'mobility matrix' from the famous Nuffield Survey into social class mobility (Goldthorpe, 1980). Mobility, in the sense used here, refers to the movement in social class position between generations. The question posed is as follows: are class boundaries 'rigid' and do people tend to stay in the class into which they were born; or is the class structure 'fluid' and is there a considerable shift in people's life chances? The answer to this question is to be found in the data in Table 2.1.

44

Sociology

Table 2.1 Class composition by class of father (percentage by column)

		1	2	3	4	5	6	7	Total
	1	25.3	12.4	9.6	6.7	3.2	2.0	6.5	680
	2	13.1	12.2	8.0	4.8	5.2	3.1	2.5	547
Father's class	3	10.4	10.4	10.8	7.4	8.7	5.7	6.0	687
	4	10.1	12.2	9.8	27.2	8.6	7.1	7.7	886
	5	12.5	14.0	13.2	12.1	16.6	12.2	9.6	1072
	6	16.4	21.7	26.1	24.0	31.0	41.8	35.2	2577
	7	12.1	17.1	22.6	17.8	26.7	28.0	36.6	2126
	Total	1230	1050	827	687	1026	1883	1872	8575

Respondent's class

Key

1 Higher professional, higher administrators, senior managers, large proprietors

2 Lower grade professional, administration and managers, high-grade technicians and supervisors

3 Routine non-manual – mainly clerical and sales personnel

4 Small proprietors and self-employed artisans

5 Lower grade technical and supervisors

6 Skilled manual workers

7 Semi-skilled and unskilled manual workers

Source: Adapted from Goldthorpe, 1980

Part of a training in research methods is to learn how to 'read' such information and so I proceed with a one-paragraph lesson. The basic idea is to follow one generation to the next in terms of their class position. The baseline measure of social class is an occupational schema reproduced at the foot of the table which breaks the population down into seven classes. A random sample of male respondents was selected and two pieces of information were sought from them: their occupation and their father's occupation. This gives every family unit a place on the grid in Table 2.1. For instance, I am an academic (classified class 1 by Goldthorpe, 1980), my father was a grocer (class 4). Thus on the table, we would appear in column one, row four. The sample of 8575 father/son pairs are assigned to the various cells in the same fashion. The other significant feature of the table is given in the heading which explains that the data are presented as a 'percentage by column'. So, for example, if we look down column 1, this gives us a picture of the 'inflow' into that particular class. Starting at the top and reading down, the evidence reveals the following picture: *of respondents in class 1*, 25.3 per cent of their fathers were also in class 1, 13.1 per cent had class 2 fathers, 10.4 per cent came from class 3, 10.1 per cent had class 4 origins, 12.5 per cent were born into class 5, 16.4 per cent had skilled manual fathers, and 12.1 per cent had leapt all the way from the bottom of the occupational structure.

Having established the nature of the data, let us now see how they are put to work in analysis. Goldthorpe used the data to test a variety of hypotheses, one of which is referred to as the 'closure thesis' (1980: Ch. 2). This is a Marxist-inspired idea which argues that the élite class has an obvious interest in maintaining its position down the generations, and has sufficient clout to ensure that its own offspring retain their position while also making it difficult for other classes to enter this topmost group. It suggests, in short, that there will be a high degree of 'self-recruitment' to class 1, and relatively little upward mobility from below, especially from the ranks of the working classes. So what is the verdict on the closure thesis? We have already examined the crucial bit of evidence, namely the inflow into class 1. A quarter (25.3 per cent) of the class 1 respondents in the Nuffield Survey do indeed come from that background, but the other three-quarters have origins elsewhere in the class structure and, moreover, the upward march seems remarkably well distributed all the way through that class structure. Indeed, respondents from manual working backgrounds make up over a quarter (16.4 per cent + 12.1 per cent) of the élite positions. On first sight, we seem to have here a ringing denunciation of the closure thesis and a picture of significant fluidity within the British class system.

We now reach the methodological point I wish to make – which is that data analysis requires second sight! Put more formally, the lesson is that data never speak for themselves and that hypotheses get tested only by taking into account rival ideas and further evidence. For instance, an alternative hypothesis accounting for the upward swell of folks into class 1 is the so-called 'room-at-the-top' thesis. This argues that there has been a significant change in the occupational structure in 'late' industrial society and that the production process has changed in a way that creates more managers, professional, clerical and service-sector workers and which destroys traditional manual work. It could be this shift in the workforce needs, rather than the efforts of individuals, which are causing the high levels of mobility. Evidence for this alternative thesis can be seen instantly in Table 2.1. If we look at the sum total of respondents in class 1 (bottom of the column), we see that there are 1230 of them. Compare this with the 680 fathers who had class 1 position (end of column one) to get a clear picture of the vacuum created by the expansion of top positions which may well have had the effect of sucking up recruits from below.

Another rival hypothesis argues that the closure thesis still holds – but was intended for a much more narrowly defined élite class than that defined in

Goldthorpe's class 1. No self-respecting Marxist, for instance, would include academics and production managers as part of the self-perpetuating élite but, as we have seen, they fall within this initial test of the thesis. Such arguments led another member of the Nuffield team to re-examine the data and look at upward mobility into the component sectors of class 1. Heath (1981) thus discovers that the 25.3 per cent rate of recruitment into class 1 from class 1, shoots up to 40.2 per cent and 44.2 per cent in turn, if one narrows down the definition of that class to 'self-employed professionals' and 'large proprietors' respectively.

We are beginning to get a picture of how data analysis and hypothesis testing actually work. The key is to identify and choose between rival theories. Thus our example started with one regularity – considerable upward mobility into the élite class. This datum could be explained in (at least) three ways:

1. the class structure is fluid
2. the workforce has transformed
3. some parts of the 'élite' are open and some closed.

Good research has the patience to hold back on affirming the former before the others get checked out. The 'closure thesis' quickly becomes the 'closure theses' as it is interrogated by different facets of the data. One idea spins off another and the spotlight falls on one part of the data matrix then another. The result is that it takes Goldthorpe 310 pages to complete an analysis of the social processes that produce Table 2.1, and this is not to mention the volumes of critique and counter-critique which followed (Pawson, 1993). Analysis is not a terminus but a process.

Verbal data

Most data analysis in the qualitative traditions takes the form of the presentation of transcripts of dialogues taken from the group under study which are then put into context and 'explained' by the researcher. I take as my example a typical and highly respected piece of ethnographic analysis, Pollert's (1981) *Girls, Wives, Factory Lives* and also draw on a critique of her research contained in Hammersley (1990: Ch. 4). We join the analysis with Pollert explaining the daily grind of factory life:

> 'Cutting off', or separating the 'inner self' from what is objectively happening on the 'outside' is one of the sorry 'skills' we are forced into, in an existence dominated by alienated relations of production. It is otherwise know as 'wishing one's life away'. Some girls actually pride themselves in the art of switching off, pitying those who were bad at it, and thinking themselves to be very lucky to be working at all:

Racquel: Yes you get bored sitting up here, very bored... You gets used to it though. I think that it's imagination a lot of the time. I get fed up sometimes, but I don't really get that fed up, because I haven't really got anything to be fed up about.

Anna (the researcher): What do you think about?

Racquel: Nothing, really. I can sit up here a whole day without really speaking. (Pollert, 1981)

Hammersley's point is that in such analysis it is vital to inspect closely the relationship between the evidence and claims, as they to do not always match. In this particular extract he perceives that Pollert makes at least three claims:

1. that the workers cut themselves off or switch off from their work
2. that they refer to this as wishing one's life away; and that it is a 'sorry' skill produced by alienating relations of production
3. that some of the women prided themselves on their ability to switch off and pitied those who were bad at it judging themselves to be lucky to be working.

His judgement is that the evidence (the dialogue between Racquel and Anna) justifies only the first of these propositions and that the other two remain unsupported. The point here is not to take sides between Pollert and Hammersley but rather to show that in qualitative analysis the data will usually allow for alternative explanations to be made. Indeed, authors of qualitative research know full well the possibility that their accounts can be challenged. It is this knowledge that differentiates them from story-tellers. Thus it is for the good researcher, as part of the analysis, to take into account potential rival theories and bring forth further evidence which will help the reader in coming to a preference for one particular 'reading'. The best qualitative analysis, therefore, takes the form of a *pattern-making exercise* (Diesing, 1971) in which particular claims are buttressed and counter-claims anticipated and rebutted by a whole patchwork of evidence.

Let me now pull together some conclusions from both the quantitative and qualitative examples. *Rule one* is a negative. Do not be misled into thinking that it is the data themselves which provide analytical power. So it is not 'hard data', 'number crunching' or 'statistical power' which gives quantitative analysis its clout. Nor is it 'rich data', 'a good story', or 'empathetic ability' which makes qualitative analysis convincing. *Rule two* is a positive. Data analysis and hypothesis testing are two sides of the same coin. One will need several hypotheses to make sense of any datum and one will need much data to make sense of any hypotheses. Data analysis, whether quantitative or qualitative, is about *utilizing evidence to discern and choose between theories*. The principal skill of data analysis is the refinement of theory.

Conclusion: The Realists and the Relativists

I began this chapter by drawing attention to a basic conundrum about the sociologist's expertise. Every explanation that the sociologist comes up with implies an act of faith. How do they know they are correct and how does anyone else know that they are correct? An obvious danger is lurking. The world is full of so-called 'experts'. Soothsayers come and go. Priests and politicians, agony aunts and commercial consultants, indeed anyone with a couple of beers down their throat is prepared to act as an instant pundit on the social world and its problems. Making claims for sociological wisdom thus requires a leap of imagination. Is this sheer bravado, mere conceit or is there some basis for this 'special knowledge'?

As we have seen, this 'quest for certainty' goes by the name of 'methodology'. Coming to grips with 'research methods' thus presents something of a challenge to the beginning student. 'Methods' is the hard bit. 'Methods' is the bit that slows down the imagination. It is the bit that is supposed to turn the pontification into justification. I have introduced the methodological domain via a series of dichotomies between principle and practice, pure and applied, structured and unstructured, qualitative and quantitative, and so on and so forth. We now reach the *big dualism*. After the effort expended on methodological strategies and tactics, do we end up with objectivity or subjectivity? Is it all truth or merely opinion?

In academic terms, we are discussing the opposition between 'realism' and 'relativism' in social research methodology. Realism is founded on the belief that the social world is real and external to our senses. It assumes that people have power and individuals have intentions, and these things are just as real as horses having hooves and water having wetness. Relativists do not believe that it is possible to know about the world in a way which is independent of the knower. They believe that beauty is in the eye of the beholder and, so too, is our understanding of good and bad, right and wrong and, of course, power and intentions. While it is clearly an oversimplification to imagine that every piece of research is either a search for objective fact or a crusade on behalf of subjective opinion, sociology has suffered tremendous mood swings in relation to these poles.

If I can give a personal view, the answer to the big question lies in the small detail of the dilemmas, problems and disputes already covered in previous sections of this chapter. It will not surprise the reader, therefore, to discover that my inclination on 'realism versus relativism' is that, for practical purposes, it is a phoney opposition in exactly the same way as were many of the detailed 'debates' already covered. That is to say, it is as plain as day that researchers do *not* have to choose between starting their investigations under the assumption that they have automatic access to the facts, nor that their findings will turn out to be only as good as any other viewpoint.

So, I come down on the side of the truth – knowing that the truths of sociological research will always be partial and provisional and never uniform and universal. I figure that certainty requires humility – and that research can only help us in choosing between theories rather than proving one. I rest content that good-quality research comes with qualifications – our hypothesis will work only for certain people in certain circumstances at certain times.

'Truth' and 'objectivity' thus remain the *goals* and *ambitions* of sociological research, and I can do no better than to conclude with Gordon's brilliant quip for preserving them:

> That these ideals cannot be attained is not a reason for disregarding them. Perfect cleanliness is also impossible but it does not serve as a warrant for not washing, much less for rolling about in a manure pile. (Gordon, 1992)

Be careful where you tread. There's a lot of it about.

Further Reading

Babbie, E. *The Practice of Social Research,* 5th edn, Belmont, Wadsworth, 1989. The best traditional 'cookbook' introduction to methods of inquiry.

Blaikie, N. *Approaches to Social Inquiry,* London, Polity, 1993. Provides a good introduction to a range of research strategies.

Hammersley, M. *Reading Ethnographic Research,* Harlow, Longman, 1990. A clear introduction to ethnographic research methods.

Pawson, R. and Tilley, N. *Realistic Evaluation,* London, Sage, 1997. An introduction, with case study examples, to the comparatively new area of evaluation methodology.

deVaus, D. *Surveys in Social Research,* 4th edn, London, University College Press, 1996. The standard text on the survey method.

Williams, M. and May, T. *Introduction to the Philosophy of Social Research,* London, University College Press, 1996. A good introduction to epistemology, ontology and matters philosophical.

3

Sociological Theory

Alan Swingewood

The aim of this chapter is to provide an introduction to some of the major theories and theoretical perspectives that have been developed by sociologists to help explain the key 'sociological questions' of social order, social change and the relationship between the individual and society. This chapter examines some of the most important contributions to these questions made by classical, modern and contemporary social theoriests. It should help you begin to understand:

■ The origins of sociological theory in the 'classical' theories of Durkheim, Marx and Weber

■ 'Modern' structural functional, symbolic interactionist, ethnomethodological and Marxist theories

■ The significance of the macro-micro distinction in social theory

■ Giddens' theory of the structuration and Bourdieu's theory of fields

■ The postmodern critique of meta-narratives

CONCEPTS

macro- and micro-theory ■ social integration ■ ideology
materialism and idealism ■ methodological individualism ■ agency
hegemony ■ culture industries ■ meta-narratives

Introduction

While the previous chapter on methodology examined theoretical issues concerned with the *production* of sociological knowledge, this chapter is concerned with *substantive* sociological theory. Substantive theories are the 'sociological maps' identified in Chapter 1 that sociologists use to help them explain what societies are and how they work and change. Substantive theories attempt to organize the apparently random nature of social life into coherent social knowledge and, at the same time, raise new questions for social research on the relations between different parts of society, such as how they are constituted and survive as permanent structures and how they affect individual actions. The central problem for sociological theory in this context, and the problem on which this chapter will focus, is the nature of the relationship between large-scale institutions, such as bureaucracies or religious organizations (the macro-dimension), and patterns of face-to-face interactions between individuals in everyday life (the micro-dimension).

Sociological theories are not developed in a vacuum, they are *ideas* which invariably arise from theorists' attempts to develop, refine, criticize or replace existing theories. There is thus a tradition, or legacy, of sociological theory, and many theoretical ideas from the 'classical sociology' of the nineteenth and early twentieth century continue to influence contemporary theory. Consequently, this chapter begins with a discussion of the legacy of the classical theories of Durkheim, Marx and Weber. It then looks at the major perspectives of 'modern' social theory; the macro-approach of structural functionalism and the micro-sociology of interactionism and ethnomethodology. It goes on to examine some of the most important attempts in sociological theory to synthesize the macro and the micro in sociology and concludes with a brief discussion of the challenge of postmodern theory.

Classical Social Theory

Durkheim

Emile Durkheim (1858–1917), the first professor of sociology, probably did more than anyone to establish sociology as an independent academic subject. He was particularly influenced by the work of Auguste Comte (1798–1857). Comte argued that, to make sense of societies, sociology had to adopt the methods of the natural sciences, especially biology, as the basis for a positivist social science. However, while sociological analysis must be based on careful observation, these observations only make sense when interpreted by theory. The idea that no real observation is possible unless it is first directed, and finally interpreted by some theory, was developed by Durkheim and is one of the valuable legacies of Comte's early sociological positivism (Comte, 1896).

Second, Comte defined society *holistically*, that is, as a system which exists *independently* of individuals and determines their actions in ways which can be understood scientifically. Durkheim followed Comte in seeing the focus of sociological inquiry being on *social structures* rather than on the *individuals* who comprised them. However, unlike Comte, he argued that, although sociology dealt with objective facts which could be observed and measured, these 'social facts' were not mere objective *things* but external, collective phenomena which were general through society, such as law and religion, and which constrained individual action but which were not reducible to being explained in 'individual' terms. As things like moral codes and language were social facts so, less obviously, were invisible moral currents generated by collective social life. One of Durkheim's most striking demonstrations of this theory is found in his major study, *Suicide* (1897/1952). Statistics from European countries showed not only that there were significant variations in the suicide rates of different countries, and social groups within these countries, but that these variations were remarkably consistent over time. For Durkheim, the stability of the suicide rates was a collective phenomenon which could only be explained in relation to other social facts. He argued that the major cause of variations in the suicide rate was the degree of social integration (or social solidarity) existing in specific social groups. For example, he explained the consistently lower suicide rates of Catholic communities compared to Protestant communities in terms of the fact that Catholic society binds the believer more effectively than Protestant society into an established set of shared beliefs and ritualized practices common to all the faithful. Protestant communities are thus less integrating and, in times of crisis, Protestants were more likely to be thrown back onto their own resources and were thus more vulnerable to suicide. The greater protection from suicide for Catholics came not from their religion as such, but from the more intense and integrating quality of their social life. By relating the suicide rate to social solidarity, Durkheim raised important questions about the ways individuals internalize the culture of a specific group and thus regulate their behaviour from within. Durkheim's concept of culture as the mechanism of social integration was to exert a great influence in the subsequent development of sociology.

Another of Durkheim's concepts in his analysis of suicide was anomie, a condition of normlessness, a breakdown in the internalizing of values and the strong social bonds generated by social solidarity. Durkheim's substantive theory focused on the disintegration of social order brought about by rapid social change and the subsequent erosion of traditional institutions and values. He argued that modern societies would not work through external compulsion but only through people internalizing values and acting through their beliefs. A mechanistic, purely external concept of society eliminates its 'soul which is the composition of collective ideals' (Durkheim, 1964: 312).

What Durkheim suggested is that social life contains social facts that function as collective symbols (for example religious rites and national flags) through which society becomes 'conscious of itself'. He defined these forms as 'collective representations', the embodiment of ideals which constitute a *symbolic* order, a universe of shared meanings. The soldier who dies for his country thus dies for the flag, a sign with no value in itself but a collective representation signifying a specific reality which succeeds in motivating action.

Thus culture and symbolic representations can strengthen social solidarity and work against the anomic tendencies of advanced industrial society. Durkheim developed a more complex notion of social facts, involving the internalizing of values and the possibility of action through beliefs. Thus, societies were *both* physical and mental entities. However, in spite of valuable insights of this idea critics argue that Durkheim did not link it with the *active* part individuals play in the 'making' of the social world. In Durkheim's theory, individuals execute their beliefs and values, but are not involved in *changing* ideas and symbols through collective action. Durkheim's theory does not really explain which social groups produce specific values. Preoccupied with the problem of social order and the concept of society as an organism Durkheim did not really address questions of power, conflict and change.

Marx

Unlike sociological positivism, Marxism identified social theory with the interests of a specific social class, the industrial working class, and defined capitalism as the inevitable prelude to the penultimate stage of social development, socialism. While Marx's first writings were largely philosophical, concerned with abstract questions of freedom, it was with *The German Ideology* (Marx and Engels, 1845) that he established the framework for what he termed 'the materialist conception of history'. In this text he defines society in terms of its forms of economic production, its structure of property, the division of labour, class structure and class struggles. Society is conceived as historical and *relational:* 'Society does not consist of individuals; it expresses the sum of connections and relationships in which individuals find themselves' (Marx, 1971). Society exists through its 'material infrastructure'; that is, the forces of production (tools, machinery) and highly organized forms of collective social labour (wage labour in capitalism). For Marx, it is this material 'base' that generates the 'superstructure' of ideas, religion, education, political systems and so on. Hence the real foundations of any society are the forces of production and those who own and control the forces of production are the ruling class. Ideas reflect class interests: 'The ruling ideas of each epoch are those of the ruling class' (Marx and Engels, 1845/1964: 37–8). Thus, free-market economics reflected the ideological values and interests of the ruling capitalist class, the bourgeoisie, and helped legitimize its domination.

Marx believed, like Comte, that human society develops through the work-ings of certain laws, which he argued were specific to a particular mode of production. However, unlike Comte and Durkheim who regarded conflict as 'pathological', he argued that social and historical development occur through contradictions and conflict. For Marx, the source of change was a contradic-tion between the technological forces of production and the relations of production, that is, the way production is organized socially. For example, within the feudal mode of production a fundamental contradiction develops between the burgeoning capitalist classes' 'need' for markets, the free exchange of commodities and a mobile labour force, and the economically static and restrictive nature of feudal economic institutions where land, for example, could not be bought, only inherited.

Thus in Marx's theory of social change, different stages in historical devel-opment were defined in terms of their mode of production, with each containing elements within it that point the way to 'higher', more advanced and complex forms of social organization. Thus industrial capitalist produc-tion involves the concentration of masses of workers in close proximity. Herded together in towns and factories, Marx believed the working class will become increasingly aware of common interests and how these interests are in conflict with those of the owning class. This will lead to political awareness and increasing conflict over the ownership of the forces of production. Marx predicted that as capitalism will not be able to resolve its internal contradic-tions, it is a social system historically doomed with the bourgeois class acting as the 'gravediggers' of their own economic and social order.

Marx's model of society, then, is a system built around the primacy of economic processes and laws of production which assumes a deterministic relationship between the forces and relations of production, between base and superstructure. Hence his statement 'the handmill gives you society with the feudal lord; the steam mill society with the industrial capitalist' (Marx, 1962: 109). Although Marx has been criticized for producing an 'economically determined' model of society, he was aware – like Durkheim – of the critical role played by ideas in the constitution of society and he frequently argued that in particular contexts ideas can play a decisive role in shaping social insti-tutions and social change. In his major work, *Capital* (1957), he noted, almost in anticipation of Weber's thesis on the link between ascetic religion and modern capitalism, that 'Protestantism, by changing all the traditional holidays into work days, plays an important part in the genesis of capital' (Marx, 1957: 276). In the same text he notes that at the end of every labour process, we get a result that already existed in the imagination of the labourer before commencement' (ibid.: 174). Thus the concept of production itself is not crudely materialistic: for production always involves knowledge, imagi-nation, skills, reflexivity. Although culture and ideas may reflect specific social conditions, like the reflexive nature of the architect, they contribute actively to its further development. Marx thus allows space for social action. Collective agents, in the form of social classes, become aware of their position in class society, their relations with other classes and develop institutions for consolidating and furthering their interests.

How does this recognition of the importance of ideas fit in with Marx's concept of system and laws of development? Society is defined as a hierarchically organized structure involving social struggles between different groups and classes. In contrast to Durkheim, Marx emphasizes the violent and abrupt nature of social change generated through conflict and contradictions. This is change at the system level but it also takes place through collective action. If Marx's work held to a rigidly deterministic theory of iron laws and inevitable historical change (as with Comte), there is no scope for either collective or individual action. However, as I have suggested, Marx's model does provide for knowledgeable collective agents to act in pursuit of goals given their consciousness of interests and the fluid, dynamic structure of modern capitalism (Sztompka, 1994). One of Marx's most important insights, which continues to influence sociological theory, was his grasp of the revolutionary nature of modern capitalism, a system constantly undergoing rapid change, dynamically transforming both the economic structure as well as all social relations, culture and ideas. The broad, macro-historical process in which collective human action takes place is never at rest but, through the workings of social struggles and contradictions, permanently challenges all traditions and fixed notions. Thus Marx's concept of modern societies, or modernity, is one in which 'all that is solid melts into air' (Marx and Engels, 1962).

Weber: Social Action and Social Change

While Marx emphasized that history was the product of economic change and collective action, Weber (1864–1920) opposed this macro-theory and advanced a theory of 'methodological individualism' rather than Marx's 'methodological collectivism'. Weber was especially critical of the concept of objectively determining laws with the assumption that culture existed merely as a passive reflection of material forces. He believed that Marx's emphasis on systems and laws diminished the active role of the individual, known in sociology as agency or action. In contrast to the rather deterministic view of the individual reacting to structural arrangements put forward by positivism and Marxism, Weber argued that society should be conceived primarily in terms of the *meaningful* social action of people. Collectivities such as classes, bureaucracies and states do not determine behaviour, but rather exist as modes of 'actual or possible social actions of individual persons' (Weber, 1978: 14). Weber argued that, rather than trying to analyse human action from the 'outside', sociology has to be based on the interpretative understanding (*verstehen*) of the meanings that people give to their actions. People are motivated to act because they believe in the reality of certain ideas.

Weber applied his methodological individualism in his study of the relation between the rise of capitalism and the Protestant religion. Capitalism was not simply the inevitable product of objective economic laws but was also the result of a pattern of motivation engendered by Protestant culture with its rejection of worldly pleasures and the promotion of the values of a disciplined work ethic, investing rather than consuming and seeking salvation through a specific course of action (doing good works) in this world. These values were internalized and translated into economic and social principles which rejected luxury, immediate gratification and the avoidance of all spontaneous enjoyment of life. Individuals were self-controlled and disciplined in relation to pleasure and use of time. Rather than a passive reflection of class interests, ideas such as these, which helped bring about a distinct and disciplined 'work ethic' conducive to the development of modern capitalism, constituted active material forces. As Weber expressed it:

> Material and ideal interests directly govern men's conduct. Yet very frequently the 'world images' that have been created by 'ideas' have, like switchmen, determined the tracks along which action has been pushed by the dynamic of interest. (Weber, 1948b: 280)

Protestantism, especially the Calvinist sects, linked material economic needs closely with ideal interests in salvation. Martin Luther's concept of the 'calling', fulfilling one's duty to God, helped to promote disciplined action, while Calvin's doctrine of predestination – with its claim that God had chosen few believers for eternal grace and no one knew who they were – produced an anxiety which could be offset to some extent by economic success in this world as a sign of God's favour. Through useful activity, self-control, commitment to the ideal of work as an end in itself, Protestants could hope for salvation. This 'ethic' was an important part of the 'spirit' of capitalism.

For Weber, then, the springs of action and hence of social change were psychological. While India and China developed markets, division of labour, money economy and trade routes, it was in western Europe that these material conditions linked up with a particular *culture* to produce a highly rationalized form of capitalism, one based on the principles of systematic and impersonal rules, calculation and predictability.

Weber's theory of social action thus linked the micro-level of everyday social action with the macro-level of large-scale historical transformation in a way that avoided a determinism based on laws of development. In short, Weber's methodological individualism attempts to integrate a broad historical sociology with a concept of action. Weber's critique of Marx was that social change is always 'open ended', based as it is on the unpredictability of human action. The impossibility of predicting how people will act in any given context means that sociology will always lack the predictability of action conditioned by laws. It cannot offer a vision of the future.

Modern Social Theory

Functionalism and its Critics

Marxism, the sociological positivism of Comte and Durkheim and social action constituted the three major classical sociologies which continued to influence the post-classical phase of sociology. As sociology grew and developed into a professional academic subject, it continued to lack a unified social theory, although for a time structural functionalism became the most widely accepted general theory in sociology.

Structural functionalism had its origins in positivism with its concept of society as an organism in which the various component parts contribute to the integration of the whole. In his *Rules of Sociological Method* (1895/1982), Durkheim distinguished functional from causal explanation, arguing that the causes of social facts must be investigated separately from the function they fulfil socially. Causes refer to origins, functions to intrinsic properties: hence the causes of the division of labour must be sought in preceding social facts, such as changes in population and urbanism, while its function is to generate reciprocity of services and thus produce social solidarity. However, examining functions in this way fails to resolve the problem of the making of institutions and the role agents play in their everyday functions. This issue is particularly marked in the work of Parsons (1902–79) who laid out the basic principles of modern functionalism in painstaking and elaborate detail notably in works such as *The Social System* (1951) and *Toward A General Theory of Action* (Parsons and Shils, 1962).

While classical sociology integrated theoretical analysis and empirical research, Parson's work reflects an emerging trend within sociology towards the 'autonomy of theory'. Parsons described himself as 'an incurable theorist' and although his work examined many empirical and historical issues – fascism, family and socialization, social evolution, education and medicine – it was at an extremely abstract level of pure theory which at times seemed to have lost contact with social and historical reality. For example, his view of society as a social system was defined in terms of 'needs' or 'functional prerequisites', the generalized conditions essential for survival including provision for an adequate relationship of the individual with the environment, differentiation of roles, communication, shared goals, socialization and the social control of deviant behaviour. These prerequisites are grouped under four headings: adaptation (activities by which a system adapts to its environment modifying and controlling it in terms of system needs); goal attainment (mobilizing resources for specific goals); integration (the solidarity of the system, its survival as a cohesive whole); and finally, latency (accumulation and distribution of energy in the form of motivation). This was popularly known as the AGIL schema (Parsons, 1967).

A system is further held together by three sub-systems including the personality sub-system (motivation, values), the cultural (action orientated to symbolic forms, beliefs, ideas) and finally, the social sub-system (interaction between actors sharing common understandings and stable roles). Although many of these formulations approximate to commonsense propositions, the broad tendency of Parsons' conceptual framework lies in its emphasis on the degree of functional integration of a system: actors successfully internalize values to maintain the persistence of the system itself. Parsons' functionalist model takes little account of the possibility that motivation and the internalization of values may produce conflict and struggle. For example, values can be divisive, working to exclude rather than include specific groups into the system. There is also the question of *whose* values prevail in given situations.

Effectively, a functionalist model of society removes contradiction; the system functions behind the backs of its agents producing a huge moving equilibrium, integrated through a central value system, 'a set of normative judgements held by members of society who define... what to them is a good society' which becomes institutionalized into normative expectations and internalized 'need dispositions' (Parsons and Shils, 1962: 225–7). Parsons' functionalism thus assumes a neatly ordered, closed social world, a vast filing cabinet consisting of systems and sub-systems, multiple divisions and sub-divisions, endless classifications with the most tenuous relation to historically produced societies, a theoretical framework in which questions of who makes values, and why and how, have been systematically removed. Moreover, system changes occur not through social struggles over resources and ideology but through modes of internal disequilibrium and re-equilibrium. Parsons' concept of actor is also too one-dimensional, too easily conforming to the existing norms and values, lacking a many-sided and reflexive self capable of engaging in the strategies and practices linked to social change and to the broader issues of power.

Critics of functionalism have frequently pointed to its apparent failure to provide an adequate explanation of social change and the related issues of conflict and social struggle. Some functionalists, however, have integrated the concept of conflict within the model by arguing that it functions as 'a safety mechanism', producing an equilibrating and stabilising impact' (Coser, 1967). However, this is to define conflict in terms of system needs and fails to address the problem Marx raised of conflict playing a productive and constituting role in the making of institutions and values. The concept of system needs removes the actor as an active force from the structure so that 'conflict' is divorced from action. Thus the functionalist analysis of education, for example, points to its role in allocating individuals to specific occupations. However, it fails to address the conflict that can develop *within* the educational system. For example, as we saw in Chapter 2, Willis' (1977) research highlighted the conflicts between working-class children and the formal structure of the school, which resulted in anti-educational sub-cultures with their own specific values.

The concept of system needs seemingly reinforces the general criticism of Parsonian functionalism as based in an 'oversocialized' notion of the individual, a cultural dope with no apparent autonomy. Parsons has always rejected this criticism pointing to his concept of 'pattern variables' for providing actors with some autonomy and choice. Pattern variables structure modes of action, by providing the actor with choices over pairs or dichotomies of values, options which decide their relations with others. They include particularism/universalism (relating to others on the basis of gender or class and so on, or as a human being); affectivity/affective neutrality (choosing emotional involvement in relations, or as a business arrangement); specifity/diffuseness (relations defined in terms of role, lawyer, teacher, or more broadly through marriage and family; quality/performance (choosing relations through persons or through ends). Action is a mixture of the pattern variables but it remains limited and formal. Thus, in one of his own examples, Parsons' argues that the doctor/patient relationship involves universalism, specificity and affective neutrality. While this has been seen as a major theoretical contribution to the sociology of sickness (see Chapter 12), it has been criticized for failing to account for the fact that doctors are increasingly treating patients as sources of income in a competitive capitalist culture, striving for status and power within a hierarchically organized medical profession and sometimes 'medicalizing' areas of life for their own interests. Such action is difficult to accommodate to Parsons' abstract categories.

Action and Interaction: Problems of the Macro-micro Link

As a macro-sociological theory, functionalism conceived society as an external system structured in equilibrium and self-regulation, a whole superior to its constituent parts, in which the active human agent exercised little significant role in constituting and transforming institutions, structures and ideas. Although Parsons refers to his concept of system as 'a system of action', it is hard to find links between action and structure other than the concept of the actor assimilating cultural values which then become institutionalized components of the system itself and regulate the scope of action.

Micro-sociology is an attempt to resolve this problem by developing a distinctive sociological concept of the active, human self. The major contribution to sociology's concept of the self came from Mead (1863–1931). Mead emphasized the fluid and open nature of social order and the capacity of individuals to create new roles and meanings. For Mead, communication is effected through 'significant gestures', self-conscious acts which distinguish human from non-human behaviour. Animals do not communicate through universal symbols such as language, but react and adjust to situations. In contrast, humans interpret the *meaning* of other people's actions; language gives them the unique capacity to 'take the role of others' and see themselves from the point of view of others. The self is thus developed through its reciprocal relation with others and the wider community, both as a subject and an object. Mead theorized the self in terms of an 'I' and a 'Me'. The 'I' is the subject which thinks and acts, while the 'Me' is a consequence of the individual's awareness of self as object existing for others. It is the 'I' that has ideas, drives, impulses (such as the desire to walk out of a very boring class) while the 'Me' takes into account the reactions of others (that wouldn't look good, the tutor has to mark your examination paper). The 'I' is a combination of biological drives and social experiences, while the 'Me' arises almost entirely from communication through language. The self is thus a 'social structure' developing through patterns of interaction with itself, with others and with the community or social group. Hence the individual player within a football team must take account of the role and structure of the whole team. The self arises by taking into account the attitude of others and assimilating the group's 'social habits', values and goals. Mead suggests that it is shortly after childhood that the individual internalizes roles, especially the collective role of the group, which he called the 'generalized other' (Mead, 1934).

Mead regarded his work as social psychological rather than strictly sociological. It was Blumer who, in 1937, extended Mead's ideas to the field of social structure, coining the term 'symbolic interactionism', to refer to those modes of action whereby individuals 'negotiate' the different social situations encountered in everyday life to produce new meanings (Blumer, 1967). What is striking in Blumer's work is the emphasis on reciprocity, that social action occurs only through the self taking account of others – their values, ideas, definition of the situation – within a fluid and open structure, where relations are never fixed and rigidly stabilized.

While this approach focuses on the 'volunteristic' nature of social life, interactionism has been criticized for avoiding institutional analysis and macro-sociological issues of social class and power. In this context the work of Goffman (1922–82) is especially important for attempting to define interactionism more precisely and for taking up the problems of the micro-macro-link. In his late essay, 'The interaction order' (1983), Goffman argued that face-to-face interaction constitutes a *specific* order defined by its own distinctive internal properties (language, symbols, rules and moral obligations) and clear boundaries. The interaction order is not a mere reflection of the macro-institutional order but exists in its own right. Goffman's (1991) early work on mental hospitals had shown how, in the face of a depersonalizing social order where patients are classified by the institution as if they were objects and divested of any moral responsibility, there nevertheless develops an informal interaction order which enables them to sustain a sense of identity and engage in morally responsible social action.

Goffman's point is that the interaction order always involves a moral dimension, trust and tact in encounters with others and a commitment to sustain the order itself. For Goffman, the queue is perhaps the best example of the working of the interaction order as external influences (such as class or status) are usually blocked, with individuals accepting the inherent orderliness of the first-come-first-served basis.

But how is this interaction order linked with the macro-order? Goffman suggests that society exists and is integrated loosely through talk, with everyday conversation acting as a ritual affirmation of a commonly shared reality. Talk plays a key symbolic role in defining, strengthening and maintaining the structure of social groups and patterns of interaction. Through talk a world of other participants is created in everyday conversation, in pubs and work, and in public ceremonies, university seminars and learned societies, each one 'a little social system with its own boundary maintaining tendencies' (Goffman, 1972: 113). Goffman's point is that while the self develops only in relation to its social context, it is constituted at the macro-level by symbolic forms and shared meanings common to the micro-level of talk. Everyday conversation, for example, is usually sustained through the symbolic and ritual elements of politeness, with its respect for the other participants that is similar to the conception of the individual in religious institutions. Thus the institutional and interaction orders are 'loosely connected' through their common basis in symbolic and ritual forms that define the individual as embodying sacred and moral value (ibid.: 73, 95).

While this example of the 'loose coupling' of the micro- and macro-orders is ingenious, it has been criticized for failing to deal sufficiently with interaction within the institutional order itself. In common with many other micro-sociologists, Goffman focuses on interaction *only* at the micro-level. However, many other sociologists argue that all interaction is hierarchically structured. Within bureaucracies, for example, administrators and managers will generate their own distinctive interaction order producing meanings and new ideas that will affect the everyday life of those in subordinate positions, in the micro-contexts of the shopfloor, hospital wards, supermarkets. In 'The interaction order' Goffman suggested that in everyday interaction individuals draw on resources from institutional contexts, those relating to class and ethnic relations for example, to sustain them in encounters with others. However, class and ethnicity play important roles in constituting the interaction orders of both macro- and micro-contexts. And, while both orders can be empirically distinguished, it is rather a question of a tight, not a loose, coupling.

Goffman's micro-sociology has also been criticized from an action point of view for its conceptualization of the reflexive nature of the self. He argued that individuals do not have a unified self but, rather, have multiple selves in their everyday lives as they constantly move in and out of varied social and linguistic contexts. However, in stressing that the self is always 'embedded' and thus conditioned by a specific context, Goffman tends to minimize the cognitive and reflexive elements that constitute the self and its actions. He examines neither the sources of motivation (the Weber problem), nor how individuals come to believe in certain values while rejecting others and how they act with others on the basis of such beliefs.

It is ethnomethodology, perhaps the most radical of micro-sociologies, that represents the most strenuous attempt to deal with the question of motivation. Developed by Garfinkel during the 1960s, ethnomethodology (*ethno* referring to the observational study of the stock of commonsense knowledge available to individuals, while *method* refers to the strategies individuals employ to make sense of the social world and communicate meaning) was concerned with 'common sense knowledge of social structures as an object of theoretical interest' (Garfinkel, 1984: 77).

Ethnomethodology was influenced by the work of Schutz (1899–1959). Schutz agreed with Weber that sociological explanation should be based on the meanings that individuals give to their actions, but he argued that Weber had ignored an important problem:

> [Weber's] concept of the meaningful act of the individual – the key idea of inter-
> pretive sociology – by no means defines a primitive, as he thinks it does. It is, on
> the contrary, a mere label for a highly complex and ramified area that calls for much
> further study. (1972: 7–8)

This 'further study' involves the attempt to explain the ways in which people actually 'accomplish' social interaction. Reciprocity of perspectives cannot be assumed – it has to be explained. From this basis, Schutz developed the concept of the life world, the everyday world of experience, 'an inter-subjective world of culture' (Schutz, 1974: 134–5). Within this world of everyday experience, meaning is constantly produced by individuals who share in a common culture and a commonsense knowledge of how the elements of the everyday world work. This emphasis on knowledge, understanding, shared meanings and inter-subjective relationships contrast with Parsons' stress on the external and constraining role of norms in the socialization of individuals and their embodiment in the personality system.

Garfinkel, following Schutz, argued that social life is an 'accomplishment' of 'the organised artful practices of everyday life' (ibid.: 11). When agents choose particular goals they do so in terms of the taken-for-granted, mundane knowledge that is available in any given situation. A sociological theory of action must not only include the agent's own account of that action, but also examine how agents draw on commonsense knowledge and the *unstated* rules and assumptions of everyday life. It is through a process of practical social reasoning that individuals come to understand and grasp the rules that govern everyday social action. Although we may believe that our activities are shaped by clearly understood rules, this is not the case. The order around us is fragile. To illustrate this Garfinkel conducted a series of 'breaching experiments' in which individuals were faced with the breakdown of their expectations. For example, he encouraged his students to act as if they were lodgers within their own homes, thus disrupting the taken-for-granted routines of everyday life bringing to light its basis in commonsense assumptions. This disrupted situation caused anger and confusion, as individuals strove to re-establish the rules of everyday life. Hence Garfinkel's view, contrary to Parsons, that social order is not the result of the workings of system imperatives, or a common culture, but the practical accomplishments of highly reflexive agents as they make and remake meanings within everyday social interaction.

However, while ethnomethodology addresses the problem of motivation by positing a knowledgeable, imaginative and reflexive self, it tends to over-emphasize this voluntarism (agents vary in their capacity for reflexivity) and to place sociological analysis too narrowly within the micro-contexts of everyday social interaction. Ethnomethodology 'resolves' the agency structure problem by dissolving the latter. Such an approach thus ignores the possibility that individuals may be *unaware* of the ways in which social structural elements, external to their immediate situation, may shape their understanding and action: class position, ideology, power relations may influence educational, religious or political values and play a key role in determining the individual's attitude to others and to society. It is this exclusion of the macro-dimension which limits ethnomethodology as a sociological theory, for interaction occurs at both the macro- and micro-level. It is the complex relation of these two dimensions of social life which constitutes one of the major problems of sociological theory. The following sections examine attempts to develop concepts and substantive theory which might link the macro- and micro-dimensions in Marxism, structuration and field theory.

Attempts at Theoretical Synthesis

Marxism: From Gramsci to Habermas

Although Marx had noted the reflexive nature of human agents and argued for the role of collective agents (social classes) in social change, his work largely concentrated on the macro-economic and social processes. Few Marxists developed concepts which could link the macro- and micro-dimensions of the social formation. An important exception was Gramsci (1891–1937) who was one of the first major Marxist theorists to address this issue by analysing the workings of the cultural superstructure. He argued that socio-historical change was not the product of impersonal laws but the result of collective human will organized in collective social institutions, such as trade unions and political parties, involving both struggles over material resources as well as ideas. Gramsci used the concept of *hegemony* (derived from a Greek word meaning the leadership of one state over another) to describe a process whereby those social groups and classes aspiring to political and economic domination must develop both narrow 'corporate' interests, such as control over economic resources, *and* broader intellectual and moral leadership, including cultural, ethical, political ideas and values. Gramsci's thesis was that while 'corporate' interests are specific to a class, hegemonic interests are general to the whole society. He cites the case of the French Revolution where the revolutionary Jacobins developed from a class which initially functioned to organize a bourgeois mode of production to a class which represented all the popular social forces, such as the middle classes, working class and peasants, in opposing the old, aristocratic feudal regime. As a concept, hegemony elucidates the ways 'rising' classes seek to dominate not merely through the use of force and coercion but through *consent*, through generating ideas which command the support of subordinate classes, such as universal suffrage, expansion of education and the legal system. In modern societies individuals actively internalize the cultural values of a dominant or rising class ('the moment of hegemony') and this points to a voluntarist element in political domination with agents consenting and thus legitimating class rule. In modern society no one class can dominate 'from above' by excluding and ignoring other groups and classes. A dominant class must listen to the voices of subordinate classes thus producing a balance or 'equilibrium'.

Force and coercion belong to the state, while hegemony belongs to what Gramsci called 'civil society' (institutions such as the family, church, trade unions which are partly independent from the state). In this sense Gramsci conceives modern society as pluralist, a balance of forces between state and civil society, although one structured in class struggles. Within this context hegemony works at both the macro- and micro-levels. For example, during the nineteenth century Alpine mountaineering clubs became very popular in Britain, especially after 1850, bringing together different 'factions', of the upper and middle classes: the landed aristocracy, industrial bourgeoisie, old and new professions and intellectuals all united around an ideology which emphasized masculine, romantic and individual values. At this micro-level the values reflected the competitive individualism of the 'rising' capitalist class. It is through these specific values that the macro- and micro-levels can be linked in a tight coupling which focuses both on class and power as well as Goffman's interaction order (Robbins, 1987).

Hegemony thus points both to macro- and micro-processes involving agents seeking to establish new values. Although the concept of internalizing values brings Gramsci close to Parsons, the theory of hegemony is anti-functionalist, for the internalization of culture leads to a critical and cognitive awareness of existing values and the possibilities for opposition and change. Within Gramsci's model, then, there is no sense of a process of total incorporation of the individual into an integrated social whole.

Another Marxist perspective, equally concerned with the problem of social integration is the Frankfurt School. Its leading theorists, Adorno, Horkheimer and Marcuse abandoned the idea of working-class revolution, arguing that modern capitalism had developed into a highly centralized economic and political system dominated by the mass production of commodities, an increasingly atomized social structure and a passive, consumerist population. Capitalism had become a 'mass society' in which the principle socializing agencies were no longer those of class and family but the newly emerging mass media or 'culture industries'. The classical Marxist theory of capitalism was no longer relevant and, in Frankfurt School theory, the concept of mass culture replaced the concept of mode of production. Culture was the new mechanism of social order.

The conceptual framework employed by the Frankfurt School was derived less from Marx than from Weber, with culture industry (films, radio, television and so on) built on the basis of formal or *instrumental rationality*, which is largely concerned with the efficient functioning of the existing society and with narrowly defined goals, as distinct from *substantive rationality*, which is concerned with 'ultimate questions' such as freedom, justice, equality. Through the culture industries, organized entirely to make profits, culture becomes commodified, marketed as efficiently as possible to entertain and socialize individuals into a state of uncritical acceptance of society as it is.

Describing their approach as critical theory, in contrast to positivism which they termed 'traditional theory', the Frankfurt School analysed the processes whereby the institutions, culture and social consciousness of modern mass society had become one dimensional. Individuals were becoming less and less autonomous and increasingly incapable of critical thought and reflexive action. Thus their conclusions were bleakly pessimistic: the culture industry worked like an 'apparatus' socializing individuals into mass conformity. Unlike Gramsci, the Frankfurt School theorized social integration as indoctrination. Their substantive theory went on to postulate the questionable proposition that all forms of industrial society (capitalist, communist, fascist) were broadly similar in structure, integrated around a centralized, cultural apparatus.

Habermas, the leading figure of the second generation of critical theorists, rejected the Frankfurt School's concept of an inert, alienated mass and attempted to develop a more rounded, comprehensive theory. He argued that Marxism must be reformulated by integrating it with systems theory (especially Parsons) and with action theory (especially Weber, Mead and Schutz). Habermas agreed with Parsons about the importance of sociology explaining how consensus is achieved in societies. For Habermas, a major problem with Marx's model of the base and superstructure is that it lacked a concept of communicative interaction;

that is, it said little about how action is orientated towards establishing mutual agreement and understanding and a consensus governed by shared norms. Habermas' concept of communicative action follows Mead in arguing that it is through 'linguistically mediated interaction' that individuals achieve understanding and co-operation with others. In contrast to Marxism, which ignored the role of language in social evolution defining society in terms of a 'productivist model' based in collective social labour, Habermas argues that society consists of 'networks of communicative actions' which involve speaking as well as tool-making agents (Habermas, 1989).

Habermas makes a key distinction between the life world and the system. Following Schutz, the life world refers to the everyday world of active subjects trying to understand each other. In this context, Habermas follows the ethnomethodologists in highlighting the ways in which people draw on a stock of taken-for-granted assumptions to order their interactions. The life world is the sphere of active subjects trying to understand each other. However, society consists of both a life world and a system. The latter refers to things which are not linked by communicative action, such as state bureaucracy and capitalist economics. Here money and power rule and it functions through purposive, instrumental action. The system works through efficiency and profit, imposing its norms and constraining discourse. Action is orientated to the specific goals of the system and the most efficient means for realizing them. These are the system imperatives such as the maximization of profit irrespective of consequences for the quality of life within the life world. In contrast, communicative action is orientated to raising issues over the quality of life and engaging in open dialogue with others.

While the life world and system are separated in modern society, there is always a tension, especially acute in contemporary capitalist societies, between them. Habermas argues that there has been colonization of the life world by the system as more areas of life become subject to the imperatives of money and power. For example, culture and education have become commodities to be organized for profit rather than developed for mutual understanding. The result is the development of 'distorted' forms of communication based on force and coercion limiting the potential for rational communicative action. However, Habermas is not as pessimistic as Weber or the generation of Frankfurt School sociologists who preceded him. He argues that system elements could be forced out of the life world to create a more rational and egalitarian society. Habermas argues that this will come not from organized working-class resistance in the classical Marxist sense, but from 'new political movements', based on things like environmental concerns and the rights of various minority groups, which seek to reclaim aspects of the life world from the colonization of the system.

By positing a tension between system and life world, and emphasizing everyday face-to-face interaction, Habermas achieved a dynamism missing from Parsonian functionalism and the theory of culture industry. However, the role given to the impersonal logic of system imperatives – money and power – in the colonization of the life world suggests an absence of voluntarist social action which, to critics, seems uncomfortably close to a reassertion of functionalist systems theory. Society is integrated behind the backs of agents even though Habermas allows for social struggles in the life world.

Two more recent attempts to resolve the fundamental dualisms of sociological theory are Giddens' theory of structuration and Bourdieu's theory of habitus and field. Unlike Habermas, both reject Parsonian systems theory, arguing for a sociology built around the notion of reflexivity.

Structuration

Giddens first announced his theory of structuration in *New Rules of Sociological Method* (1976) developing it further in a series of publications culminating in *The Constitution of Society* (1984). Structuration theory seeks to unify sociological theory through the concept of the *duality* of structure through which it becomes possible to analyse human practices as both action and structure. The focus is on the making of structures, social life as 'the production of active subjects' (Giddens, 1976: 120–1). Society is not an external, constraining system but the result of skilled, knowledgeable and reflexive agents whose actions occur within specific social contexts. Giddens is not suggesting that the agent is the sole source of society, but rather, that all so-called objective structures are substantiated in practice as agents produce and reproduce the structures which underpin and enable action to take place. Thus structure is not theorized as a fixed and inert property of a social system but is 'carried' in reproduced practices embedded in time and space: it is *both* the medium for, and outcome of, social action. This is close to Weber's concept of social action, that social institutions and structure have no existence apart from the actions they embody. For Giddens, the focus for sociological analysis is not on an objectively existing system, nor the experiences of individuals, but 'social practices ordered across space and time' (Giddens, 1984: 170–1).

Giddens defines his concepts of structure and practices in terms of 'rules' and 'resources'. Rules provide the basis for an ordered and stable social life. They can be formal and public, such as those governing elections and teaching practices, and informal, governing the varied encounters of everyday life. Rules operate on two levels of consciousness: first, a discursive level in which agents have a tacit or theoretical grasp of the rules involved in the reproduction of social practices thus enabling them to understand and give reasons for action; and second, on a practical level, an awareness of the skills and knowledge which enable agents to carry out forms of action. Resources are those elements which agents incorporate into 'the production and reproduction of social practices' such as education, knowledge, skills which enable people to interact with others and transform relations. Resources, in short, are employed to 'make things happen' within specific social contexts. Through rules and resources social life is not intentionally realized by agents but 'recursively' structured. By this term Giddens means that while social practices change a situation, they simultaneously reproduce the social order on which the rules governing action depend. This is the key to understanding Giddens' argument that structure is both the *medium* and the *outcome* of social action (ibid.: 181).

Structuration theory, unlike Parsonian functionalism and Habermasian systems theory, is built around the concept of reflexive agents capable of monitoring their actions through practical and discursive consciousness. Agents, then, are not over-socialized and passive but knowledgeable, creative and active. While Giddens is right to stress the making of structures, the problem is that structure is collapsed into agency. For structures do not exist simply as practices, but both pre-exist and endure beyond individual and collective action. In many modern European societies, for example, compulsory military service, administered through military and political institutions, exerts an external, constraining influence on specific individuals; it acts on them as a structure limiting their choices and freedom to act. This suggests a dualism rather than a duality of structure, that is, structures *can* exist independently and objectively of individuals and constrain their action rather than necessarily being bound together with action (Mouzelis, 1991: Ch. 2).

Theory of Fields

Bourdieu's reflexive sociology, in contrast with Giddens, provides a body of concepts and substantive theory which link social practices and objective structures theoretically and empirically. Bourdieu (1990) conceives society as a network of specific 'fields', or 'social spaces', characterized by complex internal differentiation and hierarchical structures. Modern society comprises many different fields (education, religion, economic, cultural, political) each with its own specific institutions, rules and practices. In all fields those agents occupying dominant positions adopt defensive 'conservation strategies' to preserve their position and status, while newcomers develop 'subversion strategies' aiming to overthrow the governing rules and establish new ones. For example, within the cultural field there are struggles taking place over the concept of art, between conceptual painters and more traditional artists, with each group seeking to control the networks of galleries, art magazines and media journalism.

While fields are objective structures they are made through human action. Bourdieu makes the important point that this process of making is only possible because agents become socialized in ways which enable them to participate in the field itself. They do so by internalizing the social structure of the field, the hierarchy of positions, its history, its traditions and institutions. This is the 'habitus', a set of acquired and durable dispositions enabling agents to understand, interpret rules and act within a field. To participate in the educational field, for example, agents must acquire specific dispositions enabling them to understand relations between students and teachers, rules governing class discussion, tutorials and relations with others. Agents are thus not adapting passively to a pre-given social world but, through the creative and imaginative use of knowledge and skills, participate and enhance their position within a field (Bourdieu, 1990).

Habitus is grounded in practical knowledge and, although it can be modified by later experiences, it becomes ingrained, internalized as second nature. Thus within the field of diplomacy the dispositions linked to an upper-class family background and prestigious education enable individuals to move with confidence and style in the highly formalized social world of official ceremonies and pomp. Bourdieu has advanced a sociological explanation for the historical development of fields and the role of agents in their structure and transformation and, while marking an advance on the work of Parsons, Habermas and Giddens, it is not without its problems. The concept of habitus suggests a rather rigid social self based almost exclusively on self-interest and egoism, concerned only with pursuing goals that enhance status and position within a field. Action seems only to be instrumental in enabling agents to maintain or increase their assets and not bound up in any kind of fundamental belief in things such as politics, economics or art. Nevertheless, Bourdieu has made a major contribution to resolving many of the dualisms within sociological theory and has reunited theoretical analysis with the empirical research, something which constituted the hallmark of classical sociology.

Conclusion: Postmodernity and Social Theory

If the history of sociological theory can be understood in terms of attempts to reconcile the fact that societies are collectivities (structures) which are produced by the intentional actions of individuals (action), then postmodern social theory represents a decisive break with that tradition. While it is possible to categorize previous contributions to sociological theory in terms of the degree to which they emphasize the determining effects of structures, or the relative independence of human agency, it is not possible to categorize postmodern theory in this way. Postmodernism falls outside these traditional categories of sociological theory.

The starting point for postmodernists, as we saw in Chapter 1, is that we are now living in an altered postmodern condition of increasing diversity and fragmentation, where many of the divisions that characterized modern societies have collapsed. However, for postmodernists, it is not enough to reflect on these changes, the form and content of sociological ideas must themselves be *deconstructed* (Derrida, 1982). Deconstruction is a specifically postmodern idea, developed from literary criticism, that involves taking apart the internal characteristics of an approach rather than trying to supplement it with an alternative set of 'better' ideas. Postmodernists deconstruct the central idea of sociology, that there are ordered and related phenomena called 'societies' which can be understood by specialist concepts and methods. As McLennan puts it, the postmodernist asks:

> What gives us the right to see society as a totality, as a unified and coherent being? Why isn't it just a motley collection of bits and pieces? And how can we ever tell if our concepts genuinely do 'grasp' or 'reflect' this thing called society accurately? Indeed, who is to say what knowledge of society really amounts to? (1992: 329)

The postmodern critique can be seen most clearly in relation to structural theories, such as Marxism and structural functionalism, which purport to incorporate all aspects of social life into a set of universal structural principles. Postmodernists are sceptical of such theories because they represent grand narratives, or 'meta-narratives'; that is, single, overarching explanations which claim a superior grasp of truth over all others. For Marx, social phenomena could ultimately be explained in terms of the economic base, while for Parsons, it was the functional prerequisites which hold the key. Lyotard (1984), one of the most influential voices of postmodernism, argued that such meta-narratives reflect an arrogant and outdated modernist assumption that it is possible to have objective knowledge based on scientifically established truths. Postmodernists thus reject not only the substance of structural sociological theories, but also the very assumption that there can ever be a single valid account of society.

While the relationship between postmodernism and social action theories is undoubtedly more complex, the same basic objections that have been raised against structural theories still apply. This is because, even though social action theorists like Goffman and Garfinkel propose very different models of society from those advanced by structural theorists, they share the same desire to produce some form of authoritative account of social life. For example, Garfinkel's ethnomethodological account of social order is proposed in opposition to, and as superior to, the model of normative order proposed by Parsons. Even though social action theorists do not appeal to scientific truth to validate their accounts, from the postmodernist point of view, they are still locked into the modernist idea of producing some form of true, or better, accounts of society. These truths may be different – here actors are seen as rational, self-motivated and artful, whereas in structural theories they tend to be passive recipients of external forces – but they are presented as truths all the same.

Postmodern social theorists, in contrast, argue for the co-existence of a range of competing and incommensurable theoretical approaches, with no overarching set of principles by which to choose between them. While this position is no doubt useful as a corrective to some of the more ambitious grand theories which have emerged in sociology, it does nevertheless pose some real difficulties. The first is the tendency towards *relativism*, which seems inherent in postmodern theorising. Relativism, as we saw in Chapter 2, is the idea that no one theory can in principle be judged superior to any other. It is problematic because if we cannot judge any theory superior to any other, neither can there be any rational grounds to reject weak or incorrect theories. Thus Weber's account of the origins of capitalism must be regarded as just as valid as Marx's or, for the matter, as the incoherent ravings of a lunatic. Taking the postmodern critique to its logical – or rather illogical – conclusions, if no account can, in principle, be judged superior to any other, then we might as well question whether there is any purpose in doing sociological research in the first place.

Second, the extent to which to which postmodernists adhere to their own principles has been questioned. For example, Baudrillard (1983) has argued that contemporary societies are characterized by the endless consumption of signs and symbols generated by the electronic media. It is no longer a question of whether or not the media reflect reality, they have *become* reality. Consequently, we are living in a state of unreality, or *hyperreality* (see Chapter 14 for further discussion of the postmodern view of the media). Whatever the merits of this theory, it is a theory nonetheless, and one which Baudrillard supports with evidence and examples. It is thus difficult to see how postmodern theorists can express their own ideas without at the same time undermining them.

Third, postmodernism has been criticized by writers like Habermas for being inherently 'conservative'. If there are no criteria for judging one point of view better than any other, then it follows that there can be no valid, or authoritative, criticism of the ways in which societies are organized for the benefit of some groups at the expense of others. However, Foucault, whose work had a great influence on the postmodern movement, counters this by arguing that Habermas' work is naive and utopian. The idea that there are some fundamental 'truths' to be uncovered about social life is one of the myths of modernity. Foucault argues that critical theory's analysis of power and inequality, although claiming some sort of objective status, simply involves contrasting one set of value judgements with another. This debate reflects a more general question in sociology. Much of the credibility of sociologists' critical analyses of social arrangements rests on their conceptualizations of power and how it operates in societies. So what is power and how have sociologists tried to explain it? This is the subject of the following chapter.

Further Reading

Giddens, A. and Turner, J. (eds) *Social Theory Today,* Cambridge, Polity Press, 1987. A series of informed essays on some of the major trends in social theory.

Layder, D. *Understanding Social Theory,* London, Sage, 1994. An excellent, clear introduction, organised around the macro-micro dilemma in social theory.

Mouzelis, N. *Sociological Theory: What Went Wrong?,* London, Routledge, 1995. Advances a distinctive critical position, emphasizing the need for conceptual and substantive rigour.

Swingewood, A. *A Short History of Sociological Theory,* 2nd edn, Basingstoke, Macmillan, 1991. A discussion of the origins and development of sociological theory.

4

Power

Christine Helliwell and Barry Hindess

The concept of power is central to many areas covered elsewhere in this volume: from the organization of work to class and stratification, from the family to gender relations, from religion to crime and deviance. Yet the concept itself is subject to considerable confusion. The aim of this chapter is to clarify some of these confusions by exploring three different under-standings of power and the divergent sociological approaches they generate. It should help you understand:

- The fact that power has different meanings which give rise to different sociological questions

- Theories of the distribution and production of power

- Theories of the legitimacy and effectiveness of power

- Theories which focus on how the effects of power are produced

- The importance of looking for the theories of power which underlie different sociological perspectives and research studies

---

CONCEPTS

false consciousness ■ zero-sum view of power ■ coercion

legitimacy ■ power élite ■ government ■ liberalism

Introduction

The *Oxford English Dictionary* (OED) provides several different meanings of the word 'power'. Of these, three are used in discussions of social life. Accordingly, this chapter is divided into three main parts, each of which deals with one of these meanings.

The first part explores the understandings and assumptions encapsulated in the *OED* definition of power as 'possession of control or command over others'. This is what most sociologists mean, most of the time, when they talk about power: the capacity to get others to do what we want them to do. In this sense, teachers have power over pupils, presidents over populations and parents over children. This conception of power as some kind of *capacity* is intimately linked to a view of power as *quantifiable*.

The second part examines the understandings and assumptions encapsulated in the *OED* definition of power as 'legal ability, capacity or authority to act; especially delegated authority'. Power here refers to the legal authority or *right* that some people have to get others to do what they want them to do. In this sense, as well, teachers have power over pupils and presidents over populations; in addition, police have power over citizens and, until very recently, husbands had power over wives. While this view of power as *right* has been less widely accepted among sociologists than that of power as capacity, its advocacy in the work of certain key thinkers has rendered it extremely influential.

While these first two meanings of power are those used in most sociological discussions on the subject, there is a third, more general and much older, meaning which has recently begun to garner support in contemporary sociology as a result of its elaboration by the French theorist Michel Foucault. The third part of the chapter explores this conception of power, focusing primarily on its use in Foucault's work. This is the conception encapsulated in the *OED* definition of power as the 'ability to do or affect something or anything'. Power, in this sense, relates to human *agency*; that is, to one's ability to 'make a difference' in the world. On this definition, all human beings have power, in that we all have the ability to alter some pre-existing situations, no matter how trivial. Students have the power, for example, to disrupt a lecture or a tutorial class; a population has the power to resist the actions of its president.

It is easy to see that the three meanings of power given above overlap with one another. In the case of the first two, one's *capacity* to exercise control or command over others (power in the first sense) can often be seen as resulting, at least in part, from one's legal *right*, or authority, to do so (power in the second sense): the power of teachers over pupils, or police over citizens, being obvious examples. In the case of the first and third meaning, anyone's capacity to control or command others (that is, one's power in the first sense) is frequently understood as being a product of their more general ability to affect things – to make things happen in the world at large (power in the third sense).

Yet, while there are obvious congruencies between these three meanings, it is nevertheless important to keep them conceptually distinct. Hindess (1995) argues that the tendency to conflate the different meanings of power (which he sees as endemic to contemporary social and political theory) has had adverse consequences for the ability of social scientists and others to understand social and political life.

Power as Quantitative Capacity

One of the assumptions that pervades sociological discussions of power is that power is some kind of quantitative entity, like wealth: something that one can have 'more of' or 'less of'. This is the understanding set out in Weber's famous definition of power as 'the chance of a man or a number of men to realise their own will even against the resistance of others' (Weber, trans. 1978: 926). Weber is suggesting here that everyone has some chance of realizing their own will (or of 'getting their own way', as we might now say), but that some have a greater chance of doing so than others. In this understanding, power is usually seen as a *capacity* – the capacity to get one's own way – with some individuals or groups understood as having more of this capacity and others as having less. Most sociological writing on power has focused on questions to do with its *distribution* – who has it and who does not, and how much different parties have relative to one another – and/or its *production* – under what conditions greater or lesser amounts of it are created. The appeal, for many social scientists, of this conception of power as quantitative capacity is that it suggests that the study of power is a straightforward empirical matter: a matter simply of measuring and comparing. In practice, as we shall see shortly, it is less straightforward than it seems.

The Distribution of Power

Most sociologists who hold to a quantitative view of power – indeed, most sociologists writing about power – have been primarily concerned with its *distribution*: with which members of a society have more of it, and which have less. This, in turn, allows them to ask questions about what happens when parties with different *quantities* of power at their disposal come into conflict, and how power operates to enable those who have more of it to exercise their will over those who have less. For example, how is it that oil barons and newspaper tycoons seem so readily to get their way with governments, even when their wishes are opposed by the majority of the population? These kinds of questions require that the different quantities of power held by different parties can be measured and compared with one another, so that it becomes possible to state definitively that some parties have more than others. Since, as we have seen, the conventional sociological understanding of power is that it is what allows one party to command or control, or to impose their own will over others, then it follows that the outcome of social interactions will accord with the wishes and interests of those with more power. All one has to do in order to predict such outcomes, then, is to measure who has the most power and find out what their wishes and interests are.

The distribution of power, in this respect, suggests an obvious analogy with wealth. However, while it is possible to establish the overall quantities of wealth which someone holds in terms of money, it is much more difficult to establish the quantities of power which different parties hold, since there is no equivalent unit in terms of which power may be measured. As a result, the question of how the power holdings of different individuals or groups within a society are to be identified and compared with each other has been a matter of considerable debate among sociologists and others.

Lukes (1974) still provides one of the most useful introductions to the issues in dispute here. His discussion takes the form of an extended commentary on the 'community power debates', a series of famous debates about the nature and location of political power in the United States which took place among American sociologists and political scientists in the 1960s and 70s. Reflecting on these debates, Lukes argues first, that power has three aspects or dimensions, all of which must be considered in any serious analysis of the distribution of power. These three dimensions are:

1. the dimension which operates to determine the outcome of direct conflict
2. the dimension which operates behind the scenes so as to exclude certain interests from direct public conflict in the first place
3. the dimension which operates on people's thoughts and desires.

Lukes attributes the first two of these views to two sets of antagonists in the community power debates; the third view is his own.

The simplest and, on Lukes' account, the least satisfactory of these three views is the 'one-dimensional' or 'liberal' view of power, which he attributes to thinkers such as Dahl (1957, 1958, 1961) and Polsby (1963, 1980). Those who hold such a one-dimensional view focus exclusively on the first dimension of power: on that dimension which operates to determine the outcome of direct conflict. Methodologically, then, we can be certain that one party has more power than another only if we have evidence to show that that party has, in fact, been able to prevail on some occasion in the face of the other's opposition. During the community power debates, Dahl and Polsby argued, against Mills (1959) and others, that one cannot determine who has power in American society simply by establishing who is the 'ruling élite' (that is, by establishing who controls or commands 'major institutions' such as business, government and the military); one must also provide clear evidence that the members of this supposed élite can indeed impose their wishes against majority opposition.

In contrast, those who adopt a 'two-dimensional' or 'reformist' view of power regard as profoundly simplistic the 'one-dimensional' stress on power as largely manifest in contexts of direct, overt conflict. For reformists such as Bachrach and Baratz (1969) power is often also exercised in such a way as to *prevent* certain conflicts of interest from coming into public play in the first place. The approach adopted by thinkers such as Dahl and Polsby, they suggest, focuses only on the 'public' face of power, thereby ignoring the manner in which certain interests are excluded from consideration in council chambers, parliamentary assemblies and other venues in which major decisions affecting the community are taken. Thus, any study focusing exclusively on who prevails in cases of overt conflict is likely to obscure an important dimension of the actual exercise of power in any society.

Lukes describes this two-dimensional view as 'reformist' because it insists not only that the interests of certain individuals and groups are not represented in political debate, but also that the exclusion of those views is illegitimate. It suggests, in other words, that political and other institutions are in need of substantial reform. Thus, on Lukes' account of the dispute between supporters of the one-dimensional and the two-dimensional views of power during the community power debates, what is at issue between them is a matter not only of method (how to identify who has power and who has not) but also of values (how power should be distributed in society).

Lukes argues, however, that both views, at least as he describes them, treat power as enabling some parties to prevail over others in conditions where there are clear differences between what each regard as their respective interests. Lukes himself believes that it is necessary to go even further. He suggests that while there are certainly cases in which power works in the relatively straightforward ways which are the concern of the one- and two-dimensional views, there are also important cases in which it does not, such as when those who suffer from the workings of power are prevented from recognizing that their interests are at risk. Some of the most influential forms of the exercise of power in the modern world, in his view, work by manipulating the thoughts of those whose interests are adversely affected. Indeed, he asks:

> Is it not the supreme exercise of power to get another or others to have the desires you want them to have – that is, to secure their compliance by controlling their thoughts and desires? (Lukes, 1974: 23)

This is the basis of Lukes' own 'three-dimensional' or 'radical' view of power.

The attempt to influence the thoughts and desires of others is a feature of most social interaction, and the individuals concerned often have a fair idea of what is being done to them. What Lukes has in mind is something less obviously mundane, in which the victims of power are unaware of its action on them. The most significant of these kinds of cases are those in which power is not exercised over individuals in any direct fashion, but operates instead via 'socially structured and culturally patterned behaviour' (1974: 22). In other words, Lukes is suggesting that *socialization* processes themselves are part of the exercise of power in any society. In such cases the exercise of power will generally go unrecognized by those whose interests are injured by its effects: it influences the thoughts and desires of its victims, but it does so largely through the workings of 'collective forces and social arrangements' (ibid.). According to Lukes, it is possible for the social scientist to work out which members of society are the victims of power, through imagining how an autonomous life – a life unconstrained and unshaped by the exercise of power over it – would be lived. Those whose lives deviate from this autonomous ideal – those who are constrained in the pursuit of their autonomous interests – are those over whom power is being exercised by others.

Lukes' 'three-dimensional' view rests on the twin understandings that not only do all individuals have the potential to achieve true autonomy if they are free from the constraining and distorting effects of power, but also that it is possible to have a society in which the third dimension of power plays no significant part. In the next section of the chapter we shall see that these two understandings are central to an extremely influential body of analysis which focuses primarily on power not as a capacity, but as a *right*, and which is thus primarily concerned with issues of consent and legitimacy.

In addition, Lukes' analysis requires that we regard all social interaction as a potential conduit for the workings of an insidious form of power. This involves two assumptions which are fundamentally Marxist in origin. First, that society can be understood as an arena of conflict between overarching social forces which themselves represent the interests of particular social groups. Second, that the institutions of capitalist society operate in such a way as to impose a distorting *ideology* or a *false consciousness* on the masses of the population, that is, to prevent them from recognizing either the true character of their position in society (for example, the fact that they are oppressed or exploited by a small minority) or the interests which arise from that position. These same two assumptions underlie the argument of the influential Italian Marxist, Gramsci, that as we saw in Chapter 3, the rule of the bourgeoisie in advanced capitalist societies is based on both coercion and consent, and that the latter is made possible by the fact that members of the subordinated classes are not aware of their interests in the overthrow of capitalist domination (Gramsci, 1971). Lukes' view is radical because, like Gramsci and other Marxist scholars such as Marcuse and Habermas, he argues that contemporary social institutions must be completely transformed if those who are the victims of social and political power are ever to free themselves of its effects.

The three approaches to the study of power delineated by Lukes all treat power as a quantifiable capacity – usually as a capacity to command or control others, that is, to impose one's will over others – and they are also concerned primarily with the *distribution* of this quantifiable entity – with who has more of it, and who less. However, each of these views differs markedly over how power should be measured, and how its distribution should thus be ascertained. Ironically, then, while the conception of power as quantitative capacity appears to promise that its distribution can, like wealth, be unambiguously determined through simple techniques of measuring and counting, it has in fact given rise to intractable dispute – as exemplified in the community power debates and Lukes' later intervention in them – over exactly how those techniques should be applied.

The Production of Power

While most sociological writing on power has focused primarily on its distribution, a number of very significant discussions have been concerned largely with questions to do with its *production*. Those writing on production also invariably assume that power is a quantifiable capacity whose possession determines the outcome of social interactions. However, their primary concern has been with the social conditions that explain why some parties have been able to have more power than others. This focus on the 'why' questions has meant that these analyses are in certain respects more sophisticated than those which focus only on the simple 'who/where' questions of the distribution of power.

We have already noted that the understanding of power as a quantitative phenomenon suggests an analogy with money or wealth. One of the most significant and forceful elaborations of this analogy is Parsons' critique of what he calls the 'zero-sum' conception of power which, in his view, informs much of the academic discussion of the distribution of power in American society (Parsons, 1969a, 1969b). 'Zero-sum' is a technical term taken from game theory. It is used to characterize a distinctive feature of competitive games, such as poker, in which a fixed quantity of assets is at stake. Because the stake is fixed, there are only a finite number of ways in which it can be distributed among the players, and so only a finite number of possible outcomes to any particular game. For those playing the game, the exclusive concern is with the distribution of the stake and, specifically, with how to maximize one's own share of it. Similarly, Parsons argues, according to the zero-sum conception of power there is only a fixed quantity of the stuff to go around, and the most important issues to be raised in any investigation of power are thus concerned with its distribution: who has it and who has not?

Parsons' central point is that it is a mistake to treat power in this 'zero-sum' way: as a fixed quantity. Doing this, he implies, is like analysing economic activity by focusing only on the circulation of money and wealth in market exchanges. Such an analysis would ignore, in particular, the *production* of goods and services. Economic commentators commonly argue that we should not allow our concern with matters of equity in the distribution of income and wealth to obscure the importance of the production of wealth. They have observed that some societies have considerably more wealth than others, and that the condition of a poor individual in a wealthy society may be superior to that of a wealthy individual in a poor one. For this reason, many sociologists of development have suggested that, in most 'undeveloped' societies, what is needed to improve the condition of the poor is economic growth – the *production* of new wealth – rather than a different *distribution* of existing wealth.

Similarly, Parsons and others argue that power is something that is not simply distributed in societies, but is also produced there: the quantity of power potentially available to any society is thus not fixed. In particular, they have observed that, even allowing for differences in population size, some societies have been able to generate considerably more power than others. Like wealth, power will often be used in pursuit of sectional interests but much of it will also be available for the benefit of society as a whole. Continuing the analogy between power and wealth, they have gone on to argue that the production of power is at least as important an issue for our understanding of modern societies as is its distribution.

Parsons argues that power is produced by the particular set of social conditions found in any society. In particular, he suggests that the amount of power in a society will depend on the extent to which it is possible to generate and to sustain the belief among the population at large that the actions and instructions of those in positions of authority are indeed legitimate. This belief by a population that those in positions of authority have the *right* to exercise power (in the first sense of control or command) over them – that their power is, in other words, legitimate – is usually referred to by sociologists (and by social and political theorists in general) as a belief in the *legitimacy* of that power or, indeed, of the ruling élite itself. In fact, the notion of legitimacy often involves rather more than this, as we shall see in the following section of the chapter. For now, however, we need to note that just as, in extreme cases of inflation, loss of confidence in money can inhibit the production of wealth and encourage increasing resort to barter, so, in Parsons' view, can a loss of belief in legitimacy inhibit the production of power and encourage the use of coercion.

Returning to the three definitions of power with which we began this chapter, we can see that Parsons' use of the term combines the first and second of these: power as control over others and as legal capacity or authority to act. Power in the sense of capacity to control or command others Parsons describes not as power, but as *coercion*, unless it occurs in combination with power in the second sense; unless, that is, it is legally authorized or 'legitimate'. A belief by the members of society at large in the legitimacy of those wielding power over them, then, is integral for Parsons to the constitution of power – to its very production – in the first place. Without such a belief there is not power; there is simply coercion.

Like Parsons, Weber sees the continuing power to control or command others as a product of social conditions or social arrangements; he stresses that it is dependent on both organization (the presence of a chief and administrative staff – and therefore some system of hierarchy – as well as a relatively complex system of administration) and compliance or co-operation on the part of those over whom the power is exercised. He goes on to argue that compliance is unlikely to survive for long unless it is accompanied by a belief in the legitimacy of the leader's power. Thus, while Parsons sees legitimacy as essential for the *production* of power in the first place, Weber sees it as necessary only for the *continuation* of certain kinds of power.

A more recent, influential approach to the study of the production of power is developed by Mann (1986). He identifies power in general as 'the ability to pursue and attain goals' (1986: 6) – that is, in the third sense identified at the beginning of the chapter. He then goes on to define *social* power – the power pertaining to relationships between people – as involving two distinct aspects: first, the power which one individual or group exerts over others and, second, the power produced by a number of people engaged in collective action, whereby their co-operation allows them 'to enhance their joint power over third parties or over nature' (ibid.). Mann's point, with respect to this second aspect, is that a group of individuals co-operating is able to produce far greater power than any individual can produce on their own. Like Weber, he stresses the importance of *organization* for the production and maintenance of social power: individuals must be organized relatively efficiently if they are to co-operate to the degree necessary for the production of significant amounts of social power. Mann suggests that in most significant forms of social power both of these aspects are present: people usually co-operate with one another to produce larger amounts of power because of the power exerted over them by others (because they are commanded to, or required to, by others). As with Weber, the production of power thus requires both hierarchy and co-operation. Mann distinguishes four types of social power – economic, ideological, military and political – which correspond, in his view, to the four fundamental spheres of organized social life. While these are different from one another in certain important respects, they nevertheless all involve the two aspects of social power outlined earlier.

Parsons, Weber and Mann all provide analyses of power which are rather different in orientation from those which focus only on questions of its distribution. Nevertheless, there is a sense in which their arguments continue to rest on the quantitative conception of power outlined at the beginning of this section. In particular, as we have seen, all are concerned with the social conditions under which 'more' power may be produced, with Parsons stressing the role of legitimacy in this respect, and Weber and Mann emphasizing also the significance of organization and co-operation. While Parsons' analogy between power and wealth makes explicit this conception of power as a quantifiable entity, so too does Mann's claim that those with 'more' economic, ideological, military or political power commonly prevail over those with less power of the same kind. We find here the conventional sociological assumption that the outcome of social interactions or disputes is determined by the quantities of power available to different parties, with those with more able to impose their own will onto those with less.

The conception of power as some kind of quantitative entity is thus pervasive throughout sociology and, indeed, throughout the social sciences in general. Yet, there are problems with this conception, and its widespread acceptance has hampered attempts by sociologists and others to come to terms with what we mean by power. The first concerns the notion of power as some kind of homogeneous essential substance – a notion which is invariably accepted by those who wish to compare quantities of power as distributed within a society or, indeed, as produced under different social conditions. Those sociologists and others engaging in such comparative/quantitative work have little choice but to accept an essentialist notion of power as something which remains unchanged across the many diverse contexts in which it comes into play. This is because without such a notion the comparative enterprise would become untenable: how does one compare quantities of one 'kind' of power obtaining in certain specified social contexts with quantities of a different 'kind' of power obtaining in others? In order to make such comparisons and so to assess who has more and who less power in society at large, or what kinds of overall societies produce greater amounts of power than others, sociologists must be able to regard all of these potentially different 'kinds' of power as equivalent in some sense – as able to be compared in a meaningful way. They do this by treating power as if it involved some kind of common substance: as if it has the same fixed, fundamental character regardless of the context in which it occurs or how it is used.

As a result, sociologists often draw a distinction between power *itself* (which remains unchanged in its essential character from one social context to another) and the *means* by which that power is exercised (which varies from one context to another). Giddens, for example, stresses the need to distinguish between power and 'resources': 'the media through which power is exercised' (1984: 16). The latter include material conditions of various kinds (land, machines, weapons) as well as what he calls 'authoritative resources' related to patterns of social organization and legitimacy. Giddens' point in stressing this distinction is that while these 'resources' may vary from context to context, the underlying power which they have in common remains the same.

While this distinction, between on the one hand, the essential, unchanging substance power and, on the other, the diverse, changing resources through which that power is exercised, is necessary to most quantitative analyses of power, it is, nevertheless, deeply problematic. In practice, the 'quantity' of power which any party is able to exercise on any particular occasion cannot so easily be separated from the resources through which it is exercised. To take a straightforward example: a would-be rapist has a much higher chance of imposing his will onto his victims if he threatens them with a weapon such as a knife or a gun than if he merely engages in verbal abuse to get his way. In other words, the quantity of power which he is able to exercise over them is directly related to the use of certain kinds of resources. In fact, a number of those analysts who hold to a quantitative understanding of power are aware of this problem, and have attempted to circumvent it. It is partly in order to do this that Mann, for instance, distinguishes (as we have seen) between political, economic and other kinds of powers; he thus avoids essentializing power and so is able to link it more closely to the particular contexts in which it operates.

The second (closely related) problem is a much more profound one, and concerns the most fundamental assumption underlying the understanding of power in quantitative terms: viz, that it is a *difference* in power which allows one party to impose its own will over others, even against the wishes of those others. Quite apart from the fact that it is much more difficult than it appears at first sight, as we have seen, to work out which party has more power in any social situation, there is a deeper problem with this assumption. This is that it is by no means always the case that the relative quantities of power (however these might be measured) held by different parties allow us to determine the outcome of any conflict between them. No doubt there will be cases in which the power available to one party is so outweighed by that available to another that the outcome of any conflict between them could hardly be in doubt. However, the experience of the USA in Vietnam or of Russia in Chechnya suggests that such cases are fewer than one might imagine. In other words, the outcome of interactions or disputes between contending parties is influenced by much more than simply how much power in the abstract is available to each: it is also influenced by such things as the tactics which each employs to achieve its goals, how they make use of the resources at their disposal and so on. The notion that the shape of social life is determined entirely by the sheer quantities of power available to different parties is clearly oversimplified.

Power as Right

While, as we have seen, almost all sociological accounts of power have been concerned with it as the quantitative *capacity* of one party to command or control, or to impose its will on others, many of these have also been concerned with power in the second of those senses: as a *right* which some parties have to command or control others. In contemporary western societies this right is generally recognized as such by those over whom it is exercised, with the result that they are willing to *consent* to being commanded or controlled. To take some obvious examples, we all consent to pay our taxes, or to drive according to the rules of the road, because we accept the *right* of our leaders to demand these things from us; they can thus be described as having the 'power' to tax us, or the 'power' to demand that we abide by the road rules. Central, then, to most modern discussions of power as right are questions to do with *consent*, and specifically with whether or not the fact that we accord power as right to certain authorities (such as the power/right of the government to tax us) means that we can genuinely be said to have consented to that power being exercised over us. At issue here is the notion of *legitimacy* which, as we have already noted, is at the core of many discussions of power.

It is helpful to distinguish between two rather different approaches to the study of legitimacy and power as right. The first of these is that taken by Weber and Parsons, in which the focus is on how a population's belief in the legitimacy of the power exercised over it is produced and sustained. In this approach, little attention is paid to the question of whether this belief is itself well founded or 'true'. Rather, what is of concern to these thinkers is the simple fact that such a belief *does* exist, and how it came into being. Weber notes, for example, that in modern democratic societies 'the chief and his administrative staff often appear formally as servants or agents of those they rule', and he adds that this fact 'does nothing whatever to disprove the quality of dominance' (1978: 215). However, what matters for Weber's analysis of political power in democratic societies is the existence of this belief and its consequences for political organization, not the fact (as he sees it) that it is based on a misapprehension about the nature of political power. Parsons takes a similar view. Rather than presenting democracy as a system in which the people rule, he treats it instead as one which promotes a pervasive feeling of obligation among the people with respect to the commands of those able to exercise power as right (that is, those in legitimate positions of authority) He suggests democracy is more effective in this respect than any other form of rule yet seen; it is partly for this reason that he regards democratic societies as having reached the highest known stage in his scheme of societal evolution (Parsons, 1971).

However, for many sociologists, the Weber/Parsons stress on the *effectiveness* of power smacks of moral bankruptcy. They are also interested in whether a population's belief in the right of their rulers to exercise power over them – and their consequent consent to that power – is well founded, or justifiable. At issue for these thinkers, in other words, is not *belief* in the legitimacy of power, but rather legitimacy itself. If, for instance, people consent to power being exercised over them because they are unaware of the real character and effects of that power, can they truly be said to have *consented* to its use, and is the power in question truly legitimate? To take a straightforward example: if the populations of the USA, Australia and New Zealand 'consented' to the sending of troops to fight in Vietnam on the basis of deliberately distorted information about the situation in that country, can we describe this as 'true' consent, and can we describe the governments of those countries as having a 'true' right to send the troops? Many members of the populations of the USA,

Australia and New Zealand clearly thought that the answer to all these questions was no, resulting in outbreaks of civil disobedience which occurred in all three countries for the duration of the war.

This notion of power as right has appeared in many sociological discussions, especially those dealing with political power as it operates in modern democracies, most particularly in the United States. These studies are concerned, in particular, with the question of whether the belief of the American people at large that their government has the right to exercise power over them necessarily renders this power right, or legitimate. In the previous section we looked at the 'community power debates' of the 1960s and 70s, in the context of Lukes' discussion of what he called the one-, two- and three-dimensional approaches to the study of power. While we focused there on the differences between the protagonists concerning questions to do with the *distribution* of power (concerning who has it, and how we can measure it), in fact, for those involved, these questions were simply a means to answering a much more important set of questions: those concerning the *legitimacy*, or the *right*, of political power in the United States. The differences between the protagonists regarding questions of the distribution of power in fact prefigured the differences between them regarding whether the widespread consent to the exercise of power by the ruling élite was justified, and whether that power could therefore be said to be legitimate.

The community power debates were sparked off by Mills' condemnation of the American power élite for operating a system of rule which he describes as one of 'organised irresponsibility' (1959: 361). In Mills' view, the 'ruling élite' – those in charge of major institutions such as business, government and the military – is concerned with the pursuit of its own interests at the expense of those of the people, and is not truly accountable to the people. He argues, then, that American democracy is not, in reality, operating in the ways in which most Americans believe it to be operating; the people thus give their consent to their rulers under false pretences. For Mills, this renders illegitimate the power exercised by those rulers.

In opposing this view, Dahl (1961) acknowledges, in his study of politics in the American city of New Haven, that the conduct of political life in America does not conform to received understandings of democracy. However, in his view, this shows that these understandings should be modified to take account of the complexity of twentieth-century democratic societies, rather than that such societies are not democratic. As he puts it: New Haven 'is a republic of unequal citizens – but for all that a republic' (Dahl, 1961: 86). In other words, while America may be a long way from the democratic goal of political equality, it is nevertheless a society in which the people rule. At the most fundamental level then, according to Dahl, the system operates in the way in which its citizens believe that it does. Their consent to that system is thus justified, and the power exercised over them by their rulers thus legitimate, or 'right'.

Bachrach and Baratz (1969) argue, in turn, that Dahl's conclusion rests on a failure to recognize that power itself may be used, covertly, to exclude the interests of those who are not well served by the American political system.

Lukes, and other adherents to the 'radical' view of power, go one step further. They suggest that in contemporary western democracies not only are the interests of many people excluded by the covert use of power but, in addition, this power operates in such a way as to mislead *those people themselves* concerning where their real needs or interests lie. Another celebrated example of this kind of argument is found in Marcuse's *One-Dimensional Man*, where he argues that liberty, in contemporary democratic societies, has been made 'into a powerful instrument of domination' (Marcuse, 1972: 21). Marcuse is, in effect, claiming that the fact that people have been misled into believing that they are free in those societies, leads them to consent to a system which is, in fact, profoundly unfree.

We can see that the concepts of *false consciousness* and *ideology*, which we discussed in the previous section, are central to this kind of argument: people consent to power being exercised over them because they have been socialized into believing that society is operating differently (more in line with their interests) from how it actually is operating. Lukes, Marcuse and like-minded thinkers argue that under such conditions, the 'consent' of the members of these societies to the power in question serves simply to perpetuate the very exercise of power which works against their own needs and interests. This is why, of course, many of those who have adopted this kind of position – most particularly Marxist scholars – have advocated civil disobedience, or even revolution, seeing this as a 'legitimate', or morally justifiable, response to such an illegitimate use of power.

A central difficulty with all of these discussions which take the second approach to the study of power as right, is that there is no straightforward basis on which we can decide, in any particular case, whether or not 'true' consent has been given by people to the exercise of power over them, and whether that power is therefore legitimate. Because there is no systematic basis for agreement between them, different scholars decide these questions, and pass judgement on any particular case, according to their own political understandings and commitments. In the community power debates for example, as we have already seen, some scholars (Dahl, Polsby) claim that the exercise of political power in the USA *is* based on the people's consent and is therefore legitimate, while others (Mills, Bachrach and Baratz, and later, Lukes) argue equally vehemently that it is neither of these things. The lack of any objective basis on which to make such judgements suggests in fact that such disputes are, ultimately, irresolvable.

There is an additional, related, problem with the 'radical' view adopted by Lukes, Marcuse and others. According to this view, the consent that matters for our evaluation of the legitimacy of political power is the consent that people would give under conditions in which their thoughts and desires were not affected by the impact of power. For example, if we wished to evaluate whether or not the consent of Australians to the exercise of power by their government in sending troops to Vietnam was 'true' consent, we would need to imagine whether they would have consented to this action were they members of a society in which Lukes' 'insidious' power was not influencing their thoughts and actions. The difficulty here is that we can identify the effects of such an insidious power only through *imagining* what a society without such an insidious power might be like. We are back in the terrain of contentious ethical and political judgements and, consequently, interminable dispute.

We have already noted that most sociological work concerned with power as quantitative capacity has focused around apparently 'empirical' questions such as who has power, who has not, and how it is produced. Furthermore, the study of power as right raises 'political' or 'ethical' questions to do with whether or not those who exercise power over others have the *right* to do so. In practice of course, as we noted at the start of the chapter, many thinkers tend to run these two senses of power together, with the result that 'empirical' and 'political' questions become entangled. Consequently, academic debates about power in the sense of quantitative capacity have usually been animated by broader political concerns, especially those to do with the legitimacy of government and the defence of individual autonomy.

To take the latter as an example, *quantitative* studies of who has 'more' and who 'less' power in a society – such as those occurring as part of the community power debates – are frequently motivated by the *political/ethical* assumption that substantial inequity in the distribution of power in society is a 'bad' thing. Such inequity is believed to be 'bad' because it enables some parties to influence profoundly the behaviour of others, or to 'get their own way' even against the wishes of others. In western societies, where an extremely high value is placed on individual autonomy, or individual freedom, this is seen by most scholars as highly undesirable.

Partly for this reason, power over others is often represented in *negative* terms in sociological and other kinds of discussion, as an imposition or constraint on the autonomy of those over whom it is exercised. The power of the modern state is regarded as being particularly important in this respect, since it is seen as constraining the liberty or autonomy of all of its subjects. In this view, power is invariably negative in its effects when exercised over people: it is seen as *taking something from* people, rather than as giving something to them. This 'negative' view of power – the notion of power as *constraint* or *imposition* – underlies the disputes over legitimacy which we considered earlier: the political power of the state is seen as legitimate if its capacity to constrain or impose on the liberty of its subjects is based on their consent, and illegitimate if it is not. Indeed, in Lukes' version of this argument, power can even be used to prevent its victims from thinking what they otherwise would have thought and so to elicit from them a consent which they otherwise would not have given. However, as we will see in the following section of the chapter, sociologists do not necessarily have to understand power in negative terms.

Power as Acting on the Actions of Others

If the study of power as quantifiable capacity is invariably caught up with broader political and ethical concerns, then criticism of that understanding of power can be expected to have widespread ramifications for social and political theory in general and, more particularly, for the issues considered in earlier sections of this chapter. This point brings us to the work of Foucault, which offers a radical alternative both to conventional understandings of power and to the alternative views offered by thinkers such as Lukes.

Foucault understands power as the ability of individuals or groups to act on the actions of others or, in other words, to act in such a way as to affect the actions of others. Giddens has a related understanding in mind when he insists that action:

> Depends upon the capability of the individual to 'make a difference' to a pre-existing state of affairs or course of events. An agent ceases to be such if he or she loses the capability to 'make a difference', that is, to exercise some sort of power. (Giddens, 1984: 14)

For Foucault, however – unlike for most other thinkers who make use of this conception of power – the ability to *act* on the actions of others is not the same as the ability to *control* or *command* the actions of others, which Foucault (1988) calls domination. Thus, in contrast to most other thinkers, Foucault is not running together the first and third meanings of power provided at the start of the chapter; in his view, people can affect or influence the actions of others without controlling those actions. Power is, here, an inescapable feature of all human interaction.

This view of power as *action* (and, specifically, as acting on the actions of others) has a number of radical implications for the study of power by sociologists and others. First, it suggests that power cannot be understood (and hence analysed) in quantitative terms. Foucault describes power as the 'total structure of actions' (Foucault, 1982: 220) that one brings to bear on the actions of others: in other words, power simply *is* (it is all of one's actions directed at other people), rather than something that one can have more or less of. A crucial point to note here is that for Foucault power *is* action, rather than something which animates – or underlies – action, as it is for many other thinkers. We have seen, for example, that Giddens distinguishes between particular resources 'through which power is exercised', and the underlying capacity – power itself – which those resources represent.

Foucault's view, on the contrary, is that power in the sense of such an under-lying capacity simply 'does not exist' (1982: 217).

Second, and following on from this, the view of power as *action* renders irrelevant questions about whether a population's belief in the right of their rulers to exercise power over them is 'truly' legitimate or right. As we have seen, these questions are a central focus for most sociologists – and most other scholars – concerned with power. But if, as in Foucault's view, power is everywhere, and is an inescapable component of all social relationships, then these kinds of questions are of little value. This is not to say that Foucault is not concerned with the *belief* in legitimacy: the fact that people obey commands because they *believe* that others have the right to issue them. In this respect *belief* in legitimacy plays a similar role in Foucault's analysis to that of Parsons and Weber: the concern is with how that belief is produced and sustained and what its effects are, rather than with whether or not it is 'true' or well founded.

In Foucault's view, then, the focus on legitimacy in most writings on power is misplaced and we need 'a political philosophy that isn't erected around the problem of sovereignty' (Foucault, 1980: 121). Just as Foucault does not conflate the first and the third of the meanings of power provided at the beginning of the chapter, neither does he conflate the second and third. In adopting a notion of power as to do with human agency, he is not assuming that it automatically follows from this that power concerns the ability to exer-cise control over others, and that it therefore necessarily involves questions to do with legitimacy or 'right'.

The radical significance of Foucault's analysis of power, then, lies not in suggesting a new set of answers to questions about how power is distributed and produced, and on what basis it can be said to be 'legitimate' or 'right'. Rather, the significance of Foucault's contribution lies precisely in his *displace-ment* of these issues from the centre of discussions about power: in effect, the most radical implication of his view of power as a ubiquitous, inescapable feature of all human interaction is that there is little of value to be said about power itself. We all act on the actions of others, but our actions in this respect (our 'powers') have nothing in common with each other: end of story. Foucault's analysis then, leads us away from the study of power *per se*, and into quite different areas of inquiry.

We can illustrate this point by reference to Foucault's discussions of the relations between power and autonomy. We have seen that the understanding of power as quantifiable capacity suggests that the power of others should be seen as an actual or potential constraint or imposition on one's autonomy, or freedom, and that this view of power as constraint or imposition – as *nega-tive* in its effects – is assumed in most discussions on power. Autonomy, in this view, is a matter of not being subject to the power of another. But if we accept Foucault's account of power as a matter of acting on the actions of others, then autonomy in this sense is illusory: we are always subject to the power of others, just as others are subject to our power.

However, while for Foucault the ideal of 'true' autonomy (and, hence, true 'consent') is an illusion (since others are always acting on our actions), this does not mean that he sees individual behaviour or conduct as *determined* by the actions – by the power – of others. On the contrary, in his view, people are always able to choose, to some degree, how they will conduct themselves in any situation. Indeed, for Foucault, the effective exercise of power *requires* that individuals possess a significant degree of freedom. This is because for people to be able to act on the actions of others – that is, to exercise power over others – those others must themselves be able to act and, indeed, to reciprocate that exercise of power. In fact, as Foucault argues in *Discipline and Punish* (1979), power often has the effect of *enhancing* the capacities of those over whom it is exercised. The exercise of discipline, for example, can provide individuals with new skills and attributes, help them to control their own behaviour in trying conditions, and promote their ability to follow commands and to act in concert with others. Foucault's concept of power, then, is profoundly radical in a further sense: it construes power as most usually *productive* in its effects, as *adding to* the capacities and abilities of individuals. This is in marked contrast to conventional depictions of power which, as we have seen, almost invariably assume it to be *negative* in its effects: to *take away from* – to constrain and distort – people's 'true' capabilities. Moreover, while questions of *production* are important in Foucault's analysis, the focus is on how the *effects* of power are produced. In this respect, his work differs also from that of other thinkers for whom the issue of production is important – such as Weber, Parsons and Mann – where the focus is on the production of *power itself*.

The fact that power depends on the freedom of its subjects means, in Foucault's view, that where there are relations of power there is also the possibility of resistance. Nevertheless, in marked contrast to Lukes' notion that we can judge the effects of power on people's thoughts and desires by imagining a world in which those effects are not present, Foucault's understanding of power appears to invoke no such utopian possibilities. Indeed, his work has often been criticized on precisely these grounds (for example Taylor, 1986; Fraser, 1989; McCarthy, 1992). However, the difference between these two positions is less clear-cut than it might seem. Thus, while he insists that power depends on the freedom of those on whom it is exercised, Foucault also recognizes that conditions will often be such that those who are subject to the effects of power will find that their 'margin of liberty is extremely limited' (Foucault, 1988: 12). This is what Foucault calls 'domination', using that term to designate 'what we ordinarily call power' (ibid.: 19) – that is, the capacity of one or more persons to impose their will even, in Weber's words, 'against the resistance of others who are participating in the action' (1978: 926).

While Foucault makes no secret of his hostility to states of domination, his own later studies of power are more concerned with an asymmetrical relationship of another kind, that is, with *government*. Foucault (1991) uses the term 'government' in a very general sense to refer not only to the regulation of the population and the territory of a state by a legally constituted authority – that is, by *the* government – but also to the regulation of oneself, of a household or organization, or even of a collectivity such as the poor, the sick or the unemployed. Rather than operating in the manner of domination to determine directly the behaviour of individuals, government, in Foucault's view, aims to affect their behaviour *indirectly* by influencing the manner in which they regulate their own behaviour. A change in interest rates, for example, or in the tax regime, can have a substantial impact on the conduct of numerous individuals without any of them being told directly what to do.

While this overarching concern with the regulation of conduct is central to all of his discussions on government, Foucault pays particular attention to the predominant modern understanding of government as identified with the state. His aim here is to distinguish this form of government both from the other forms which coexist with it in the contemporary era (government of oneself, of one or more others, and of a household or organization) and from the forms of government which existed in earlier times (for example, the rule of the prince, feudal magnate, church or emperor over the populations of late medieval Europe). In this context, Foucault is more concerned with the different *effects* of each of these forms of government, and with how these are produced, than he is with those questions of the *legitimacy* of governmental power which have so preoccupied other scholars. For this reason, his discussions of government have focused especially on the different *rationalities* associated with different forms of government. By rationalities he means the ways of thinking about the nature of government and its objectives, about the character of the population to be governed and the organizations and collectivities that exist within it, and about the knowledge and practical resources that government can draw upon and the obstacles that stand in its way.

Particularly important here is Foucault's treatment of liberalism, since he sees liberalism as the most influential of all rationalities of government in contemporary western societies (Foucault, 1997: 73–9). Liberalism is a way of thinking about government which is distinguished by its emphasis on individual liberty. Conventional academic accounts of liberalism treat its overarching commitment to liberty as a matter of principle: frequently debating whether such a commitment can be justified and whether the forms of government to which it gives rise can therefore be regarded as legitimate. In addition, most such accounts treat the stress on individual liberty as implying that liberal forms of government will be characterized by a strictly *limited* interference in, and regulation of, the lives of citizens.

Foucault's account of liberalism as rationality of government presents a very different view of the role of liberty in liberal government. The stress on individual liberty is seen here, not as a philosophical/ethical stance giving rise to certain forms of government, but rather as a *means* by which government itself can be effected. Liberal ideas are thus understood in this model as representing less a political/ethical commitment than a body of knowledge concerning how the citizens of modern states can most effectively be governed. The importance of liberalism, for Foucault, lies not in questions of the legitimacy of liberal government but rather in its *effectiveness* as a practical means of governing modern populations, that is, to regulating the conduct of individuals. In this view, liberal government is characterized not so much by the *restriction* of government in the name of liberty, as by the *exercise* of government via that same stress on liberty (Rose, 1995, 1996; Hindess, 1996).

Thus, where liberal government is conventionally understood as concerned with minimizing the impact of state activities on the pre-existing freedom of individuals, the Foucauldian view understands it both as actively *producing* certain forms of freedom and as using them for its own purposes. This is what Rose and Miller have in mind when they describe liberal government as a matter of 'governing at a distance' (Rose and Miller, 1992: 173), that is, as a matter of producing certain kinds of 'free' individuals who are thus able to regulate or govern their own behaviour in line with governmental norms. Foucault's treatment of liberalism in these terms has been taken up and developed by a number of contemporary sociologists and others concerned with investigating the role of government (in its broadest sense) in contemporary western societies. Rabinow (1989), for instance, has argued that the development of urban planning in nineteenth-century France is linked to this kind of 'government at a distance': thus public spaces and buildings were designed in such a way as to instil in individuals a sense of constantly being watched (and judged) by others and so, in turn, to induce a process of self-monitoring and self-regulation, or self-government, in those individuals. Likewise, Hunter's studies of the development of systems of mass compulsory education in contemporary democratic states such as Britain and Australia have emphasized the governmental concern with ensuring that individuals acquire appropriate means of analysing their own behaviour and the behaviour of others (Hunter, 1988, 1994). Here, education is seen as a matter not only of academic and vocational training, but also of forming individuals whose capacities and habits of thought are such that they normally can be relied upon to govern themselves. Dean (1998) has suggested that many welfare programmes can be seen not only as delivering various benefits to the members of groups such as the unemployed and the aged, but also as shaping the desires and aspirations of those people by attributing to them particular statuses, rights and obligations. In his view, even the 'free' decisions of the unemployed have been turned into components of government labour market programmes, that is, into means whereby the unemployed themselves may be governed.

These brief and schematic remarks on government seem to have taken us a long way from the study of power as such. This is because those sociologists and others who have followed Foucault's lead in this area have shown little interest in the kinds of questions more conventionally associated with the study of power: questions to do with its distribution and production or with its legitimacy. Foucault's discussion of power allows us to recognize that ways of acting on the actions of others are, first, considerably more diverse and, second, frequently far more complex and sophisticated than can be accounted for by a focus on power as either a capacity or a right. As we have seen here, a Foucauldian focus on how the effects of power are produced – rather than on power itself as the explanation for such effects – enables those who adopt this kind of approach to avoid many of the problems associated with an understanding of power as either capacity or right, and so to break away from the intractable disputes concerning how we should identify and measure power, and how we should determine its legitimacy.

Nevertheless, we should note that Foucault himself (and many who write in a Foucauldian vein) fall back into using, on occasion, something that looks very like the conventional conception of power that his work elsewhere so trenchantly critiques. Thus, we have already noted that he uses the term 'domination' to mean almost exactly what other thinkers refer to as power in the sense of capacity: it is presumed in his use of this term that some parties are able to exercise power more effectively than others (and so to reduce their margin of liberty). This returns us to the familiar problems outlined earlier for the view of power as quantitative capacity: how do we decide in any context who is suffering from such effects of power or, in Foucault's terms, from 'domination'?

We have also seen that, just as Lukes and others offer the utopian prospect of social relations in which the distorting effects of power are not present, so Foucault imagines the possibility of social relations in which the effects of domination are reduced to an absolute minimum (Foucault, 1988: 18–20). This, of course, raises the question of what, if any, relations of domination could be seen as legitimate or as unavoidable. Foucault does not deny the legitimacy, for example, of hierarchical relations of the kind that appear in many teaching situations, provided that the pupils are not subjected to 'the arbitrary and useless authority of a teacher' (ibid: 18). But the problem here, as many pupils will have discovered for themselves, is that the difference between an exercise of authority which can be justified on pedagogic grounds, and one which is 'arbitrary or useless', is a much more difficult one to draw than it appears at first sight and must inevitably depend on personal evaluation. We are back in the familiar terrain of ethical and political judgements and consequent intractable dispute. It seems that in spite of his wish to leave behind conventional notions of power, Foucault is unable to relinquish them entirely, smuggling them into his model under a different name.

Conclusion

The concept of power as used by sociologists is far less clear-cut than most of us imagine it to be. As we have seen, sociologists can mean three rather different things by the term, each of which gives rise to a distinctive kind of analysis. For example, in analysing class, gender and 'race' – the next three topics discussed in this book – sociologists will inevitably use one or more of the three understandings of power discussed in this chapter. Those who see power as the quantifiable capacity of one party to get others to do what they want them to will generally be concerned with questions such as whether we can speak of members of the upper class, men or 'racial' majorities as a 'dominant' social group and working-class people, women or 'racial' minorties as a 'subordinate' social group. Those who assume some notion of power as the right of one party to get others to do what they want might focus on questions such as how societies operate to instil into working-class people, women or ethnic minorities a sense that the statuses they fill are the right and 'natural' ones. In fact, many analyses in these areas will use power in both of these senses, sometimes without any acknowledged awareness of the differences between them and the different assumptions which each involves. Significantly, analyses based on either or both of these understandings will often see power purely in negative terms, as an undesirable aspect of social relations that enables one social group to reduce the scope of action of another.

Students who understand power in a Foucauldian sense will tend to question the categories of class, gender and 'race'. On this view, categories such as 'the poor', 'the unemployed', 'blacks', 'whites', 'Asians', 'men', 'women', 'transvestites' are means by which the members of contemporary societies are governed. Analyses of these types will see power largely in productive terms: as promoting individual dispositions, ways of thinking and patterns of behaviour identified with each of these categories. As we have seen, for Foucault, the fact that power is productive in its effects is not to say that it is necessarily positive or good. In particular, when power veers towards domination, then it may well be resisted by the dominated groups.

This brings us to the final point of this chapter. While Foucault's view of power as an inescapable element of all human action appears to release sociologists from intractable disputes about power as capacity and right, it still retains conceptions of power in these terms under the different name of domination. It is tempting to conclude from this that conventional conceptions of power as capacity and right may be unavoidable simply because they accord with the harsh empirical reality that, whether we like it or not, some people are always going to dominate others. On this view, if Foucauldians are going to use the term 'power' to mean something different, they must find a new name for this reality. However, there is an alternative explanation for Foucault's resurrection of the conventional conceptions of power, one to which we have alluded in our discussion of power as right. On this view, the conceptions of power as capacity and as right reflect the high value placed on individual autonomy in modern societies. As such, they are so deeply implicated in contemporary western ways of understanding and organizing social relations that no matter how hard we try, we can never quite free ourselves from them.

Further Reading

Hindess, B. *Discourses of Power: From Hobbes to Foucault,* Oxford, Blackwell, 1995. Offers a critical examination of the treatment of power in western political thought and an extended discussion of Foucault's radical alternative to conventional approaches to the study of power.

Lukes, S. (ed.) *Power,* Oxford, Blackwell, 1986. An excellent edited collection which brings together a range of different accounts of power, including Lukes' own reflections on the argument of his 1974 book.

Wartenberg, T. *The Forms of Power: From Domination to Transformation,* Philadelphia, Temple University Press, 1990. Combines a useful account of the historical development of the concept of power with a critical discussion of its main contemporary interpretations.

Wrong, D. *Power. Its Forms, Bases and Uses,* 2nd edn, Chicago, University of Chicago Press, 1988. Still the most useful survey of mainstream sociological understandings of power.

5

Class and Stratification

Rosemary Crompton

Social classes are groups of people sharing a broadly similar market, or economic, situation. Class is one of the most fundamental concepts used in sociology to explain differing life chances. The idea had its origins in the classical sociology of Marx and Weber, examined in Chapter 3, and continues to be particularly relevant to areas of research considered later in the book, such as education, work and organizations, crime and deviance and health. This chapter aims to explain theories of class, the major strategies for measuring class inequalities and the debates surrounding the relevance of class in contemporary societies. It should provide understanding of:

■ Marxian and Weberian theories of class and their legacy in modern sociology

■ How sociologists go about measuring class inequalities and criticisms of these methodologies

■ Changes in the class processes of modern societies

■ Some of the major issues surrounding the 'end of class' debate

■ Changing patterns of inequality in contemporary societies

CONCEPTS

social stratification ■ class conflict ■ status ■ class consciousness
lifestyles ■ deskilling ■ social mobility ■ polarization

Introduction

'Class' is a word which has a number of different meanings in sociology as well as in everyday life. Beyond a fairly basic level of complexity, all known societies are stratified – that is, differentiated according to one or more principles of classification, which is usually hierarchical. These principles have included age, ritual purity (as in the Hindu caste system), citizenship and the division of labour, and religious and military hierarchies. Thus the term 'class' is often used to describe the ranking of a group in a formal hierarchical order – for example the 'class' of plebeians in ancient Rome. These hierarchies were woven into the fabric of society and carried with them legal and quasi-legal rights and obligations (relating, for example, to the right to practice a particular occupation). The linkage of 'class' with hierarchy persists today, in that class is a term which is widely used to describe unequally rewarded groups, such as the Registrar General's 'social classes' in Britain. These are employment aggregates corresponding to broad divisions within the occupational order – manual workers, white-collar workers, managers and professionals, and so on. In contemporary societies, however, such groupings are not characterized by any formal, legal distinctions, rather, they summarize the outcome, in material terms, of the competition for material resources in market capitalism. This chapter begins by discussing concepts of class. It then examines the measurement of 'class' inequalities and recent changes which have affected class processes. The next section considers the recurring question of the 'end of class' and the chapter concludes with discussion of the 'underclass' and the deepening inequalities in Britain over the past two decades.

Concepts and Definitions

Marx saw 'class' categories as relating to the ownership of property, and production relationships. However, as we saw in Chapter 3, Marx argued that 'classes' were not mere social categories, but also transforming social forces and 'all history was the history of class conflict'. Marx saw all complex societies as characterized by the relationship between antagonistic classes. Out of these conflicts came major social changes culminating in changes in production and property relationships. In feudal Europe, for example, the Church and feudal lords, who controlled access to land and property, exploited the major producers, the peasantry, through the direct appropriation of a portion of that which they produced either directly, in the form of produce, or through taxes. The antagonistic relationship between lord and peasant was intermittently expressed through wars and peasant revolt but, in Marx's analysis, the revolutionary (that is, epoch-changing) class of the feudal era was the rising bourgeoisie, the merchants and nascent capitalist manufacturers, who sought to remove the restrictions on production and the market (such as restrictions on the movement of labour and capital), which maintained the feudal order (Marx and Engels, 1962). Thus they struggled for a fundamental transformation of society from feudalism to market capitalism.

A significant element of Marx's conceptualization of class was that classes were identified according to their relationships in production – owner and non-owner of the means of production such as land and property, controller and non-controller of labour power. Thus 'classes' for Marx are identified not simply according to the extent that they possess a particular attribute – such as money or social honour – but rather, in terms of their *relationship* to other classes. This 'relational' conceptualization may be distinguished from a 'graduational' view of class which Wright argues merely describes. Although the groupings identified by Marx are characterized by material inequalities, classes were for Marx defined primarily by their relationship to other classes rather than the extent of their material and/or social inquality relative to other classes (Wright, 1980, 1997).

The concept of 'class', therefore, may be used to describe hierarchical groupings characterized by material and social inequalities, prestige rankings, and actual social forces with the capacity to transform societies. There is no 'correct' definition of the term although it is, of course, legitimate to debate the correct interpretation of a particular social theorist's use of the concept. Theoretical debates about the use of the concept of class have sometimes been very prominent in sociology, particularly during the 1970s and 80s. In the context of these theoretical debates, a contrast was often drawn between 'class' in particular and the more general concept of 'stratification', which, as we have seen, describes the general principles according to which societies are differentiated. This was often associated with the attempt to isolate the impact of 'class' – understood broadly to refer to groups emerging from the patterning of property, production and market relationships – from other stratification principles such as prestige (status), ethnicity, gender and age – and indeed, 'class' was sometimes seen as the ultimate determinant of these other axes of differentiation (see discussion in Bradley, 1996). In practice, of course, the complex nature of modern societies is reflected in the complexity of their systems of stratification, which are invariably multi-stranded.

Classical Theories

In sociology, Marx and Weber have had the major impact upon theoretical approaches to class, and sociological debates still reflect the contrast between these two. Both were concerned with the transition from pre-capitalist to modern industrial capitalist societies, and the consequences of this transition for social organization and institutions. Marx was an active revolutionary, and his analyses of the class structure were undertaken as part of the development of a political agenda. He developed a distinctive materialist theory of history which, as we have seen, argued that the ownership and control of the material means of production (for example, land in feudal societies, factories in industrialism) was associated with distinctive societal types and class-related patterns of exploitation and inequality. Modern capitalism was a particularly dynamic type of society, in which the 'two great classes' were the bourgeoisie (the private owners and controllers of the material means of production), and the proletariat (those who, having no ownership or rights in the means of production, are dependent upon the sale of their labour power in order to survive).

However, capitalism is not just a 'two-class' society, as there are other classes besides the bourgeoisie and proletariat, including the petty bourgeoisie (small employers, often of family labour), the small peasantry and the lumpenproletariat (people without regular employment existing on the fringes of capital). Capital itself is divided between industrial capitalists, financial capitalists, and landowners (Marx, 1962). Nevertheless, Marx believed that it would be the conflict between the bourgeoisie and the proletariat which would bring about the transition to the next historical stage of society; first to socialism, then to true communism. This conflict would come about because of the inherent contradiction between the forces and relations of production in capitalism – that is, between the increasingly social nature of the production process and the private ownership of the means of production. In this conflict, the proletariat would be the revolutionary class, whose conscious endeavours, like those of the bourgeoisie during the feudal era, would eventually bring about a new stage of societal development.

Weber, as we saw in Chapter 3, was critical of this exclusively materialist view, arguing that influential ideas and social movements can also be sources of important historical changes. In a similar vein, he argued that although 'classes' were defined largely in material terms, societal *ideas* about 'better' and 'worse', 'higher' and 'lower', were also significant factors in social stratification. Here the concept of 'status' was central to his thinking. He used it to describe:

1. social honour or prestige
2. an associational group or 'consciousness community'
3. non-market claims to material resources.

Thus for Weber, the feudal estates just described, whose claims rested upon tradition and customary rights rather than 'market forces' as such, represented status groups rather than, as they did for Marx, classes. Indeed, Weber considered that classes – groups characterized by their differential access to the property and labour markets – were characteristic only of capitalist societies. Unlike Marx, Weber saw the development of class consciousness as essentially contingent – that is, consciousness might or might not develop depending upon circumstances. However, classes and status groups were very likely to come into conflict with each other, as the pretensions of status honour (and claims to privileged positions) would be offended by the bargaining which accompanied market (that is, class) situations.

In summary, theories of class and stratification have long been regarded as central sociological concepts. Because the class concept is flexible and has a number of different meanings, a number of different, if related, topics are involved. In the most general stratification terms, at the macro-level the concepts are seen by some sociologists to capture the transition from systems of inequality characterized largely by ascription (status) to achievement (class) (Parsons, 1954). In the 1960s and 70s, such optimistic arguments were associated with the notion that a true (and essentially 'fair') meritocracy was in the process of being created (Kerr *et al.*, 1973). In opposition to these arguments, Marxist-influenced writers have found the value of the class concept in both explaining the broad contours of social change and indicating how societies might develop in the future. At a more micro-level, however, class and stratification theories have been used in order to identify actual and potential sources of social conflict and to explain why some social groups have been more or less successful than others. This latter dimension lies at the root of the inescapable association of class and inequality, and the capacity of stratification concepts to describe and explain inequalities of power, ownership, and control, and access to scarce goods and resources. Not surprisingly, therefore, class and stratification concepts have always been associated with the measurement of material and social inequalities and it is to this dimension that we now turn.

Measuring 'Class'

Classes are made up of individual human beings, who must therefore be allocated to a class according to some kind of principle or other. Many theorists working in the area of class analysis would argue that the question of how to allocate individuals and thus measure and describe 'social classes' cannot be separated from the question of class consciousness – that is, the extent to which individuals in the same class situation share a sense of their common interests, and thus think or behave in a similar manner.

As has already been noted with reference to the discussion of Marx and Weber's work, one major difference between modern industrial and pre-industrial societies is that the majority of the population are directly or indirectly dependent upon paid employment in order to survive. Access to positions in the labour market and employment are closely related to levels of material inequality, and class relationships – of ownership and non-ownership, power and control – are obviously reflected in work and employment relationships. Therefore, employment position has been widely used in order to allocate individuals to 'classes', and the structure of employment has been divided up in various ways in order to generate them (Marsh, 1986). We may describe this as the *employment aggregate* approach to class analysis.

A number of different class schemes are available. In Britain, the Office of Population Censuses and Surveys (OPCS) currently supports two occupational classifications: Registrar General's Social Class (RGSC), as well as a more detailed Socio-Economic Grouping (SEG). (The Office of National Statistics is currently undertaking a review of social classifications, and they will be revised in the 2001 census.) Other nation states also have their own versions – for example, the Nordic Occupational scheme, used in the Scandinavian countries. The RGSC has six categories, ranging from higher professional and managerial through to unskilled manual workers, which represent, in broad outline, the hierarchy of occupational advantage and disadvantage in Britain. The OPCS schemes have been widely used in social policy applications. Another scheme, which is widely used in advertising and market research, is Social Grade (A, B, C1, C2 and D). This scheme is maintained by the advertising industry, and includes an assessment of 'lifestyle' as well as a separate categories for the self-employed and unemployed. Both the OPCS schemes and Social Grade have been devised with practical applications in mind – to chart social inequalities, to monitor the spending and reading habits of individuals and families.

Sociologists have also constructed class schemes for their own purposes. In Britain, probably the best-known practitioner of 'employment aggregate' class analysis is Goldthorpe, who devised his scheme as part of his work on social mobility. Employment status (whether employed or self-employed) is a key category of the Goldthorpe scheme. In his early work, Goldthorpe was closely associated with the theoretical approach that had been developed by Lockwood (Lockwood, 1958; Goldthorpe *et al.*, 1969). Lockwood had identified the Weberian category of 'market' situation (together with 'work' situation) as key factors in locating occupations within 'classes'. Goldthorpe's *original* formulation of his class scheme carried over this 'Weberian' aspect of Lockwood's approach.

This neo-Weberian characterization was thrown into sharp relief with the development of an explicitly Marxist programme of employment aggregate class analysis by Wright (1976). Wright's explicit aim has been to develop the empirical investigation of a number of Marxist-derived theories – for example, the 'proletarianization' of the labour force. In British sociology, Wright's approach was incorporated into a major empirical investigation of the 'class' (that is, employment) structure carried out in the 1980s (Marshall *et al.*, 1988). Marshall and his colleagues used the same data set to compare outcomes using the Registrar General's 'common sense' class scheme, Goldthorpe's neo-Weberian class scheme, and Wright's Marxist class scheme. They not only found a number of apparent anomalies in Wright's scheme (Wright's 'autonomous worker' category, for example, grouped together lawyers and forklift truck drivers), but also that Goldthorpe's scheme corresponded most closely to political preferences and voting intentions. Goldthorpe's 'Weberian' scheme, therefore, was declared the 'winner'. The presentation of evidence of Marshall *et al.* may be read as an empirical evaluation of three different class schemes: Goldthorpe's, Wright's, and the Registrar General's, within the employment aggregate approach to 'class analysis' (see Marshall, 1988). However, as the three schemes were designed for different purposes (and it is certain the RGSC was not designed with reference to sociological understandings) it is not surprising that the outcomes of the schemes should vary. Recently, however, Goldthorpe and Marshall (1992) have asserted that the Goldthorpe scheme is not characterized by any particular 'theory' of class. Rather, they now assert that it focuses upon *employment relations,* as it combines employment status (whether employer, self-employed or employee) together with the employee relationship – that is, whether the employee has a 'service' or 'labour' contract of employment. In particular they reject any notion that work tasks and roles play any part in the construction of the scheme. Goldthorpe has modified his scheme over the years, largely as a consequence of practical requirements (such as the separate identification of agricultural and farming occupations) in order to achieve cross-national comparability in his comparative study of social mobility (Erikson and Goldthorpe, 1992).

In practice, although Goldthorpe and Wright are frequently presented as representing different theoretical traditions (Weber and Marx), the methodological assumptions underlying their empirical approach – that is, the comparative analysis of national, large-scale, sample surveys – are in fact very similar. Over the years this has resulted in a considerable convergence in these apparently conflicting approaches to employment aggregate 'class analysis'. Despite their being constructed according to different principles, the 'Marxist' class scheme of Wright and the (Weberian) class scheme of Goldthorpe in fact give very similar measures of the same phenomena (Emmison, 1991). Indeed, as Wright has recently argued: 'as a practical set of operational categories, the ("Marxist") class structure matrix... does not dramatically differ from the class typology used by Goldthorpe' (Wright, 1997: 37).

The 'employment aggregate' approach to class analysis has been useful in identifying the contours of major inequalities – for example, in health, and access to educational opportunities – and describing attitudinal and behavioural differences such as political affiliation and voting patterns. However, it should not be taken to represent 'class analysis' as a whole as there are a number of empirical and theoretical problems associated with this approach.

The first difficulty with the aggregate employment approach is that the focus upon employment means that some very significant class categories are inadequately considered – in particular, major owners of capital (Westergaard, 1995). The number of such major owners in the population is too small for them ever to be counted in sufficiently large numbers within a sample survey. However, the impact of this class is out of all proportion to its numerical significance, and the study of large capital holders should obviously be incorporated into the field of 'class analysis'. Second, there is the problem of gender. Given the persistence of occupational segregation by sex, then the 'class structure' as revealed by an employment aggregate class scheme is very different for women and men. Men tend to predominate in skilled manual and higher professional and managerial occupations, women in lower professional and white-collar occupations. However, it may be argued (as Goldthorpe has done) that, although the 'class' (that is, occupational) structure is different for men and women, the class differences for women in 'women's' jobs and men in 'men's' jobs are of a similar order – that is, 'service-class' women differ from 'working-class' women in the same way that 'service-class' men differ from 'working-class' men – even though there may be differences between 'service-class' men and 'service-class' women. More intractable problems, however, are presented by the growth of long-term unemployment. Individuals who have never held a permanent, full-time job, as well as households headed by individuals who are long-term unemployed, are difficult to classify using the 'employment aggregate' approach. Thus many commercial agencies, for example, prefer to use a measure such as social grade (rather than sociological class measures) as this scheme allows for the identification of those on state benefits.

Another problem is caused by changes in the occupational structure itself. This may lead to the reclassification of certain key occupations – for example, the Registrar General once placed clerks in Social Class II but they have been moved to III – as well as the problem of allocating new occupations to an appropriate category. Even more problematically, the criteria by which occupations are allocated to categories may themselves change over time. For example, as we have seen, a crucial element of the Goldthorpe class scheme is employment relations, in which the presence or absence of job security and, above all, a career is central. Goldthorpe regards the career as an attribute of the job, rather than the individual: 'It is not so much that reward is being offered in return for work done, but... "compensation"... in return for the acceptance of an obligation to discharge trust "faithfully"' (1982: 169). Once on the career escalator, it is assumed that individuals did not get pushed off it as long as they abided by the rules – although some might move to faster tracks. However the last fifteen years have seen a transformation of the 'service' relationship which breaks with many of the assumptions central to Goldthorpe's definition. The growth of self-employment and short-term contracting, together with individualized and performance-related pay systems, serves to make individual 'employability' potentially more significant than the job-related employment conditions (see Chapter 10 for further discussion).

There is, therefore, a range of problems associated with the employment aggregate approach, which stem from the difficulties of devising a reliable measure of a rapidly changing and developing employment structure. However, it has been more generally argued that changes in the relative significance of 'work' as employment may be undermining the utility of the 'class' concept in sociology – and indeed, the project of class analysis as a whole. Authors such as Pahl (1989) and Saunders (1987) have argued that 'work' as employment, and thus 'class', is declining in its significance at the end of the twentieth century. The shift to the service sector and the development of new production systems is leading to an erosion of work hierarchies and the decline of work-centred social identities (Clark and Lipset, 1991; Beck, 1992). More particularly, it is argued that consumption and 'lifestyles' are becoming more central to people's lives than 'class'. Thus whereas class might have been an appropriate concept for the analysis of industrial societies in the late nineteenth and first half of the twentieth century, this is no longer the case in the era of increasingly individualized contemporary society.

Class Processes: Recent Developments

Foremost among those who criticized the impetus towards classification in (structural) sociological approaches to 'class' was the historian E.P. Thompson (1968). In the 1960s, sociologists such as Parsons (1954) and Dahrendorf (1969) had described the 'class structure' as corresponding to an abstract structure of social roles and positions. In contrast, Thompson argued: 'I do not see class as a "structure", nor even as a "category", but as something which in fact happens' (1968: 9). For Thompson, 'structure' and 'action' could not be separated: 'Classes do not struggle because they exist, but exist because they struggle' (Joyce, 1995: 127). Thus his major work is on the *making* of the English working class; the 'class' does not exist outside its making.

Social history in Britain has been enormously influenced by Thompson, even though recent discussions have gone beyond his (contested) materialism to embrace the 'linguistic turn' in which 'class' is defined largely in relation to experience and consciousness, and indeed, the notion of structure disappears altogether. Not surprisingly, however, there developed an affinity between historical approaches stressing the unity of structure and action, and sociological commentaries on class with a similar emphasis. Giddens (1973, 1981) examined the processes whereby classes become stable and enduring social aggregates by reproducing themselves intergenerationally. Giddens has not carried out any subsequent work in the field (Giddens, 1990: 298). The significance of Giddens work on 'class', therefore, lies largely in its emphasis upon the sociological study of class *processes*. This position was rather different from the focus on the *measurement* of social class, and class-related attributes, which was a major feature of the employment aggregate approach of authors such as Goldthorpe.

At the time, however, Giddens' work was seen as making a contribution to the theoretical elaboration of the class concept and, in particular, the growing debate between sociological 'Marxist' and 'Weberian' approaches to class (see Crompton and Gubbay, 1977). The 1970s were characterized by a surge of interest in Marx's work, including both French structural Marxism (as represented by the work of Althusser and Poulantzas), as well as a more culturalist version influenced by the Gramscian notion of 'hegemony' described in Chapter 3. Marxist accounts of the class structure were complemented by a renewed interest in the labour process stimulated by Braverman's work (1974). Braverman's account of the 'deskilling' or 'proletarianization' of the contemporary labour force seemed to offer an avenue whereby relations in production might be mapped onto the job structure – a strategy which, as we have seen in the previous section, was taken up by Wright. The revival of interest in Marx meant that the 'Marx vs Weber' debate assumed a high profile and came to represent *the* major polarity within class analysis.

However, more important was the (largely unacknowledged) split within the sociology of 'class analysis' between, on the one hand, employment aggregate practitioners concerned mainly with the analysis of national data sets, and, on the other, socio-historical and other case studies focusing largely upon the processes of class formation, emergence, and consciousness. The latter were particularly concerned with the impact of major social changes which had occurred very recently – for example, the increasing employment of married women, economic decline and rising unemployment, deindustrialization and the shift to the service sector, and the corresponding growth of 'middle-class' occupations. Within this approach the emphasis was above all on *change* (see for example Lash and Urry, 1987), whereas within the employment aggregate approach (particularly as represented in the work of Goldthorpe and his associates), there developed what appeared to be a contrary emphasis upon *stability*, rather than change.

The view is taken here that the field of 'class analysis' as a whole must incorporate both change and continuity, as well as a range of methodologies including large-scale surveys and case studies as well as socio-historical and contemporary research (Crompton, 1993). The remainder of this section, therefore, will explore the impact of changes in the organization of productive activity and in the labour market which have had important impacts on the 'class structure'. These include the expansion of the middle class and the decline of the working class, together with an associated increase in social mobility and the increasing employment of women.

The Decline of the 'Working Class'

As we have seen in the previous section, the strategy of using the employment structure as a proxy for the class structure is a longstanding convention. Changes in class structuring are indeed reflected in labour markets and the occupational structure, and one of the most notable of these changes since the end of the Second World War has been the decline of manual work in manufacturing which has been long associated with the idea of the 'proletariat' or 'working' class, together with an increase in service-related employment of all kinds (in education, health, financial services, leisure, and so on). In Britain, using the Registrar General's measure, the 'working class' (skilled and unskilled manual workers) has declined from 64 per cent to 42 per cent of the employed population since the Second World War. Since the end of the 1970s, deindustrialization has resulted in the further decline of manufacturing industry, and between 1971 and 1993, employment in manufacturing declined from 36.4 per cent to 20.4 per cent, while employment in services grew from 52.6 per cent to 72.8 per cent.

Economic and political change, therefore, has brought with it the proportional and numerical decline of the 'working class'. The shrinking of the working class over the last twenty years has effectively eclipsed a topic which flourished during the Marxist revival of the 1970s – the apparent failure of this class, in the advanced industrial societies, to develop a consciousness of its revolutionary political role and act accordingly. As Savage (1996) has argued, the 'working class' has been the reference point against which other classes have been identified, and its apparent decline came to be associated with notions of the 'end of class' itself. More particularly, the working class was the main focus of arguments relating to 'class dealignment' – that is, the apparent decline of the link between class and voting behaviour (the working class being more likely to vote for socialist parties, the middle and upper classes to vote for right-wing parties). In Britain, the failure of the Labour Party to be elected during the 1980s and early 1990s was seen as being a consequence of a shift in the allegiance of the skilled working class in particular. As a consequence, the 'end' of class politics was widely heralded. In fact, the data suggest that there has been a 'trendless fluctuation' in the working-class vote, rather than any permanent shift in voting behaviour (Heath *et al.*, 1991). Nevertheless, as we have seen in recent years, the changes in the occupational structure brought about by economic and industrial restructuring have been reflected in the strategies of both of the major political parties – both of whom seem to be largely preoccupied with gaining the middle-class vote.

The increased employment of married women, as well as the enhanced participation of women in the labour force more generally, has also affected approaches to 'class analysis'. As feminists have argued, a whole range of concepts in the social sciences – and class analysis in particular – were developed so as to incorporate the assumptions of the 'male breadwinner' model of the gender division of labour, in which men were held to be responsible for market work and the public sphere, whereas women were located in the domestic sphere. This convention had been incorporated into the employment aggregate approach via the collection of 'men only' samples in empirical investigations of class and stratification during the 1960s and 70s, as well as the designation of the male breadwinner as the 'head of household', 'even when the female partner was in employment'.

Besides the problems associated with this practice, the growth in women's employment from the 1960s also served to undermine other assumptions relating to 'class'. Chief among these was the question of causal primacy in respect of the major determinants of material inequalities and associated structures of stratification. To put this argument crudely, did 'class' also determine the shape and extent of other major inequalities such as gender and ethnicity, or should these attributes and their social structuring be regarded as independent dimensions of stratification? Marxist theory had provided a set of arguments to the effect that the subordination of women was, indeed, largely to be seen as a consequence of successive types of class domination (Engels, 1940) and, following this view, in the 'state socialist' countries the 'liberation' of women had been officially announced following their incorporation into the paid labour force (Buckley, 1989). This approach to the 'woman problem' took no account of the domestic division of labour, as feminists argued. Besides the lack of any substantial change in the domestic division of labour, the increasing employment of women in the 'public' sphere also served to highlight the extent to which women had been excluded from better paid and higher level jobs, as well as the way in which 'women's' work had been devalued (Cockburn, 1983; Walby, 1986). Increasingly, it was argued that women's subordination was largely a conse- quence of patriarchal, rather than class, processes (for further discussion, see Chapter 6). A parallel set of arguments has been developed in respect of 'race' (Anthias and Yuval-Davis, 1992). 'Class analysis' came increasingly to be regarded in some quarters as an over-deterministic mono-theory, in which the multiple sources of social inequality had been reduced to the simplicities of 'class'.

Parallel with this emphasis upon alternative sources of social inequality, it was also increasingly argued that 'class' had lost its salience as a source of indi- vidual and social *identity:*

> In the traditional models, people were socialised into worlds of home and work in which they 'knew their place'. They joined a class, learned its values, developed its attitudes and behaved accordingly – again throughout their lifetimes. These fairly rigid boundaries have now gone. (Thrift and Johnston, 1993: 84, cited in Savage, 1996)

Rather than 'class', it was argued, other sources of identity, such as those of 'race', lifestyle, age and gender, were becoming more significant. The loss of class identity was explicitly linked to political developments including the supposed decline of class politics. Political life, it was argued, was becoming increasingly concerned with specific issues (for example, the environment, 'race'), rather than class, and these politics were organized and pursued by new 'social movements', rather than class-political parties (Offe, 1985). However, it may be suggested that what they are describing is a society shaped by a relatively stable *status* order, and that there are rather more grounds for arguing for the contemporary decline of the status, rather than the class, order.

The linked social processes of the erosion of the traditional working class, the apparent decline of class voting, the increase in women's employment and the growing emphasis upon other sources of inequality and identity have all served to contribute to the growing tide of arguments relating to the 'end of class' (Hall and Jaques, 1989), which will be considered in the next section. For the moment, I shall briefly examine a further important outcome of the process of class restructuring – the expansion of the 'middle classes'.

The 'Middle Classes'

The decline of manufacturing and the corresponding increase in service-sector employment brought with it a growth not just in routine clerical work, but also in administrative and managerial, technical and professional occupations. The 'middle classes' have always been regarded as somewhat problematic from within a Marxist framework. Do their interests lie with those of the working class, or with those of the bourgeoisie? These debates have not just been couched at an abstract level (see Poulantzas, 1975), but have also focused upon the type and nature of these expanding 'middle-class' occupations. It was argued that much of the growth in middle-class occupations was in fact more apparent than real as those at the lower level were deskilled and routinized. Indeed, it was suggested that this process of 'proletarianization' was in fact extending beyond lower level white-collar workers to include managerial occupations (Braverman, 1974; Crompton and Jones, 1984). Contrary to some of the more apocalyptic earlier predictions, it would seem that a widespread process of 'deskilling' has not in fact taken place, although many white-collar jobs in retail and other services *are* extremely routine, poorly paid, and insecure and would nowadays be located in the 'working' or lower levels of most class schemes. There still remains, however, the wider problem of the societal consequences of middle-class expansion.

Goldthorpe has argued that the expansion of the 'service' (that is, middle) class is a source of social stability, largely because service-class families will seek to secure and pass on their advantages to future generations (Goldthorpe, 1987; Erikson and Goldthorpe, 1992). In contrast, others have argued that the extent of internal differentiation within the middle classes is such that such cohesion cannot be reliably anticipated (Lash and Urry, 1987; Savage *et al.*, 1992; Butler and Savage, 1996). Goldthorpe has argued that besides status in employment (that is, whether employed, self-employed or an employee), the crucial differentiating feature of the 'class structure' is whether the employee is in a 'service' or a 'labour contract only' employment relationship. The 'service' relationship, as we have seen, is held to be an attribute of the job, rather than the individual, or of the kind of work they do. Thus the service relationship encompasses a heterogeneous range of occupations. It is a feature of the service relationship that it contains important prospective elements, including salary increments, security of employment, and 'above all, well-defined career opportunities' (Goldthorpe, 1996: 315). Labour contracts, by implication, carry with them no such advantages.

Savage and his colleagues have in contrast argued for an 'asset-based' approach which identifies considerable diversity within the middle classes. Three different types of asset are identified: property, cultural capital (a concept Savage takes from Bourdieu and which mainly includes formal qualifications) and organizational assets or 'property in positions'. He argues that these assets give rise to different patterns of interests and thus the possibility of intra-class conflict, rather than homogeneity and stability (see also Urry, 1996).

In this section, we have moved from considerations relating to the measurement of social class towards greater emphasis on the processes of class formation and structuring, focusing in particular on the impact of recent changes in work and employment. However, questions of measurement, location, and labelling cannot be avoided, even by those emphasizing the 'processual' approach to class analysis. Thus we have come full circle back to a major question which occupied us in the second section – that is, how do individuals get allocated to social classes? This suggests that common threads run through different approaches to class and stratification.

The 'End of Class'

The 'end of class' has been a recurring theme of post-war sociology. In the 1950s and 60s, academic sociology in Britain was engaged in debates with the normative functionalism of US sociology, as well as a critique of 'industrialization theory' – that is, the argument that all 'industrial' societies were moving along a similar path towards a destination in which class conflict would be a thing of the past (Kerr *et al.*, 1973). During the late 1980s and early 1990s, however, 'class' seems to have become 'decentred' as a focus of sociological debate and, at worst, treated as an irrelevance.

When people like the ex-Prime Minister, John Major, asserted that Britain has become (or is becoming) a 'classless' society, what they usually mean is that 'social background' is becoming less important to individual success and that societies like Britain are becoming more meritocratic. This kind of argument hails back to the debates about the increasing 'openness' of 'industrial societies' in the 1960s and 70s, in which it was argued that individual effort, rather than inheritance or nepotism, was becoming increasingly more important as far as eventual social destination was concerned (Blau and Duncan, 1967).

Considerable 'long-range' mobility is indeed possible in contemporary societies. Nevertheless, surveys of individuals in top positions regularly reveal that by far the majority originate from privileged backgrounds (Scott, 1991). For example, an analysis of the 100 top people in Britain revealed that 66 went to public school, and 54 to Oxbridge. Moreover, these figures had changed very little since a similar sample was investigated in 1972 (*The Economist*, 1992). Changes in the occupational structure – in particular, the growth of administrative, managerial and professional occupations – mean that there has been a considerable increase in upward occupational mobility so that, overall, many people will have moved into jobs where their rewards are better than those of their parents. However, a series of empirical investigations has demonstrated that, whereas absolute rates might have increased, *relative* mobility rates – that is, individual chances of upward mobility relative to social origin – have not changed (Goldthorpe, 1987). Thus mobility chances are unevenly distributed through the employment class structure, and those of people in the lower classes are worse than those of those in the higher.

Another factor which has contributed to the perception of a more open society is the continuing decline of the traditional status order. Institutions such as the established church, and the monarchy, are no longer treated with the automatic deference which once prevailed. Even though Britain may not be a meritocracy, meritocratic *ideas* have been very influential. On the whole, it is no longer acceptable for elevated positions to be acquired on the basis of birth or breeding alone. This tendency is reflected in the survey of 'top people' described above, in which twice as many had received higher education than in 1972. Reflecting this trend, *The Economist* (1992: 21) commented: 'Fewer dumb aristocrats have got to top jobs on the basis of little education and much family influence.'

It has been argued that changes in production and markets, which have seen both the decline of old classes and the rise of new ones, means that this emerging structure cannot be conceptualized using class concepts which were developed with reference to nineteenth-century industrialism. This is not just a problem for the class schemes of the employment aggregate approach, as the 'processual' approach to class analysis is also concerned with the identification or class character of newly emerging groups. The decline of class politics, together with the proliferation of issue politics and the coming to the fore of new 'identities', such as those associated with sexualities, gender and ethnicity, have all been used to argue that 'class' is no longer important. Contemporary societies, it is argued, are characterized by an increasing 'individuation' (Giddens, 1991b; Beck, 1992), in which the collectivities of 'class' have been left behind and 'old' class and stratification patterns and their associated ideologies have no place in increasingly fluid, late modern, or 'postmodern', societies.

It may be suggested that much of the debate relating to class and stratification reflects broader themes within sociological theory – in particular, the structure/action debate discussed in Chapter 3. In rather different ways, both

Marx and Weber used the class concept to link structure and action, and to match patterns of power, control, and material production to the propensities for collective action. However, Hindess (1987) and Pahl (1989) have criticized 'class analysis' for its failure to link structure and action theoretically and empirically. Thus Pahl, for example, argues that the class concept has ceased to 'do any useful work' for sociology and should be abandoned because the structure → consciousness → action (SCA) chain had not been 'adequately theorised' or demonstrated. Indeed, he argues, 'lifestyles', are more important determinants of attitudes and behaviour than 'class', and changes in production processes are making the development of class consciousness extremely unlikely. Thus non-'class' indicators such as age or income might be more useful as far as social policy is concerned.

Much of the thrust of Pahl's argument, it may be suggested, in fact concerns the usefulness of employment-derived class schemes as social indicators and/or indexes of attitudes and behaviour. Similarly, for Clark and Lipset (1991), the shift to the service sector, the increased proportion of managerial and technical occupations, as well the decline in class-related voting and the growing significance of 'lifestyle' issues, suggest that where class theories may once have mapped onto the employment structure in a fairly satisfactory manner, it is doubtful if this is still the case given recent changes. If this is so, is 'class' any more a useful concept?

These critiques have generated substantial debate (see *International Sociology*, 1993; Goldthorpe and Marshall, 1992). Criticisms relating to the failure of class consciousness and action to materialize relate largely to orthodox Marxist accounts of class. Here, as Pakulski (1993) has suggested in the context of Clarke and Lipset's arguments, we may in fact be witnessing the 'failure' of a particular version of Marxist class analysis, rather than of the sociology of class and stratification as such, while Mullins (1991) has argued the 'failure' to link structure and action is not peculiar to class analysis, but rather, reflects underlying problems in social theory. In fact, it may be argued that recent sociological criticisms, such as those of Pahl, and Clark and Lipset, derive from an overly narrow perception of class analysis. In particular, these critics have failed to make a distinction, between 'employment aggregate' and 'processual' approaches to the investigation of class and stratification (Crompton, 1993, 1996, 1998).

The Underclass

The deindustrialization and economic restructuring of many contemporary societies have resulted in a substantial rise in the level of unemployment, as well as the proliferation of self-employment, temporay contracts and casual working. The growth in the numbers of the severely disadvantaged has been followed by arguments to the effect that this disadvantage is a consequence of their own actions – or rather, lack of them. The 'underclass', it is argued, has had its capacities eroded by state benefits to such an extent that it no longer wishes to work or support itself, and a life of indolence, petty crime, and single parenthood is a much more attractive option as far as it is concerned. Such people have become apathetic, fatalistic and rejective of the values of the wider society (Murray, 1990).

Sociologists in Britain and America have responded to these arguments by exploring the structural *processes* of 'underclass' development. At the macro-level, Wilson (1987) argued that, in the United States, the loss of manufacturing employment, together with the exit from the ghettos of the urban black middle classes, had contributed to the formation of the black 'underclass'. As Wilson argues, what differentiates the very poor of today from the very poor of a previous era is the dual problem of marginal economic position, together with social isolation in highly concentrated areas of poverty. Thus studies of underclass formation have increasingly focused upon the meso-level of the locality (Wilson, 1993). In Britain, Morris' (1995) study of Hartlepool, for example, carefully explores the intertwining of employment opportunities, social networks, and households which structure patterns of advantage and disadvantage in the search for employment at the local level. Her research reveals a complex picture of unemployment and insecure employment, no-earner and two-earner households and different patterns of household budgeting, which belies the homogeneity of the 'underclass' label.

Much systematic empirical research on the 'underclass', therefore, has taken the form of case studies which have served to reveal the structural processes resulting in increased social polarization. This approach may seem very different from the statistical manipulations of 'employment aggregate' practitioners. Nevertheless, large-scale survey analysis has also made an important contribution to the 'underclass' debate. Gallie (1994) and Marshall *et al.* (1996) have suggested that the long-term unemployed are no less committed to the idea of employment than those in employment, that the attitudes of the very disadvantaged are not more 'fatalistic' than the better off, nor are they socially marginalized on a range of attitudes relating to authority, attitudes to economic success, and so on. This kind of evidence presents a direct challenge to those such as Murray who have characterized disadvantaged groups as existing 'outside of' society.

The underclass debate, therefore, may be used as an example of the need to draw upon a range of sociological approaches to class and stratification in order to explore the different dimensions of the debate. It may also be used as evidence of the continuing relevance of 'class thinking' for the understanding of contemporary social divisions. This does not mean that individual identities are not significant, nor that individuals will not consciously seek to develop and make sense of them, but it should always be recognized that they invariably do so within a socially structured context.

Conclusion: Deepening Inequalities

From the end of the 1970s, inequalities in many developed societies have widened considerably. Technological innovation has meant that fewer people are required in order to achieve a rising level of manufacturing output. In Britain, for example, the low level service jobs which have been a major source of occupational expansions over the last two decades are on the whole low paid, part time and often temporary.

Women's employment has become increasingly important in maintaining household living standards. However, the increasing number of women moving into higher level and well-paid jobs means that the positive impact of women's employment is much greater in some households than others. Thus there has been a widening gulf between households in which there are two earners, and households in which there is none. Households without a full-time earner have lower average incomes, in real terms, than in 1979. In respect of male, full-time wages, the Rowntree Report has shown that:

> Between 1966 and 1977 all wages grew at much the same rate. After 1978, the experiences of the three parts of the distribution diverged: wages for the lowest paid hardly changed, and by 1992 were lower in real terms than in 1975; median wages grew by 35 per cent; but high wages grew by 50 per cent. (Joseph Rowntree Foundation, 1995: 20)

Over the last fifteen years, therefore, the material impact of occupational success or failure has become increasingly important, as the gap between the lowest and highest paid has widened. One consequence has been that educational credentials have become ever more important in the labour market. The Rowntree Report (1995: 20) argues that the 'stakes have become higher for young people entering the labour market, with greater differences between those who do well (linked to high educational levels) and those who do not than there were twenty, or even ten, years ago'.

While the recent increase in social inequality could be seen as a 'natural' development arising from social changes and the declining demand for unskilled labour in manufacturing industry, there can be little doubt that government policies aimed at increasing marketization have also increased levels of inequality. Indeed, it could be argued that one major reason for the persistence of the perpetually criticized structure → consciousness → action links in the sociological class analysis chain is that the capitalist class *does* manifest all the signs of being both conscious of its material interests and capable of protecting them. Capitalist interests are not difficult to identify, and the legitimacy of this interest (enterprise success and profitability) is widely accepted in society and supported by the state. Not all capitalists need to be organized in order to represent the interests of the whole, and short-term conflicts of interest may be accommodated. In contrast, oppositional forms of organization do not possess the same 'taken-for-granted' legitimacy. Workers have to be persuaded that their interests have to be articulated (and are distinct from those of the capitalists), and organization is rarely successful unless all workers are involved.

In Britain in the 1980s, legislation was introduced which facilitated the payment of lower wages to workers who were often poorly paid in the first place. They included the removal of rights granted by the Employment Protection Act of the mid-1970s; the privatization of public-sector services, as a consequence of which those workers who did not lose their jobs were often rehired at lower rates of pay, subsidies to encourage low wage rates for young workers and the removal of wages council protection in low-paid industries. At the same time, the abandonment of wage and salary controls allowed the incomes of the very highest earners to spiral up to previously unheard-of levels. Sustained high levels of unemployment, together with legislation against trade union strategies such as picketing and the closed shop, have further eroded the basis of collective action and thus the capacity to protect wage levels. By 1988 trade union membership in the United Kingdom had declined by fully 24 per cent from its peak level of 13.3 million members in 1979 to just over 10 million.

During the same period, direct tax cuts disproportionately benefited the better off. Between 1979 and 1986, it has been calculated that out of the £8.1 billion in tax cuts, nearly half went to the richest 10 per cent and almost two-thirds went to the richest 20 per cent. Rising unemployment, declining wage levels, and demographic changes mean that the increase in households headed by single parents, and the proportion of households dependent on social security benefits has risen – social security payments accounted for a fifth of all income in 1992 and 1993 (Goodman *et al.*, 1997). Since 1980, social security benefits have been indexed to prices, rather than wages. As wages (except those of the lowest paid) have risen faster than prices, then the value of benefits, in relative terms, has been declining.

The restructuring of other institutions has increased inequality by opening up opportunities to 'earn' very high incomes. Among the most important examples here are deregulation of the financial sector in 1986, together with the selling off of state-owned utilities. Financial deregulation resulted in an explosion of finance-related jobs, some of them very highly paid indeed. The 1996 annual report of KPMG, one of the 'Big Six' accountancy firms, revealed that the earnings of their 586 partners ranged from £123,000 to £740,000 a year (Adonis and Pollard, 1997: 87). For the very highest of flyers in the financial sector, yearly bonuses can run into millions of pounds. The directors of privatized industries found themselves able to award themselves huge salaries.

Increasing social polarization over the last two decades, therefore, has a number of different sources. In part, the morphology of inequality has changed – women's earnings, for example, have become much more important than they once were. Class processes remain crucial to the maintenance of educational advantage and, given that educational qualifications have become more important in getting a good (that is, secure and well-paid) job, then this aspect of class inequality has become more important. In addition, the institutional filters of class in Britain have been adjusted so as to increase levels of inequality and benefit the better off, that is, in the interests of capital, rather than labour. It could well be that all of these trends suggest, as Westergaard (1995) has argued, a hardening of class inequalities rather than the 'death of class'. At the very least, it seems that the questions that class analysis was designed to address remain as important as ever.

Further Reading

Bradley, H. *Fractured Identities*, Cambridge, Polity, 1996. A wide-ranging attempt to synthesize the inequalities of class, gender, 'race' and age.

Butler, T. and Savage, M. (eds) *Social Change and the Middle Classes*, London, UCL Press, 1996. A range of papers focusing on different aspects of the continuing expansion of the 'middle classes'.

Crompton, R. *Class and Stratification*, 2nd edn, Cambridge, Polity, 1998. A revised and updated edition of the 1993 textbook, covering the different theoretical and methodological approaches to the study of class.

Lee, D. and Turner, B. *Conflicts over Class,* London, Longman, 1996. Organized around the debate relating to the 'death of class'.

Scott, J. *Stratification and Power*, Cambridge, Polity, 1997. A contemporary version of the 'Weberian' approach to class analysis by an author who has carried out extensive research on the 'ruling class'.

6

Gender Relations

Mary Maynard

The study of women and of gender relations has been a major growth area in sociology over the past three decades, influencing sociological theory and methods as well as many core areas of sociological research, such as family, education, work, health and the media. The aim of this chapter is to examine the ways in which gender has been conceptualized in sociology and illustrate the part played by social institutions in the construction of gender relations. It should help you to understand:

■ The importance of including a gender perspective in sociology and some of the different ways in which gender has been theorized

■ The significance of the sexual division of labour in shaping the life chances of women and men

■ Feminist arguments concerning sex and violence as gendered social control

■ How the state, the law and citizenship construct men and women differently

■ The limitations of the 'traditional' division between radical, socialist and liberal feminism

---

CONCEPTS

feminism ■ gender blindness ■ patriarchy ■ sex and gender
sexual division of labour ■ domestic labour ■ sexual harassment
welfare state ■ citizenship ■ post-structuralism

Introduction

It is salutary to remember that for most of its history sociology has been gender blind (Abbott and Wallace, 1996). There has been little recognition that differences in the experiences of women and men, together with changes in the relationship between them, could have profound and significant implications for the ways in which social phenomena are conceptualized and investigated. For instance, as the example of class considered in the previous chapter illustrates – prior to the 1970s much empirical sociology focused on men and boys as its subjects. Areas researched tended to concentrate on the so-called public spheres of life, those existing outside the private sphere of the home, such as the workplace and the school. It was assumed either that the experiences of women could be simply inferred from those of men or that men had the normal or customary kinds of lives, with those of women being treated as unusual and deviant. Such narrowness, which effectively excluded one half of the population from investigation, also had implications for the formulation and development of important sociological ideas. For example, concepts such as social class, alienation, work and citizenship, along with others that have been central to sociological theory, were all drawn from male perceptions and understandings about the essential features of social life. Overall, then, for the first 100 or so years of its existence sociology was largely written from the standpoint of men.

The situation began to change with the resurgence of organized feminism in the late 1960s. The women's movement had a more immediate influence on sociology than on other academic disciplines, both because much of its subject matter is concerned with everyday life and because it has always been a particularly popular area of study for women. In a relatively short period of time the study of women began to develop from a peripheral minority interest into a major area of activity and debate. This has had implications at all levels of sociology, from topics chosen for research, to theoretical perspectives, to methods used for investigation.

This chapter examines some of the insights to be gained in understanding contemporary western societies when gender relations are taken into account. It first considers the kinds of criticisms which have been made of mainstream sociology by beginning with an overview of the recent history of the sociological study of women, men and gender relations. This will examine why a feminist intervention was required, what this might be said to have achieved and debates as to how gender itself is conceptualized. The chapter then considers the issue of power and gender inequality. In this, it will focus on three particularly important areas which have been researched: life chances and the sexual division of labour; sexuality and violence; and the law, citizenship and the state. These areas have been chosen both for their topicality and for their ability to highlight the gendered nature of social life. Finally, the chapter examines some of the current issues which promise to mould the future of gender research in the twenty-first century.

Why Study Women and Men?

Criticisms of the gender blindness of sociology have taken three forms, which have elicited three responses (Maynard, 1990). The first of these addressed the *invisibility* of women in most sociological work. Here the emphasis was on the extent to which sociology's focus on men's lives and experiences led to the neglect of women and the production of biased and one-sided knowledge. The aim was to undertake studies of women in areas where they had been previously ignored. This 'additive' approach, which characterized the early stages of the development of gender awareness in sociology, involved studying women in most of the sub-areas taken to be constitutive of the discipline. So, for example, work was produced on women's education, paid employment, health and illness, deviancy, youth culture and their relationship to social policy and the state. The approach was 'additive' because it simply added extra research about women onto that which already existed about men. It has been criticized subsequently for failing sufficiently to challenge sociology's basic assumptions and concepts, with women being tagged on rather as an afterthought. However, such arguments tend to play down the important role played by such studies in raising the profile of women in sociology, thereby ignoring the significant impact that they had at the time.

The second kind of criticism of sociology's gender blindness arose from the first. As research on women began to proliferate, it became clear that simply adding women into the subject would not suffice. There were whole areas of women's experiences which they did not share with men and concerning which sociology remained silent. It also became apparent that many of the perspectives and concepts at the very heart of sociology required substantial revision or transformation if they were to be applied in any meaningful way to the lives of women. So, new aspects of social experience and activity, alongside new ways of thinking sociologically had to be introduced (Maynard, 1990). For example, new themes addressed ranged from housework, motherhood and childbirth to sexuality, pornography and male violence. The inclusion of such areas of social life radically extended the parameters of the sociology of gender, as well as increasing the scope of sociology overall.

In addition, some ideas and terms had to be revised. For instance, the meaning of 'work' had to be extended to include both unpaid as well as paid labour. Leisure, previously regarded as activity carried out away from paid employment, had to be redefined to include housewives and those with a 'dual burden' of both labour market and domestic commitments. Some now refer to the family as the 'household' in order to take account of single people, single parents, those living together in unmarried relationships and others who do not conform to stereotypical notions of the nuclear family. In these ways, taking account of gender has involved challenging previous taken-for-granted assumptions about what counts as the 'proper' subject matter for sociological discussion. The terms and topics which structured the practice of the discipline have been re-evaluated and some have had to be redesigned.

A third way in which the gender blindness of sociology has been tackled focuses on the theoretical and methodological perspectives which have been central to the discipline. In terms of theory, for example, previous insistence on the precedence of social class in understanding inequality has been challenged (Walby, 1990). Instead, feminists have focused on women's unequal relationship to men and the resulting patterning of inequality which constructs men as the dominant group and women as subordinate. Feminist theorists are particularly concerned with the power relations between men and women (Davis *et al.*, 1991). They have adopted the concept 'patriarchy' through which to analyse the depth, pervasiveness and interconnectedness of different aspects of women's subordination (Walby, 1990). Although there are many kinds of feminist theory, emphasizing different aspects of patriarchy and the reasons for women's unequal positioning *vis à vis* men, all are concerned to explicate the mechanisms through which women are controlled, together with the circumstances under which resistance might also be possible. Thus, a rich and wide-ranging literature has been established, presenting an important challenge to the established ungendered orthodoxy in sociological theory.

Feminists have also been responsible for generating some heated debates about sociological research practice (Stanley and Wise, 1990). Many have argued, for instance, that qualitative rather than quantitative methods, and especially the in-depth interview, are more appropriate when studying women. This is because they facilitate the collection of rich and detailed material, as opposed to the limited data obtained via less intrusive methods, and encourage the participation of those being researched in the research process itself. Feminists have also expressed concern about the relationship between the researcher and the research participant. As we saw in Chapter 2, some have been critical of textbook guidelines which recommend that social distance be maintained between them, pointing out that this gives the researcher untold power to exploit subjects with a view to extorting as much information from them as possible. Feminists have contributed to the argument that the act of researching is as much a social process as are the experiences of the people sociologists study. It is, therefore, important to acknowledge and take account of this fact, rather than pretending that research proceeds as an unsullied and value-neutral activity.

The Concept of Gender

So far this chapter has used the term gender in an unproblematic way. However, the meaning of the concept is contested. The most usual sociological formulation distinguishes gender from sex. Whereas sex is taken to denote the anatomical and physiological differences which define biological femaleness and maleness, gender refers to the social construction of femininity and masculinity. Further, gender is not regarded as being a direct product of biological sex. Rather, gender roles, behaviour and identities are seen as being differently created and interpreted by particular cultures and in particular periods of historical time. In other words, what it means to be feminine or masculine is not fixed but changes. It is subject to a variety of cultural definitions and understandings.

This sociological conception of sex and gender, however, is not without its critics. For example, some feminists have questioned the assumption that gender is culturally constructed, while sex is still seen as having an innate biological basis (Ramazanoglu, 1995). Such an approach is essentialist because it implies that how we interpret and give meaning to biological phenomena is unproblematic, inherent and independent of cultural discourses and practices. Further, this way of thinking perpetuates the opposition between nature and culture which permeates western societies. It precludes the possibility of analysing the various ways in which bodily functions and processes (for instance, pain or pleasure) may influence the gendered experience of social life. Ramazanoglu (1995), for example, argues that ideas about the body are social, although not entirely independent of biology. It is important to take account of people's bodily existence (for women, such things as menstruation and childbirth), without assuming that this determines their behaviour.

Other feminists have questioned the very existence of gender and the categories 'women' and 'men'. Jackson (1998) has suggested that there are two main ways in which this has occurred, through materialist and postmodern feminisms. Materialist feminists focus on social structural relations between women and men (Delphy and Leonard, 1992). Following Marx, these are conceptualized as a class-like relationship in which women are unequal and exploited. Instead of seeing men and women as two natural biological groupings with relatively inevitable unequal social positions, the sexes are regarded as being socially distinguishable only because one dominates the other. Anatomical distinctions between the sexes have been made socially relevant because of, and as a justification for, unequal gender relations. It is the inequality of gender which gives salience to the otherwise socially insignificant differences of biology.

In contrast, postmodern feminists concentrate on the ways in which the categories 'men' and 'women' are culturally constructed through discourse. Butler (1990), for example, deconstructs our understandings of both sex and gender. She argues that if gender is not inherently linked to physiology and anatomical bodies, there is no reason to believe there are only two genders and that this binary opposition is based on a heterosexist world-view. Bodies become gendered through being socially classified as biologically different and through the continual process of people acting in gendered ways. For Butler, gender has no pre-given essential existence. Femininity only exists to the extent that it continues to be performed. It is, thereby, rendered diverse, fluctuating and volatile, rather than a stable and relatively homogeneous identity. Because performing gender brings gender itself into being, Butler regards the latter as being much less stable than is usually accepted. Gender does not have an existence outside the performance. By focusing on its ambiguities, her intention is to signal the possibility of new forms of non-hierarchical relationships. However, along with other postmodern feminists, she has been criticized for her portrayal of 'women' as a construct with no existence or unity prior to discourse (Jackson, 1998).

Other commentators have also been concerned with gender and diversity but in a rather different way. For example, black and Third World women have criticized early work on gender for focusing on the concerns of white, middle-class, educated, western women, thereby neglecting the experiences of women from other backgrounds, countries and cultures (Ramazanoglu, 1989; Collins, 1990). They argued that the significance of race and racism in their lives qualitatively effected their experiences of being women and, thus, needed to be taken into account during any analysis concerning gender. Similar concerns were also voiced by other groups of women, indicating that factors such as age, sexual orientation, disability and socio-economic status were also important in structuring the experience of being a woman. Thus gender inequality and women's subordination are no longer regarded as relatively straightforward and uncontradictory. Some women may be able to exert power over others by virtue of their race, sexuality or wealth and some may even be able to exercise power over some men. Analyses which unproblematically supposed a unified notion of gender oppression have been deconstructed and critiqued.

Another new development in the sociology of gender has been to focus on men and masculinity. It may seem strange to describe this as a 'new' area of study, particularly when the current interest in gender arose largely in response to the fact that sociology had previously been concerned almost exclusively with men. Yet, although it is the case that men historically have been the main subjects of empirical and theoretical work, they were studied in a purely genderless sense. There was little direct focus on the social construction of 'men', being male or having masculine characteristics and behaviour. For these reasons, it has been argued that, in focusing on men and masculinity, researchers are paying attention to an area of study which is long overdue. Now that the significance of gender for women has been subject to scrutiny, it is time to repeat a similar kind of exercise for men.

The critical study of men and of masculinities is currently a major area of growth in the sociology of gender (Hearn, 1992; Connell, 1995). Concern has been expressed that such work detracts from the many projects on women which still need to be undertaken, that it involves providing sociological justifications for unacceptable male behaviour and that it is an attempt by men to 'muscle in' on the study of gender, by intruding on women's hard fought for and jealously guarded space (Hanmer, 1990). Yet, the best work in the field raises a variety of problems of how men are, how they behave, how they should behave, why men have power, how that power is socially structured, what different kinds of men and masculinities there are, and how current arrangements can be changed (Hearn, 1996). Its significance for sociology is, therefore, immense.

Life Chances and the Sexual Division of Labour

The previous sections have considered some of the reasons why it is important to include a gender perspective within sociology, along with conceptual debates to which these give rise. One significant factor is that gender plays a major part in structuring the opportunities which are available to social groups, the kinds of experiences they are likely to have and the ways in which they are represented in a range of societal institutions, from the mass media to the welfare state and social policy. Despite widespread rhetoric about equal opportunities policies and legislation, major inequalities between women and men still remain in western societies, as the following sections illustrate.

Gender Inequalities in Education and Employment

Historically, sociologists have always emphasized material factors in the analysis of inequality, focusing on such issues as pay and the kinds of employment undertaken, relationship to the means of production, educational opportunities, and access to resources such as money, housing and consumer goods (Brannen and Wilson, 1987; Rees, 1992; Drew *et al.*, 1998). Feminists have argued that all these aspects of social life have a gendered, as well as a class and race, dimension. However, the evidence indicates that the picture is neither static nor uncontradictory. For instance, early work in the area of schooling showed girls generally performing better than boys at the beginning of their school career, a situation which was reversed during its later stages (Acker, 1994; Skelton, 1997). For older school students, research focused on such topics as girls' under-achievement in science and technology subjects, the ways in which boys command more of a teacher's time in the classroom and the comparative lack of strong role models for girls (Skelton, 1993; Acker, 1994). The overall picture of girls' education emerged as one of under-achievement and lack of confidence in the face of boys' bravado and domination in the classroom.

The gendered educational experience which girls received has also been linked to the gendered nature of their future position in the labour market. More women than ever before are working in paid jobs and they are doing so for longer, less intermittent periods of time, due to the trend to return to work between the births of children (Rees, 1992; Drew *et al.*, 1998). Yet they still appear to fare less well than men in terms of such factors as hours worked, pay received and the kinds of jobs they undertake. This is partly because many women work part time. In Britain, for example, 28 per cent of all those at work did so in 1995, although there are important ethnic differences between women, with fewer Asian and Afro-Caribbean women thus employed (Witz, 1997). It is also the case that the labour market remains gender segregated, both horizontally and vertically. Not only are women and men employed in different occupations and industries, women are concentrated in a much smaller number of jobs, particularly those in catering, retail, banking and other services, than are men (Rees, 1992; Witz, 1997). Further, the existence of a 'glass ceiling', whereby men continue to dominate in management, especially senior management, means that even when women increase their presence in a particular occupation, they may still fail to achieve their full potential within it. The existence of these forms of gender segregation are regarded, by feminist sociologists and policy makers alike, to be the single most important reason for the persistence of gender inequalities, particularly wage differentials, in the labour market (Witz, 1997).

Recently, however, the situation with regard to women's and men's position in education and the labour market appears to have been changing, although the implications of these changes are still not entirely clear. One aspect of this, which has caused much public comment, is girls' educational performance. In Britain, this is because they have been achieving an increasing number of good passes in public examinations, now surpassing the boys, although there are still fewer of them doing physics and chemistry (Walby, 1997). As a result, concern has switched from that about girls and science to one about boys' more general under-achievement and especially their relatively poor performance in linguistic and verbal skills.

Changes in the nature of the labour market also have a gendered aspect. For example, the manual occupations in which men have been traditionally over-represented, such as manufacturing and construction, have generally collapsed (Rees, 1992). By contrast, part-time work in shops, offices and other kinds of so-called 'women's work' has increased. Taken together, these educational and employment trends have raised the spectre of a potentially increasing number of unemployed, and unemployable, young men, mainly those who are from working-class backgrounds. Commentators have talked about a 'crisis of masculinity', created, in part, by the dismantling of the traditional male breadwinner image and the notion of 'jobs for life'. Under such circumstances, it is feared that those young men who are particularly disadvantaged will increasingly resort to lives of crime and violence (MacDonald, 1997). Such concerns underline the importance of sociologists including studies of men and masculinity, as well as women, in their gender analyses. However, caution needs to be exercised, lest the impression be given that, overall, women are no longer disadvantaged in relation to men. The significance of this is affected by class and race, as well as by gender factors.

Gender Inequalities in Family/Household

One area which emphasizes the nature of women's disadvantage, and on which feminists have done a lot of work, is that of the family/household. In this, they have focused on the notion of 'reproduction', using this as the central organizing concept through which women's material position within the household is to be understood, in a way analogous to the sociological use of 'production' to analyse capitalistic relations at work (Jackson, 1997). For feminist sociologists studying gender, the idea of reproduction has three meanings. The first refers to women's childbearing and mothering capacities. The second relates to the ways in which women's domestic servicing makes it possible both for the current generation of workers (husbands/partners) to work and looks after, nurtures and cares for the next generation of workers (their children). The third connotation of the term reproduction is concerned with how women's roles and expected activities within the household serve to make them subordinate both to their own husbands and partners and to men more generally. In other words, women's unequal situation within the household helps to make them also unequal outside it.

Part of the reasoning to support these arguments rests on the distribution of, and time spent on, domestic tasks within the home. Extensive research has shown that the majority of women still undertake the bulk of household jobs compared to men, even when they are themselves in full-time employment (Morris, 1990; Robertson Elliot, 1996; Drew *et al.*, 1998). Another aspect of gender inequality in the family/household relates to the unequal ways in which resources are managed, controlled and distributed. For instance, whatever mechanisms are adopted for money management, men usually have more personal spending money, while women generally keep little money for themselves (Pahl, 1989). Since husbands generally earn considerably more than their wives, they have potentially greater power in determining how any income should be spent and subsequent purchases used. In this context, studies have focused on the use and ownership of computer and video technology within the home, the amounts and types of food consumed and allocation of time for leisure and other pursuits. Men have been found to exercise a major amount of control in all these areas (Gray, 1992; Morgan, 1996). Why should this be the case?

Feminist sociologists have argued that the key to this question lies in the unpaid nature of the housework women undertake (Jackson, 1997). This is socially beneficial in several related senses. It benefits men who are able to exploit women's labour power and keep women dependent on them, by receiving services for which they do not have to pay, apart from contributing to their wives' maintenance. Further, the work that women do in the home creates men's leisure; it constrains their own free time while also making that of others possible. Women's unpaid domestic work, it is argued, also benefits capitalist employers in the labour market. This is because, if men had to pay for these services they would expect to be compensated by a rise in wages. In fact, it is only when such work is performed within households that domestic tasks are unpaid. Outside the home these can be undertaken as paid jobs and the services provided purchased on the market.

This section has focused on education, employment and the household and the ways in which one's gender can bestow both material benefit and constraint. Indeed, gender is an important influence on access to opportunities and resources, throughout the life course (Arber and Ginn, 1995). However, more attention needs to be paid in this area to some of the differences which exist between women, as well as the things they are likely to share. For instance, Afro-American and Afro-Caribbean women have been critical of some aspects of sociologists' preoccupation with the family, particularly when their analyses suggest that it is the basis of women's oppression (Collins, 1990). This is because families can provide protection from and resistance to racism. There are also important ethnic differences between women with regard to employment. For example, in Britain, Afro-Caribbean women are much less likely to be working part time than white women (Witz, 1997). Further, whereas for white women, pay and conditions of work vary greatly between full- and part-time employment, the same is not true for Afro-Caribbean women. Thus, the picture often presented concerning the material aspects of women's lives frequently fails to tell the whole story.

Sexuality and Violence Towards Women

The issues of sexuality and of violence towards women are examples of two interrelated areas which have been introduced into sociological analysis as a direct result of a feminist concern with gender. Previously, sexuality was commonly regarded as a private and personal matter and largely ignored by sociologists. Because it was treated as something innate or natural, sexuality was not seen as a legitimate topic for sociological investigation, being, at best, a subject for biologists or psychologists (Dobash and Dobash, 1980). Similarly, men's violence towards women tended to be explained away as the acts of a few 'sick' or psychologically deranged individuals, who had probably been provoked by women's provocative and inciteful behaviour. It was implied that such violence was a relatively rare occurrence and that it was perpetrated outside the home by abusers who were unlikely to be known to their victims.

Violence Towards Women

Sociological work on violence to women arose as a direct result of the contradictions faced by those who were both politically active in the women's movement in the 1970s and involved in feminist academic work at the same time. As the significance of violence in women's lives started to emerge at a grassroots level, support networks and groups began to be established for them (Dobash and Dobash, 1992). Yet, the extent of the violence that women appeared to be experiencing in everyday life did not appear to be mirrored in the appropriate official statistics, which recorded relatively small numbers of incidents (Maynard and Winn, 1997). It is now widely accepted that such figures significantly under-estimate the amount of violence that actually occurs. This is because many women do not report their attacks to the police, especially if their attacker is known to them, as is frequently the case. In addition, police have often been reluctant to intervene in those cases they define as 'domestics'. Evidence from Australia, Britain, Canada and the United States indicates their unwillingness to get involved if an incident takes place in the private setting of a woman's home because of a tendency to regard it as simply 'trouble' in a personal relationship (Hanmer *et al.*, 1989).

By contrast, feminist sociologists have been able to uncover the extent to which violence against women is hidden, by using female interviewers and adopting more sensitive research techniques. For instance, early quantitative work by Russell in the US found that 44 per cent of a random sample of 930 women had been the subject of rape or attempted rape during their lifetime; 21 per cent of those who had been married had been beaten by their husbands at some time; and 16 per cent had experienced incestuous abuse before the age of 18 (Russell, 1982, 1984). Kelly's (1988) in-depth interviews with 60 women found that the majority had experienced violence, the threat of violence, sexual harassment or pressure to have sex. These studies, along with similar research, suggest that violence towards women is far more extensive than official figures might lead us to believe. They demonstrate that, whereas sexual violence is often trivialized or treated as insignificant, it represents an important, complex and ever-present part of gender inequality in many women's lives (Hester *et al.*, 1996; Kennedy Bergen, 1998).

Sexual Violence

The term 'sexual violence' is used in feminist analyses for very specific theoretical reasons. It represents an attempt to link together a number of different forms of violence and the ways in which they occur and are experienced. Thus 'sexual violence' refers to acts which are directed at women because their bodies are socially regarded as sexual. Kelly defines sexual violence to include: 'Any physical, visual or sexual act that is experienced by the woman or girl, at the time or later, as a threat, invasion or assault, that has the effect of hurting her or degrading her and/or takes away her ability to control intimate contact' (1988: 41).

This widely used definition, which feminists have based on the accounts and experiences which women themselves have offered during the course of research, encompasses a wide spectrum of behaviour including the threat or fear of force, as well as its physical use, together with emotional abuse. It includes rape, sexual assault, woman beating, sexual harassment, incest, child sexual abuse and pornography. They are linked by virtue of the fact that they are overwhelmingly *male* acts of aggression against women and girls, often use *sex* as a means of exercising power and domination, and their effect is to intrude upon and curtail women's activities. They all, therefore, compel or constrain women to behave or not to behave in certain ways. In other words, both the reality and the threat of violence act as a form of gendered social control.

For example, for feminist sociologists, sexual harassment involves a variety of behaviours, some involving physical contact, some of a verbal or psychological kind, ranging from suggestive remarks, looks or joking to unwanted touching or patting, to direct sexual propositioning. What distinguishes sexual harassment from friendly banter or flirtation is that 'it is not mutual; it is not welcome; it offends; it threatens' (Halson, 1989: 132). It may even lead a girl or woman to alter her activities by taking a different route to school or changing her job.

Pornography is also included by some feminists in their definition of violence. Dworkin (1981), for instance, is famous for her arguments that pornography is at the heart of male supremacy. It portrays women's bodies as belonging to men and presents women's sexuality in an objectified, debasing and humiliating way. Dworkin sees this as constituting the foundation of women's oppression, because it legitimates women as the property of men and as subordinate to them. It is a violation of women as human beings and an encouragement to men to treat women as inferior and in abusive ways. For Dworkin, then, it is not just a question of whether pornography contains or causes violence towards women (although she argues both to be the case). Rather, she claims that pornography is itself violence to women and that it pervades and distorts every aspect of western culture.

It is only recently that researchers on violence have begun to address the issue of race. Mama (1992) points out that, in Britain, due to racism, ethnic minority women are very reluctant to call the police, even when serious or life-threatening crimes are being directed against them When the police are present, they tend to avoid enforcing the law and there is evidence to suggest that the police themselves perpetrate crimes, particularly against Afro-Caribbean people (Maynard and Winn, 1997). This means that ethnic minority women suffer a lack of protection within the community and can be particularly isolated if they live in white areas. However, although much progress has been made in highlighting the extent and severity of male violence, a great deal still remains to be done in terms of how it is treated and dealt with (Elman, 1996; Maynard and Winn, 1997; Jasinski *et al.*, 1998). Most material is still overwhelmingly about male violence towards white, apparently heterosexual women, thus ignoring issues of racism and heterosexism in its findings. It is, therefore, important that the parameters of research are broadened in the future in order to be able to investigate any factors which may effect women's differing experience of violence.

The Law, Citizenship and the State

The idea of the state refers to the mechanisms for government exercised over a particular population of people. These are usually defined territorially and nationally, although the definition of where the boundaries lie may shift and change over time. Hence, the state has been defined as a body of institutions centrally organized to distribute and redistribute resources and as a form of control (Anthias and Yuval-Davis, 1989; Randall and Waylen, 1998). As such, it has a variety of tools for enforcement at its disposal. For example, both the military and the police have access to the physical means of social control. The state also operates through the more subtle means of ideological persuasion, particularly because it can use institutions, such as the education system and the media.

As the state in so-called democratic countries is said to have legitimate authority over its citizens, it has been seen as important to investigate the extent to which this is equal for men and women. Three linked and significant areas have been given particular investigation. The first looks at the operation of welfare states, particularly in the context of a growing sense of their power since the 1980s to regulate, define, provide for and monitor individuals' lives (Sainsbury, 1994). The second area has been concerned with the law, how it tends to ignore women's experiences and views, thereby disempowering them. Drawing on arguments from the previous two, the third area focuses on the notion of citizenship in liberal democratic countries, how far it constructs men and women differently and the consequences of this for women.

Welfare and Social Policy

A welfare state is a system under which the state more generally undertakes to protect the health and well-being of its citizens, especially those in financial need, by means of the provision of services, grants, pensions and so on. Since the mid-1970s, sociologists and social policy analysts have become increasingly interested in the ways in which welfare states function and who their most likely beneficiaries are. Feminist work on social policy and welfare states has sought to bring women and gender to the centre of this analysis. The work has had two particular emphases. First, it has documented the inequalities between women and men as recipients of welfare benefits, for example in pensions and unemployment provision (Sainsbury, 1994). It has highlighted the role of familial and gender ideologies in influencing state provision of benefits and services. The tendency to treat the household as an undifferentiated unit, thereby assuming that any resources will be distributed equally within it, has been especially criticized, as has the assumption that women are largely dependent on men who are willing to support them. By examining the nature of informal care and care in the community, feminists have also shown how this is mainly undertaken by women, is unpaid and reinforces a sexual division of labour which increasingly absolves the state from obligations towards the elderly, sick and disabled (Ungerson and Kember, 1997; Sevenhuijsen, 1998). Their work on lone mothers has also highlighted the plight of women and their children, who are inadequately provided for by the state (Duncan and Edwards, 1997). All this work has broadened the analytical focus of welfare state research in comparison to mainstream analysis.

Second, feminist work on welfare and social policy has also studied the historical assumptions built into the structures of various welfare states, which remain largely intact today (Sainsbury, 1994). These tend to be based upon the expectation of full male employment, that the majority of married/co-habiting women would abandon paid work to be financially supported by a male breadwinner, and stable and intact families (Lister, 1998). But, of course, these sorts of conditions are less fulfilled today than in previous decades. In the 1990s, a significant level of unemployment is the norm, more married women than ever have employment and extra-marital births, and both cohabitation and divorce are substantially on the increase. This means that the assumptions on which welfare entitlements are based tend to be outmoded. As a consequence, many women who rely on such entitlements live in poverty. The central cause of this is the devaluing of women's caring and domestic work in the family, together with the assumption that women are, and should be, financially dependent on men. It is only by adopting a gendered approach to welfare analysis that the particular difficulties which women face on this score come into view. However, much still needs to be done to integrate feminist findings into current policy provision.

Women and the Legal System

The state has also been slow to respond to the wealth of evidence, now amassed, concerning violence towards women. Feminist researchers' claims that the violence which they were beginning to uncover was but the tip of an iceberg were dismissed, amidst accusations of exaggeration, provocation and lying on the part of women (Maynard and Winn, 1997). Subsequently, the feminist contentions have been upheld, with the seriousness of rape, domestic violence and child sexual abuse being more recognized. Yet, although violence towards women has received an increasingly high public profile, the practical response of state agencies has been very patchy. It even appears that the very laws passed with the precise aim of assisting women in their fight against male violence have been relatively ineffective (Maynard and Winn, 1997). Research on domestic violence legislation describes how reactionary interpretations of such legislation in courts of law have limited what can be achieved. This is because of the unsympathetic attitudes towards women held by the courts and by the police who are the gatekeepers to the legislation. Thus, although domestic violence legislation has undoubtedly improved the formal legal rights of battered women, the real improvement in their position is substantially less (Hester *et al.*, 1996).

There are also other problems with the ways in which the legal system deals with violence against women. For instance, researchers have referred to the police and courts of law as a rape victim's 'second assailant', where the women themselves are put on trial. Women, it has been found are reluctant to report rape because of the ways in which questioning and medical examinations are carried out (Lees, 1997). In court they have to give details of the whole process of the rape, talking intimately and publicly about parts of their body. Their accusations of rape may well be dismissed if there is no sign of bruising or struggle, even though resistance may put a woman's life in jeopardy. Attempts are made by those defending the accused to establish that a woman consented to intercourse, that even when she said 'no' she meant 'yes' and that she dressed provocatively to encourage sexual attention. In other words, women may be treated as unreliable witnesses (Lees, 1997).

This is also largely the case with the way in which courts treat children who have been sexually abused. Some sociological research has suggested that there is a common belief that children lie about sexual abuse and that they are likely to make false accusations (Smart, 1989a). Consequently, the child does not enter the witness box on neutral terms, but has been partly disqualified in terms of the perceived legitimacy of its evidence. Commentators argue that the way in which the procedures of the court operate in child sexual abuse cases, as in those of rape, are precisely designed to find ambiguities and flaws in the victim's story (Smart, 1989). Further, as in rape trials, the child's evidence must be corroborated by independent evidence, from doctors, social workers or witnesses, which is often impossible, before a conviction can be secured. For the courts, when it comes to the question of the violence committed against them, the word of the woman or child alone is not sufficient.

Citizenship

The issues raised in relation to the state, social policy, legislation and the operation of courts of law, alongside those previously considered concerning women's material circumstances and the violence committed towards them, all have implications for current debates about the gendered nature of citizenship. The concept of citizenship is important because it suggests that individuals can claim certain rights from the state which, in turn, has obligations towards them. Much of the recent social science discussion on the subject, as is so often the case, is concerned with class and omits gender. Most commentators draw on the work of Marshall (1950), who distinguished between three elements of citizenship – the civil or legal, the political and the social. Each is associated with a set of rights guaranteed for the individual by the state and made available through its judicial, political and welfare institutions. However, those researching gender point out, not only have women been slower in attaining many aspects of citizenship, some of them still do not apply to women at all (Walby, 1997). Women still tend to be an under-represented group in mainstream political processes and government (Walby, 1997). They may have the right to own property and make contracts along with men, but do they have liberty of the person and the right to justice? (Walby, 1997; Lister, 1998). If we return to some of the sociological evidence already cited in this chapter, it appears they do not. Not only may the widespread existence of sexual violence and abuse, rape and the extensive availability of pornography be regarded as infringements of women's personal liberty but, as has been seen, the courts and other institutions of the state scarcely provide adequate protection of women's rights in this area. What kind of citizenship rights do women have when they are regularly warned not to dress too eye-catchingly or walk alone at night for fear of provoking male attack? (Lees, 1997). Gender research shows, therefore, that the benefits supposedly bestowed by citizenship are not as available to women as they are to men.

There is also a tension between social citizenship for women and their location in the family as primary carers. One of the problems is that social citizenship often depends on being fully employed for access to rights. Those who do not contribute via employment can fall back on only very meagre levels of support. With regard to pensions, for example, women who work part time or spend long periods caring for children, husbands or elderly relatives may not have direct access to the same level of pensions as do men. It is for such reasons that Lister (1998) argues that women's financial dependency on men is an obstacle to their social citizenship. She shows how governments, when discussing the 'problem of dependency', consider only the public form of dependency on the state and neglect the extent of their private dependency in the family. Yet, it is the latter which leads to gender inequalities in welfare payments. Arguing that those women who care for elderly and disabled people at home might be regarded as the ideal model of the modern active citizen, Lister bemoans the fact that this seems to be the very opposite of the case (Lister, 1998). Further, excessive demands on women's time to undertake unpaid work in the household not only undermines their citizenship in a social sense, they also limit the extent to which women can participate fully in political life.

Current Concerns

The previous discussions have illustrated some of the ways in which adopting a gender approach in sociological analysis can help in understanding important aspects of contemporary society. In particular, focusing on the different life experiences of women and men is a way of highlighting both the nature of and the degree to which inequalities exist between them. As has been acknowledged, however, it is also necessary to take account of the fact that there are also differences and inequalities within the categories of women and men. One current and major concern within the sociology of gender is to pay more attention to this issue of difference on both an empirical and a theoretical level. This will involve becoming more sensitive to dimensions of things like 'race', ethnicity, sexuality and disability, and the ways in which they interlink with questions of gender.

Other matters are also at the forefront of sociological concerns about gender at the start of a new century. Although there are many which could have been chosen for discussion, three have been selected, in particular, both for their potential to influence the sociology of gender itself and for their likely impact on the gendered nature of society. They relate to gender and sociological theory, ageing and ageism, and the impact of the new information technologies on women.

With regard to theory, it was customary, until recently, to analyse and explain women's subordinate social situation in terms of three major perspectives, each with their own historical tradition and legacy. The first of these, liberal feminism, is depicted as focusing on individual rights and on the concepts of equality, justice and equal opportunities. In this, women are presented as being prevented from achieving equality with men by certain social barriers. It is, therefore, argued that specific legal and social policy changes are the necessary tools for rectifying women's inferior position. The second position, that of Marxist feminism, is identified by a concern with women's oppression as it is tied to forms of capitalist exploitation of labour. Here women's paid and unpaid work are each analysed in relation to their function within the capitalist economy. Third, radical feminism is 'radical' because, unlike the previous two, it challenges existing theoretical frameworks and attempts to formulate new ways of theorizing women's relationship to men. In particular, men's social control of women through various mechanisms of patriarchy is emphasized, especially violence, heterosexuality and reproduction, where men as a group are seen as responsible for maintaining women's oppression.

It is now recognized, however, that this perspectival approach is far too simple and that it is increasingly difficult to categorize feminist thought in this way. Different ways of thinking have developed, for example black, materialist, lesbian and eco-feminisms. Further, adoption of new theoretical frameworks means that it is more appropriate to view feminist theorizing about gender as a complex, dynamic and evolving process, rather than in terms of static stereotypes (Maynard, 1995). The emphasis now is much more on theory as an active process of understanding and less on the 'mugging up' of pre-given ideas.

Two general theoretical trends, those of psychoanalysis, particularly the thinking of Lacan, and post-structuralism, through the ideas of Foucault, have been especially influential in this process. Together, they have led to an increasing emphasis on language, culture and discourse. As a consequence, explorations of the meanings of 'difference' for women have begun to involve not just a concern for diversity of experience but also a postmodern emphasis on diversity within the individual. This involves the deconstruction of an individual's subjectivity. One's 'self' is no longer presented as rational and unified, so that what constitutes womanhood is seen as fragmented, pluralistic and continually changing (Butler, 1990; Maynard, 1995). In terms of gender theory, this has involved rejecting any claim that there can be *a* specific *cause* of women's oppression (be this male violence, capitalism's need for a docile workforce or discriminatory laws). Instead, arguments are made about the unevenness of power and relationships between men and women being far from the same and uniform (Ramazanoglu, 1989). Not all of women's experiences are negative, neither are they always and necessarily those of being oppressed. Developments such as these are indicative of considerable changes taking place in what constitutes feminist theory, when compared to the earlier 'perspectives' approach.

The other current interests must be dealt with rather more briefly. There has been a call for a focus on age and ageism, amidst concern that older women have been ignored and marginalized in gender analysis (Arber and Ginn, 1995). Despite much room for further improvement, more attention has been paid to differences in gender experiences related to such factors as race and sexuality, than has been given to ageing. Feminists have mainly studied younger women and those in their child bearing and child rearing years. Their virtual silence concerning those in older age groups has contributed to the negative stereotyping of the latter as 'past it' and as constituting continual social problems due to their lack of money, poor housing and ill-health. Little is known about the 'normal' experience of ageing for women (or men), since most research only concentrates on the difficulties they cause. Yet, most western countries have an increasingly ageing population. Further, a high proportion of the older population is female, due to a longer life expectancy and a tendency to outlive male partners (Arber and Ginn, 1995). Many of these women live an active life and contribute to society, certainly until their mid-70s. Gender relations are clearly not static throughout their life course and a great deal more research is needed to explain how the lives of older women in society are both experienced and constructed.

Finally, the analysis of gender must not be immune to the changes currently being wrought by the information revolution (Spender, 1995). Whether directly or indirectly, large-scale electronics communications media are changing both leisure and working lives. The pace of work, its location and distribution, alongside the nature of free time (from what is done to with whom) is being transformed, whether one is concerned about electronic banking or virtual sex (Star, 1996). While there has been much debate about the benefits or otherwise of this new technology, little of this has been gender sensitive. Yet, there are, arguably, two areas of immediate concern to women, which necessitate research. The first is the extent to which many women are excluded from and silenced within electronic networks and other technological work (Star, 1996). This occurs because, within the home, boys have more access to, and are more likely to be socialized into, new technology than girls, and because they receive more training at school and at work. Women's marginalization also occurs as a result of the reproduction of violence towards women, where fantasy games which may involve rape and pornography are readily available electronically. The technology, then, ceases to be gender neutral and becomes suffused with masculine values and culture.

A second concern is the extent to which the new technologies are entering the work environment. It is now perfectly possible, and increasingly likely, for some jobs to be done from terminals or computers at home (Star, 1996). Further high-tech developments have aided the generation of a global economy in which both production and services are increasingly moved from the 'first' world to vulnerable and impoverished workers in the 'third' (Mitter, 1991). The possible implications of this for women cannot be overlooked. In less developed nations it is likely to mean sweatshop labour in appalling conditions of work (for further discussion of gender and global changes, see Chapter 15). In the more developed ones it could lead to women's increased isolation into 'homeworking', in which they are expected to combine with child care and which remains outside health, safety and other labour regulations. This is an area which clearly requires further research.

Conclusion

This chapter has explored some of the sociological insights to be gained from taking account of gender. Clearly, much progress has been made and a new and thriving sub-area of the discipline has been established in little over twenty years. However, it is important that sociologists do not simply confine their gender awareness to a separate and specific field of study. For it is obvious, from the material and arguments covered here, that gender permeates and has repercussions for every aspect of social life. Thus a concern for gender relations needs to be included in every aspect of sociologists' work. While the in-depth work conducted by gender researchers is significant in its own terms, this has fundamental and far-reaching implications for the whole of sociology.

Further Reading

Abbott, P. and Wallace, C. *An Introduction to Sociology: Feminist Perspectives*, 2nd edn, London, Routledge, 1996. An introduction to feminist perspectives in sociology, demonstrating how conventions are challenged when gender is taken into account: covers education, the household, health, work, crime and politics, theory and method.

Hallett, C. (ed.) *Women and Social Policy,* London, Prentice Hall/Harvester Wheatsheaf, 1996. An introduction to the key topics and issues in social policy as they affect women, both as users and as providers of welfare services, including employment, poverty, housing, education, health care, community care and male violence.

James, S. and Busia, A. (eds) *Theorizing Black Feminisms*, London, Routledge, 1993. A collection of essays providing an overview of 'black' women's thinking about feminism.

Robinson, V. and Richardson, D. (eds) *Introducing Women's Studies*, London, Macmillan, 1997. A comprehensive overview of a range of important issues relating to women and gender; focuses, among other topics, on sexuality, the family and marriage, work, race, history, violence, reproduction and motherhood, methodology and language and literature.

Walby, S. *Gender Transformations,* London, Routledge, 1997. Examines how increased opportunities for women in Europe and America have been accompanied by new forms of inequality.

7

Racism and Ethnicity

Robert Miles and Stephen Small

While sociologists reject the idea of naturally occurring biological races, they are interested in the ways in which ideas and beliefs about 'race' are important sources of inequality and identity. The aims of this chapter are to question the concepts of 'race' and 'race relations' and explain and illustrate the concept of 'racialization' and 'racialized' inequalities. It also considers how 'racial' inequalities relate to inequalities of class and gender considered in the previous chapters. This chapter should help you understand:

- The distinctions between 'race' and ethnicity and 'race relations' and 'racialized relations'

- What sociologists mean by racism and new racism

- Some of the major theoretical approaches that have been developed to examine 'race' and ethnicity

- How the idea of racialized inequality can be applied to the example of Britain

---

CONCEPTS

ethnicity ■ 'race relations' ■ ideology ■ new racism
nationalism ■ colonialism ■ discrimination

Introduction

If asked to identify the most important problems of the day, a large proportion of the populations of developed countries would include in their list the problem of racism and the disadvantage that results from it. They may also make a reference to immigration and to the need for 'strict immigration control'. In this chapter we use the example of Britain to show how sociologists analyse these concerns. In Britain, there has been a long tradition of politicians, journalists and the 'ordinary man and woman in the street' claiming that 'immigrants' create social problems such as crime and violence, deteriorating housing conditions and housing shortages. The objection to 'immigrants' is not just about material concerns. They are blamed for simply being here, for challenging the 'British way of life' by refusing to adapt to 'British culture' expressed in terms of language, law, religion, dress, food and moral values. The argument may be given a further twist by claiming that these same 'immigrants' are living in Britain illegally, and that there are many millions more seeking to enter Britain illegally for the sole purpose of enjoying the benefits of the National Health Service, schooling or housing available in Britain. Generally, the central claim is that 'immigrants' (identified as the Other) create problems for 'decent citizens' (that is, Us).

These arguments may be accompanied by the statement that British people are neither 'prejudiced' nor 'racist'. Rather, it will be suggested that they have always been, and remain, tolerant of 'immigrants'. But, so the argument continues, their tolerance has a limit. That limit is reached when 'too many immigrants' are admitted to Britain and when 'they' fail to 'adjust' to the 'British way of life'. Then, it is 'natural' for 'our own people' (Us) to become hostile to 'immigration' and to the 'immigrant presence' (the Other). Such hostility is not racism, it will be said. Rather, it is an inevitable human reaction to being 'overrun', to the destruction of 'our way of life'.

While these views no longer attract widespread public support to the same degree as in the past, they continue to shape opinion, especially when 'immigration' becomes the focus of political attention. Moreover, historically, there is little new in these claims. As social historians have demonstrated (Fryer, 1984; Holmes, 1988) a review of the press and of political debate in Britain in the nineteenth century or in the 1930s reveals similar arguments. What differs is the group that is identified by the term 'immigrant': in the mid-nineteenth century it was 'the Irish', in the late nineteenth century it was Russian and Polish 'Jews' and in the 1930s it was German 'Jews'. Other groups have become stigmatized in this way at specific moments, including Germans and Italians. Since the mid-1950s, any reference to 'immigrants' in Britain has been understood to refer to 'coloured people', to those migrating to Britain from the Caribbean, Africa and the Indian sub-continent. Yet, while there is diversity in terms of the group signified as a problematic presence, to varying degrees each has also been identified as a distinct 'race'. This language of 'race' has had a particular resonance and significance with respect to post-1945 migration to Britain because of the way in which the immigrant presence has been signified by reference to human physical features such as skin colour, but all these earlier migrant populations were similarly labelled as 'races'.

Over the last four decades, it has come to be seen as self-evident that Britain has a 'race relations' problem as a result of the fact that 'coloured immigrants' are resident in very large numbers. It is thus suggested that 'race relations' are the 'natural' outcome of different 'races' living together in Britain. Underlying this suggestion is the subsidiary assumption that 'race relations' are the inevitable outcome of the 'natural' differences between different 'races' in terms of their mental and biological constitution, and the cultural practices, institutions and behaviour that are believed to follow from this. Hence, it is concluded that Britain's 'race relations' problem results from immigration: and if 'we' had not allowed 'them' into 'our country', we would not have such a problem.

Students approaching an analysis of 'race relations' by accepting these assumptions are building their conceptual foundation on shifting sands and risk legitimating dominant (and in some instances racist) discourses and the practices that derive from them. Many sociologists believe that it is preferable to commence the analysis of 'race relations' by questioning the language of 'race relations' and the assumptions which underlie such language (for example Miles, 1982; Miles and Torres, 1996). Many of the words just used are based on misleading claims and assumptions. Rather than accept them at face value, these sociologists urge students to challenge them in order to expose their unquestioned assumptions. Doing this raises questions about the motivations and intentions of those in positions of power who use them so uncritically. Accordingly, this chapter will begin by providing some definitions of the key concepts that will be used. It will then look at some of the major theoretical approaches to the study of 'race' The following sections look at patterns of racialized inequality in Britain and issues of immigration and citizenship.

Concepts

'Race' and Ethnicity

Words like 'race relations', 'race' and 'racial' in have been placed in quotation marks because these are commonsense words whose meaning and significance are hotly contested. For many sociologists, these words, and the assumptions underlying them, create problems of understanding and analysis. The words 'race' and 'racial' presume the existence of discrete biological 'races', and imply that anything which is 'racial' results primarily from, and is explained by, this supposed fact. For example, the idea of 'racial conflict' suggests conflict results primarily, even inevitably, from contact between 'races' in and of themselves, rather than because of factors such as economic and political competition. However, the vast majority of scientists, genetic and social, agree that discrete biological 'races' do not exist (Hannaford, 1996). That is to say, most scientists do not believe that the human population is divided into a number of distinct types of species in such a way that evident physical characteristics or even hidden genetic characteristics correlate in a determined way with social, psychological and cultural characteristics. They also agree that the physical distinctiveness that does exist across human populations bears little relationship to the racialized identities of communities scattered across the world today.

Even though they are regarded as synonymous in much commonsense discussion, most sociologists are agreed that the terms 'race' and ethnicity should be clearly distinguished for analytical purposes. Use of the idea of 'race' usually indicates a belief in the existence of naturally occurring groups, each exhibiting real and imagined biological and mental attributes and characteristics which are regarded as fixed. While the idea of 'race' necessarily both self-identifies and other-identifies (to identify the Other as a distinct 'race' entails simultaneously identifying Us as another 'race'), a great deal of academic work has focused upon the ways in which it has tended to be imposed upon populations as part of a process of subordination, rather than being sought after and embraced. Research on the ways in which Africans have been regarded as the 'black race', and as biologically and culturally inferior, illustrates this process (Miles, 1982). More recently, interest has been shown in the ways in which self-identified, superior 'race' identities have been constructed and sustained (for example Roediger, 1996).

The concept of ethnicity refers to specific social and cultural attributes (such as language, religion, dress, food, music, beliefs of origin and genesis) and to the social and cultural (and negotiable) boundary between two or more self-identifying collectivities who claim a historical existence by reference to such attributes. Hence, ethnic groups are identified by a pattern of cultural signifiers which sustains claims of difference and distinctiveness through historical time: in some instances, the claims of distinctiveness may be supported by beliefs about natural difference (that is, by a belief in the existence of 'races'). Ethnicity tends to be embraced rather than imposed and is fluid and flexible because the identifying social and cultural attributes can and do change through time. Most of what was called 'race' in the past is now usually referred to as ethnic or ethnic relations: the description of 'racial group' is replaced by that of ethnic group (and 'race relations' by ethnic relations).

Given the limitations of the idea of 'race' as an analytical category, this development has significant advantages. This is because the conceptual language no longer reproduces an echo of a racialized discourse in such a way that commonsense beliefs in the existence of 'races' are implicitly or explicitly legitimated. Yet it needs to be recognized that beliefs about 'race' are still

employed in self- and other-identification: members of a group may simultaneously self-identify in relation to some combination of, for example, religious belief, language, cuisine and dress *and* the imagination of itself as a
'race'. And, of course, ideas of 'race' are still often central to negative other-
identification: for example, people of Irish origin resident in Britain distinguish themselves and are distinguished by others by reference to a range of
cultural attributes but they are also other-identified negatively by a belief in
their existence as a distinct 'race' as evidenced by their supposed mental
inferiority. What is sociologically significant is not only the variation in what
is signified but also the economic, political and ideological forces that shape
these variations.

'Race Relations' and Racialized Relations

Close to the idea of 'race' is the notion of 'race relations'. This notion often
leads to an oversimplified focus on 'race' by positing the existence of a distinct
category of social relations (that is, relations between supposedly distinct
'races') while ignoring the relevance of economic and political processes and
the consequences of the routine operation of key institutions in contemporary
life. Many sociologists now reject the term 'race relations' because there are
no 'races' and so there cannot be any social relations between them. But if
'race relations' are not the relationship between biologically different 'races',
why are certain types of social relation defined as such? In order to answer this
question, it is necessary to turn our attention to economic and political
processes and to the ways in which structures, images and ideologies operate
to sustain inequality. Additionally, we need to consider the impact of the ideological dimension of resistance to such inequality. In this kind of analysis there
is no presumption that 'race' is a variable in and for itself. Rather, it is argued
that ideas and beliefs about 'race' have shaped these relationships, alongside
the impact of, for example, class and gender.

This approach is usually described as the *racialization problematic* (or framework). This framework is a set of assumptions and concepts which explore the
multiple factors that shape what has previously been described as 'race relations'.
Some of these factors entail explicit reference to 'race', for example, beliefs about
the existence of 'races', and discrimination based on such beliefs. But other
factors – such as competition for economic and political resources (education,
jobs, housing, elected office) – may seem to have no 'racial' reference. The
racialization problematic enables us to draw out the relationship between these
seemingly unrelated variables, and to assess the significance of each of them.
What this conceptual approach requires, rather than presumes, is that there is a
need to question and explain the social and cultural boundaries and identities
by which groups called 'races' have been, and continue to be, defined. We
believe a historical and comparative approach is the best way to do this.

The key concept within the racialization problematic is the process of *racialization* (and hence the notion of racialized social relations) which has been defined in a number of ways (see Small, 1994 for an overview). We use it to refer to a historically specific ideological process, and to the accompanying structures, that results in certain social collectivities being thought of as constituting naturally (often biologically) distinct groups, each possessing certain ineradicable features. The groups racialized in this way vary. The example with which most people are familiar with is the racialization of diverse ethnic groups from the Caribbean, Asia and Africa in order to constitute a 'black race' which stands in contrast (even in conflict with) the 'white race'. This particular instance of racialization is founded in part on colonization and imperial conquest. It also refers to the associated institutional arrangements: the legal system (in slavery, and post slave societies, including legislation on immigration), the economic system (the plantation economy, and the distribution of jobs), as well as housing (with, for example, African-Caribbeans, Pakistanis and Bangladeshis generally confined to inferior housing).

People of African and Asian origin are not the only populations to be racialized by Europeans (who simultaneously racialized themselves). There have been many instances of racialization of Europeans by other Europeans (Miles, 1993: 80–104). During the nineteenth century, the Irish were widely racialized by the British while, during the twentieth century, the racialization of Jews was a prelude to the Holocaust. Moreover, the laws and policies introduced to promote equal opportunities and multiculturalism sustain the process of racialization even though their objectives are clearly very different: for example, the very title of the legislation legitimates the ideas of 'race' and 'race relations' while the content of the legislation includes a legal definition of a 'race'.

The concrete examples elaborated in the following text demonstrate that this is not simply a matter of changing the words, or playing semantics; rather it is a matter of challenging the assumptions, and of improving the analysis, by identifying as central a number of variables that are usually neglected or obscured. It is useful to distinguish several aspects of this process of racialization. Racialized structures are the institutional pillars of society. They are the routine, recurrent and organized features of contemporary life. The idea of racialized structures has two key components.

First, it refers to the distribution of valuable resources such as political power, employment, education and housing. Primarily this aspect involves who owns what, works and lives where, and has good health. Second, it refers to the normal, recurrent and routinized procedures of institutions that shape and constrain our daily lives, from politics (voting and political representatives), economics (businesses, employment), education (universities, schools), health (hospitals) and other spheres of social life (family, media, music, sport). These behaviours and actions sustain the distribution of resources. The practices of key institutions in contemporary societies shape and determine who succeeds and who fails, who is rewarded and who is punished.

Ideologies are systematic statements about the way in which society is organized, or ought to be organized, if it is to function well. Ideologies are racialized in several ways. Ideologies that make explicit reference to 'race' are the
most obvious examples of racialized ideologies, closely followed by those in
which 'race' is indirectly referred to, or implied. But all ideologies are racialized in that they have differential consequences for populations labelled for
example as 'black', Asian and 'white'. For example, the 'Keep Britain White'
slogan is an explicit expression of a racialized ideology, asserting as it does a
racialized conception of Britishness and of immigration control. Not far away
from such ideologies are those in which the policies of multiculturalism, anti-
discrimination and equal opportunities are blamed for deteriorating 'race relations'. Here it is suggested, or stated, that such policies favour 'black' people
who are thereby privileged illegitimately.

There are also less explicit racialized ideologies, for example, those with a
coded racialized reference. In these ideologies, while no reference is made to
'race', the words themselves are heavily saturated with such meanings and
interests as the result of a specific history in the course of which a particular
social group is attributed with a fixed nature and/or whose presence is associated with a set of (usually undesirable) social consequences. When people
refer to crime in the 'inner city', the 'immigration problem' or to 'reverse
racism', and when they claim that multiculturalism devalues their culture,
these all have a 'racialized' reference.

There are also ideologies without any racialized reference, but in which we
can identify the hostile intentions of those advocating them, or the likely
adverse consequences of the ideology for 'blacks' and/or Asians. Some policies
around policing exemplify this type of ideology. For example, the practice of
'Stop and Search', which gives the police to stop and search persons suspected
of crimes on rather slender suspicion, is defended by arguments about the
need to act directly to deal with street crime. This policy – and the one which
preceded it (the 'Sus law)' – has been enforced with disproportionate impact
on young black men of Caribbean origin (Smith and Gray, 1987).

Racialized identities are the collective identities embraced by people previously and contemporarily described as 'races'. As Europeans created for themselves the idea that they are a 'white race', they also created the idea of the
'black race' which categorized and controlled people originating from Africa,
or the Asian race for those from the Indian sub-continent and the
surrounding region. In some contexts, the category of 'black' or 'coloured' has
been used to refer to all those considered to be 'not-white' while in other
contexts these groups have been subdivided, as with distinctions by nation,
for example, 'Indians' or the 'brown race'. The racialized identity of whiteness
serves as a platform on which to organize; and so, too, does the racialized
identity of blackness. These identities serve to defend and promote the interests of those people labelled by them, and/or embracing them. Hence, social
movements of 'blacks' or 'Asians' have emerged expressing their collective

strategies of resistance around racialized identities and many continue to do so. In this regard, they fulfil a number of group interests. However, they also mask the very real differences within these groups, along lines of class and gender differentiation, religion, language or political interests.

These various aspects of racialization interact in ways that shape one another. Racialized structures shape representations and ideologies. Poverty causes material hardship for 'blacks' and 'Asians' and media institutions have employed images of such people in poverty and on welfare dependency. Control of government institutions affect the policies that prevail, just as control of businesses hinders or helps opportunities. These same institutions are positioned so as to restrict or expand the incidence of racialized discrimination. In African-Caribbean communities, the never-employed, the unemployed, the unskilled and the skilled continue to face hostility. Similarly, racialized images and ideologies can influence social structure: African-Caribbean and Asian communities continue to be the subject of negative media images which can increase hostility not only from 'white' people but also from some sections of African-Caribbean and Asian communities towards each other (for some examples, see Gabriel, 1994). The psychological consequences are immense. At the same time, ideologies of 'colour-blindness' create the appearance of equality and fairness, while hiding practices of discrimination.

Racism, New Racism and Racisms

The concept of racism is especially problematic for a number of reasons (cf. Miles, 1989, 1993). First, despite the fact that it is now widely used as if it had a universal existence and reference, the word 'racism' was created in the 1930s. Precursors such as 'race prejudice' embody a similar meaning but the specific origin of the word 'racism' has had implications for its use and meaning in later historical periods. Given that the word was created to refer to the scientifically justified belief in the existence of an ordered hierarchy of biologically distinct 'races' that was used to legitimate fascism in Germany during the 1930s, some sociologists have argued that, in so far as such a belief is in decline, then racism is in decline. Moreover, if the meaning of the concept is so firmly grounded in its immediate referent, then it cannot have an object in earlier historical periods: simply stated, there cannot have been racism before the rise of science as a form of human knowledge in Europe.

Second, in the light of what is now widely known to have been done in the name of racism in earlier historical periods (the events of European colonization and of the Holocaust are especially significant), the ideology of racism is widely discredited. As a result, the concept of racism has taken on a very negative connotation and the accusation that someone is a racist is extremely condemnatory. Thus, explicit references to an alleged 'racial inferiority' of the

Other are rare in the formal, public arena and, when they are made, they attract widespread media attention and censure.

In the light of these historical developments, there are two main sociological approaches to the scope of the concept of racism. On the one hand, there are those who, in effect, sustain the original definition of the concept which refers to the ideology that the world is divided into a number of separate 'races' (for example, Europeans, Africans and Asians) who are endowed with different physical and mental attributes, that 'race' determines culture, and that Europeans are superior both mentally and culturally. On the other hand, there are those who revise or extend the definition in various ways. They claim that the original referent is only one specific form of racism, this being identified as biological or scientific racism.

The revision has taken two main forms. First, there are those who retain the idea that the concept refers to a specific form of ideology and who argue that there are a variety of historically specific racisms which refract the particular context in which they are formed and expressed. Second, there are those who extend the definition in such a way as to include both beliefs and practices which lead to the subordination of specific racialized groups. In some versions of this argument, evidence of the existence of racism is found in the comparative material disadvantage of, for example, 'black people' or 'Asians' irrespective of any beliefs held about the group.

The debate concerning the scope of the concept of racism has been particularly lively over the past two decades. The concept of a *new racism*, formulated initially by Barker (1981), has been especially influential. The emergence of this concept is grounded in the previously mentioned declining expression of biological or scientific racism, at least in the formal spheres of social life. It is argued that this 'old racism' has been superseded by a new racism which is characterized by an assertion of the naturalness of both a desire to live among 'one's own people' (Us) and hostility towards a culturally distinct immigrant presence (the Other) that threatens the existence of 'our way of life'. This concept was incorporated into the influential analysis of the Centre for Contemporary Cultural Studies (1982). Gilroy argues (1987) that hostility to people of African Caribbean and Asian origin in Britain in the 1980s was dominated by hostility to their religion, family values and language, rather than to their skin colour. A similar emphasis upon cultural signifiers is found in Modood's claim that there is less discrimination against people of African and African-Caribbean origin because their cultures are closer to that of 'white' Britons, and more against British Muslims in particular and British Asians in general because their cultures are seen as being more 'alien' (Modood, 1992). While retaining the essence of the idea of a new racism, a rather different emphasis is found in the assertion that hostility is dominated by a concern with profit and prosperity in the context of a 'new world order' of global capitalism: 'Racism is no longer about racial or cultural superiority... Racism is about prosperity, and prosperity is white, Western, European' (Fekete and Webber, 1994). One can conclude from this that there are many different racisms which differ in motivation, content and outcome.

It is important to recognize that contemporary social reality is complex. For example, it is problematic to say that a person who opposes equal opportunities policies for people of African-Caribbean origin or who is in favour of tighter immigration control is necessarily articulating racism because these views may be grounded in a variety of beliefs and assumptions. For example, the former may be motivated by a genuine belief in treating all individuals equally without regard to ethnicity or 'race'. But neither can we say that a person who expresses support for 'colour blind' policies is necessarily 'anti-racist' or 'non-racist'. The intentions people have, and what they actually do, can be markedly different from what they say they will do. In so far as the concept of racism is used to refer to a particular ideology, this complexity creates particular difficulties for the sociologist when seeking to determine whether any particular set of assertions warrant description as an instance of racism.

Because of this difficulty, our preference is to use the concept of racism to refer to a specific kind of ideology: this at least avoids the problem of reading intentions and beliefs from actions and outcomes. But we also criticize those writers who have used the concept of racisms without also attempting to specify what each specific instance of racism has in common with all other instances to warrant description as a racism. Put another away, if historically there are many different racisms, each instance must express a set of core characteristics that allow it to be described as a racism. Thus, elsewhere, one of the current authors has proposed the following definition (Miles, 1993: 99, but see also pp. 100–2):

> Racism is a form of ideological signification which constructs a social collectivity as a discrete and distinct, self-reproducing population by reference to certain (real or imagined) biological characteristics which are purported to be inherent, and which additional attributes the collectivity with other negatively evaluated (biological and/or cultural) characteristics. Racism, therefore, attributes meaning to the human body, either somatically or genetically, in order to construct an Other which reproduces itself through historical time and space.

Moreover, an analysis of racism which is grounded in this kind of definition will need to identify not only the features that an ideology must exhibit in order that it may be identified as an instance of racism but also the wider historical and structural factors that shape its existence. An analysis of this kind will therefore seek out the links between racism as ideology, and broader economic and political structures. This will have a historical dimension because we have inherited a system of beliefs about 'race' and mental and physical abilities, and a commonsense language which we use to describe present differences between racialized populations.

Yet understanding racism is not simply a matter of looking at beliefs inherited from the past. Current beliefs and ideologies are shaped by past beliefs but also by current social arrangements, especially economic and political structures. Social structure is important, because racism (in the past and at present) has been a moment in the reproduction of economic, political and social structures which continue to shape our attitudes and behaviour, with significant consequences. For example, ideas of 'race' helped channel and shape patterns of colonization and conquest, the various systems of slavery instituted across the Americas, as well as the circumstances and conditions surrounding the independence of countries like India and Pakistan, Ghana and Nigeria, and Jamaica, not to mention the mass murder of Jews in Europe prior to and during the Second World War. In all these different situations, the ideology of racism was used by the dominant groups to identify other populations as naturally inferior and therefore deserving of domination and exploitation.

Contemporary racisms are also shaped by the division of the world into distinct nation states and by the ideology of nationalism (Anderson, 1983; Balibar and Wallerstein, 1991; Miles, 1993). Once again, there is a historical dimension to this relationship. Commencing in the late eighteenth century in western Europe, the rise of a new ruling class, the bourgeoisie, was accompanied by an appeal to the 'common people' to see themselves as members of a single nation with common interests. This process of nation state formation was legitimated by the belief that (as with supposed 'races') nations too were naturally occurring populations. The languages of 'race' and nation were thereby closely intertwined, and supported by a binary opposition between Us and Other. As populations were persuaded to think of themselves as unitary, homogeneous nations, a process that was accompanied by a significant degree of real cultural change (regional languages were, for example, eliminated), rights of political participation and of eligibility for welfare benefits were gradually granted to most members of the nation.

Post-1945 migrations have highlighted the significance of these arrangements: should the new arrivals have equal access to these rights and resources reserved for members of the nation? In the case of Britain, as we shall see shortly, many of the migrants were British subjects who did therefore have the right to work, political participation and access to welfare benefits. But racism was used to identify them as illegitimate competitors: the language of 'our own people' became simultaneously a nationalist and a racist discourse, defining the nationalized Us by reference to 'whiteness'. In this instance, racism and nationalism articulated to identify a racialized Other whose presence marked the necessity of redrawing the boundary of who belonged and who should not belong to the nation. The relationship between racism and nationalism, and its structural consequences, should therefore be viewed as historically contingent: the precise interrelationship between these two ideologies varies from one set of circumstances to another.

Theories

Sociological debate is shaped by the emergence and decline of different theo-rietical approaches which themselves express changing social conditions. In British sociology, for example, the origin of theoretical discussion about 'race' can be traced back to the late 1960s when 'race' and 'immigration' were becoming identified as major social problems. Two texts expressed the emer-gence of the *sociology of 'race relations'*: Banton (1967) and Rex (1970). While the underlying presuppositions of these two texts differed in significant respects, they shared the objective of defining 'race relations' as a legitimate object of sociological investigation and explanation. Moreover, both sought to understand the British situation through frameworks that were historical and comparative: British 'race relations' were thereby compared with 'race relations' in the USA and South Africa. The crucial difference between the two texts lay in their understanding of the nature of racism: Banton argued that the ideology of racism was no longer widely expressed while Rex argued that it was a defining feature of a 'race relations' situation and that it continued to be a major ideological force in Britain, even if its form and content had changed.

As we saw in Chapter 5, during the late 1960s and early 1970s, British sociology was shaped by a renewal of interest in Marxist theory and in the interconnections between the centre and periphery of the world capitalist economy. Out of these developments emerged other theoretical perspectives which came to constitute specific challenges to the sociology of 'race relations' during the late 1970s and 1980s. These can be described collectively as *Marxist theories of 'race'*: because the Marxist tradition itself encompasses a variety of perspectives, these were reflected in different analyses of the British 'race' problem, but they were agreed that:

1. 'race' was the object of analysis
2. understanding the relationship between class and 'race' was the central theoretical and empirical priority
3. racism remained a central determinant of inequality in contemporary capitalist societies.

Their concern to explain the disadvantage and discrimination arising from racism within the broader framework of Marxist theory distinguished these writers from both Rex and Banton.

In the light of the influence of political movements in the USA, this theor-etical development was divided into 'black' and 'white' sub-sections, the former arguing that 'black people' needed to assert political (and therefore theoretical) autonomy in order to overcome the legacy of colonialism. Refer-ences to 'white sociology' and 'black Marxism' became commonplace for a time, reflecting the influence of these different perspectives. Examples of contributions to Marxist theories of 'race' include the writings of the Centre for Contemporary Cultural Studies (1982) and Ben-Tovim *et al.* (1986).

What can be called the *theory of racialization* emerged during the 1980s (Miles, 1982, 1989) out of a critique of what (despite their fundamental differences on many other matters) the sociology of 'race relations' and the Marxist theory of 'race' were agreed on, namely that 'race' was the object of study. The main features and themes of this theory have been outlined in preceding sections. But it was not the only theoretical development of this decade: there were three others.

First, the sociology of 'race relations' gave birth to the *sociology of ethnic relations*. This reflected in part the influence of the academic discipline of anthropology, grounded in the ethnographic study of colonized people, many of whom had migrated from periphery to centre of the world economy. Studies of the culture and way of life of African-Caribbean and Asian migrants during the 1970s revealed them as social groups embodying distinct histories and cultural traditions and therefore not just the victims of racism and discrimination (for example Watson, 1977). The concepts of ethnicity and ethnic group entered the theoretical language, stimulating a debate about the distinction and relationship between 'race relations' and ethnic relations (Banton, 1983; Anthias and Yuval-Davis, 1992). Moreover, the exploration of the production and transformation of cultural traditions (and their simultaneous maintenance across time and space following migration) has highlighted the distinctiveness of ethnic groups resident in Britain following the colonial migrations of the 1950s and 60s. As a result, not only is the idea of a single 'black community' unified by the collective experience of racism now undermined by a distinction between African-Caribbean and Asian ethnic groups, but this dichotomy is itself fractured by the revelation of the significance of, for example, religious belief and practice to those whose migrant origin lies in the Indian sub-continent (Modood, 1992).

The second development arose from the growth of feminist theory within the social sciences. The sociology of 'race relations' and Marxist theories of 'race' were not immune from the silence about gender that characterized much of the academic discipline of sociology. The key theoretical developments took place in relation to Marxist theories of 'race', concerned as it already was with the articulation between the social divisions of class and 'race': it was but a small step to add gender to this articulation. But what we might describe as the *theory of class, 'race' and gender* was far from being a unitary theory.

The political division between 'white' and 'black' feminists was reflected in the debates of the 1980s and early 1990s: 'race' was conceived as fragmenting gender as much as it was conceived as dividing class (for example Centre for Contemporary Cultural Studies, 1982; Bryan *et al.*, 1985). The idea of triple oppression along with that of simultaneous articulation or intersectionality shaped these expressions of the relationship between 'race', class and gender (Centre for Contemporary Cultural Studies, 1982; Cheney, 1996). Whereas the first concept assumed men and women who were 'black' or 'Asian' experienced a similar racism, and all women experienced a similar sexism, intersectionality rejected this as an oversimplified accumulation. Instead it was argued that 'black' and 'Asian' women's experience of racism was uniquely gendered, their experience of sexism uniquely racialized. One example of this is the primary purpose rule in immigration law which required 'black' and 'Asian' women to demonstrate that their primary purpose in getting married to a UK citizen was not for purposes of immigration. Both triple oppression and intersectionality continue to be stated, or suggested, in works that explore patterns of dominance against 'black' and 'Asian' women, as well as women from other ethnic minorities (Brah, 1996).

The third development arose out of the theoretical critique of Marxism itself. A number of sociologists (for example Touraine, 1981; Gorz, 1982) had argued, long before the collapse of communist states in central and eastern Europe forced a wider critique of Marxist theory, that class relations were no longer the key force shaping historical development. Such an argument had a particular attraction to self-identified 'black' sociologists who were asserting that 'race' was an autonomous social force, reflected in the existence of a 'black' community shaped by a distinct historical experience and culture (for example Gilroy, 1987). The arena of cultural studies provided fertile ground for the development of the *theory of the autonomy of 'race'*.

Focusing as it does on cultural production and consumption in everyday life, cultural studies has facilitated the analysis of the production of collective identities through adherence to a specific lifestyle (expressed in dress, language, religion, music): 'race' is theorized as one social division which sustains such a collective identity by means of both a resistance to exclusion and marginalization determined by racism, as well as the celebration of a positive cultural tradition. Such a perspective has merged with certain of the theoretical currents that have been labelled as postmodernism (Hall and du Gay, 1996).

Most attempts to classify races gloss over, even obscure, connections and overlaps between categories or groups which are presented as absolutely separate and distinct: the preceding distinctions between different theories is no exception. In particular, the theoretical developments of the 1980s are closely linked. Some postmodernist perspectives have adopted the concepts of identity and ethnicity, even if they have been employed in a distinctive manner (Rattansi and Westwood, 1994; Hall and du Gay, 1996). There is no fundamental obstacle to the integration of a racialization perspective with one which highlights the interrelationship between class and gender inequalities (Anthias and Yuval-Davis, 1992; Brah, 1996; Sudbury, 1997).

Those writers who reject theories which take 'race' as their point of origin and as an explanatory concept do so because they doubt that such a theory can offer a satisfactory explanation of the structures and patterns of social relations described in this chapter. They argue that any explanation of these structures and patterns must relate the unfolding of social practices and beliefs associated with the idea of 'race' to associated patterns of economic and political power, and gender differences, nationally and internationally. Even though there are many individual, and indeed collective, examples of people acting on the basis of a belief in the existence of 'races' without regard to economic or political consequences, the broad contours of racialized structures, processes and ideologies are best explained in relation to these broad patterns (for example Small, 1994).

Racialized Inequality in Britain

At the turn of the century, British African-Caribbeans and British Asians find themselves collectively at a significant disadvantage, as compared with British 'whites', deprived of many basic resources and facing racist hostility. Racialized inequality is revealed in the differences in the share of, and access to, valued resources. However, an overview of racialized inequality is not straightforward, given the many differences *within* the various racialized groups in Britain. Although commonsense discussions argue that British African-Caribbeans are not doing as well as British 'whites', or that British Asians are doing better than both, the evidence reveals a more complex picture. There are major differences within these broadly defined groups (for example, between British Asians who originate from the different countries of the Indian sub-continent and between British Africans and African-Caribbeans). While these differences are clearly real, collectively all negatively racialized groups face some institutional discrimination.

British African-Caribbeans and Asians are more likely to be unemployed, under-employed (that is, to have more qualifications than their job merits), to receive low pay, and/or Social Security benefits. They have comparatively worse jobs, worse work conditions (shifts, night work, part-time work) and less pay and security (Jones, 1993). In the 1980s, African-Caribbean and Asian males earned 10–15 per cent less than 'whites'; and almost twice as many African-Caribbean and Asians, as compared with 'white', households were likely to be reliant on child benefits (Brown, 1984: 242). Compared to 'white' people, African-Caribbeans are less likely to be self-employed, and more likely to be in manual and lower paid jobs while 'white' men are more likely to be employed as corporate managers and in skilled and semi-skilled jobs. For example, Brown reported that, while 19 per cent of 'whites' were found in the top socio-economic group, only 5 per cent of African-Caribbeans were. And the proportion of 'whites' in other 'non-manual' jobs was double that for African-Caribbeans (Brown, 1992: 157). This is true despite the fact that more African-Caribbeans were economically active in the late 1980s. While they are more likely to be unemployed, African Caribbeans and Asians are less likely than 'whites' to claim unemployment benefits (Jones, 1993: 119).

British African-Caribbean and Asian people are overwhelmingly an English urban population where they are more likely to live in sections of the inner city, and to be residentially segregated from 'whites'. Five English metropolitan areas – London, West Midlands, the North West, Yorkshire and Humberside – account for more than 90 per cent of all African-Caribbean people in Britain. Similarly high numbers of Asians live in these conurbations. Compared to British African-Caribbeans, and to Pakistanis and Bangladeshis, British 'whites' are more likely to live in owner-occupied housing (66 per cent of the latter own their own homes compared to 42.3 per cent of the former) (Owen, 1994: 6). African-Caribbean, Pakistani and Bangladeshi households are more likely to be over-crowded and to share a bathroom, and less likely to own cars. The evidence on educational performance displays considerable racialized disparities, with African-Caribbeans, Pakistanis and Bangladeshis generally less likely to receive qualifications.

But not all British African-Caribbeans and Asians experience this pattern of disadvantage: there is clear evidence of class, occupational and educational differences among these populations. Surveys in the 1990s have found that British African Asians and Indians, as well as Africans, reveal greater levels of educational and economic success than do African Caribbeans, Pakistanis and Bangladeshis (Jones, 1993). Those who are financially better off include business owners and managers, the self-employed, professionals (such as academics, doctors and social workers), local and central government workers, civil servants and politicians. There is also a small but highly visible number of wealthy individuals such as sports personalities, television celebrities and musicians. In part, this reveals the higher class origins of these immigrants in the countries from which they migrated. This being said, the absolute number of those experiencing these materially privileged circumstances is tiny, and when compared to the rest of the British population, the relative number is even smaller. For women the number is smaller still.

While the explanation for this pattern of inequality cannot be reduced to a single factor, racialized discrimination is certainly a determinant. Racialized discrimination is widespread, and continues to constrain the aspirations of African-Caribbean and Asian people, at all class positions, and both genders. This includes violence and physical attacks, verbal abuse and exclusion. A series of studies carried out since the mid-1960s shows that racialized discrimination in employment, housing and education persists at high levels (described in Brown and Gay, 1985). This is despite three Race Relations Acts (passed in 1965, 1968 and 1976) which have made such discrimination illegal and provided institutions (for example the Commission for Racial Equality) and procedures to identify and prevent it, and have also sought to encourage a wider social commitment to multiculturalism and to equal opportunity policies, particularly in the area of employment. Both government and private employers publicly and officially support equal opportunities policies but, by postponement and prevarication, they ensure that they are not fully or effectively implemented (McCruddon *et al.*, 1991).

While racialized discrimination is widespread, the forms that it takes are far more diverse than in the past. Patterns of direct individual and institutional racialized hostility are accompanied by indirect and furtive forms. This means overall a continued move from direct, overt and conspicuous racialized discrimination in which it is relatively easy to identify motives predicated on racialized beliefs (for example, immigration legislation or violence accompanied by racist abuse) to indirect, covert and inconspicuous discrimination in which motives and intentions are less obvious. Those who harbour hatred and hostility employ code words and double meanings to camouflage the vehemence and virulence of their attitudes and actions: apparently neutral language such as 'our own kind' and 'British people', appeal to a racialized nationalism (according to which 'whiteness' is a precondition of being considered British), while a greater emphasis on networks, word of mouth, internal adverts, and 'acceptability' criteria for recruitment in employment can be highly effective in excluding racialized minorities. The pursuit of their distinctive cultural practices, including language, religion, dress, music (sometimes in resistance against racialized hostility) is labelled culturally myopic and anti-British.

While all racialized groups face some common restraints, different groups have been targeted for attack or victimization of various sorts. Asians are more likely to be targeted for violence by neo-fascist groups such as the National Front while young African-Caribbean men have a greater likelihood of experiencing police violence. Murders of African-Caribbeans have continued as have violence and abuse, with the latter too frequently finding themselves and their properties attacked (Hesse *et al.*, 1992). One of the most widely publicized recent deaths was that of Stephen Lawrence, savagely murdered at a bus stop. This particular case became well known because it led to a high profile campaign for justice by the African-Caribbean and Asian communities. There is also a high level of accusations of racialized intimidation by the police and a number of deaths of young African and African-Caribbean men in police custody, many of them in suspicious circumstances (*The Voice*, 1995).

In the face of these patterns of disadvantage and discrimination, African-Caribbean people continue to resist in various ways (Sivanandan, 1990). This resistance entails collective and individual strategies, as well as physical and ideological strategies, many of which are articulated around the organizations and institutions of the African-Caribbean communities and the cultural patterns prevalent within them. The various forms of resistance present today reflect, in part, traditions of resistance by African Caribbeans and Asians to European conquest and colonization, but also their relationship to British political structures and traditions of resistance.

Various goals and strategies are articulated at both local and national levels. In education, health and welfare, the criminal justice system and housing, various groups fight poor facilities, inadequate finances and homelessness, and establish alternative community-based services (Sivanandan, 1990; Solomos and Back, 1995). Some groups seek integration and incorporation in the present system while focusing on overcoming discrimination and injustice; others seek a fundamental change in the organization of society, expressing socialist or communist aspirations; still others see the way forward in developing distinctive racialized institutions and communities (Small, 1994; Brah, 1996). Strategies also vary: some seek broad alliances with 'white' people, as in the Anti-Racist Alliance; others call for the consolidation and expansion of 'black' organizations and the regeneration of self-reliance and self-dependence, as in the case of Southall Black Sisters or the National Black Caucus.

The contribution of women has differed from those of men, as have their modes of organization, because of their experience of gendered and racialized inequality and exclusion. They have been involved in industrial and workplace struggles, in immigration and legal defence campaigns and they have mobilized to combat male violence within their own communities (Brah, 1996). While ethnic minority men have faced racialized and class hostility, ethnic minority women have also faced sexism from most men and racism (much of it from 'white' women). Social analyses have also tended to ignore or understate their unique position. For example, by saying that the inequality between 'white' women and ethnic minority women is less than that between 'white' men and ethnic minority men, one gains the impression that ethnic minority women are doing well (Jones, 1993: 70). In fact, the average earnings of women are lower than that of men. In this way ethnic minority women occupy a position at a unique intersection of hostilities, and the strategies they have developed have varied accordingly.

Immigration, Nationality and Citizenship

British immigration legislation is thoroughly racialized: the passport held by British citizens corresponds to a significant extent to skin colour. Until the early 1960s, one passport was held by all citizens of the United Kingdom and Colonies, regardless of origin and skin colour, and its possession guaranteed, at least in principle, identical rights, privileges and obligations. Today there are three different passports: British Citizen, British Overseas Citizen and British Dependent Territories Citizen. Only those holding the first category of passport have the right to enter and work in Britain. These passport holders are overwhelmingly 'white'. Holders of the second and third type of passport – who are overwhelmingly of ethnic minority origin – have no rights to enter or work in Britain. Over a period of little more than ten years, successive British governments deprived millions of people of British citizenship. These measures have largely stopped the migration and settlement of South Asian and African-Caribbean people in Britain.

Between 1880 and the beginning of the Second World War, immigrants to Britain were mainly of European origin: with the exception of Irish migrants, these immigrants were legally aliens (Holmes, 1978, 1988). A large proportion of these immigrants originated from Ireland, which was a British colony until the 1920s, but there were significant minorities from central and eastern Europe, Italy and Germany. After the Second World War, and in the light of the urgent demand for labour to rebuild and restructure the British economy, attention focused initially on these 'traditional' sources of labour. While Ireland once again supplied such labour, the countries of north-west Europe were unable to do so, and attention turned to a variety of refugee and displaced populations. These included, for example, members of the Polish Army that had fled to Britain during the war, and male and female refugees from various central and eastern European countries who were living in British-maintained refugee camps in Germany and Austria. The latter constituted the source for the European Volunteer Worker Scheme which was set up by the post-war Labour government (Kay and Miles, 1992).

But while considerable energy was invested in a variety of labour recruitment schemes orientated towards aliens from Europe, a small number of (mainly male) migrants from the Caribbean arrived in Britain largely as the result of their own initiative. These included men who had worked in Britain or had served in the British armed forces during the Second World War. In common with the population of all British colonies and of those ex-colonies that gained political independence but became members of the British Commonwealth, citizens of the British islands in the Caribbean were legally British subjects. As such, they had the right to enter, live and work in Britain. Yet, despite the existing labour shortage, there was considerable panic within the British state concerning their arrival and a secret Cabinet committee was set up in 1950 to investigate the possibility of controlling the entry of 'coloured people' into Britain. The underlying concern was that such immigration would create a 'race relations' problem in Britain. While no legislation was passed at this point in time, a variety of administrative and bureaucratic devices were used to limit the migration not only from the Caribbean but also from India and Pakistan (Miles and Phizacklea, 1984).

Migration from the Caribbean and the Indian sub-continent continued throughout the 1950s, encouraged by British employers, including the National Health Service and London Transport. The evidence shows that this migration was shaped by the level of labour demand in the British economy (Peach, 1968), and facilitated not only by the legal status of the migrants as British subjects but also by the relatively poor economic circumstances in the countries of origin. The resulting settlement in the major urban conurbations of England, and to a much lesser extent Wales and Scotland, provoked an increasingly active and hostile political response as the decade proceeded, stimulated by racism and by conflicts over access to housing and welfare benefits. A small number of politicians, as well as right-wing groups of various kinds, played an active role in this process, alongside, in some instances, members of the trade union movement.

By the early 1960s, 'immigration' had become defined as a national problem requiring political action: the claim was that 'immigration' had created a 'race relations' problem in Britain which could be solved only by the introduction of controls (Miles and Phizacklea, 1984). In practice, what was being demanded was a discriminatory system of control. The discourse of 'race relations' entailed a coded reference to 'coloured immigrants', with the result that the demand was not for immigration control in general (and anyway there was already a system of control in place to regulate the entry of aliens into Britain) but rather for control over the entry of British citizens from the Caribbean and the Indian sub-continent. Thus, when legislation was passed in 1962, it specifically excluded from its terms of reference citizens of the Irish Republic who had retained the right of entry into Britain since 1945. Further legislation, accompanied by administrative action, followed during the 1960s, the most important being the Commonwealth Immigrants Act 1968. Its objective was simultaneously to remove the right of entry into Britain of UK passport holders who did not also have a parent or grandparent born in Britain while ensuring that citizens of independent Commonwealth states such as Canada, Australia and New Zealand who did have a parent or grandparent born in Britain retained the right of entry.

The legislation of the 1960s was consolidated and further 'rationalized' by the 1971 Immigration Act. It also anticipated the consequences of Britain's entry into what has since become the European Union. British entry meant that citizens of other member states had the right to live and work in Britain, and this entailed removing the restrictions that applied to citizens of the relevant European nation states (other than the Republic of Ireland) who, in terms of British law, were aliens. Put another way, while the 1971 Act reinforced the controls over 'coloured' British citizens, it also removed controls over the entry of citizens of France, Germany, the Netherlands and so on. The racialized preference for European and 'white' immigration was therefore reinforced. Yet, while legislation by the late 1960s had effectively ended the entry of 'coloured people' seeking work, the spouses and children of earlier migrants from the Caribbean and the Indian sub-continent had not been formally banned from joining family members now effectively settled in Britain. This continuing migration flow became the object of political agitation during the 1970s and 80s which was expressed in very similar terms to those that dominated the agitation during the 1960s (for example the idea that 'immigration control is necessary to maintain good race relations'). As a result, the 'immigration problem' remained high on the political agenda, and further restrictions were imposed on this particular group of migrants with the intention of limiting the categories of people eligible to enter Britain, and discouraging by a variety of bureaucratic mechanisms the arrival of those who retained the right.

During the 1980s the old theme was given a new dimension as a result of the increasing flow of refugees into Europe caused by a variety of political and economic crises in Africa and the Indian sub-continent (Joly and Cohen, 1989). Individuals seeking asylum have a particular status in international law, mirroring a parallel status in humanitarian considerations. But the latter was not recognized in the reaction of the British state. Rather, those entering Britain seeking refugee status were identified as yet another group of 'coloured immigrants' who, in this instance, were pretending to be refugees but who were 'really' 'economic migrants'. They were therefore identified as being guilty of subterfuge, their presence denoting illegality: the language of 'bogus refugee' came to be widely used. A variety of legal and administrative changes (including the withdrawal of all forms of social security in certain circumstances) in the early 1990s were intended actively to discourage those seeking asylum from entering Britain.

During the 1980s, the British state's continued identification of 'strict immigration control' as a major political priority meshed with a wider debate about immigration and immigration control within the European Union. In accordance with the principles embodied in the Treaty of Rome (1957), some member states of the European Union sought to remove the existing restrictions on the movement of people across the internal borders of the EU in order to ensure that people moved as freely as capital and commodities. This proved difficult to achieve within the political structures of the EU, with the result that the states committed to this objective initiated negotiations between themselves following an initial meeting at the small town of Schengen. The so-called Schengen group eventually negotiated the Schengen Treaty in 1990, to which a majority of EU member states are now signatories, although effective implementation of the commitments remains uneven (Miles and Thranhardt, 1995).

The central objectives of the Treaty are to remove all controls on the movement of people across the internal borders of the signatory states, to increase the controls on movement across their external borders, and to increase surveillance to identify illegal migrants within the territories of the signatory states. This initiative has been widely described as the creation of a 'Fortress Europe' (Sivanandan, 1990), a description that is not entirely appropriate (Miles, 1993: 194–216). British governments have been consistent in their opposition to the Schengen group and its objectives, claiming that it is essential to sustain 'strict immigration controls', even on its borders with other EU member states. Thus, the intensely racialized debate in Britain about the need for 'strict immigration control' has been reinforced by the need to take a position with respect to this particular dimension of the evolution of European integration, ensuring that the issue of immigration remains high on the political agenda.

Conclusion

It has been argued in this chapter that the usual starting point for an analysis of 'race relations' is seriously flawed, because it starts with a set of 'common-sense' ideas and beliefs about 'race'and 'immigration' which cannot withstand close scrutiny. Hence, it has been suggested that the language, concepts and theories used in debates of 'race relations' should be questioned rigorously and that there is no place in sociological analysis for the use of the idea of 'race' as an analytical concept. Such an approach will lead to a more complex analysis of the structures, processes and ideologies in play in what are popularly called 'race relations' situations and, in particular, to an understanding of the relationships between those variables which appear to be explicitly 'racialized' (for example racist beliefs, prejudice, cultural differences) and others which appear to have no explicit racialized content (for example, economics, politics and power relations). This mode of analysis will help us understand the motivations and benefits of the key institutions involved in shaping patterns of racialized social relationships, as well as private employers, and the media.

In a world of increasing interdependence and competition – and a dizzying array of factors that shape racialized and ethnic relations – international factors can only become more important. While 'race relations' are experienced, interpreted and often described at the local level, the latter is increasingly being shaped by national and especially international factors. However, while it is indispensable to have an understanding of the historical unfolding of these processes, it has been argued here that the legacy of the earlier conceptual framework of 'race relations'should be transcended. Rather than seeking to understand 'race relations' it is better to conceptualize social relations which have been racialized, and to understand the factors that shape such processes locally, nationally and globally.

Further Reading

Anthias, F. and Yuval-Davis, N. *Racialized Boundaries,* London, Routledge, 1992. A good example of the use of the racialization framework to analyse the interrelationship between different modes of exclusion.

Brah, A. *Cartographies of Diaspora, Contesting Identities,* London and New York, Routledge, 1996. An excellent example of a recent attempt to draw upon postmodern themes and preoccupations to analyse racism and ethnic relations in Britain.

Miles, R. *Racism After 'Race Relations',* London, Routledge, 1993. A series of essays which explore the way in which the concept of racism can be used to analyse British and European history.

Small, S. *Racialised Barriers: The Black Experience in the United States and England,* New York and London, Routledge, 1994. A comparative analysis of experiences of racism.

8

Families, Households and Domestic Life

Stevi Jackson

While families seem to be a taken-for-granted part of everyday life for most people, the change and diversity of patterns of domestic life in contemporary societies has resulted in the concept of 'the family' being called into question by some sociologists. This chapter aims to examine contemporary debates about the 'family' and domestic life. While the sociology of class examines inequalities between families, sociological studies of families and households are also interested in inequalities within them. Like the sociology of gender relations, contemporary studies of family are strongly influenced by feminist theories; the influence of families also plays an important part in other areas of sociological research, such as education, work, deviance and health. This chapter should help you understand:

- The changing, and increasingly critical, orientation of the sociology of the family and domestic life

- Challenges to the concept of the family

- Inequalities within families generated by the economics of domestic life

- Sociological interpretations of marriage, parenthood and childhood

---

CONCEPTS

nuclear family ■ symmetrical family ■ household ■ marriage
domestic labour ■ domestic violence ■ childhood

Introduction

From the standpoint of everyday life families are taken for granted as part of the social landscape. After all, most of us have direct experience of family relationships and have spent at least part of our lives living with those we count as 'family'. Yet 'the family' is also the focus of a great deal of public concern and political debate, frequently represented as a cherished but endangered institution, threatened by changes in the moral climate, high rates of divorce and single parenthood. Here, as elsewhere, sociology fosters a degree of scepticism about commonsense views of the world and offers fresh insights into public issues. Sometimes the questions sociologists raise are disquieting, for they invite us to look critically at valued personal relationships; to consider, for example, sources of power and inequality within families. We might ask whether the popular image of the 'normal family' corresponds with empirical reality: indeed the concept of 'the family' itself is now being called into question, and there is an increasing tendency to talk of households or families rather than 'the family' in the singular.

Some of the difficulties presented by the concept of 'the family' are obvious once we reflect on the multiple meanings which the term has in our everyday language. When someone says that they like 'all the family' to sit down together for the main meal of the day, they usually mean those family members who live together. When we say that 'the whole family' attended a wedding or funeral, usually this implies a wider group of relatives – uncles, aunts, cousins and so on. When we say that a treasured possession has been 'in the family' for generations we are speaking of the family through time, tracing relationships back to our forebears. When a couple talk of 'starting a family' they usually mean having children, implying that a couple on their own are not a family, but with children they become one. We also recognize different types of families such as lone parent or lesbian and gay families – but the two parent, heterosexual family remains the dominant, normative ideal.

While the meaning of 'family' varies, this does not usually cause us problems in our daily lives; we usually understand what is meant from the context in which the word is used. Sociologists, however, have developed a more precise vocabulary to define different senses of the lay concept of 'family' or to describe different family forms. The term *kin* is used to mean relatives and *kinship* is usually thought of in terms of networks of people related to each other. Those who can trace their descent back to a common ancestor collectively form a *lineage*. A heterosexual couple with children is a *nuclear* or *conjugal* family while an *extended family* includes additional kin. Those who live together and in some way recognize their home as a shared space entailing some degree of collective responsibility and housekeeping are a *household*. Family members who live together constitute a household as well as a family, but not all households are based on families.

The existence of this sociological lexicon does not entirely dispel the ambiguity surrounding the concept of 'the family' itself; it remains a protean term covering a complex array of relationships and practices. This ambiguity goes some way towards explaining why many sociologists are wary of the concept of 'the family'. However, recent challenges to the concept are more fundamental, a result of radical shifts in sociological perspectives on family life over the last three decades of the twentieth century. During this period there have been changes in the way family life is lived, and also in the way sociologists conceptualize it. There is no longer a clearly defined field of study describable as 'the sociology of the family', despite continued socio-logical interest in family relationships and domestic life. In what follows, I shall consider how the old sociological certainties about the family came to be undermined before evaluating the current debate about 'the family'. Data about changing patterns of family life will be introduced along the way. I shall then examine aspects of current research and thinking on families and households in more detail, concentrating on economic relationships, marriage, parenthood and childhood.

Whatever Happened to the Sociology of the Family?

During the 1950s and 60s, sociologists assumed that the family was a key social institution, a fundamental element of social structure. It was taken, for example, as the basic unit of stratification in studies of class and social mobility, as a central agency of socialization, and as a mechanism by which individuals were integrated into wider ties of community and society. Until the early 1970s, at least in the USA, the dominant perspective on the family was functionalism, associated in particular with the work of Parsons. While some of these theorists argued that the family performed similar functions in all societies and throughout history, Parsons was more interested in demon-strating that the nuclear family was functional for advanced industrial society (Parsons and Bales, 1956).

According to Parsons, the modern family has shed some functions – such as productive work – and become more specialized, concentrating on the socialization of children and the 'stabilization of adult personalities'. The nuclear family had also become relatively isolated from wider kinship ties, thus adapting to the instrumental (pragmatic and goal-orientated) ethos of industrial society, with its emphasis on individual achievement. These values conflict with the 'affective' (emotional) bonds, and more collective orienta-tion which govern relations among kin. The potential strain between these two sets of values is minimized by loosening wider kin ties and by a special-ization of functions within families: husbands, who work in the outside world, take on instrumental roles while wives, who stay at home, specialize in affective roles.

This picture of emotional housebound women and rational male bread-winners now looks hopelessly sexist and outmoded, but Parsons' analysis may be more understandable in its historical context. In the period following the Second World War there had been a reassertion of women's supposedly 'traditional' domestic role. Most women gave up paid work to rear children and, since this was a time of full employment, most married men expected to earn enough to support their families. Even then, however, not all families conformed to the model. What Parsons was describing was the white middle-class suburban family. Other forms of family tended to be ignored or dismissed as deviant 'problem families'. Yet there were already changes taking place. In particular, in many western countries the proportion of married women in the labour market was increasing, despite the ideal of domesticated femininity. For example, British women's labour force participation rates rose from 21.74 per cent in 1951 to 38.8 per cent in 1966. A few sociologists began to pay attention to women's dual commitments to home and employment (see Myrdal and Klein, 1956), but such issues remained peripheral to the sociology of the family.

British sociologists were often sceptical of the functionalist orthodoxy and inclined towards empirical studies, often locating families within wider communities (see Morgan, 1996). Yet even here the issues studied sometimes related to the Parsonian agenda, such as research on the relative isolation of the nuclear family and the degree to which wider kin networks were maintained (Young and Wilmott, 1962; Bott, 1971). Although there was some discussion about the extent to which patterns of family life were class related, it was widely assumed that there was a trend towards looser kin ties and a more privatized style of family life accompanied by more egalitarian, companionate marital relationships. This, according to Young and Wilmott (1973), heralded the arrival of the symmetrical family. While inequalities between husbands and wives were recognized in some studies, it was assumed that they were disappearing.

The idea of egalitarian marriage also featured in one of the major American challenges to functionalism in this period. Berger and Kellner (1964) argued, from a phenomenological perspective, that rather than marital roles being pre-defined, marriage was an arena in which individuals could construct their own social reality. They suggested that husbands and wives experience their marriage as their joint creation in which they inhabit 'a fully shared world of meaning' (1964, 1971: 18). Where Parsons had at least recognized that women's experience of family life differed from that of men, Berger and Kellner theorized any such differences out of existence. What they shared with functionalism, and with British empirical sociologists, was an assumption that marriage and the family 'worked'. The picture of family life painted by most sociologists prior to 1970 was a rosy one.

Challenges for the Sociology of the Family

By the 1960s, however, there were already dissident voices. In the USA the feminist writer Friedan (1965) identified 'the problem with no name': the discontent of suburban housewives, the boredom and emptiness of their lives. Komarovsky's (1962) study of blue-collar couples revealed divergences between husbands' and wives' expectations and experiences, with many wives unhappy with the lack of emotional intimacy and companionship in their marriages. In Britain, Gavron (1966) considered the plight of 'the captive wife', trapped into social isolation by her domestic and maternal responsibilities. Studies such as these presaged the sustained feminist critique of the family which was to emerge in the 1970s. By the time Bernard published *The Future of Marriage* in 1972, there was sufficient evidence for her to argue that in any marital union there were two marriages – 'his' and 'hers' and that his was considerably better than hers.

Feminist research and theory was to have a major impact on the way in which sociologists thought about family life, but others were also contributing to the critique. Far from being a cosy domestic haven, the privatized nuclear family was seen as stultifying and damaging. In his 1967 Reith Lecture, Leach announced that 'the family with its petty privacy and tawdry secrets is the source of all our discontents'. Anti-psychiatrists such as Laing (1971) saw the close confines of the family life as giving rise to highly charged, disturbed and disturbing interpersonal relationships. Marxists saw the retreat to the family as symptomatic of the alienation characteristic of capitalist society, and argued that the family could not possibly satisfy all our emotional and social needs (Zaretsky, 1976).

Most of these critics still took it for granted that the typical modern family was the isolated nuclear family. It was widely believed that extended families had been the normal living arrangement prior to industrialization, an assumption which underpinned the idea of a functional fit between industrial society (or, for Marxists, capitalism) and the nuclear family. In the 1970s and 80s new historical research began to cast doubt on this assumption, revealing that households based on extended families had not been common in pre-industrial western Europe. This does not mean, however, that nothing changed as a result of the rise of industrial capitalism. It has become clear that the history of family life is much more complex than was once thought (see Anderson, 1980).

The meaning of the 'family' has itself changed – for much of our pre-industrial history it was used to refer to all those living under one roof under the authority of the head of household, whether or not they were related. Most productive work, prior to the rise of industrial capitalism, was centred on such 'families' engaged in farming or craft production. Men, women and children all contributed to household production. Families often contained unrelated employees (known as 'servants'), usually young people. These servants worked, lived and ate alongside other family members. Households varied greatly in size – more prosperous families with many servants could be very large, while the poorest were small. Demographic factors, such as the prevalence of remarriage after all too common widowhood, also produced diversity in family forms. Moreover, historians became aware of the ways in which household composition varied as a result of local economic conditions and changed over the life course. Surveying these data, Anderson (1980) concluded that there has never been a single family form in western society.

Historians also began to think of family members as participants in economic and social processes, engaged in the active pursuit of strategies which enabled them to survive in changing times. Hence it became possible to think of family organization having an effect on social change rather than simply being affected by it. Feminists, and those influenced by them, suggested that pre-existing patriarchal relations helped shape the form of industrial capitalism – as did the tactics men used to retain their privileges under changed conditions (Hartmann, 1976; Walby, 1986). Older forms of patriarchal control based on control of family production and labour were eroded, but were ultimately replaced by new forms based on the ideal of the male breadwinner and dependent, domesticated wife.

Industrialization created a split between family life and commercial enterprise. Among the bourgeoisie in the early nineteenth century women withdrew from active participation in the family business and a new 'domestic ideology' defined the home as women's 'natural' sphere (Hall, 1992). A version of this ideology was subsequently adopted by sections of the working class who fought to establish the principle of the male breadwinner earning a family wage (Walby, 1986; Jackson, 1992). However, women were never entirely excluded from paid work and the direction and pace of change was uneven, with class and regional variations in the organization of domestic life. Nonetheless there were patterns beneath these variations, in particular persistent inequalities between men and women.

Such inequalities also emerged in research on contemporary families as sociologists began to pay more attention to what went on within families. As new critical perspectives emerged, sociologists found themselves investigating an institution which was itself changing. The increasing participation of married women in the labour market, along with much higher rates of unemployment than were prevalent in the 1950s and 60s, has eroded the norm of families dependent on a sole, male breadwinner. Over 70 per cent of all women of working age were economically active in 1996, including about half of those with pre-school children. The isolated housewife is now much rarer than the woman struggling to cope with the double shift of paid and domestic work. Moreover, perhaps because of these changing employment patterns, people are now marrying and having children later than they did two or three decades ago.

From the early 1950s until the early 1970s there was a trend towards early marriage and parenthood; since then, this trend has been reversed. In 1971, 87 per cent of British women were married before they were 30 and the median age of marriage for women was 21.4; 78.5 per cent of babies born in that year had mothers under 30 (figures from Coleman, 1988; Kiernan and Wicks, 1990; Central Statistical Office, 1993). By 1994 the average age at first marriage was 28 for men and 25.8 for women. More women now delay childbearing until they are in their thirties and more are apparently choosing not to have children. Cohabitation prior to or instead of formal marriage has become common: between 1981 and 1995 the proportion of women under 50 cohabiting doubled to 9 per cent of all women and 25 per cent of non-married women. Divorce rates rose swiftly in the 1970s, and subsequently more slowly, stabilizing at rates much higher than those of the 1950s and 60s Whereas there were only 2 divorces per 1,000 of the married population in 1961, there were over 13 in 1995. On current trends as many as two in five marriages are likely to end in divorce. High rates of divorce have swelled the ranks of one parent families – and also step-families, since most of those who divorce subsequently remarry or cohabit. Moreover, more children are now born to unmarried parents, over one-third in 1995. As a result of these trends, 20 per cent of children live with a lone parent and a further 7.9 per cent live in step families (figures from Office for National Statistics, 1997). While these figures are British, the trends they record are not specific to any one country, but are observable in most other contemporary societies.

One effect of all these changes has been to increase the variability of family forms. Britain has also become ethnically more heterogeneous and patterns of family life differ from one ethnic group to another. The diversity of family life has become a central issue in sociological analysis, and a major basis for problematizing the concept of 'the family'. In the next section I will explain why 'the family' has been called into question and consider whether these doubts are sufficient to justify the abandonment of the idea of the family as a social institution.

The Trouble with 'the Family'

Since the 1980s, many sociologists have suggested that the 'the family' is a term which represents an abstract idea, an ideological construct, rather than the way people actually live (Barrett and McIntosh, 1982; Bernardes, 1997). Some wish to retain the concept of the family (see, for example Delphy and Leonard, 1992), but even those who still define the family as an institution nonetheless conceptualize it very differently from earlier generations of sociologists. Three main objections to 'the family' have been raised:

- the term is essentialist, as it presupposes an essential basic unit discernible in all cultures at all times
- it treats as a unity something which is in fact internally differentiated, thus concealing inequalities within it
- it masks the diversity of family forms existing in society today.

I will deal with each of these in turn, but it is the third of these – diversity – which is most often taken to signal the demise of the family as a useful conceptual tool.

The Charge of Essentialism

If used incautiously, especially in cross-cultural and historical analysis, the term 'the family' can imply a universal phenomenon. Asking whether the family is universal or, how it has changed since pre-industrial times, effectively decides the issue in advance: that even if it varies in form there is still some essential entity identifiable as the family which exists across time and in all societies. The commonly used terms 'nuclear' and 'extended' family also suggest a basic nucleus which is, under some circumstances, extended to a wider orbit of kin. This essentialist view has often entailed treating 'the family' as a clearly bounded unit set apart from wider society, something which is affected by differing or changing social structures but which has no effects beyond its own boundaries. This is why sociologists in the past talked of the effects of industrialization on 'the family' without considering that family relations might affect wider social relations.

As we have seen, the term 'family' has not had the same meaning throughout history; household and family relations have not always intersected in the ways they do today. Cross-culturally, there is even greater variability. Anthropological evidence suggests that here is no simple, single entity that can be defined as 'the family' and compared across cultures. What we are dealing with is not a fixed structure but a complex set of relationships and practices – who counts as kin, who lives with whom, who can or should marry whom, who should perform which activities inside the domestic unit – all of which vary cross-culturally (see, for example Edholm, 1982; Harris, 1990). This suggests that the concept of 'the family' as we understand it is historically and culturally specific and should be used, if at all, only in the context of contemporary society.

Differences within Families

If families are constituted through a complex of relationships and practices, it follows that individuals are differently located within families and not all members of the same family experience it in the same way. In particular, families are differentiated by gender and generation. The term 'the family' can often mask these differences. We should not, for example, speak of the effects of poverty on 'the family', without considering that these effects might not be felt equally by all family members family. Nor should we assume that 'the family' or even 'a family' acts collectively. Even when family members do something together, they may not be engaged in exactly the same activities in precisely the same ways. To take one example, Morley's (1986) study of families watching television revealed distinct gender differences in viewing practices. Men generally controlled the remote control device and gave the television their full attention while women often combined viewing with domestic chores, such as ironing. This example suggests that work and leisure are unequally distributed within families and that families are also sites of power relations: Morley sees the remote control device as a symbol of power, rather like a medieval mace, which sits 'on the arm of Daddy's chair' (Morley, 1986: 148).

Differences within families, however, do not provide grounds for denying that the family is an institution. After all, most social institutions are internally differentiated. Moreover, we are not dealing here with accidental differences, but with regular, patterned gender and generational hierarchies, as will become clear later in the chapter. Family relationships appear to be structured, institutionalized relationships despite the diversity of domestic arrangements existing in society today.

The Problem of Diversity

It is certainly the case that the abstract idea of 'the family' does not correspond with the lived reality of family life. In one sense 'the family' is an ideological construct, and one with considerable emotional appeal – which is why it is often invoked by politicians to win us to their cause and by advertisers to encourage us to buy their products. Clearly the advertiser's image of comfortable, middle-class, two parent, two child families does not reflect reality. But this ideal does have real effects; it encourages to look to the family to meet our personal, social and emotional needs; it serves as a perpetual excuse for the paucity of public services; it encourages us to blame ourselves or our partners if our own family life does not live up to expectations. In a sense, then, this representation of 'the family' is 'anti-social' (Barrett and McIntosh, 1982).

Moreover, the popular image of the family is an ethnocentric one, based on 'white' families, which obscures ethnic differences in patterns of family life. Such differences have long been evident in countries such as the USA and are are now coming to be recognized as an important source of family diversity in Britain. Here South Asian households are more likely to contain more than one family with children than either Afro-Caribbean or white households. However, the proportion of nuclear family households among South Asians is also high – more than double that found among the white population. African-Caribbean women are more likely to head single parent households than white or South Asian women. In 1989–91, nearly half Afro-Caribbean mothers were lone mothers, compared with around 15 per cent of 'white' mothers and less than 10 per cent of those of South Asian descent (Central Statistical Office, 1993, 1994, 1995). Conceptualizing 'the family' from a 'white' perspective can easily lead to a failure to appreciate cultural differences and to branding 'black' families as deviant.

The main reason for the disjunction between the ideal of 'the family' and lived experience, or so it is argued, is that there is no normal or typical family but rather a diverse and shifting array of different forms of household (Barrett and McIntosh, 1982; Bernardes, 1997). The most telling evidence for this point of view is that only a minority of households today are inhabited by nuclear families of two parents and dependent children, and the proportion of such households is declining. In 1996 such households comprised only 23 per cent of all British households and accounted for 40 per cent of the total population (Office for National Statistics, 1997). These figures might suggest that the family is in terminal decline and is becoming a minority lifestyle. But is it?

Such a view can only be sustained if we view this statistical snap-shot as the full picture and if we define the family in very narrow terms. Families are not static entities, but dynamic ones, changing over the life course as people marry, rear children and see their children leave home – or as couples divorce or remarry or one of them dies. Even if there were no divorce or untimely death, each individual would live in a nuclear family only at certain stages of the life course. Most households are, in fact, based on family ties, on marriage or parenthood: in 1996, 70 per cent of all households, contained 85 per cent of the population (Office for National Statistics, 1997). Most of the remaining 30 per cent of households are accounted for by people living alone; over half of these individuals are over the age of retirement, and most of them will at one time have married and reared children. The 13 per cent of households inhabited by single people under retirement age are a much more mixed group. They will include those who have chosen a single life and those who are single by default, young people who will marry and have children in the future and older people who have married and parented at some stage in their lives. Only 2 per cent of households are lived in by two or more unrelated adults, and again their composition is very diverse. They might include, for example, lesbian or gay couples, those who choose a communal way of life and young people flat-sharing as a relatively transitory arrangement.

Looked at this way, we gain a rather different picture of family life: it is certainly shifting and dynamic, but most of the population live in households based on family relationships for much of their lives. Moreover, if we look only at households, we forget that family ties persist after family households have broken up. For example, my mother, my sister and I all live in separate households in different cities, but we still count each other as family. We should not conflate families with family-based households: significant family relationships, carrying with them all manner of social expectations and obligations, exist across the boundaries of households as well as within them (Finch and Mason, 1993). Nuclear family households may be a minority, but most of us have families.

Focusing only on households rather than families can be used to downplay the importance of family relationships. Delphy and Leonard argue that this strategy gives the misleading impression that 'households are only sometimes, contingently, or as a matter of choice, based on family relationships' (1992: 5). The idea of family diversity thus conceals the regularities of family life and can also divert attention from the structural inequalities, the hierarchies of gender and generation within families. Even if we are wary of the concept of 'the family' *per se*, it must be accepted that the most crucial elements of family life, the bonds of marriage and parenthood are *institutionalized* through social expectations and legal regulation.

These debates around the concept of the family have made sociologists much more aware of the complexity of family life, of the interplay between family, household and kinship networks. Sociologists have become much more sensitive to differentiation and inequality within families. Morgan uses the apt analogy of the kaleidoscope to capture this complexity:

> With one turn we see a blending of the distinctions between home and work, family and economy, and the idea of the household comes into focus. With another turn, the apparently solid boundaries of the household dissolve and we see family and kinship, and possibly other, relationships spreading out across these fainter boundaries. With each twist of the kaleidoscope we see that these patterns are differently coloured according to gender, age and generation and other social divisions. (Morgan, 1996: 33)

The effect of this can be dizzying, and also makes it difficult, if not impossible, to summarize the full range of sociological work on family life. In order to simplify matters I will concentrate here on the key relationships through which families are constituted: those between husbands and wives and between parents and children. I will start, however, with the economics of domestic life – an area once largely ignored by sociologists but which is now recognized as vitally important.

The Economics of Domestic Life

Family ties entail economic co-operation, support and dependency, but also inequality and exploitation. Economic obligations often extend beyond family-based households and include wider kin, but here, and for the remainder of the chapter, I shall concentrate on family-based households, those founded on heterosexual couples and/or parent–child relationships. In exploring these economic relations I begin by looking at the income coming into families and how it is allocated.

Most married women now have paid work, although there are ethnic differences here: in Britain 71.9 per cent of 'white' women were defined as economically active in 1993, compared with 66 per cent of women of African and African Caribbean descent, 61.4 per cent of those of Indian descent and 24.8 per cent of those of Pakistani or Bangladeshi descent (Central Statistical Office, 1995). For most women, total dependence on a male worker is now unusual and women's earnings make a vital contribution to household finances. However, women's jobs are generally lower paid than men's, and many women, especially those with young children, are employed part time. Because men usually earn 'full' wages while women often earn only a 'component wage', one insufficient to run a household, most married women are at least partly financially dependent on their husbands (Siltanen, 1994). A number of studies have found that even where women make a substantial contribution to household income, the importance of their earnings may be played down so that the man is still defined as *the* breadwinner. Women's wages, however essential, are often seen as covering 'extras' (Mansfield and Collard, 1988; Pahl, 1989; Brannen and Moss, 1991).

Recent research has challenged the assumption that families are units in which all resources are distributed equally (Brannen and Wilson, 1987; Jackson and Moores, 1995). There is growing evidence that 'while sharing a common address, family members do not necessarily share a common standard of living' (Graham, 1987a: 221). Since husbands generally earn more than their wives, they tend to have more power over the disposal of family income – although the degree to which men exercise direct control over domestic expenditure varies depending on the strategy couples adopt for apportioning money. Whether women control the bulk of domestic finances, have housekeeping allowances, draw from a common pool, or cover certain costs from their own wages, they usually spend little on themselves. Men, by the same token, almost always have greater access to personal spending money. The 'extras' women spend their earnings on are usually for their children or the family as a whole rather than for themselves. Hence women often contribute a higher proportion of their wages to housekeeping than do men (Pahl, 1989).

During the 1980s researchers in the UK uncovered considerable evidence of hidden poverty in families dependent on men. One telling indicator of this is that some studies found that a substantial proportion, sometimes as many as half, of previously married single mothers felt that they were as well off or better off financially than they were when with their partners (Graham, 1987a). This is surprising given that, during this period, two out of three lone mothers lived on state benefits and that households headed by lone mothers were three times more likely to be poor than two parent households. It was not only men's spending on personal consumption that accounted for this, but also the greater degree of control lone mothers had over the total family budget. They could plan their expenditure, decide their priorities and make economies in the interests of their children and themselves without having to take a man's desires and demands into account. In part this represented a freedom to go without, since women were often prepared to make personal sacrifices in order to provide more for their children, but lone mothers sometimes found that exercising their own preferences led to a more economical lifestyle (Graham, 1987).

The domestic distribution of money is unlikely to have changed substantially in the 1990s and serves to demonstrate a more general point, backed by a range of research, that consumption within families rarely takes place on the basis of fair shares for all (see Jackson and Moores, 1995). The same can also be said of patterns of work and leisure. Families are often seen as sites of leisure but, for women, home is also a place of work.

Work within Families

Men's participation in routine housework has increased slightly since the early 1980s but, as we saw in Chapter 6 on gender relations, women still carry most of the burden of domestic labour, whether or not they are in waged work. Men may help more around the house, but the domestic division of labour in both Britain and the USA remains largely unaltered (Mansfield and Collard, 1988; Hochschild, 1989; Brannen and Moss, 1991). Women have less free time than men and are more likely to spend it at home so that they are constantly 'on call' even when not actually working, resulting in fragmented, interrupted periods of leisure (Chambers, 1986; Sullivan, 1997). Men have greater freedom to enjoy leisure since they do not have to consider who is taking care of the children or whether there are clean clothes ready for the next day. Someone else is doing the work and taking the responsibility.

It is only since the 1970s, as a result of feminist critique, that sociologists began to take housework seriously and to investigate women's experience of it. British studies carried out in the 1970s and 80s revealed that women's feelings about housework were profoundly ambivalent. Women commonly expressed dissatisfaction with this work, finding it monotonous, repetitive, isolating, tiring and never-ending. They were often well aware that they carried an unfair burden, especially when they also had paid jobs. However, in stating these grievances, women usually stopped short of an overall critique of their situation; they rarely dismissed housework as a whole as unrewarding, and were even less likely to challenge the sexual division of labour which made housework their responsibility (Oakley, 1984; Westwood, 1984). The work itself may be the focus of declared dissatisfactions, but women value the ideals of caring for others and creating a home. In her study of women factory workers, Westwood heard all the usual complaints about housework. Yet the women also saw it as 'their *proper* work' which was invested with meaning and status because it was 'work done for love' which demonstrated their commitment to their families. Thus boring, routine work was 'transformed into satisfying, caring work' (Westwood, 1984: 170).

It has been suggested that only 'white' middle-class women dislike housework. The research I have cited shows that there is little class difference in women's feelings about the work itself and, in the case of Westwood's research, little difference between 'white' and Asian women. Thorogood (1987) found a high degree of dissatisfaction with domestic chores among Afro-Caribbean women, and those of them living independently of men felt a major advantage of this arrangement was that it reduced the amount of housework they had to do. More recently, Brah found that many young Pakistani women in Birmingham (both married and single) felt over-burdened with domestic work. As wives or daughters they were often caring for large households which, because of poverty, lacked the domestic appliances more privileged women take for granted (Brah, 1994). While 'black' women may find family life a welcome refuge from a racist society (Collins, 1990), this does not mean that they escape from an inequitable division of domestic labour or that they like housework itself any more than 'white' women.

Housework has also been the object of much theoretical interest, especially in the 1970s. Marxists and Marxist feminists were primarily interested in the contribution housework made to capitalism through the reproduction of labour power – servicing the existing labour force and rearing the next generation of workers. A major limitation of this approach was that it concentrated on the contribution of domestic labour to capitalism and did not consider the extent to which men benefit from it. Other theorists, notably Delphy and Leonard (1992) and Walby (1986) have argued that housework takes place within patriarchal relations in which men exploit women's labour. Marxist feminists objected to the idea that men benefited sufficiently from women's work to justify the term exploitation (see, for example Barrett, 1980). More recently, however, some neo-Marxists have argued that household labour does involve exploitative relations (see Gibson-Graham, 1996). The empirical evidence suggests that men gain a great deal from women's household labour. Men do not simply evade their share of housework, they have their share done for them.

Most recent work on the distribution of domestic labour is less concerned with grand theory and more focused on specific situations and the effects of changes and variations in working practices. There is less emphasis on women's experience of housework *per se* and more on the continued inequities imposed by the 'double shift' (Hochschild, 1989; Brannen and Moss, 1991). Among the well-paid professional classes, women's increased labour market participation has led to the re-emergence of paid domestic labour, the employment of nannies and cleaners (Gregson and Lowe, 1994). Some attention has also been paid to those who are in some way resisting male-dominated patterns of domestic organisation. In a study of heterosexuals committed to anti-sexist living arrangements, Van Every (1995) found that the traditional division of labour was avoided in a number of ways: individuals doing chores such as washing and ironing only for themselves; sharing cooking and cleaning; buying in domestic help or services. The strategies used, however, were constrained by income, by the differential earning capacities of men and women, and also by the expectations of others outside the household. There has also been a little research on lesbian and gay couples and families suggesting a more equitable division of labour than is typical in heterosexual partnerships (Dunne, 1997; Heaphy *et al.*, 1997).

Work within families is not always confined to domestic labour. Small businesses are now part of the social landscape and are often based on families. There is a particularly strong tradition of family-based enterprise among Asian communities in Britain. Of those in employment in 1994 over 20 per cent of Pakistani and Bangladeshi people and around 18 per cent of Indian people are self-employed, and most of these are men (Central Statistical Office, 1995). Here family obligations can mean wives and daughters working for little or no remuneration within family enterprises (Westwood and Bhachu, 1988; Afshar, 1989). This is not a situation peculiar to Asian women. In general, the wives of self-employed men, from plumbers to accountants, may provide free labour to their husbands' businesses – and three-quarters of the self-employed are men.

There are also grey areas where housework shades into work connected to a husband's business or employment such as entertaining his colleagues or clients and taking telephone messages. A woman may thus find herself married to her husband's job (Finch, 1983). Since patterns of paid work affect the performance of unpaid domestic work, another area of investigation is the practice of homeworking. Twenty-nine per cent of employed men and 24 per cent of employed women work from home at least some of the time (Office for National Statistics, 1997). For women homeworking is usually poorly paid and is a means of combining domestic responsibilities with earning a small wage (Phizacklea and Wolkowitz, 1995). Men who work at home are often in professional and managerial occupations and it seems unlikely that they are taking on extra housework as a result. Given Finch's (1983) observations on the ways in which men call on their wives' labour in carrying out their paid work, it is more probable that these male homeworkers are increasing their wives' workload. However, this has yet to be researched.

Children as Economic Actors

Research on the economics of family life has generally focused on husbands and wives, but it has recently been recognized that children and young people are also economic actors located within family divisions of labour. Children may perform domestic labour (Brannen, 1995), help out in family businesses (Song, 1966) or be earning their own pocket money outside the home (Morrow, 1994). However, the situation of most children is that of economic dependants within families. As such, they have things bought for them rather than buying them for themselves and exercise consumer choice only if their parents allow them to. Gifts of money and pocket money are given at adults' discretion and adults may seek to influence how it is spent. Adult-mediated consumption is one facet of parents' power over children (Leonard, 1990). Hence independent employment can be attractive to children themselves, although often seen as a problem by adult society. I shall return to the position of children in families later, but first I shall survey some of the research on the more personal aspects of married life.

Marriage as a Personal Relationship

The changes in patterns of marriage discussed earlier in the chapter do not indicate a wholesale flight from matrimony. Cohabitation may now be common, but most of those who cohabit later marry and cohabitation, in any case, is not so very different from formal marriage. Despite increasing numbers opting to delay or eschew marriage, most young people still expect to marry. The majority of British marriages still involve a bride and groom who are both under the age of 30, and the traditional pattern of women marrying men older than themselves persists (Office for National Statistics, 1997).

The 'normality' of marriage is central to the maintenance of 'compulsory heterosexuality' (Rich, 1980), making lesbian and gay relationships appear to be a deviant and unnatural choice. Some gay rights organizations are campaigning for the right to marry, although others see this demand as a capitulation to the heterosexual norm (see Rahman and Jackson, 1997). It may also be the case that, among the heterosexual population, expectations about marriage are changing. Giddens (1992) has suggested that we are witnessing a move away from marriage as life-long commitment to an idea of the 'pure relationship' – a more provisional, contingent form of intimacy in which relationships last only as long as they fulfil individual desires. While high divorce rates may be an indicator of this, there is no evidence that individuals *entering* marriage treat it as provisional: most expect and want it to last. Giddens may, however, be correct in noting a trend in aspirations, led by women, towards a more egalitarian ideal. Recent research suggests that young women now hope for greater equality and autonomy in their marriages (Sharpe, 1994).

Although the decision to marry is in part a pragmatic one, within the western cultural tradition being 'in love' is seen as an essential precondition for marriage. Marrying other than on the basis of free choice and romantic love, particularly the practice of arranged marriage within Asian communities, may be judged very negatively from the standpoint of the dominant white culture. Yet Asian parents usually select their children's spouses with considerable care, and young people have varying degrees of choice in the matter (Westwood, 1984; Afshar, 1989; Sharpe, 1994). The ideal is that love should develop within marriage. While the reality does not always match the ideal, this is equally true of marriage founded on romantic love.

Research on 'white' couples suggests that romantic love does not deliver what it promises. 'Togetherness' is central to the modern western ideal of marriage, but it is often one-sided; the disjunction between 'his' and 'her' marriage (Bernard, 1972) persists. Mansfield and Collard's study of newly weds, carried out in the 1980s, found that husbands and wives defined the ideal of 'togetherness' differently. The men wanted a home and a wife, a secure physical and emotional base, something and someone to come home to. The women desired 'a close exchange of intimacy which would make them feel valued as a person and not just as a wife'. They 'expected more of their husbands emotionally than these men were prepared, or felt able, to give' (Mansfield and Collard, 1988: 179, 192). These findings are not unique: similar patterns emerged from a number of British and North American studies in the 1980s, while more recent studies suggest that women put a great deal of emotional labour, as well as domestic labour, into maintaining marital relationships. Here, as well as in the economic aspects of marriage, they give more than they receive (Duncombe and Marsden, 1993; Langford, 1998).

These emotional imbalances, along with economic inequities, suggest that marriage is a power relationship. Traditional sociological approaches to marriage either ignored this issue or considered it only in terms of decision making and weighted wives' decisions over choice of food purchases as equal to husbands' decisions about relocating the family home (see, for example Blood and Woolfe, 1960). Research over the last three decades has suggested that power in marriage is complex and multi-dimensional and that it is rooted in the structural relations of male domination (Bell and Newby, 1976; Edgell, 1980; Komter, 1989). It is not, however, always subtle and can be brutal. Violence against wives is by no means a modern phenomenon, but it has only recently been recognized as a widespread social problem.

Even as late as the 1960s and 70s, many social scientists considered wife abuse to be the result of individual male inadequacy or provocation from nagging wives. The first in-depth British sociological study on marital violence (Dobash and Dobash, 1979) challenged this view, revealing a pattern that was to become very familiar in subsequent research: violence was used systematically by men to keep women under control; it occurred across the full range of the class spectrum; it often entailed serious injury and it was very difficult to escape from. Some recent research has suggested that men and women are equally likely to resort to violence in marital disputes (for example Berliner, 1990). Such studies, relying on quantitative methods, 'counting' violent incidents without considering their context, severity or effect, are seriously methodologically flawed (Nazroo, 1995). Women may hit men and throw things at men, may fight back in self-defence when attacked, but most evidence indicates that domestic violence is primarily male violence. It is estimated that between 80 and 90 per cent of domestic assaults are perpetrated by men on women (see Maynard and Winn, 1997).

One indicator of women's refusal to accept maltreatment, as well as emotional and economic deprivation, is that almost three-quarters of British divorces are initiated by women (Office for National Statistics, 1997). This may reflect women's greater need to formalise financial and child custody arrangements once a marriage has broken down (Delphy and Leonard, 1992), as well as their greater marital unhappiness. Divorce, however, only ends a particular marital relationship. It does not necessarily undermine the institution of marriage itself. Most of those who divorce subsequently remarry, or enter into heterosexual cohabitation – many only to separate or divorce again. Discontent with marriage seems to be experienced as disillusionment with a particular relationship, rather than with the institution.

Parenthood and Childhood

Earlier sociologists tended to follow lay assumptions in regarding parenthood as the logical outcome of marriage and treated both parenthood and childhood as relatively unproblematic. The gender differentiation of parenting was largely taken for granted and the status of children within families was rarely questioned. This has now changed, with far greater critical attention being given to the social construction of motherhood, fatherhood and childhood.

It is perhaps self-evident that parenthood is differentiated by gender. Consider the meanings of the phrases 'to mother a child' and 'to father a child', where mothering implies nurturing and fathering no more than the act of conception. Transforming fathering into fatherhood – a relationship with the child – requires an ongoing relationship with the child's mother. Hence sociologists have long held that fatherhood is a social institution whereas motherhood was, in the past, often taken for granted as the natural outcome of bearing a child. Both motherhood and fatherhood, however, are fully social and given form and meaning by the culturally and historically specific situations in which they are practised. Since women carry more of the burden of child care, it is not surprising that there has been more research on motherhood than on fatherhood. However, there has recently been some investigation into the social meanings and experiences of fatherhood.

While becoming a mother has traditionally been seen as the fulfilment of women's 'natural destiny', not all women are seen as fit mothers. Although there is now less stigma attached to unmarried motherhood, there is still a tendency to scapegoat lone mothers, especially if they are young (Phoenix, 1990; Laws, 1994; Millar, 1994). This is evident, for example, in the way in which teenage pregnancy continues to be defined as a major social problem, even though its incidence has declined steadily over the last two decades (Office of National Statistics, 1997). Young motherhood is thought of as an accident resulting from ignorance rather than a rational choice or, if seen as a choice, is deemed to be motivated by a desire to scrounge from the state or jump housing queues. The recent availability of forms of assisted conception have raised new questions about who should be allowed to bear a child. For example, in Britain in 1991 the use of artificial insemination by lesbians provoked a mini moral panic around 'virgin births', with subsequent calls for restrictions on the availability of other reproductive technologies.

Sociological investigations into motherhood have revealed a gap between the ideal of motherhood as something which comes naturally to women and the actuality of motherhood as it is experienced (see Richardson, 1993). First-time mothers often feel ill-prepared for the realities of looking after a child, do not automatically experience a surge of maternal feeling and often find that the positive aspects of motherhood are undercut by sleepless nights, the constant demands of a needy infant and social isolation. Even as children grow, women many continue to experience a loss of identity: they have ceased to be recognized as individuals and have become, instead, someone's mother. There are also contradictions within the idea of motherhood: it is supposed to be natural and yet there is a long tradition of advice from experts telling women how to be mothers. This advice changes over time, as views on children's needs change; motherhood is never defined in its own right, but always in response to children's perceived needs.

Fatherhood, like motherhood, has been redefined over time in relation to changing ideas on childhood. Until the early nineteenth century the emphasis was on children's duty to their parents rather than parental responsibilities to them. It was the father, as familial patriarch, who was held to be the parent to whom children 'naturally' belonged. Gradually, with the emergence of the modern idea of children as a category of people with specific psychological needs, mothers came to be regarded as more important to children's well-being and women gradually gained more rights in relation to their children and were increasingly awarded custody of them in the event of divorce. Women only gained full legal equality as parents in 1973 and their rights have always been conditional on being seen as a good mother. Those deemed unfit, and hence at risk of losing their children, were often those who flouted patriarchal convention: in the 1950s the adulterous wife, more recently, the lesbian (Smart, 1989a). Since the 1980s, however, there has been a move in the direction of reinstating paternal rights and responsibilities which has been reflected in legal decisions and policy changes.

The 1989 Children Act enshrined the idea of joint parenthood after divorce, on the assumption that children need social contact with their fathers. Here fatherhood is constructed as a caring relationship. The 1991 Child Support Act, however, was targeted at purportedly 'feckless' fathers who abdicated their financial responsibilities for their children. In obliging absent fathers to provide financial support for their children, it represented fatherhood as an economic obligation. The different assumptions underpinning these two pieces of legislation may reflect a wider uncertainty about the role of fathers in contemporary families and contradictory trends in patterns of fatherhood today. On the one hand, many absent fathers have little or no contact with their children; on the other some evidence suggests that fathers are becoming more involved in child care (see, for example, Smith, 1995). We should be wary, however, of accepting uncritically the idea of the 'new father'. It may now be routine for fathers to attend the birth of their child and to participate in caring for them, but the primary responsibility remains with mothers. When men are at work, they are often working long hours and may have little opportunity to care for their children (Lewis, 1995). When mothers return to full-time work after maternity leave it is they, rather than fathers, who take responsibility for alternative child care arrangements (Brannen and Moss, 1991). Moreover, those fathers who are keen to claim residence or contact with their children after divorce have not necessarily taken much part in caring for them before the divorce; sometimes they are building a new post-divorce relationship with their children on the basis of little prior involvement with their day-to-day care (Neale and Smart, 1997).

Not surprisingly, many feminists are sceptical about reinstating fathers' rights while women still bear most of the burden of caring for children. Other feminists, while sharing these concerns, are wary of asserting that mothers' rights over children should automatically take precedence over those of fathers. Delphy, for example, argues that this might reinforce the traditional view that child care is women's business and thus undermine demands for equality. Moreover, she suggests that mothers' rights can easily become rights *over* another category of people – children – with children becoming a commodity to be fought over (Delphy, 1994).

Children in Families

It is only recently that sociologists have given attention to children and child-hood other than from an adult-centred perspective. Within the traditional socialisation paradigm children were thought of as incomplete adults whose experiences were not worth investigating in their own right, but only insofar as they constituted learning for adulthood (Thorne, 1987). Thinking of childhood as a developmental stage and psychological state masks the fact that it is still a social status, that children are neither citizens nor legal subjects but are under the jurisdiction of their parents. It may be that parents today have less power and autonomy than in the past because child rearing is regulated by experts and state agencies. Nonetheless, parents retain a great deal of latitude to rear their children as they wish, to set acceptable standards of behaviour, to decide what their children should eat and wear and how they should be educated and disciplined. Others' interference in these matters is regarded as violation of family privacy and an assault on parents' rights; public regulation generally only intrudes where parents are deemed to have abused their power or not exercised it effectively enough – where children are 'at risk' or delinquent.

Modern families are often described as child centred. Certainly children's needs are given a high priority, but these are defined for them by adults. This is in part tied to the responsibility placed on parents to raise children 'properly'. This responsibility is far reaching and is heightened by increased public concern about risks to children. Often such concerns reflect risk anxiety as much as actual dangers – for example widely expressed fears of sexual assault and murder by strangers, despite the lack of evidence that risks to children come primarily from this quarter (see Scott *et al.*, 1998). Risk anxiety, however, does have material effects in that parental fears can lead to further limits on children's autonomy. In 1971, 80 per cent of British seven and eight year olds went to school on their own; by 1990 only 7 per cent were doing so (Hillman *et al.*, 1990). Other factors, such as increased car ownership may contribute to this trend, but parental fears about safety figure significantly in decisions on where children are able to go without adult supervision.

Home and family life is frequently thought of as a place of safety for children, but this is not always so. Children suffer many serious accidents in the home, especially where housing conditions are poor. Moreover children are far more likely to be assaulted and sexually abused within the family circle than outside it. Although this is widely known, it is still the shadowy figure of the 'pedophile' which haunts the popular imagination. There is now a large and growing body of research on child abuse, especially sexual abuse, which suggests that it is men children know who are more likely to abuse them. Like violence against wives, this can be seen as a result of the power structure and privacy of family life which can effectively place children entirely at the mercy of violent men.

Conclusion

I have not attempted to cover the whole field of sociological work on family life, but the research which I have reported challenges the cosy image of the family as a haven of harmony and security. Sociologists have demonstrated that family life is organized hierarchically, with men having power over women and adults of both sexes having power over children. We now know a great deal about the ways in which this situation is experienced by women, but rather less about men's understanding of their position in the family and less still about children's perspective. There has recently, however, been a move towards considering the world from children's own point of view (see, for example, Brannen and O'Brien, 1994). Ongoing research in this area is likely to offer us a new point of view on family life.

There are other areas which require further investigation. Despite the recent emphasis on diversity in family life, there is still little work on sources of variation other than demographic ones. Most existing research concentrates on white families, so that much remains to be done on the specific, and changing, forms of domestic organization found among Britain's diverse ethnic minority populations. We are also only just beginning to address issues raised by alternative forms of family life, such as lesbian and gay families and those consciously seeking to build anti-sexist living arrangements (Weston, 1991; Van Every, 1995). Sociologists are still finding aspects of family life which are so taken for granted that they are only now being subjected to critical scrutiny, such as the institutionalization of heterosexuality (Richardson, 1996). New issues are also being raised by wider social change – for example the implications of assisted conception for the ways in which we understand parenthood and kinship (Stacey, 1992; Strathern, 1992). The field of family studies is continually evolving to take up new issues. Meanwhile, family life will continue to change, as it always has, throwing up new challenges for sociologists seeking to understand the shifting kaleidoscope of household, family and kinship.

Further Reading

Bernardes, J. *Family Studies: An Introduction*, London, Routledge, 1997. A basic text emphasizing the diversity of family forms and questioning monolithic conceptualisations of the family.

Gittins, D. *The Family In Question*, 2nd edition, London, Macmillan, 1993. An accessible, introductory overview of debates and research on family life from a feminist perspective.

Jackson, S. and Moores, S. (eds) *The Politics of Domestic Consumption: Critical Readings*, Hemel Hempstead, Prentice Hall/Harvester Wheatsheaf, 1995. A reader bringing together critical work on the everyday practices of domestic consumption: includes readings on money, food, leisure, the media, domestic technologies, and the cultural construction of home.

Jamieson, L. *Intimacy*, Cambridge: Polity, 1998. An interesting new perspective on familial relationships focusing, as the title suggests, on the quality of personal relationships and how patterns of intimacy may be changing.

Morgan, D. *Family Connections: An Introduction to Family Studies*, Cambridge, Polity, 1996. An interesting and readable overview of sociological research on family life over the last two decades, showing how it intersects with wider sociological concerns.

9

Education

Robert G. Burgess and Andrew Parker

Education is a distinct form of 'secondary socialization'. Educational institutions are specifically created and legally sanctioned to transmit knowledge, skills and values; they also play an important part in determining people's position in society. Although most contemporary societies place great stress on equality of opportunity, a great deal of sociological work has suggested that education not only reflects, but also helps to reproduce, inequalities of class, gender and 'race' discussed in earlier chapters. This chapter aims to illustrate how sociologists have examined how schools work and their relationship to wider society. It should help you understand:

- The significance of functionalist, interactionist and Marxist theories to the development of the sociology of education

- The relationship between education, social class and social mobility in post-war Britain

- Ethnographic studies of stratification within schools and the influence of class, gender and 'race' on classroom interaction

- Sociological analyses of the effects of increasing marketization, competition and accountability in contemporary education

---

CONCEPTS

consensus and conflict models ▪ post-structuralism
postmodernism ▪ social mobility ▪ culture of deprivation
cultural reproduction ▪ marketization
'New Right' ▪ post-Fordism ▪ surveillance

Introduction

Most of us know something about education as a consequence of our exposure to it as pupils in school, and as students in college or university. Education is a 'commonsense' part of our society; a built-in set of expectations which we are all obliged to fulfil at specific points in time; a process whereby certain 'types' of knowledge are legitimized and mediated via teacher/instructor–student/pupil relations. These expectations are largely determined by statutory government guidelines and/or 'orders' which, in turn, structure institutional policy and practice. The sociology of education has attempted to analyse and explain the role of education within our society, to examine how it works, what it achieves and who benefits from its provision.

Education is one of the major institutions of modern societies, but what kind of questions have been asked by educational sociologists? First, at the structural level, sociologists have been interested in asking questions about the relationship between education and other major institutions such as family, class and work. For example, how do things like class and ethnic background influence educational attainment? What is the relationship between people's education and the jobs they end up doing? Second, sociologists have looked behind the statistics and wider social processes to examine the day-to-day practice of education. How do schools and classrooms 'work'? How, for example, do the attitudes of teachers and pupils influence each other? Third, sociologists have examined the influence on educational institutions of the social and political contexts in which they are located. For example, to what extent do centralized educational systems (such as those of France, Germany and Japan for example) and decentralized systems (such as those of England and Wales) result in different educational processes (Archer, 1979)? In the last two decades there have been vast amounts of legislation concerned with educational change worldwide. In England and Wales, for example, the Education Reform Act 1988 brought about changes in curriculum, assessment and testing. Sociologists of education have been interested in exploring the nature and effects of these developments. For example, how have policies aimed at making schools more 'efficient' and 'accountable' affected educational practices?

This chapter is organized around the questions raised above by providing specific illustrations of these general themes. It begins by introducing some of the major theoretical approaches in the sociology of education. It then looks at the relationship between education, inequality and social mobility and goes on to examine sociological research into what actually happens in educational settings and how this gives rise to further questions about different experiences of education. The chapter concludes by examining the changing context of educational policy, and how this affects the processes and practices of schooling.

Theoretical Perspectives in the Sociology of Education

The sociology of education has been influenced by a number of theoretical standpoints offering different explanations of what education is and how it operates. Three major theoretical perspectives can be identified as central to the way in which sociologists have analysed educational systems and their related contexts: functionalist (or consensus) theory, social action theory and Marxist (or conflict) theory. Feminist and multicultural theories have been influential in studies of educational experiences in the last 20 years and more recent commentaries on educational issues have alluded to aspects of post-modern thought.

In investigating education, the questions sociologists ask and the ways in which evidence is interpreted are necessarily influenced by their underlying theoretical perspectives. Functionalists, for example, have been keen to analyse the school as a social system; to establish the relationship between the structure of society as a whole and education as part of that structure, and to examine the effectiveness of education as an agent of socialisation. Durkheim was the first major theorist to make a thorough examination of the role of education within contemporary society. For Durkheim, as well as teaching specific skills, education is the central means by which society perpetually recreates the conditions of its existence by a systematic socialization of a younger generation:

> Education is the influence exercised by adult generations on those that are not yet ready for social life. Its object is to arouse and to develop in the child a certain number of physical, intellectual and moral states which are demanded of it by both the political society as a whole and the special milieu for which it is specifically destined. (1956: 71)

Education thus provides an important link between the individual and society. An appreciation of history, for example, helps children to see society as something 'larger' than themselves. Durkheim argued that this moral education was becoming more important in an increasingly individualized, competitive and secular modern world. The idea that schools play an important role in transmitting cultural values has been a theme of continuing importance in the sociology of education.

Like Durkheim, Parsons (1961) sought to identify education in terms of the societal function it serves, depicting it as a context in which individuals are taught the fundamental rules and values of society thereby facilitating the maintenance of moral order and consensus. For example, in order to prepare children for the orientations of society at large, schools promote the value of achievement and success, with responsibility for development in these areas being primarily located with children themselves. In turn, schools also function to select people for work roles which are appropriate to their abilities.

Functionalism has been widely criticised for presenting an essentially 'conservative' and uncritical view of education. However, this is not a *necessary* consequence of the functionalist approach. For example, Durkheim was insistent that for education to be an effective source of socialization it had to provide *real* equality of opportunity. As we shall see in the following section, within this tradition a great deal of work has been directed towards documenting and explaining the structural causes of education's failure to achieve these ideals.

Social action theorists, on the other hand, have adopted a more 'interpretive' approach towards educational practice. They have looked closely at the ways in which educational institutions are organized and structured; how those who work within them interpret, negotiate and carry out their roles, and how the resulting web of interrelationships impacts upon processes of teaching and learning. This approach has been most strongly influenced by symbolic interactionism which, presenting clear challenges to the work of functionalists, focuses on the subjective meaning of individual action rather than issues relating to societal structures and systems. These contentions reflect an ongoing structure/agency debate in sociological theory which was discussed in some detail in Chapter 3. A major focus within the social action approach has been to explore the relationship between educational processes and children's identities. For example, once a child has been identified as a 'troublemaker', 'clown' or 'high-flyer', is there then a tendency for their actions to be interpreted in terms of this label? Interactionists also consider the extent to which such labels might then be internalized and become the basis for the way in which children think about themselves and the social world.

While functionalist and social action theorists have adopted the notion of 'social inequality', particularly equality of opportunity, as a key feature of their work, Marxist (or conflict) theorists have traditionally presented a more radical analysis of educational institutions and systems, highlighting issues of social class, power relations and inequality, locating schooling as a process of unequal distribution of societal resources and opportunities. As a result the school system has been portrayed by some as part of a state machine eager to allocate pupils from specific social class backgrounds into certain roles within society, particularly within the world of work. Althusser (1972) provides an example of this approach by locating education as the central component of state policy with regard to ideological dominance of the masses in mature capitalist societies. For Althusser, education has taken the place of religion (the Church) as the key ideological focus of such societies and, in so doing, serves as the primary method by which the relations of capitalist production (capitalist relations of exploitation) are reproduced:

No other ideological State apparatus has the obligatory (and not least, free) audience of the totality of the children in the capitalist social formation, eight hours a day for five or six days a week out of seven. But it is by an apprenticeship in a variety of 'know-how' wrapped up in the massive inculcation of the ideology of the ruling class that the *relations of production* in a capitalist social formation... are reproduced. The mechanisms which produce this vital result for the capitalist regime are naturally covered up and concealed by a universally reigning ideology of the school, universally reigning because it is one of the essential forms of the ruling bourgeois ideology. (1972: 261)

Such analyses have attracted a good deal of criticism as a consequence of the way in which individual action is portrayed as being constrained by the economic logic of capitalism and its inherent structures. However, this has not deterred sociologists from utilising Marxist theory to explain the inner workings of educational systems. In their book, *Schooling in Capitalist America,* Bowles and Gintis (1976) offer a strong critique of the way in which the bureaucratic and hierarchically ordered format of schools resembles that already established within the workplace and how socialization is necessarily carried out in an institutional atmosphere of subordination and domination. Outlining a clear relationship between the economy and education Bowles and Gintis go on to advocate that pupils in school learn to be workers via a 'correspondence' between the social relations of production and the social relations of education.

Critical perspectives have also been adopted by feminist researchers to investigate patterns of inequality on the grounds of gender (see Riley, 1994; Weiner, 1994; Arnot *et al.*, 1996), and by those exploring issues of 'race', racism and ethnicity to evaluate the impact of multiculturalism within and upon the educational system (see Mac an Ghaill, 1988; Gillborn, 1990; Foster *et al.*, 1996). While vestiges of functionalist, social action and Marxist 'theoretical' approaches remain apparent within contemporary studies of schools, it is evident that there has been a shift away from fundamental questions concerning selection, socialization, social class and social mobility to those dealing with broader and more complex notions of educational process, policy and practice. In this sense, contentions and concerns over issues of social class, gender and 'race' and ethnicity are still high on the sociological agenda within the context of education, yet in more recent years these issues (and indeed, a host of others) have come under increasingly critical scrutiny by sociologists who have begun to cite instances of cultural and educational fragmentation and diversity as a clear indication that we now live in a postmodern age requiring different forms of sociological analysis.

Such developments are evident in contemporary analyses of educational settings and the kinds of theoretical perspectives being utilized. The work of Foucault, for example, has been adopted by a number of sociologists in order to present post-structuralist accounts of educational experience. In particular, Foucault's assertions regarding the 'geneology of power/knowledge' and the emergence of powerful societal *discourses* (bodies of ideas, concepts and theories which define social phenomena) have proved influential in this respect (cf. Foucault, 1979, 1986; Sarup, 1993). Drawing on the work of Nietzsche,

Foucault's 'genealogical' analysis emphasizes the relationship between knowledge and power and how this relationship manifests itself by way of *discourses* or *discursive formations* through which particular modes of thought are rendered legitimate and others denied (see Storey, 1993; Hall, 1997). While the term 'discourse' is commonly associated with language and linguistics, for Foucault it additionally encompasses notions of *practice*:

> Discourse, Foucault argues, constructs the topic. It defines and produces the objects of our knowledge. It governs the way that a topic can be meaningfully talked about and reasoned about. It also influences how ideas are put into practice and used to regulate the conduct of others. Just as discourse 'rules in' certain ways of talking about a topic, defining an acceptable and intelligible way to talk, write or conduct oneself, so also, by definition, it 'rules out', limits and restricts other ways of talking, of conducting ourselves in relation to the topic or constructing knowledge about it. (Hall, 1997: 44)

Ball (1994) utilizes a post-structuralist approach (in conjunction with critical policy analysis and critical ethnography) to evaluate the impact of the 1988 Education Reform Act on the UK education system, and more specifically on classroom practice and teachers' lives. Pinpointing at the outset of his work how he intends 'to examine some of the "power networks", discourses and technologies which run through the social body of education: the local state, educational organisations and classrooms', Ball's (1994) explicit aim is 'to theorize educational reform and thereby achieve an unmasking of power for the benefit of those who suffer it'. In considering 'policy as *discourse*', Ball attempts to uncover the way that a 'free-market' ethos has been legitimised within the context of educational provision, the consequences of which have ultimately come to shape the organizational *practices* of modern-day schools.

In their analysis of gender relations within schools, Weiner *et al.* provide a more detailed explanation of how the notion of *discourse* might serve to provide sociologists with a kind of analytical framework. For them, Foucault

> uses discourse to explain ways of thinking about the world that are so deeply embedded in practice that we are unconscious of their existence. Discourses are structuring mechanisms for social institutions (such as schools), modes of thought, and individual subjectivities... Further, Foucault's understanding of power–knowledge relations allows for the relationship to be established between knowledge (say, relating to the curriculum, policy and so on) and power (who creates, controls, receives specific knowledges). (1997: 621)

There is an affinity between post-structural and postmodern theory and, indeed, the two are sometimes used interchangeably. However, postmodernism is a much more difficult term to pin down. There is debate in sociology about whether it is a 'movement', 'condition' or a 'system of ideas', and also whether or not contemporary society has in fact witnessed a dissolution of those social forms associated with modernity bringing about a postmodern or post-industrial phase (see Sarup, 1993). For those who advocate this position, postmodernism appears to represent key changes concerning the way in which we think about society and the events and occurrences which go on within it. First, as we saw in Chapter 3, postmodernists refute the existence of any overarching theoretical explanation, grand theory or meta-narrative (particularly Marxism) about how society has developed and proffer radical scepticism about the philosophical basis of knowledge. Second, it is argued that changes such as the development of a global economy, the emergence of flexible and highly responsive service industries, faster modes of travel and communication (the evolution of the information super-highway) and the subsequent breakdown of old state/relational 'boundaries' have transformed the condition of modernity.

While education has remained largely divorced from this overall debate there is evidence to suggest that it too is 'going through profound change in terms of purposes, content and methods' which seemingly exhibit features of postmodernity (Usher and Edwards, 1994: 3). Many of these changes can be compared to those taking place within broader industrial contexts in terms of their impact on institutional relations and workplace practices (see Ball, 1990, 1994) Analysing such changes within the context of Canadian schools, for example, Hargreaves (1994: 3) suggests that the contemporary crisis of schooling and teaching can essentially be defined in terms of the contradictions posed by the experiences of teachers who, on the one hand, inhabit an occupational world dominated by the intensities, diversities, complexities and uncertainties of post-industrialism, while, on the other hand, working in and around 'a modernistic and monolithic school system that continues to pursue deeply anachronistic purposes within opaque and inflexible structures'. The following sections explore some of the research carried out within the theoretical perspectives outlined, starting with the sociology of education's long-standing interest in the relationship between education, social class and equality of opportunity.

Education, Social Class and Social Mobility

The relationship between social class, social mobility and education has always been of interest to sociologists of education. Social mobility refers to the movement of people between social class categories and rates of social mobility are often taken as 'indicators' or 'measures' of the degree of fluidity and openness in societies. The idea of creating greater equality of opportunity in Britain, for example, was embodied in the 1944 Education Act. This made education compulsory up until the age of 15, guaranteed all children a place in secondary school, with access to the more academic grammar schools being determined by the results of a national 11+ examination which children took in their final year of primary education. The hope was that better schools and more equality of opportunity in education would lead to greater social mobility by identifying talent and enabling it to flourish irrespective of social origin. A major focus of sociological studies was to examine the impact of these reforms, particularly their impact on social mobility.

Early work in the 'political arithmetic' tradition by sociologists at the London School of Economics suggested that there was comparatively little upward social mobility from the lower parts of society to the top (Glass, 1954). The more recent and more sophisticated research of Goldthorpe *et al.* (1980) – using the employment-aggregate class scheme described in Chapter 5 – suggests a rather more complex picture. Goldthorpe and his associates found that there had been a significant increase in *absolute* social mobility. However, this was largely due to an increase in professional and managerial occupations 'sucking up' more people from the lower classes which, in effect, meant that there had been little change in the *relative* mobility of people from different socio-economic origins. The work of Halsey *et al.* (1980), which compared cohorts of men educated before and since the educational reforms, found that although educational opportunities had improved for all classes, the differentials between classes had hardly changed. For example, although the rate of university entrance was 3.5 times higher for upper and lower classes, the chances of the sons of 'service-class' fathers (Classes I and II) going to university remained over seven times greater than that of the working-class boys (Classes VI to VII) (see also Heath and Clifford, 1996).

In more recent years class has lost its central place in the sociology of education and, according to Mortimore and Whitty, 'teachers who dared to mention the subject have been branded as defeatist or patronising for even considering that class can make a difference' (1997: 1). However, data from the 1980s and 90s continue to suggest a systematic relationship between low social class and comparatively poor examination performance (see for example, Denscombe, 1993). In this context sociologists are still suggesting, as they have done for the last 30 years, that improvements *within* schools to increase educational attainment will only be partially successful if carried out in isolation. Whitty argues that 'where schools have seemed to make progress, the *relative* performance of the disadvantaged groups has often remained similar or worsened even when the absolute performance of such groups has improved' (1998: 4). For Mortimore and Whitty, 'the priority of any government must be to implement strategies to deal with poverty and associated disadvantage: schools cannot go it alone' (1997: 12).

Education is crucially important within the context of social inequality and social mobility as formal qualifications (or the lack of them) have come to be key determinants of an individual's position in the occupational structure. In general, the higher people's level of qualifications, the higher their income. For example, data from the General Household Survey of 1991, showed that the average earnings of men and women with degrees was double that of those with no qualifications (Table 9.1). However, despite formal equality of opportunity access to education, levels of educational attainment continue to be *systematically* linked to socio-economic background. For example, over half of those with Social Class I backgrounds obtained a degree or similar qualification compared to just 8 per cent from Social Class VI (Figure 9.1). Similarly, those with no educational qualifications increased from 7 per cent in Social Class I to 60 per cent in Social Class V.

Table 9.1 Median weekly earnings (£) by holders of given qualifications, by sex, Great Britain 1991

Qualifications	Male	Female
Degree (or equivalent)	440	332
Other higher education	330	296
GCSE A–C grades (or equivalent)	252	193
No qualifications	220	193

Source: General Household Survey (1991).

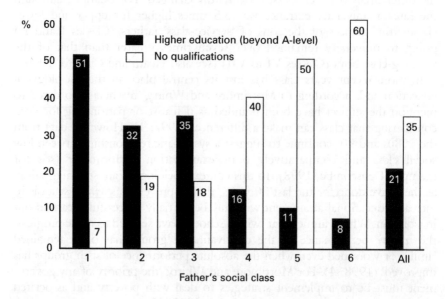

Figure 9.1 Percentage of persons with higher or no educational qualifications, by father's social class, Great Britain, 1990–91 (General Household Survey, 1991)

Early sociological explanations of the relationship between educational performance and socio-economic background focused not on the school but on factors in wider society, particularly the working-class home (see Foster *et al.*, 1996). Material deprivation, such as sub-standard housing, lack of resources, and the comparatively poorer health of working-class children, were seen as particularly important influences. Douglas (1964), in a major longtitudinal study which followed 5000 children from primary to secondary school, found clear links between reduced educational performances and 'unsatisfactory' living conditions. However, while material deprivation was seen as an important influence, many felt that it could not explain the whole problem. For some theorists, another important part of the answer was to be found in the comparative deprivations of working-class culture, particularly the different expectations, values and child rearing practices of middle-class and working-class parents. Douglas' research found that middle-class parents showed more interest in their children's education, were more likely to visit the school, and placed greater emphasis on educational attainment. The idea of cultural deprivation was reinforced by research suggesting that working-class forms or 'codes' of speech (which tended to be more restricted and context-tied than middle-class patterns) were less compatible with the demands of educational institutions (see Bernstein, 1975). Halsey *et al.* (1980) attempted, as far as possible, to separate out material and cultural influences. They found that cultural influences, especially parental attitudes, were the principal determinant of a boy's progress up until the age of 11 (when selection was made) but that after that material circumstances became an increasingly important determinant of school-leaving age and the qualifications obtained.

One of the earliest accounts of the way in which working-class children used a grammar school education to be upwardly mobile was reported in a classic study by Jackson and Marsden (1962). This study, based on 88 children from a town in the north of England, focused on one question: what occurred within the school to perpetuate social class differences in achievements among children of similar ability? The study charted the way in which children from working-class backgrounds experienced the educational system. It demonstrated how talented working-class children who passed the 11+ examination at the end of primary school and went into the selective grammar schools under-achieved by leaving school early and not proceeding into higher education. It showed that mobility from the working to the middle classes carried with it social isolation. The relationship between home and school was an 'us versus them' phenomenon, whereby the working-class child did not make the transition between the culture of the working-class community and the middle-class school which was experienced as an alien world in which they felt they did not belong. The grammar school system thus helped to reproduce social class divisions. The study raised important questions, such as the relationship between social class background and academic performance, the content of the school curriculum, the quality of teacher/pupil interaction and the ways in which assessments were made of pupils, that were subsequently investigated by sociologists of education. The study was seen as something of a landmark, not just in the sociology of education but in sociology generally, linking back to class analysis on the one hand and forward to ethnographic studies of schools.

Studies of Schools

Prior to the 1960s it was rare for sociologists to engage in any small-scale studies of schools and the ways in which they operated. However, in the early 1960s sociologists and social anthropologists developed a series of studies in which the methods of investigation that had been used to study small-scale societies, social situations and social events were used to examine the dynamics of schooling. A programme, directed by Gluckman at the University of Manchester, used techniques of observation and participant observation, in-depth interviewing and documentary analysis to develop detailed studies of schools. These were the precursors of a number of ethnographic studies in schools that were to be conducted over the next 30 years. Gluckman's programme looked at patterns of school organization by focusing on a boys' grammar school (Lacey, 1970), a boys' secondary modern school (Hargreaves, 1967) and a girls' grammar school (Lambert, 1976). A major theoretical influence was the interactionist approach, which focuses attention on the ways individuals' perceptions of themselves are shaped by the expectations of others. The studies focused on the internal organization of these schools, especially the impact of stratification within schools – that is, streaming groups in terms of different ability – on pupils' identities, behaviour and achievement. These were the themes associated particularly with the 'classical' accounts of Hargreaves and Lacey.

Lacey (1970) identified social processes associated with streaming and developed a model of 'differentiation' and 'polarisation'. The former referred to the way in which pupils were separated and ranked according to specific academic criteria within the school, while the latter indicated the way in which pupil anti-school sub-cultures might develop in response and opposition to the academic value structures in place. This model of differentiation and polarization was central to Lacey's study: those who conformed to teacher expectations and demands and who valued academic success were rewarded, while those who did not were perceived by their teachers in increasingly negative terms. As these processes were linked to streaming, Lacey was able to associate differentiation and polarization with the streams to which pupils were allocated. Hargreaves (1967) reported a process of sub-cultural differentiation in 'Lumley' School, whereby the higher the stream in which pupils were allocated, the better their behaviour, while the 'anti-school' culture was manifest in the lower streams. Like Lacey, Hargreaves proposed a model of the way in which the sub-culture of the school operated. The dominant values of the A and B streams of 'Lumley' were said to be 'academic', while those of the C and D streams were predominantly 'delinquescent', that is based on rule breaking and lack of interest in academic work. The study demonstrates how the A and D streams become the poles of differentiation. In the former there was a *correspondence* between school and peer group values, while in the latter they were in *opposition*, with disruptive behaviour being associated with high peer group status.

The clear emergence of the theme of differentiation and polarization in the studies by Lacey and Hargreaves influenced further research into the fundamental processes that occurred in schools and the social implications of their internal academic organization. In a later study Ball (1981) examined the organization of 'Beachside', a comprehensive school where entry was non-selective. In 'Beachside' new pupils were placed in one of three ability bands, band 1 being high and band 3 being low. Although allocation to bands was supposed to be based entirely on 'academic' criteria, like Jackson and Marsden 20 years earlier, Ball found that a significantly higher proportion of working-class children were allocated to the lower ability bands.

While the majority of pupils were conformist and co-operative when they first came to 'Beachside', Ball found a clear divergence in the behaviour of children in the different bands developed. The banding system had the effect of separating pupils into a number of groups who had access to different kinds of subject knowledge, different teaching methods and had different kinds of relationships with their teachers. Pupils were found to make relationships within their own bands and Ball suggested that an anti-school culture, similar to that which had been found by Hargreaves and Lacey, was prevalent among band 2 pupils, who were regarded by teachers as behaviourally problematic, in contrast to band 1 pupils, who fulfilled the ideal pupil role and band 3, who were expected to have learning problems but not create difficulties. However, these processes of differentiation could not be explained entirely by banding. During Ball's research, 'Beachside' changed its system of banding to mixed-ability teaching. While pupil behaviour improved, teachers continued to make clear distinctions between 'bright' and 'dull' pupils, thus reproducing the 'stratification' of banding in a mixed-ability context of the classroom. For example, while the 'brighter' children were encouraged to enter for national exams, some of the less able were 'cooled out' and advised to set their sights lower.

In another celebrated ethnographic study of a comprehensive school, Keddie (1971) examined pupil–teacher interaction in humanities subjects where the same syllabus was taught across different streams. She argued that teachers would change the content of the 'same' lesson, 'withholding' some of the more complex material from C stream children. They were also less responsive to questions from children in the low streams, thus differentiating in their teaching methods on the basis of their preconceived assumptions of the 'given' abilities of children in different streams. Keddie gives a number of examples to illustrate this process. For example, in one lesson, children in one of the C streams were discussing the solitary confinement of the 'wolf child':

Teacher: The interesting thing is the boy was fostered out. He was illegitimate you see. If you think about it he must have had the beginnings of speech – so what do you think happened?

Boy: The woman who put him in a chicken coop made him go backwards.

Teacher: Very good...

Boy 2:   Well done.

Boy: How do you unlearn?

Teacher: Well you simply forget – in school – tests show that.

Boy: (Makes some untranscribable objection.)

Teacher: You need to keep practising skills.

A noticeable feature of this sequence is that the teacher's response renders the question unproblematic: 'Well you simply forget'. (Keddie, 1971: 153)

For Keddie, the curriculum is not a 'given'; rather it is socially constructed in different ways according to teachers' preconceived assumptions about the abilities of children in different streams. The consequence of this is that children in the lower streams have restricted opportunities to access knowledge which may have been crucial to their educational success.

While ethnographic studies of schools have made an important contribution to understanding educational processes, it is important to recall the observations made in Chapter 2 about ethnographic methods. Pawson illustrates how qualitative data are usually also open to interpretations other than the one being put forward by the researcher. In the context of Keddie's work, McNamara (1980), for example, complains that while Keddie's interpretation is plausible, the teacher may have simply wanted to keep the lesson moving, been running out of time, or the topic may have been the subject of next week's lesson. This observation does not, of course, detract from the value of ethnographic studies, of schools or anything else, but it does direct attention to the way in which the researcher deals with alternative interpretations

While studies of the internal organization of schools still dominated the sociology of education in the 1970s and early 1980s, other ethnographies emerged, offering a variation in theoretical approach. The first, signalling an increasing interest in cultural production, was influenced by Willis' *Learning to Labour* (1977), which adopted a more radical perspective towards education, working-class youth and cultural reproduction. It drew on both Marxist and interepretive theory to address the central question of how and why working-class 'kids' get working-class jobs. The study's ethnographic methods – discussed in Chapter 2 – documented the school and post-school experiences of a small group of adolescent males in an industrial city in England. Willis' findings mapped out the detailed construction of sub-cultural masculinity in and around these working-class locales, the stark realities of which allowed him to conclude that issues of social class and social mobility were as much to do with structural constraint and sub-cultural determinism as they were to do with education *per se*. The 'lads' Willis studied developed a counter-culture of resistance to the school which rejected education, teachers and conforming pupils. Willis found that the strategies the lads had used for coping with the authority and boredom of school, such as insubordination, time wasting, having a laugh and distinguishing between 'us' and 'them', were also serving them in the repetitive and supervised world of manual labour. There is thus a correspondence between school and work. However, this process did not come from the school socializing them into obedient, compliant pupils as suggested by Bowles and Gintis (1976). Paradoxically, it was the *rejection* of the school and the *active* development of an oppositional counter-culture that had prepared them for the demands of unskilled labour. Willis has been criticised for drawing his conclusions from such a small and unrepresentative sample and for not taking into account a much wider range of responses to school (Brown, 1989). However, with its emphasis on culture and resistance and recognition of the importance of both agency and structure, Willis' study was an important development in the sociology of education, providing a theoretical model which influenced other 'culturist' research studies.

It is interesting to compare the work of Willis with that of Hargreaves from the previous decade. Both consider the plight of working-class pupils in the lower 'streams' of secondary schooling and both uncover the existence of a delinquent, anti-counter-school sub-culture among their respondents. While Hargreaves sees the development of disaffected sub-cultural attitudes as a response to individual and collective notions of institutional 'failure', Willis regards them as a proactive form of pupil resistance whereby the anti-academic nuances of working-class culture fight against the school's imposition of middle-class values and belief systems. The differences between these studies are not only indicative of theoretical bias but also of a broader disciplinary shift in the early 1970s which came to be known as the 'new sociology of education' (cf. Young, 1971). Moving away from a preoccupation with notions of educational access and organization and what needed to be done to allow working-class children to benefit from the opportunities on offer, this shift marked the point at which education itself came under scrutiny in terms of the kinds of *knowledge* it promoted. In this respect, the 'new' sociologists:

> Began to challenge the whole nature of the education provided in schools. This was itself now seen as a barrier to the achievement of educational (and social) equality. One aspect of this was the argument that the knowledge and skills purveyed, or at least those accorded high status, stem[med] from the culture of dominant social groups. In other words, the very knowledge schools offer[ed] reflect[ed] the unequal social structure of the wider society. (Foster *et al.*, 1996: 10)

Thus, the 'new sociology of education' heralded the point at which sociologists switched emphasis away from the individual circumstances and backgrounds of pupils, towards issues concerning the inequality of power between the social classes and how this power was used to define the constituent elements of 'education'.

Another development, indicative of broader sociological concerns, was that educational sociologists became increasingly interested in issues of gender and 'race'. Indeed, while social differentiation and inequality had been key themes from the early post-war period up until the 1970s, in practice the majority of studies had focused upon specific groups of white, working-class anti-school boys, a pattern which, as Mac an Ghaill (1996) points out, was something of an anathema to the arguments put forward by a fast growing feminist and anti-racist lobby. As a consequence, the 1970s and 80s saw the sociology of education shift its focus away from issues of social class to explore what Mac an Ghaill (1996: 167) describes as 'the differentiated schooling experiences of girls and of Asian and Afro-Caribbean students' (see also Weiner, 1994). Without doubt, such initiatives located issues of gender and 'race' at the centre rather than the periphery of educational debate, but as Mac an Ghaill (1996) stresses there is a sense in which a subsequent preoccupation with issues pertaining to gender and 'race' then served to displace notions of social class to the extent that theorists were distracted from the development of a more holistic analytical framework involving the complex 'articulation' of all three themes. Nevertheless, these advances in the investigative remit did constitute a clear change for sociologists working within education. What they also provided were the grounds on which some understanding might be gained of what actually went on in classrooms. What they also provided were the grounds on which some understanding might be gained of what actually went on in classrooms, and it was this influence that dominated the 1980s.

Sociologists 'inside' Classrooms

Up until the 1980s many sociological studies focused on how schools functioned and operated as a whole. However, many later studies examined some of the taken-for-granted routines of the classroom, redering them 'strange' in order to understand them. Delamont (1981), for example, argued that there were specific strategies that could be used to help understand teacher–pupil interaction. She suggested the placement of these strategies into four categories. First, different kinds of classrooms should be examined in which different subjects are taught. This has resulted in sociologists studying classroom activities, not only in schools, but also in higher education institutions and also in different subject areas. Second, comparative studies can provide a stimulus for looking at familiar classroom settings – too few cross-cultural studies have been conducted, especially between Britain and Europe (see Burgess, 1998). Third, non-educational settings can be compared with educational settings, as in studies of youth training where classroom learning is compared with work-based learning (see Banks *et al.*, 1992). Fourth, the familiar aspects of schooling, such as the way gender is used to organize classroom activities, should not be taken for granted but used as a basis for questioning routine procedures in schools and classrooms – a theme that has been taken up in several studies (see Riddell, 1992; Weiner, 1994).

Such strategies have been useful in helping sociologists understand the process of schooling. For example, many researchers have examined initial encounters and routines in classrooms in order to find out how teachers attempt to organize and determine pupil behaviour. Measor and Woods (1984), in their study of pupils transferring from primary to secondary school, reported that the pupils went through a honeymoon period with teachers, whereby each presented their best fronts to each other before 'coming out' by probing, testing and negotiating rules. These phenomena were explored in several studies where sociologists examined how teachers established routines in the classroom and how pupils 'tested out' teachers (see also Beynon, 1985). Another major study by Galton and Delamont (1980) followed pupils who were transferring from first to middle schools. Using ethnographic studies in classrooms, they examined the ways in which teachers went about establishing rules in initial lessons with classes, thus providing further evidence on some of the fundamental processes identified by Measor and Woods in their school transfer study.

Of course, not all classroom interaction results in pupil conformity. In a study of a secondary school in South Wales, for example, Beynon and Atkinson (1984) report on ways in which pupils challenged the authority of women teachers. Similarly, a number of sociologists have looked at the ways in which such situations are used by pupils to disrupt classroom activity, where 'mucking about', 'doing nothing' and 'having a laugh' are cited as ways in which pupils develop subversive behaviour in classrooms to challenge teacher authority and control (see Corrigan, 1979).

Many of these themes have persisted throughout the 1980s and 90s with sociologists not only exploring fundamental processes of education, but also the ways in which gender and sexuality and 'race' influence schooling (cf. Epstein, 1994; Foster *et al.*, 1996; Haywood and Mac an Ghaill, 1996; Parker, 1996).

Gender

Gender has been a systematic source of inequality in education. Until recently, girls fell behind boys in secondary education despite outperforming them in primary education. Research in classrooms has suggested that, in addition to institutional disadvantages (discussed in Chapter 6) which have contributed to women's subordinate position in society, girls were also disadvantaged in patterns of classroom interaction in mixed schools. Spender (1983) found from tape recordings of lessons that not only did boys typically dominate classroom interactions with girls, they also received more attention from teachers, their contributions were generally taken more seriously and their work judged more favourably.

Stanworth (1983) also looked at the way in which boys and girls were treated differently by teachers in lessons. She found that both male and female pupils indicated that boys received more teacher attention in terms of being asked questions and being praised in the classroom. She argued that such teacher actions resulted in discrimination between boys and girls and the way in which pupils evaluated themselves and how pupils and teachers evaluated each other. The effect of this was to reinforce existing patterns of gender inequality by girls leaving school with an implicit understanding of their place in the world as second-class citizens. These uncompromising critiques of the consistently gendered nature of classroom interaction have themselves been subject to critical evaluation. Stanworth's conclusions have been criticized for being based entirely on secondary interview data, while Spender did not specify most of her methods, making evaluation and replication impossible (Delamont, 1986). A subsequent study by Randall (1987) failed to find the same gender bias from teachers, with girls receiving the same, and sometimes more, attention than boys.

A recent development now interesting educationalists is why girls have not only caught up with boys but seem to be overtaking them academically in many subjects. This appears to be a global trend. Research in the Caribbean, for example, found that girls were outperforming boys in most subject areas (Parry, 1996). Recent research exploring the 'problem' of boys' under-achievement has suggested that some of the factors previously believed to favour boys, such as teachers' greater tolerance and boys' overconfidence in their own abilities, may in fact be working to their detriment.

However, the position is rather more complex than the simple statement 'girls are now outperforming boys' suggests. For example, in Britain in 1995, girls outperformed boys at all Key Stages for Reading/English; however, results for Mathematics were broadly similar and boys did slightly better in Science at Key Stages 2 and 3 (Arnot *et al.*, 1998: 4–7). The results of national examinations at 16 (GCSEs) must also be carefully unpicked. In the decade prior to 1995, boys actually improved their overall exam performance (measured by number of A*–C passes), but the increase was not at the same rate as it was for girls (Arnot *et al.*, 1998). At this point an important caveat must be inserted. Preliminary research by Stobart *et al.* (1992) suggested that tiered entry for GCSE Mathematics masks some interesting gender biases. Girls may be entered for 'intermediate' maths, where they can gain no more than a C grade, rather than 'higher' maths which is aimed at students who should achieve grade A*–C. Stobart *et al.* suggest this may be due to a lack of perceived confidence in female abilities and so pupils and teachers decide to 'play it safe' and enter the girls for an exam which may curtail their future plans (1992: 269). Present statistics on A*–C pass rates do not presently show subject choices and so some gender differences may go undetected. One further consideration at GCSE is that where students have the ability to choose options there is still a marked gender gap in levels of entry. For example, Chemistry and Computer Studies are more likely to be taken up by boys (Arnot *et al.*, 1998: 12). This divide is still more marked at final school exams (A levels). According to Arnot *et al.*'s research, only History seemed to have an equal take-up rate; in terms of performance, males and females achieve broadly similar results at the A/AS level (1998: 15).

Weiner *et al.* (1997) are not convinced however that the 'future is female'. Despite real gains in terms of educational achievement for girls, they note that a discourse pervades the discussion that still centres on male concerns. Female achievement at the expense of the boys seems to be the key message. New Right thinkers contend that the demise of the traditional family has left boys without the future role of 'breadwinner' and thus boys have retreated into a macho anti-intellectual world and that a return to a bygone era would restore order and a sense of identity to men (Weiner *et al.*, 1997: 627). Confirming this male-orientated scenario, recent media attention has focused specifically on the under-achievement of boys in relation to national literacy standards, whereby supplementary forms of school attendance (such as 'booster' classes, summer schools and extra-curricular teaching) have been advocated as some kind of educational remedy (Lepkowska, 1999).

Weiner *et al.* (1997) go on to suggest that the present discourse also avoids questions concerning women's lack of promotion prospects, the continuing gendered nature of employment and pay differentials. Thus, the pervasive presence of male domination within schools and broader institutional work patterns and hierarchies would seem to suggest that genuine equality appears some way off.

'Race' and Racism

Wright (1992), in a study of four multiracial inner city primary schools, found that although most staff were committed to the idea of equality of educational opportunity, some of their preconceived assumptions led to social processes where some black children were 'racialised'; that is, discriminated against, usually unintentionally, on the basis of beliefs about 'racial' attributes (see Chapter 7). For example, some teachers' preconceived ideas about Asian girls as quiet and submissive rendered them more or less 'invisible' in class, while the low expectations of both the behaviour and academic potential of Afro-Caribbean boys resulted in more conflict with teachers, more disciplinary actions and more expulsions from class. Wright argued that the relative disadvantage experienced by some black children might hold back their emotional and educational development.

In an earlier study of secondary schools, Wright (1986) focused on the inter-action between teachers and Afro-Caribbean students, which was often charac-terised by confrontation and conflict. The result was that Afro-Caribbean pupils were often placed in ability bands and exam sets below their academic ability. Similarly, Gillborn (1990), studying a co-educational 11–16 comprehensive school, found that while teachers tried to treat all pupils fairly and equally, they actually perceived them differently and this led to different treatment. Afro-Caribbean pupils, in particular, experienced more conflict with teachers and were more likely to be reported and put into detention. Research has shown that children of African-Caribbean descent are more than twice as likely to be expelled from secondary school than white or 'Asian' children (Figure 9.2).

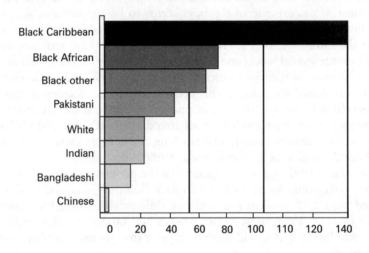

Figure 9.2   Exclusion per thousand from secondary schools in England, 1993–94 (OFSTED)

While the research just outlined used interactionist ideas to focus on the part played by schools, and teachers in particular, to prescribe identities, other studies have adopted an approach closer to that of Willis' and focused on the ways in which some black students, rather than being merely the passive victims of labelling, drew on their own cultural traditions and *actively* created a culture of resistance to the school or college. In an ethno-graphic study of 25 African and Asian students, Mac an Ghaill (1988) found that while the students disagreed about the extent of racism in education, these beliefs did not then determine their attitudes to education in the manner assumed in labelling theory. Like Willis, Mac an Ghaill's study emphasized resistance to the culture of the school through the development of a distinct sub-culture. Resistance was, therefore, the main theme within their schooling. This did not necessarily manifest in anti-education attitudes. Some students developed strategies to reconcile their resistance to the culture of the college and the content of much of the curriculum while maintaining their educational aspirations by playing the game. Fuller (1983) also gave examples of groups of female Afro-Caribbean students who found ways of resisting many of the institutional demands of the school, and what they believed to be a racist curriculum, while remaining committed to the value of education itself and the importance of obtaining academic qualifications. A more recent ethnographic study by Sewell (1997) came to very similar conclusions to Mac an Ghaill and Fuller. He found that students were 'positive about education but many rejected the schooling process' (1997: 102). However, although students adopted a number of coping strategies, Sewell maintains that, unlike the females in Fuller's study, some male students found it impossible to operate within the school system and confrontation with teachers became inevitable.

Some writers, such as Troyna, have adopted a fervently anti-racist stance towards issues of theory and practice within educational contexts and in doing so contested the way in which 'multicultural' policy has been traditionally structured (see Troyna and Hatcher, 1992; Troyna, 1993). For Troyna, the idea of attempting to modify individual attitudes towards issues of multiculturalism and developing a climate of cultural awareness in schools is merely a form of curricular 'benevolence'. Instead he advocates the implementation of anti-racist educational policies which directly address and contest issues of societal racism. According to Troyna, such policies should constitute a form of political education which highlights issues of racism.

However, this critique of the inherently racist character of schools and classroom interaction has itself been criticised on both empirical and theoretical grounds. Foster *et al.* (1996) argue that there is currently no convincing evidence by which discrimination against black students can be established. They argue that ethnographic studies alleging racist attitudes are subject to the selective interpretation discussed earlier in relation to Keddie's research. That is, evidence is filtered through a preconceived assumption that schools are racist. For example, an incident involving censure of a black child is put forward as evidence of racial discrimination when other explanations might be possible. In fact Foster (1992) has argued that teachers' views of students owe rather less to cultural stereotypes and rather more to the behaviour and abilities of students in the classroom. However, this in turn has to be balanced against research by Mac an Ghail (1988) and others that did find evidence of cultural stereotyping on the part of teachers.

For postmodernists (and post-structuralists), simply trying to compare the experiences of black, Asian and white students, for example, is fundamentally misconceived. Not only do such crude categories ignore many other minority groups, but also the differences that lie *within* these categories (Brah, 1992). In this context Gilroy (1992) has argued that anti-racist strategies, which focus exclusively on the dichotomy of 'black' and 'white', should be replaced by a cultural politics of difference; that is, recognizing and attempting to understand the diversity of cultural identities in contemporary societies. Postmodernists are similarly critical of studies which compare the experiences of 'girls' and 'boys' as if they were homogeneous categories. Rather, research should take into account the plurality and diversity which exists in contemporary classrooms and examine, for example, the *different* ways in which girls are defined and positioned in classroom interaction (Jones, 1993). This is but one aspect of a much wider critique of 'modernist sociology' by postmodernists who argue that the increasingly fluid and diverse nature of contemporary societies makes attempts to explain education (or anything else) in terms of blanket categories, such as class, gender or 'race', increasingly difficult to sustain.

From Policy to Practice

While studies of schools have contributed greatly to understanding routine educational processes and, in particular, the ways in which inequalities of class, gender, 'race' and culture may be reproduced, it is also important for sociologists to examine the changing contexts in which schools and other educational institutions exist. The policies of the state which shape the conditions under which pupils and teachers interact are particularly important in this context. The systematic sociological study of education in Britain began by investigating the effects of the major policy reforms brought about by the Education Act of 1944, aimed at providing greater equality of opportunity and access to education. In many contemporary western societies there has been another important shift in educational policies over the past couple of decades and it is to this issue that the chapter now turns.

The whole infrastructure of education, like many other institutions and organizations in contemporary society, has undergone a period of intense modification over the past decade with issues of marketization, competition and accountability coming to the fore. Sociologists are interested in examining how these policies develop, the processes of restructuring arising from them and their impact on the practice of education.

In Britain many of these changes were embodied in the Education Reform Act 1988 (ERA) which introduced a national curriculum (bringing the UK in line with most other European societies), standardized attainment tests, school governance and the establishment of city technology colleges and grant-maintained schools, (neither of which would be under the control of local education authorities in England). Much of this legislation involved reducing the power and status of local authorities while re-orientating education towards a market-driven economy of greater diversity and consumer choice.

Although the full impact of the ERA 1988 on schools has only recently become apparent, the changes it has brought can be more fully understood when viewed within the context of economic development in Britain over the past two decades. For example, one of the main features of the Act is the way in which, since the late 1970s, state educational policy has become more prescriptive in accordance with the increasing demands of economic productivity. While at first glance notions of 'education' and 'economy' may appear unrelated, clear and established links exist between these two entities which have been ever-present since the 1940s and 50s when, as both functionalist and Marxist theories articulated, education was explicitly located as a central instrument of post-war reconstruction. The general impetus here centred around the dissolution of previously pervasive class-based notions of an 'academic' versus 'vocational' split in schools with the intention of promoting egalitarian practices of educational 'equality' (see Floud and Halsey, 1961). However, more recent manoeuvres to rekindle the education–economy relationship have come about as a consequence of broader political and economic changes in society and, in particular, the emergent demands of a global economic culture. The commercialization and marketization of education, with schools and colleges being reorganized more like businesses, reflect this pressure.

Education, Marketisation and the 'New Right'

Often cited as a stimulus for such change in Britain was the wave of economic and cultural renewal which came about as a consequence of the election of the Conservative government of the late 1970s, whose processes of policy implementation and economic practice were guided by what has come to be known as the 'New Right' (see Brown, *et al.*, 1997; Whitty, 1997a). The explicit aim of the 'New Right' was to create an atmosphere of 'incentive' and 'enterprise' among individuals within society in order to engender a competitive market ethos, whereby people would strive to better themselves financially and alleviate notions of state dependency – the idea being to place the onus on individuals and individual institutions to become more responsible and accountable for their own livelihood without relying too heavily on financial support from public sources. Like a host of other institutions, education was part of this overall plan. It too would have to 'market' itself, 'compete' for clients and thereby gain state funding according to the levels of success incurred. Central to this restructuring process, Whitty argues:

Have been moves to disempower centralised educational bureaucracies, and to create in their place devolved systems of schooling entailing significant degrees of institutional autonomy and a variety of forms of school-based management and administration. (1997a: 299)

Similar changes were occurring within other western (post-) industrial societies, particularly the USA (see David, 1991). Moreover, there is evidence to suggest that since the late 1980s other nations such as Australia (Kenway, 1993), New Zealand (Grace, 1991), the Netherlands (Sleegers and Wesselingh, 1993), Spain (Bonal, 1995) and Canada (Elliott and Maclennan, 1994) have experienced some form of educational upheaval on a national scale in line with 'free market' economic forces.

In the case of Britain the consequence of such change, Brown *et al*. (1997) suggest, is that a devolution of financial staffing and policy issues has been carried out with regard to individual institutions (that is, schools), where assumptions have been made about the potential of educational establishments to 'compete' irrespective of their intake and the added pressure of 'parental choice' (see also Brown and Lauder, 1991). To this end, teachers have experienced considerable change, not only in the content of their work but also in relation to their occupational role. For example, schooling has become the subject of league tables in national newspapers with the result that teachers and schools are able to compare their position with national trends. Whereas at one time pupil assessment was simply structured around issues of 'certification' and 'selection' (Broadfoot, 1996), now such procedures are utilized to monitor school effectiveness and performance, as Torrance points out:

> The government's basic position seems to be that improving educational standards is of paramount importance in improving economic competitiveness within an increasingly competitive global economy, and that a new national assessment framework will help to raise standards by setting publicly accessible targets; measuring whether or not they have been met; encouraging schools to compete with each other by publishing the results; and allowing parents to choose their children's schools and tying finance in part to students numbers. (1997: 320)

An example of how this practice works is provided in Table 9.2, taken from recent report from the National Commission on Education (1996), where Jobson *et al*. (1996) comment on the work of Crowcroft Park Primary School in Manchester in terms of results in standard attainment tasks. The results give an indication of the way in which a school can compare itself to national results in Reading, Mathematics and Science.

Table 9.2   Crowcroft Park Primary School

| | Teacher Assessment Year 2 (percentage) | | | | | | | |
| | Level 1 | | Level 2 | | Level 3 | | Level 4 | |
	1993	1994	1993	1994	1993	1994	1993	1994
Reading national results	18		51		28		0	
Crowcroft Park	14	13	43	60	29	13	14	13
Maths national results	17		70		11		0	
Crowcroft Park	11	0	50	39	70	30	0	0
Science national results	12		70		14		0	
Crowcroft Park	0		63		37		0	

Source: Jobson *et al.* (1996), p. 49.

Sociologists have viewed the impact of educational change on policy and practice in terms of wider social processes. Some, for example, have suggested that such changes are confirmation of the fact that society has entered a post-industrial and/or post-Fordist age as a specific result of the revolutionary forces at work in the fields of technology and communication and the implications these have cumulatively posed for each nation state in terms of economic control (Menter *et al.*, 1997; Whitty, 1997b). In attempting to locate the nuances of the Australian education system within the context of this 'new-look' post-industrial scenario, Kenway succinctly maps out the broader consequences of 'market' ideology:

> As states struggle to transform their national economies and as they direct their resources accordingly, what we see is a shedding of welfare responsibilities. In the case of education... what we see is a transfer of certain responsibilities and costs away from the state to civil society. Accompanying this shift is an organisational and psychological reorientation of the education community within the state, encouraging a market/consumer orientation which feeds into the state sponsored privatisation momentum. ...What also becomes evident is that information and communications technologies and scientific discourses are deployed to promote and legitimate such adjustments. Policy making becomes increasingly caught up in the marketing and policing of images... Indeed, images and meaning have been generated which not only attract and attach people to this market discourse but which also persuade them that it is working in the interests of all. (1993: 114)

The terms post-Fordist and post-industrial are notoriously contentious, and remain open to a range of interpretations and will be discussed in more detail in the following chapter. However, in general terms, they refer to the way in which contemporary society and the institutions within it appear to have broken away from the highly stringent and routinized 'working' practices characteristic of earlier decades (Whitty, 1997b). In applying this kind of analysis to educational contexts, Ball (1990) argues that schools themselves have become post-Fordist in the sense that they have moved away from the narrow mind-set of previous years in terms of the mass production of single-skilled 'workers' and look instead towards the production of innovative, multi-skilled individuals whose diversity equips them to cope more readily with the 'flexible' demands of the global economy (see also Kenway, 1993). In turn, what a number of commentators have intimated is that the restructuring of educational bureaucracies has, to some degree, allowed the promotion of cultural differentiation to take place whereby different types of schools (that is, city technology colleges, maintained schools, non-maintained schools), accommodate the differing needs of various communities and interest groups, thereby demonstrating choice and diversity in accordance with post-industrial expectation.

Accountability, Control and Teachers' Lives

The restructuring of education in England and Wales might represent something of a contradiction with regard to notions of decentralisation. Indeed, as we have noted, the national curriculum itself constitutes a highly prescriptive educational format which, in terms of teacher autonomy and professionalization, may be viewed as much for its contribution to state control and surveillance as it is for its perceived educational benefits (see Whitty, 1997a). Sociologists are interested in exploring how these changes get implemented in schools and what effect they have on teachers' working lives.

Ball (1990) focused on the ways in which senior civil servants, inspectors of schools and Secretaries of State for Education moulded the ERA 1988, the aim of which was to reconstitute education under the 'twin bases' of increased central state control on the one hand and 'free market' parental choice on the other. Subsequent research set out to chart the impact of such measures on everyday educational practice. Bowe and Ball (1992), for example, identified ways in which clear managerial tensions emerged in some schools as a direct consequence of New Right policy changes, many of which were centred around notions of fragmentation within the context of teacher/senior manager relations and the development of an 'us and them' institutional sub-culture on the part of teachers (see also Ball, 1994). In this sense, the implementation of the ERA 1988 has meant that teaching as a profession has undergone a number of fundamental changes which collectively, Ball claims, have asserted 'a massive and complex technology of control over teachers' work in all its aspects' (1994: 12). These changes have, as Whitty points out, brought with them a host of new demands, pressures and responsibilities:

Classroom teachers face a number of new pressures – increased workloads, attempts to use them more flexibly to counter the effects of budget restrictions, performance-related pay and the substitution of full-time, permanent, qualified staff by part-time, temporary, less-qualified and less-experienced (and therefore less-expensive) alternatives. (1997a: 305)

Some of these concerns were explicitly born out in the feelings of the 88 teachers interviewed during a research project set up by Pollard and his associates (1994) which was designed to examine the impact of the ERA at Key Stage 1 in infant schools in England and Wales where the national curriculum was first implemented. The overall findings of this project suggested that the teachers concerned sensed a severe lack of autonomy and certainty with regard to the implementation of educational reform. Pollard and his colleagues asked about how teachers occupational roles had changed as a result of the national curriculum and assessment. Many of those interviewed felt very negative about their experiences of educational change, as the following quotation indicates:

I'm just more stressed now. I feel pulled in different directions and I feel the need to fulfil attainment targets and to cover the core subjects as a constant unspoken pressure. The relaxed atmosphere I used to have in my class has gone. I can't spend so much time with individual children and I don't feel able to respond in a spontaneous way to some initiative introduced by the children. I no longer have the luxury of being responsive and creative. (Pollard *et al.*, 1994: 85)

While some teachers felt more secure in the knowledge that a standardised curriculum format was in place as a consequence of the ERA (1988), such views were in a minority with many regarding the national curriculum as something which promoted feelings of professional loss in terms of autonomy in pedagogic (teaching) decision making (see also Whitty, 1997a). The different responses of teachers to the greater surveillance and examination of their working lives were brought together using five concepts: compliance, incorporation, mediation, resistance and retreatism. These were defined as follows:

- *Compliance*: acceptance of the imposed changes and adjustment of teachers' professional ideology accordingly so that greater control is perceived as acceptable, or even desirable
- *Incorporation*: appearing to accept the imposed changes but incorporating them into existing modes of working, so that existing methods are adapted rather than changed and the effect of change is considerably different from that intended
- *Mediation*: taking active control of the changes and responding to them in a creative, possibly selective, way

- *Retreatism*: submission to the imposed changes without any change from professional ideology, leading to deep-rooted feelings of resentment, demoralisation and alienation
- *Resistance*: resistance to the imposed changes in the hope that the sanctions available to enforce them will not be sufficiently powerful to make this impossible (Pollard *et al.*, 1994: 100).

While some teachers acted as mediators by taking ownership and control of innovations and trying to use them to develop new forms of practice in peda-gogy and assessment, others were involved in retreatism by taking early retirement or some other action, the most common response being 'incorpo-ration'. In spite of the negative feelings aired, resistance, in the form of refusal to implement the national curriculum or assessment, was found to be virtually non-existent. Such evidence clearly illustrates the difficulty with which some teachers in England and Wales have adapted to the demands of the ERA (1988) and its aftermath. This situation has been exacerbated by the fact that schools have also had to contend with continued policy modifica-tions along the way, some of which have come about as a consequence of governmental change.

The lasting impact of the 1988 reforms can be seen in the fact that Labour politicians abandoned their previous policy of developing a common, comprehensive education for everyone and adopted the 'New Right' language of testing, educational standards and parental involvement. More recent educational initiatives from Labour politicians have, for example, stipulated a rationalization of the national curriculum to facilitate improved numeracy and literacy standards (Qualifications and Curriculum Authority, 1998). Likewise, a more prescriptive curricular format has been put forward for the training of teachers in order to raise pupil performance in schools with early dismissals for failing teachers (DfE, 1998). While these changes may be viewed in terms of the ongoing battle to socialize and educate children on egalitarian grounds, they might also be interpreted as a further contradiction to the deregulation rhetoric emanating from state agencies in Britain. Such instances of contra-diction are not confined to the implementation of policy or the practicalities of educational delivery. They also exist in and around current theoretical inter-pretations of the changes, particularly the debate about modernity and post-modernity. On the one hand, images of diversity, choice, fragmentation and plurality appear to favour a postmodern interpretation, displacing what Whitty (1997b: 123) has termed the 'oppressive uniformity' of modernist thinking within educational spheres. On the other hand, they can be seen as a further twist in the longstanding 'modernist' tale of class, deprivation and educational disadvantage. As Whitty observes:

> Rather than benefiting the urban poor, as many of the advocates of quasi-market systems of public education claim... the emphasis on parental choice and school

autonomy in recent reforms seems to be further disadvantaging the disadvantaged. It is certainly increasing the differences between popular and less popular schools on a linear scale – reinforcing a vertical hierarchy of schooling types rather than providing the promised horizontal diversity. (1997b: 124)

Of course, in reality, it will be some time before such theoretical postulations can be confirmed or dismissed by sociologists of education, and a number of years before the consequences of more recent educational policy measures can be fully observed and interpreted. Needless to say, it will be issues like these which will dominate sociological analyses of educational developments into the new millennium.

Further Reading

Ball, S.J. *Policy Making and Education*, London, Routledge, 1990. A major study in the tradition of 'policy sociology' which raises key issues in terms of the impact of the ERA (1988).

Halsey, A.H., Lauder, H., Brown, P. and Stuart Wells, A. *Education: Culture, Economy, Society*, Oxford, Oxford University Press, 1997. This text provides an up-to-date and global compilation of various themes and perspectives within the sociology of education.

Mac an Ghaill, M. *The Making of Men: Masculinities, Sexualities and Schooling*, Buckingham, Open University Press, 1994. An engaging account of the complexities of male identities and the role schools play in the transformation of boys to men.

Foster, P., Gomm, P. and Hammersley, M. *Constructing Educational Inequality*, London, Falmer Press, 1996. A challenging and critical review of much of the research carried out in the sociology of education in the past half century.

Usher, R. and Edwards, R. *Postmodernism and Education*, London, Routledge, 1994. An accessible text which attempts to describe, explain and analyse education in relation to postmodern thought.

10

Work and Organizations

Glenn Morgan

Contemporary societies are dominated by the twin imperatives of work and organization. Our social and economic system revolves around the production of goods and services within organizations. This chapter aims to examine the relationship between work and organizations and social transformation, from classical sociologists' attempts to understand the impact of industrialization to contemporary sociologists' analyses of the effects of new technological developments and the opening of global markets. Changes in work and organization have important implications for power relations, patterns of inequality and the question of globalization. This chapter should help you understand:

- The centrality of changes in work and organizations in the transition from traditional to modern society.

- Classical sociologists' interpretation of industrialization and social change

- What is meant by Fordism and sociological interpretations of the 'Fordist era'

- The changes in contemporary societies giving rise to 'post-Fordism'

- Recent developments in economic sociology

CONCEPTS

industrialism ▪ industrialization ▪ division of labour

bureaucracy ▪ markets ▪ Fordism ▪ Post-Fordism

global commodity chain

Introduction

As consumers and citizens, we rely on private and public sector organizations to provide us with material goods such as food, clothing and housing as well as services such as education, leisure, health care, credit, and protection from crime. As workers, we rely on the existence of organizations to provide us with the income that will enable us to pay for goods and services. For people living in industrialized and urbanized societies, their lives consist of interacting continuously with organizations in order to sustain their identities as workers, citizens, consumers, parents, students and so on.

It does not take a great deal of historical understanding or sociological imagination to realize that the world was not always like this, and indeed, that many parts of the world still do not match this model. Education, the subject of the previous chapter, can provide an example of this change. In Britain, over 30 per cent of the age cohort now attend university and most people stay in some form of education until they are 18. Sixty years ago, the standard age of leaving school was 13 and the numbers who continued through to university were nearer 3 per cent. One hundred and sixty years ago, there was very little schooling of any sort for the majority of the population, most of whom would be working in factories, mines or agriculture by the time they were 7 or 8 years old. For the great majority of the population, there were no special organizations known as schools, colleges or universities. What they learnt, they learnt from their families and friends in the local settings where they lived and worked. These conditions still exist in parts of Africa, Asia and Latin America. Education to university level is confined to the élite and wealthy, while the majority receive only basic instruction, gaining most of their knowledge and understanding of the world from friends and families passing on oral traditions.

The world in which we live has been transformed by the growth of formal organizations. If we are to understand that world, we need to be able to analyse the roles which organizations play, how they are structured and how that affects the ways in which people live and work. These issues were central to the concerns of the early sociologists as they sought to define the nature of the new societies which were emerging from the impact of industrialism, urbanism and the ideas of the Enlightenment. Their writings show a commitment to the integrated analysis of social change in which work and organizations are a central element. This approach has been developed further through the twentieth century as societies and economies have undergone further changes. The chapter is designed to introduce students to these issues. In the first section, I discuss how the classical sociologists conceptualized work and organizations in the context of social transformation. I then describe how these ideas were further developed in the 1950s and 60s as sociologists sought to understand how western societies appeared to have overcome the class conflicts and social instabilities which seemed endemic in earlier periods of industrialization. However, the relative stability of these years was over-taken again from the 1970s onwards with what appeared to be a new set of changes and uncertainties in the world of work and organizations. The final section examines the changing theoretical framework which is now evolving to take account of this process.

The Rise of Industrial Societies: Work and Organization in the Classical Sociologists

Changes in work and organizations were central to the transformation of western European societies over the course of the nineteenth century. At the start of the century, most of the population were working on the land and living in small rural communities. The notion of work as a distinct sphere of activity which took place outside the home and in a social context distinctive from that of family was only just beginning to emerge in both country and town (see Laslett, 1965; Pahl, 1988). By the end of the century, there had been a major shift away from the land and the country to the factory and the town. This shift involved not just the development of manufacturing and the emergence of an industrial working class but also the emergence of new functions for the state, such as education, the maintenance of professional armies, the collection of taxes and customs duties and the regulation of conditions in workplaces and public spaces (Mann, 1993). Although these shifts proceeded at a different pace and in a different manner in different European societies, there was a common sense of transformation in Europe that was affecting all the great powers from Britain in the west to Imperial Russia in the east. This sense of a set of forces overwhelming national differences was frequently conceptualized in dualistic terms as a shift from one set of social principles to another; for Marx, it was from feudalism to capitalism; for Durkheim, it was from a mechanical solidarity of similarity to an organic solidarity of interdependence; and for Weber it was from traditional authority structures to bureaucratic structures geared around the efficient pursuit of organizational goals.

These dualisms and the way in which they were conceptualized by the classical sociologists captured distinctive aspects in the process of industrialization and its impact on work and organizations (Giddens, 1971). Three aspects were of crucial importance: the division of labour, new forms of power and inequality and the dynamics of modern markets. This section will consider each of them.

The Division of Labour

The classical sociologists were concerned with how the social transformations they observed affected the division of labour; that is, the differentiation of tasks involved in the production of goods and services. In pre-modern societies, the division of labour tended to be limited. Within peasant economies, most aspects of social life were co-ordinated through the co-operative activity of the family members. Family relations also permeated the political order in such systems and ties based upon family or 'proto-family' clientelistic relationships constituted key principles of political ordering. Modern societies are characterized by a vast extension in the division of labour which generally separates the informal processes of household work from the processes of the formal economy where wages are earned (Rattansi, 1982). As well as the process of economic reproduction being taken out of the household, functions such as education, health care, welfare and leisure become separated from the family and concentrated in specialized organizations.

The differentiation of social functions leads to more specialized organizations which require specialist workers. Specialization within the organization can have two distinct effects. It can be a mechanism for creating highly skilled employees for whom specialization requires a high level of knowledge and understanding of the work context. It can also be a mechanism for creating extremely fragmented tasks that require only unskilled workers to fill them. Specialization and differentiation inevitably lead to increased problems of integration and co-ordination both within the organization and across society as a whole. This in turn leads to a further extension in the role of bureaucracy and management as a central means for controlling and co-ordinating the disintegrating effects of complexity and differentiation. Thus, as Durkheim (1893/1984) recognized, the enhanced division of labour potentially creates greater interdependence among people while also creating greater individualization and therefore fragmentation.

Technology is an essential element in this process. Technology embodies human knowledge and human intentions adapted to what it is possible to think and do in certain periods of time. Once certain forms of technology become established, they create trajectories of development which encourage the refinement and improvement of practices and processes around the basic model. The classical sociologists saw that technology was changing the limits of what it was possible for societies to produce. However, they also realized that this implied changes in the nature of social relationships between owners, managers and workers as well as between different groups in the workforce. The increasing importance of specialized organizations, the potential fragmentation of tasks within organizations, the necessity for processes of co-ordination and control through management and bureaucracy and the impact of technology were essential parts of the changing social division of labour in the nineteenth century.

Power and Inequality

The second set of key issues revolves around power and inequality in the division of labour. For the classical sociologists, these processes involved conflicts and tensions as different groups within society sought to adapt and respond to industrialism. The types of inequality between the various ranks in feudal society were transformed as societies industrialized. The main routes to power and prestige were increasingly determined by the dynamics of the industrial and financial sectors of the economy. The new division of labour was necessarily shaping a more complex structure of power and inequality. In the nineteenth century, the classical sociologists saw mostly deepening and increasingly visible divisions within society. In the new urban areas, those dependent on paid employment were crowded together in unhealthy and insanitary conditions. The sort of employment which they could get was often short term, casual, poorly paid and frequently dangerous. The struggle to overcome these effects was often led by male trade unionists from the skilled crafts and middle-class reformers for whom a decent standard of living also implied adherence to a model of family life in which the woman stayed at home and the man worked in the paid sector of employment. Although many women continued to take on paid employment, this often remained casual and poorly paid and their dependence and subordination to men was institutionalized within the emergent industrial system. Even for male workers outside the skilled crafts or those sectors such as mining, dockwork (where spatial proximity helped induce collective consciousness), trade unionism was not well developed in most countries until the twentieth century. Thus inequalities within the working class, that is, between male workers in different sectors of the economy and between male and female workers as a whole were significant and continuously militated against collective political or social action. The broader inequalities which existed between the entirety of this class and the other groups in society were often less significant than these intra-class differences.

Industrialization generally involved a transformation in the nature of the rich, from a group predominantly based on landed power to one based on ownership and control of industrial and financial resources (Scott, 1982). Whereas feudal society was theoretically based on a system of reciprocal obligations and duties, industrialism tended to release the rich from this sense of obligation in the name of the market and individual responsibility. Thus at the same time as the differences between rich and poor became clearer, so the willingness of the rich to recognize any obligations to the poor tended to decrease (although the extent and nature of employer paternalism varied across and within European societies with important implications for the nature of the social order, see for example Bendix, 1956; Moore, 1966). Maintaining social order in the factory and in the cities in the light of the changing nature of inequality led to a range of responses from states and employers.

The classical sociologists took different attitudes towards these processes and their long-term impact. The depth and visibility of inequality in industrial systems gave Marx cause for optimism that this would lead to working-class political action and the eventual overthrow of capitalism. For Durkheim, inequality was the impetus for social reform led by the state and professional groups in order to create a greater organic solidarity. Weber had a darker and more complex vision in which the quest for amelioration of inequality through socialism would not necessarily lead to greater freedom but rather accelerate the trend towards the 'iron cage of bureaucracy' trapping individuals more tightly in its grasp. While they might differ about diagnosis and prognosis, the classical sociologists shared a concern with understanding how power and inequality were being reshaped under industrialism.

The Market

Central to the dynamic changes in the division of labour and structures of power and inequality was the role of the market; that is, an arena where people freely exchange commodities usually for money. The classical sociologists recognized that market relations embodied complex and sometimes contradictory forces. On the one hand, markets operate on the basis of individual choice – the freedom to buy and sell goods, services, land, labour power. On the other hand, people may lose freedom in the sense that markets cannot work unless there is a category of the population who have no choice other than to sell their labour power. This means that they must have been stripped of the ability to produce their own means of subsistence, for example by maintaining a plot of land, and forced to enter the money economy. Nor can markets work if there are traditional or legally based restrictions on what can be bought on the market, how goods and services may be produced and how they may be priced. Traditional societies have often involved a range of proscriptions over market-type relations. For example, the idea that one's labour belonged to oneself and could therefore be sold voluntarily on the market only established itself gradually from the sixteenth century onwards. In feudal systems, the serf was the property of the lord who had first call on the labour of his vassal. The right of the serf to move parishes was severely proscribed and considered a crime. There was no right to sell one's labour to another since it belonged not to the serf but to the lord. Selling it to another was therefore selling something one did not own and equivalent to stealing. Even the right to consume was not based simply on money. Sumptuary laws were common in feudal societies. These laws stated who could and could not wear certain types of clothing, usually furs and other signs of rank and status.

Market societies are based on the formal abolition of these restrictions. Property becomes defined from the point of view of the individual owner who can sell land, labour and other goods under market conditions and not subject to traditional proscriptions. Similarly, in formal terms, it is possible to buy anything legal on the market without any restrictions. The idea that anything can in theory be traded on the market becomes corrosive of traditional social relationships. What and how it is actually 'morally' acceptable to buy and sell is rather different from the theory. Even advanced capitalist societies possess diffuse and complex forms of social relationship which define what it is morally acceptable to sell (Thompson, 1968; Zelizer, 1994), leading to frequent agonized debates either about particular issues, such as whether or not it is right that people should be able to buy private health care or education? The formal abolition of these restrictions does not mean that the expectations or obligations disappear as easily. Even in the sphere of wage labour, debate continues as to what is being sold. The argument about how much effort and commitment is purchased by the employer in return for the wage continues to rage (see for example Kunda, 1992). Workers and managers often seek to create obligations and duties about who can do what task (Bendix, 1956; Fox, 1985).

Nevertheless, markets introduced a dynamism into social and economic relations that had not been there previously. Marx referred to the bourgeoisie as the most revolutionary class in history because in spreading market relations, it undermined all traditional systems of social order. Durkheim viewed the market and individualism as closely interlinked. The decline of traditional societies wiped away the limited horizons which people previously had, leaving them with no clear sense of their identity. The sense of meaningless which Durkheim described as 'anomie', or over-developed individualism, undermined stable social order. He therefore looked for ways in which new codes could be created to settle people in their social position and avoid conflict and disorder. Weber, in contrast, feared a society in which market rationality increasingly took over and left no room for individuals.

Social Transformations, Work and Organizations in the Classical Sociologists

In summary, the classical sociologists looked at work and organizations through the lens of their interest in the broader process of social transformation that was occurring in nineteenth-century Europe. This led them to identify aspects of the new order which were common and shared across Europe. The extension of the social division of labour and its embodiment in new forms of organization and technology, the struggle over power and inequality played out within the work setting and the dynamics of the market distinguished nineteenth-century Europe from its predecessors. Yet these authors were also convinced that they were living through a process that had not by any means reached its end-point. For Marx, this was only a stage en route to proletarian revolution, the overthrow of capitalism and the establishment of socialism. In Weber, the advance of the 'iron cage' of industrial bureaucratic rationality was likely, but not inevitable. There may be new social movements based on inspirational charismatic leadership where old ideals may be reborn, or society may solidify into 'mechanised petrifaction'. In Durkheim, the transition from mechanical to organic solidarity was in danger of creating anomie, a situation where individuals were left without values and meaning. Societies needed to develop intermediary institutions that would provide this framework, thereby allowing individualism to flourish without becoming self-destructive egoism.

For these authors, the study of work and organizations was part of their wider understanding of how societies were being transformed. It was therefore concerned essentially with processes of change and how processes inside the organization interacted, reproduced and changed the wider social context. As a result, they sought to identify the essential elements of this transformation in the division of labour, power and inequality and market dynamics. In doing so, they tended to emphasize the homogeneity of the processes which they identified. National contexts might speed up or slow down these processes but this was of marginal interest compared to the sense that this was going to happen everywhere eventually. 'De te fabula narratur' ('About you, the story is told') Marx wrote in the Preface to the first German edition of *Capital*, warning the rest of the world that his account of the dynamics of capitalism in Britain described what was going to happen to them in the future – 'the country that is more developed industrially only shows to the less developed, the image of its own future' (Marx, 1970: 9).

Approaches to Work and Organizations in the Fordist Era

By the middle decades of the twentieth century, industrial capitalism had been established for over 100 years across most of western Europe and the USA. War and economic depression had dominated the politics of the twentieth century up to the 1950s, reinforcing some of the warnings of the classical sociologists about the divisive impact of industrialism. However, during the 1950s, it appeared as if the system was at last achieving some sort of stability. Real incomes began to rise in the western economies, unemployment fell, the scope of welfare services, such as health and education, as well as unemployment and pension benefits were widened. Commentators began to refer to the 'affluent society', the 'welfare state' and 'the end of ideology'.

Sociologists at the time responded in a variety of ways to these changes. In the USA, which was by far the most successful of the capitalist economies, there was a widespread sense that the conflicts of the past had been overcome and society was now entering a phase of relative industrial peace. The sociological theory of structural functionalism, described in Chapter 3, was a product of this way of thinking with its emphasis on stability and consensual values. The idea of 'industrialism' as a system of production which relied on large firms using increasingly advanced technologies with a workforce which was generally well paid and co-operative was propounded, as we saw in Chapter 5, as representing the end of class-based politics. The authors of one of the most famous texts of the era even went so far as to suggest that industrialism would force a convergence in political and social structures across not only western societies but also those in the Soviet bloc (Kerr *et al.*, 1973).

Other authors were more sceptical. Marxists continued to argue that there remained fundamental class conflicts in capitalist societies. While some argued that what had occurred was an ideological blinkering of the working class, others challenged the actual premises of the argument. They noted that there remained high levels of industrial conflict, sometimes visible and formal (in strikes and other types of dispute) and sometimes invisible in absenteeism and 'industrial sabotage' (Hyman, 1975). Weberian sociologists, however, tended to be more cautious about what was happening; in the most widely quoted study of the period in Britain, 'The Affluent Worker' project, Goldthorpe and colleagues argued that workers had made a pragmatic adjustment to the realities of the assembly line (Goldthorpe *et al.*, 1968). In return for relatively high wages, they would co-operate up to a point with management. However, they maintained the right to argue about what were acceptable conditions of work in the light of the wages which they were offered. Their pragmatic acceptance was also dependent on continued high wages. It was therefore a conditional acceptance of the system for as long as it gave them the resources and time to pursue their interests outside work.

This era was described as *Fordism,* taking its name from the American car manufacturer, Henry Ford, who had developed the world's first mass production car plant. The key characteristics of Fordism revolved around the way in which it resolved the problems of order and control in an unequal society both at the workplace level and more generally in society. At the level of the production system, managerial control was high and workers were relatively deskilled. To make this work, employers had to be able to pay these workers high wages. High wages were viable where firms were making high profits. Firms achieved this in a number of ways. One way was by growing big and using economies of scale to reduce costs. Another was to co-operate with other firms on the limits to competition; in other words, to operate informal price setting cartels. All of this required governments which were willing to co-operate with business by stimulating mass market demand. Trade unions were brought into this process at various levels. Within the firm, they negotiated wages and control. Within the broader social context, they were 'social partners' in varying forms of corporatism (that is, high level agreements between employers, government and the trade unions to compromise over their conflicting demands). Essential to most versions of this corporatism was the creation of a welfare state which offered access to health, education, pensions and other benefits. The expansion of the state sector and state services relied on the maintenance of a taxation base which could supply the revenue. The tax base and the actual material benefits of the system varied across different countries although the basic structure remained similar.

The Fordist structure did not resolve questions of inequality and power in society or in the workplace. Instead, it tended to displace their effects on to either excluded groups or on to society more widely. For example, the Fordist system was built on the model of the male breadwinner dominant within the patriarchal family. Large manufacturing firms employed mainly men in their more well-paid manual jobs. Women found work in part-time or casual employment, while retaining the primary responsibility for children and the home more generally. The welfare state reinforced this by also being built on the presuppositions of the male breadwinner model; most unemployment insurance and pension systems provided few benefits to the pattern of labour market participation experienced by women. Furthermore, the sort of conditions which enabled the Fordist compromises were not possible in many more competitive sectors of the economy, such as small manufacturing firms, the retail and personal service sectors where wages and benefits tended to be low and work was often part time and temporary. As well as women workers (and some white male workers), migrants from South East Asia, the Caribbean, eastern Europe and Africa tended to congregate in these jobs. This reflected a broader process within the Fordist system which was the dependence on cheap raw materials (most obviously oil) and food from the non-developed part of the world. Fordism's expansion was on the basis of the subordination of most of the rest of the world to its requirements. This went along with a total disregard for the ecological consequences of the mass production system.

Post-Fordism and the End of Organized Capitalism?

From the 1970s onwards economic crises in the west, new technologies and the opening of world markets made it increasingly difficult to sustain the foundations of Fordism, giving rise to an emerging model of work and organizations described somewhat unoriginally as post-Fordism (Lash and Urry, 1987). In order to understand this, we can return to the previous themes of the classical sociologists.

The Division of Labour

The transformation of the 1980s and 90s have been centrally about the division of labour both within and across firms and across societies. Research has identified a number of important changes in the nature of work. First, the application of new information technology to manufacturing and service processes has changed the distribution of labour within organizations. Large numbers of routine manual, clerical and managerial jobs have been lost as control and co-ordination functions have been embedded in technology. The result has been reductions in the number of managerial levels and increases in the amount of skill required by key workers. This process has also led to a growing differentiation between the core workers within the firm and the peripheral workers. The latter may be on short-term, part-time or temporary contracts. As Castells says:

> The traditional form of work, based on full-time employment, clear-cut occupational assignments and a career pattern over the lifecycle is being slowly but surely eroded away. (Castells, 1996: 268)

These changes are associated with an increased technological flexibility in the production process which enables more rapid changes in products and processes in response to market pressures.

Table 10.1   Characteristics of Fordism

Level of analysis	Key features
Labour process	Mass production: assembly lines; semi-skilled workers
Mode of macro-economic growth	Based on economies of scale and investment in mass production systems: rising wages and increased mass demand
Social mode of economic regulation	State involvement in (a) managing conflicts between labour and capital (b) managing economic growth through Keynesianism (c) maintaining welfare system
General pattern of social organization	Based on consumption of standardized products: predicated on stable nuclear families with male heads of household; social order managed by centralized bureaucratic state.

Source: Adapted from Jessop 1994.

The restructuring process within the firm has led to changes in the relationships between firms. In the Fordist era, large firms tended to do everything in-house. However, as the pressure has increased on firms to cut costs, there has been a tendency to buy goods and services in from the outside. Outside contractors can be squeezed by their dependence on the large firm and thereby forced to hold down wages or reduce employment benefits. This process may occur in relatively low skilled areas such as catering and cleaning as well as in the production of components for manufacturing systems. It may also have a spatial dimension with firms purchasing from overseas where wages are low and controls on work conditions non-existent.

These processes are subject to diverse interpretations of their significance. On the one hand, some authors argue that these changes represent the end of mass production and, with it, the end of the oppressive conditions of large-scale hierarchical organizations peopled by semi-skilled workers subjected to close supervision and control. In this context, the changing nature of work and organizations is also perceived to open up new possibilities for political and social movements which will reduce inequalities inside and outside the workplace. This is generally associated with those approaches that emphasize the growing importance of co-operative networks for economic production.

The changing division of labour between firms has reflected a growing interest in patterns of co-operation between firms and their implications for social and political order and competition. Sabel and Zeitlin (1997) have argued that there are two broad types of industrial production which have co-existed for some time. The first is the Fordist mass production system based on big firms, high differentiation between managers and workers accompanied by high levels of inequality and detailed control systems over workers. The second is the form which arises from pre-industrial traditions of craft work. This is generally based on small and medium-sized firms, with low levels of differentiation and inequality between managers and workers. This tradition relies on high levels of skilled worker input to the production process in order to develop high-quality outputs. It is usually locally based with high levels of co-operation between local governmental institutions (for example training) and firms, as well as high levels of co-operation between firms. This latter model which is referred to as 'flexible specialization' can be identified in various specific locations, usually described as 'industrial districts' to reflect their specialization in a particular sector of industry. For example, in Italy, particular towns and regions specialize in specific sectors such as ceramics in Sassuolo, knitwear in Modena, wool textiles in Prato. Within these local networks, close inter-firm relations interact with high levels of specialization and skill to produce a pressure towards continuous process and product innovation (Langlois and Robertson, 1995) that is particularly important in current competitive conditions. This leads some authors to suggest that as economic competition favours industrial districts and their ability to produce high-quality outputs, flexible specialization as a mode of organizing production will become common (see Piore and Sabel, 1984; Sabel and Zeitlin, 1997), thus in practice leading to a reduction in inequalities and a greater emphasis on co-operation within and between firms. From this perspective, industrial districts and the networks of co-operation within them give rise to higher levels of social co-operation, less use of centralized authority structures and narrower spreads of inequality in wealth and income. They are generally based on strong local political institutions which take an active role in shaping economic life. This approach offers an optimistic view of the future for organizations and work, based on the gradual decline of hierarchy, control and inequality.

An alternative approach argues that the localism of industrial districts and firms is embedded within a larger structure, dominated by multinational corporations. From this perspective, the outputs of industrial districts are generally merely inputs to a more complex chain of production organized by multinationals. Multinational corporations are the main mechanism through which this is achieved as they increasingly locate production facilities around the world according to calculations about advantages deriving from labour costs, labour discipline, labour skills, access to local markets, provision of tax breaks and incentives, and access to locally specific knowledge and networks. Multinational economic co-ordination also occurs through what Gereffi has termed 'global commodity chains' (Gereffi and Korzeniewicz, 1994; Gereffi, 1995; see also Dicken, 1998). This concept describes how firms produce goods and services by co-ordinating the provision of the various elements that go to make up the product from conception and design through to manufacture to distribution and sale. Each of these elements may be produced in-house or purchased from outside. In either case, the elements may come from the home base or from another part of the world. As Gereffi and others have shown, more and more industries are now operating and controlling commodity chains which are global in their scope and orientation (see the articles in Gereffi and Korzeniewicz, 1994; also Dicken, 1998, Chs. 9–12). What this results in is a system where rich western consumers purchase from their high-street stores such as Gap, Toys R Us and Sportshoes Unlimited products such as clothes, toys, and trainers, which are produced in countries such as China, Vietnam and India with low wages, child labour, no trade union rights, and poorly monitored health and safety or welfare systems. From this perspective, therefore, multinationals reproduce and reinforce global inequalities. Their actions may be influenced by public opinion or state regulation but their ability to shift production around the world makes this influence limited. The result is that key economic decisions are being made further and further away from the people most directly affected. Even democratic nation states find it hard to influence the decisions of these multinationals which are basically reached behind closed doors according to a logic of capital accumulation that has little to do with social welfare and are characterized by high levels of inequality between their top directors and workers in far-flung subsidiaries. They are also not tied to local political systems and move their investment according to a logic of capital accumulation that has little to do with social welfare.

It has been argued that while these alternative models are useful for high-lighting the issues, they do not grasp the complexity of the different forms of production, work and organization that exist in practice. In this context Boyer and Durand (1997) propose a more complex typology which identifies a number of different routes out of Fordism which have distinct implications for work, organizations and patterns of social and economic inequality.

Flexible specialization

Workers exert control over machines and potential compromises between capital and labour occur at the level of the company or the local labour market (for example the industrial district).

Toyotaism

This 'reorganises production, maintenance and management tasks so that operators are responsible for controlling production equipment, rather than the reverse, with a tight set of incentives at the company level inducing worker commitment'.

Uddevallaism

This is named after the Swedish car factory which rejected the traditional Fordist assembly line and became a symbol of the Scandinavian 'work humanisation' movement; it 'combines the most radical reorganisation of the division of labour (elimination of the assembly line, fixed station assembly and greatly extended cycle times) with a capital–labour compromise situated at the national level (centralized negotiations over wages, training and work time)'.

Market-pushed neo-Fordism

Based on the introduction of new technologies to impose more control by machines of workers – workers are forced to accept changes for fear of unemployment.

Corporate-pushed neo-Fordism

Similar to the previous model but based on compromise between capital and labour within the company or sector.

Social democratic neo-Fordism

Based on a nationwide compromise between capital and labour which provides the framework within which new technologies and restructuring at the firm level is implemented.

Within this framework, particular national contexts have evolved specific forms of Fordism. While the crisis of this production model is general, the nature of the changes and the trajectories after Fordism will differ. There is a path dependence created by national institutional features which limits the opportunities available to particular countries (see for example the country studies in Whitley, 1992; Crouch and Streeck, 1997; also Hollingsworth and Boyer, 1997). This also implies that the impact on inequality of these various routes will also be different. Thus Boyer and Durand are implicitly criticizing those authors who believe that globalization undermines the capacity of national governments or social actors to take decisions which will affect the nature and distribution of inequality in a society (see also Weiss, 1998).

Table 10.2 Routes out of Fordism

Types of post-Fordism	Control of technology at firm level	Role of the market
Flexible Specialization	High level of control by skilled workers	Mediated at local level by collective institutions e.g. for training
Toyotaism (from the Japanese model)	Operators responsible for continuous production improvement	Mediated by long-term and close linkages with suppliers
Uddevallism (from the Swedish model)	Job rotation and teamwork	Bargaining over wages and conditions conducted at national level
Social Democratic Fordism	Management control of technology and work process but role of trade unions accepted	State continues to provide benefits to workers to mediate market pressures
Corporate-pushed Fordism	Management control of technology but recognition of importance of core workers	Core workers in firms protected from market pressures
Market-pushed neo-Fordism	Replacement of labour by technology predominant thrust	Unrestricted market forces

Source: Adapted from Boyer and Durand 1997.

Power and Inequality

The second main theme identified in the classical sociologists was the inter-relationship between work and organizations and structures of power and inequality. In the modern transformation which has been described, the impact on power and inequality is also of central significance. I will examine this in four contexts; within firms, between firms, between those in employment and those out of employment and finally between societies as a whole (the international dimension of inequality).

First, the changing nature of work and organizations is impacting on power and inequality within firms. The basic distinction which has already been described is between those employees who constitute the core workforce and those who constitute peripheral workers. The core workforce are those with high levels of managerial, professional and technical skills whose continued commitment to the organization is necessary for its success. This group will generally receive high levels of material rewards, such as income and fringe benefits linked to performance outcomes. Organizations have reduced the absolute numbers of their employees which can be counted as core as they have got rid of layers of management and administration. Core employees are often rewarded through performance-related pay and share options. The distribution of these rewards tends to be increasingly skewed with senior management in particular benefiting, thus increasing levels of inequality within the firm, even within the core workforce. Castells notes US research which indicates that while the 'median wage for men working full-time has fallen from $34,048 in 1973 to $30,407 in 1993, the earnings of the top 20 per cent grew steadily and real per capita GDP rose 29 per cent' (Castells, 1996: 275).

There is a great deal of evidence that shows that this division between core and peripheral workers reinforces and reproduces existing social divisions. Women are far more likely than men to be in part-time employment or on short-term contracts and constitute the great bulk of the peripheral work-force. In the UK, the 1993 Labour Force Survey found that 85 per cent of part-time workers were women. The young and the elderly also find it more difficult to gain positions in the core workforce as do members of ethnic minorities. The core workforce within organizations is still predominantly white and male at all levels.

Second, the distinction between core and periphery is also reproduced between certain sorts of firms. As previously noted, large firms often use small firms as mechanisms for retaining flexibility. When orders are high, large firms may subcontract out to small firms more of their production. When orders are low, subcontractors may find themselves without business. Large firms with networks of suppliers can use their position to squeeze down contract prices and in so doing, force small firms to reduce wages and employment conditions. Subcontracting also reduces the strength and power of trade unions by splitting potential members into smaller units which are geograph-ically and organizationally distinct, thus making union organization and collective bargaining less likely. Thus within the one location, firms which are interdependent in the production chain may be characterized by very different workforces with different wages and employment conditions.

Where subcontracting also crosses national boundaries, as is often the case, the result may be that wages and employment conditions are forced down even further by the use of young female labour and, in some cases, even child labour. As cross-national global commodity chains become more common, differences between levels of wages and rewards within the one commodity chain become dramatic.

Third, the process of restructuring has led to a stripping out of manage-ment and bureaucratic levels as well as a reduction in the number of employees involved in manufacturing and services. As well as specific redun-dancies, entry points into employment have reduced. Young people tend to spend longer in training and searching for paid employment than previously, often going through extended periods of part-time and casual employment before settling into a career position. Women who may have left the labour market in order to have children find it difficult to return to work other than through forms of part-time and temporary employment. Men and women who have been made redundant from declining industries find that they cannot get back into similar types of employment; some may have to face retirement in their early fifties. The restructuring of work reinforces other tendencies of social exclusion, creating an underclass of under-employed people who shift in and out of precarious positions on the periphery of the labour market. Furthermore, as societies seek to reduce welfare expenditure, many of those not in formal employment are pushed back to reliance on either family networks of support or the informal, black economy which may in certain cases shade into illegal activity.

Fourth, the restructuring of work and the development of global commodity chains has complex effects on inequality at the global level. The first basic distinction is between those areas of the world which are integrated within global commodity chains and those which are not. In the main, exclusion from these chains tends to mean exclusion from any access to even a small amount of the benefits of trade and development as well as aid funds. Countries in Africa and Asia which have nothing to sell on world markets are of little interest to governments, international agencies or funding sources until war, terrorism or famine forces them on to the international news agenda. They become trapped in a spiral of decline, unable to access any modern technologies either for production purposes or for health care – Castells refers to these as 'the Black Holes of Informational Capitalism' (Castells, 1998).

Where multinational companies have an interest in a particular area because of its natural resources, its labour or its markets, then there is the potential for a transfer of financial resources, in terms of either cash or production facilities. This transfer has a complex impact on societies (Dicken, 1998). In some societies, this transfer is effectively placed in the hands of a small and corrupt élite which siphons off a substantial share for luxury consumption while maintaining low wages, poor working conditions and high levels of labour discipline. In these circumstances, inequalities within the receiving society tend to increase. As some of the east Asian countries such as the Philippines (during the era of the Marcos presidency) and Indonesia (under Suharto) have found, there is a limit to people's willingness to accept these conditions. Given certain sorts of compromises within the élite of such societies, however, (and, in particular, social constraints on corruption) this transfer may become the basis for a sustained process of development. East Asian societies such as Singapore, Taiwan and Hong Kong show how it is possible to take advantage of these transfers and move from low-skilled assembly work for others up to constructing the whole product and even branding and selling it on one's own behalf (Wade, 1990; Gereffi, 1995; Weiss and Hobson, 1995; Castells, 1998). In these circumstances, there tends to be a wider spreading of the benefits of wealth and the creation of a substantial middle class which helps consolidate the home market. However, this process is frequently accompanied by increased commercial pressure on urban and rural communities, with the consequent deterioration in infrastructures and damage to the ecology of whole areas in the rush to industrialization (see Castells, 1997, for a discussion of these trends and emerging forms of resistance) as well as an over-expansion of lending and investment that can lead to the crisis which hit many east Asian economies in the late 1990s.

The divisions between societies are also powerful motors for the extension of international labour migration. Workers from the developing countries have moved into Europe and North America, through both legal and illegal means. Remittances from these migrants (that is, funds either sent or taken back by workers from their host state) to their home country are massive. Harris notes a number of estimates of the scale of these remittances from a World Bank figure in 1989 of $66 billion to an IMF estimate for 1990 at $33.8 billion. He estimates an average annual remittance of between $700–$1000 per year which for many less-developed countries is a major contributor to foreign exchange and therefore to the purchase of imports (Harris, 1996: 142). These remittances mitigate to a small degree the absolute inequalities between societies but at the expense of both breaking families apart and increasing inequalities within the receiving society. Migrant workers from the developing world generally move into the occupational structure in positions which the indigenous population has rejected although Cohen points out that there are different sorts of what he terms 'diaspora' with different consequences for the inequality and power (R. Cohen, 1997). For example, many east Asian migrants (from China and Korea) into the USA have had sufficient capital to set up small businesses in inner urban areas. Similar processes have occurred among some east Asian communities in the UK.

This restructuring process has seen an increased differentiation in the world division of labour. Patterns of power and inequality across societies have been affected by the actions of multinationals and global economic co-ordination. Divisions between the poorest and the richest societies have increased, as have divisions within some of the poorer societies as the benefits of industrialization are unevenly distributed.

Markets

The opening up of world markets has had a major influence on the processes just described. The Fordist system was based on the ability of the *governments* of nation states to manage demand within their own borders. The sale and purchase of goods across national boundaries was limited by the way in which national governments manipulated tariff barriers and the availability of currencies. Balance of payments crises for individual states arose where purchases from abroad exceeded overseas sales. Governments could respond by reducing internal demand. Where this still failed to work, then the currency could be devalued, discouraging imports and increasing the competitiveness of exports (Van der Wee, 1991; Foreman-Peck, 1995; Panic, 1995). Within national contexts, markets for goods and services could be regulated to achieve broader social and political objectives such as the maintenance of employment and social stability.

Once governments could no longer control their markets in this way, the edifice began to collapse. The impetus to open up national borders came from the desire first to purchase goods at the cheapest price available on the world market and second the desire to borrow capital in larger amounts and at cheaper rates than national financial systems were providing. However, these benefits were at a price, in particular the threat to home industry of loss of markets and the potential instability of currencies, capital flows and investment arising from integration into the world system (see for example Strange, 1986, 1995; also Kapstein, 1994; Stubbs and Underhill, 1994; Morgan, 1997; Underhill, 1997). This also contributed to the crisis of the welfare state as 'the price of welfare' (that is, how much it cost in terms of taxes) became incorporated into the price of commodities. Countries with higher levels of welfare faced the problem of their products being more expensive than those with minimal welfare systems. This has led to efforts at restructuring the welfare state and shifting its focus away from redistribution towards an emphasis on training and what is known as work-fare (that is, making benefits conditional on willingness to participate in training and other job schemes) (Jessop, 1994; Esping-Andersen, 1997).

The ability of governments to control markets has therefore reduced. It has become more difficult to sustain industrial sectors such as mining or agriculture because of their social function. If they cannot adapt to the market, they will go out of existence and the people who work for them will be made dependent on states where welfare budgets are shrinking. The state sector itself is also under threat. Privatization has left most western societies with a vastly reduced public sector and that which is left has often been subjected to 'market testing'. Whole societies have been forced to open their boundaries by the power of international institutions such as the IMF and the World Bank to dictate the terms on which loans can be made available. The consequences of marketization have been dramatic in countries such as Russia where unemployment and the destruction of formal systems of welfare (and even wage payments) have led in many areas to a return to a barter economy and rising mortality and disease levels among the population.

However, there remain differences in how individual countries respond to this process. Boyer's emphasis on the national specificities of production systems discussed earlier (Boyer and Durand, 1997) reflects the concerns of a number of other authors in identifying 'national business systems' (Whitley, 1992) or 'social systems of production' (Hollingsworth and Boyer, 1997). The capacities and capabilities of organizations are shaped by their institutional context. Thus global market pressures are always adapted within local contexts. For example, societies with highly developed capital market systems on the Anglo-American model are more open to global competition than societies based on what is termed 'alliance capitalism' (that is, where ownership is concentrated in interlinked banks and firms who hold shares long term rather than trading them frequently for short-term profit gains; Whitley, 1992; Orru *et al.*, 1997; Scott, 1997). Alliance capitalisms are also usually able to achieve levels of co-operation between firms and the state in terms of running down declining areas of production or developing new capacities (Wade, 1990; Streeck, 1992). For example, in Japan, the Ministry of International Trade and Industry (MITI) has been instrumental in helping and persuading firms to move out of declining industries such as textiles and ship-building and into expanding ones such as electronics and computers (see Johnson, 1982). Similarly, some societies have developed work systems that are based on a highly skilled workforce supported by the education and training system (see Lane, 1989; Streeck, 1992; Sako and Sato, 1997; Storey *et al.*, 1997); such systems seem more capable of adapting to market change and higher consumer expectations than systems based on mass production and Fordism. Thus the ability of Japanese and German car firms to respond to changing consumer tastes (such as for higher quality products, safer cars with lower petrol consumption) in the late 1970s was at least partially due to the fact that workers in these firms were highly trained and skilled in resetting production systems. By contrast, British and US firms took much longer to adapt, partly because workers were less skilled and levels of conflict with management were higher, leading to resistance to change.

Towards the New Economic Sociology

What sort of theory is required to make sense of these changes in work and organizations? There are at least three main ways in which the approach described here differs from that of the classical sociologists and the traditions developed from their work.

Nations, Globalization and Change

The classical sociologists described the nineteenth-century transformation without much acknowledgement that this process could only be enacted through specific national contexts which in turn would shape the outcome.

The sort of dualistic thinking which the classical sociologists used (for example the contrast between feudalism and capitalism in Marx, between mechanical and organic solidarity in Durkheim, between traditional and bureaucratic authority in Weber) tended to conceal the issue of *national* differences. However, many sociologists place these national differences at the centre of analysis. It is precisely in the strength of the empirical research which can now connect national systems of organization and work to deeply embedded aspects of the institutional order that most progress is being made within this new economic sociology (Whitley and Kristensen, 1996, 1997; Boyer and Durand, 1997; Crouch and Streeck, 1997; Hollingsworth and Boyer, 1997).

Even when the degree of inter-connection within nation states and across them increases as it has done over the last twenty years, the process of globalization which occurs is not an abolition of the significance of space and territory but its incorporation into a broader set of social relationships (Amin and Thrift, 1995). Smith and Meiskins (1995) identify this in terms of a triple effect. There is the national context of organizations, there is the context of the international capitalist system and the role of particular firms and territories within that context and finally there is the overall global political order in which certain nation states are dominant and set rules for others to follow either through the use of explicit military force or through informal economic power (for a discussion of globalization see Chapter 15). The new economic sociology is concerned with understanding the interaction between these national and international forces (Dicken, 1998). In this respect, it goes beyond the classical sociologists.

Markets as Social Constructs

The classical sociologists tended to assume that there were certain economic processes which could be defined as beyond and outside human intentionality which acted as determinants of social action. In this respect, they underestimated the importance of social processes in determining the nature and extent of the economy. The new economic sociology is not simply concerned to show how institutions 'affect' economic processes but rather how the two are integrally connected. For example, there has traditionally been a tendency to treat economic performance as a given, while the internal aspects of the organization can be considered as social processes, the consequences of those actions become goods and services on markets where outcomes are determined by relative efficiencies. However, markets themselves are socially constructed in many different ways. We can observe this for example in the way in which the public sector has been reconstructed over the last two decades. For example, in Britain under successive Conservative governments, an 'internal market' was constructed in the National Health Service, whereby hospitals and doctors were given budgets to buy and sell treatments which previously were provided as of right (see Ferlie *et al.*, 1996 for a discussion of these changes). The 'rules' of this market have been constructed by politicians and others seeking to implement policy objectives through creating a market which works in a particular sort of way (see Morgan and Engwall, 1999 for further examples). Even within what are seen as the traditional competitive industries, there are rules which determine who can compete and what they are trying to achieve. Smith's (1990) analysis of auctions shows how what appears to be a pure market process is in fact constructed through participants' use of shared understandings and rules of behaviour about who can bid what in particular contexts. In traditional economic analysis, the market acts as a self-regulating process, rewarding the efficient and deselecting the inefficient. Increasingly, sociologists are revealing how these processes have to be enacted by social actors, which in turn opens up the market as an arena of power and conflict in which groups struggle to impose their definition of how it should work, who should be considered winners and losers and how participants should benefit from their roles in the market (see Swedberg, 1994; Quack *et al.*, 1999).

Action and Structure

Finally, the new economic sociology is entangled within the preoccupations of sociological theory with the relationship between action and structure which was discussed in Chapter 3. Only Weber of the classical sociologists really explored the ways in which actors shaped structure rather than being shaped by it. In the current period, this is a major preoccupation that defines a range of positions. At one extreme, there are those who emphasize the 'systemic' nature of institutions and organizations which means that it is extremely difficult for actors to influence outcomes. At the other, there are those who point to the ways in which the co-ordinated effort of key groups in a society can lead to change and development. For example, the efforts of certain key nobles to industrialize countries like Japan and Germany in the late nineteenth century were successful because in those societies there was still a great deal of power centralized in and exercised by the landholding aristocracy around the court. Similarly, the industrialization strategies led by the state in South Korea, Taiwan and Singapore worked because these states (for different reasons) were extremely powerful and not subject to significant resistance. Under certain circumstances, élite groups have been able to take control of the state and use its powers to reshape the basic institutions of society towards a new structure. Moreover, this may often relate to the broader international environment in which states are located. The support of the USA in the form of cheap credits, access to open markets without demanding reciprocity, and technology transfer to Japan, South Korea and Taiwan during the Cold War was crucial in enabling them to develop their industrial structure further.

Conclusion

In this chapter, I have argued that the sociology of work and organizations is an integral part of understanding how societies work. In the writings of the classical sociologists, the understanding of work and organizations was part of an attempt to understand how life was being transformed through industrialization. These changes were related to changes in the division of labour, changes in power and inequality and changes in markets. As a result of these changes, new structures of work and organizations were emerging and giving rise to new forms of social order. In this perspective, the sociology of work and organizations is part of the broader sociological agenda about how societies are changing and adapting to processes of industrialization.

This tradition has been re-awakened in part by the sense that the world is currently undergoing a transformation of equivalent significance to that of the nineteenth century. This new set of transformations, which has to do with the establishment of global markets, new forms of technology, the incorporation into the world economy of new areas and the increasing competitiveness of firms within and across nations, is impacting and overturning existing patterns of the division of labour, power and inequality and markets. Yet the response to these upheavals clearly varies across countries. National business contexts create a form of path dependency for institutions and organizations. The aim of research is to understand more about how these dependencies constrain action or encourage it. This approach builds on the classical sociological accounts of transformation in the nineteenth century but with a new appreciation for national and territorial distinctiveness, the social basis of markets and the interaction between action and structure. Much of its research and its theorizing is essential to broader concerns about the nature of social change into the next millennium, and it is impossible to understand issues like class, power, inequality and globalization without referring to the growing literature within the sociology of work and organizations.

Further Reading

Amin, A. (ed.) *Post-Fordism,* Oxford, Blackwell, 1994. An examination of the changing nature of work and organization placed in the context of new forms of politics and culture.

Dicken, P. *Global Shift: Transforming the World Economy,* 3rd edn, London, Chapman, 1998. An examination of how networks, multinational corporations and the state link together in particular industries.

Morgan, G. *Organisations in Society,* London, Macmillan, 1990. A review of the main theories of organization and their links with classical sociological theories and themes.

Thompson, P. and McHugh, D. *Work Organisations: A Critical Introduction,* 2nd edn, London, Macmillan, 1995. A thorough account of the changing geographical and organizational structure of production.

11
Crime and Deviance

David Downes

While criminology is confined to violations of the criminal law, the sociology of deviance has a much wider focus, examining any behaviour perceived as breaking the rules of a social group. Sociologists are not only interested in explaining why deviance occurs, but also why and how some actions are defined as deviant and why and how sanctions are applied to offenders. In this undertaking they draw on a wide range of theoretical perspectives including some of those examined in Chapter 3, such as functionalism, interactionism and Marxism. This chapter aims to explain and illustrate the development of the major sociological approaches to crime and delinquency. It should help you understand:

- The distinction between the sociology of deviance and criminology

- The development of strain theories from the work of Durkheim to the study of delinquent sub-cultures

- Interactionist theory and the focus on social definitions of deviance

- 'Social' and 'situational' control theories and their implications for crime prevention

- Radical deviance theory

CONCEPTS

victim survey ▓ anomie ▓ delinquent sub-culture ▓ moral panic
secondary deviance ▓ critical criminology

Introduction

The term 'deviance' covers the spectrum of socially proscribed behaviour: any form of conduct which elicits social sanctions that may range from mild censure to capital punishment. The attempt to explain and understand not only the 'bad' but the 'mad' and the 'odd' and how they are so designated and controlled constitute the field. Students of deviance have regarded blindness (Scott, 1969), stuttering (Lemert, 1967) and nudity (Douglas, 1977) as within their intellectual domain, although crimes, delinquencies and mental illness are the usual topics of theory and research.

The scope of deviance is thus far wider than that of crime and, as a result, the sociology of deviance differs in several ways from criminology. Most importantly, its subject matter is not defined by what happens to be sanctioned by the criminal law at any time or place. Although all societies prohibit theft and non-governmentally sanctioned violence, there are immense differences between societies, and within the same society over time, in the legal status of forms of sexual conduct, drug use and freedom of expression for example. It is thus analytically preferable to build the realities of flux, diversity and ambiguity into the subject, rather than to opt for the illusion that the criminal law provides the entire basis for inquiry. The criminal law is an essential part of the field, not its foundation. It is social definitions and controls which form the basic unit of analysis in the sociology of deviance, and they are only given legal form under certain conditions.

In practice, the fields of criminology and the sociology of deviance have much in common, and they have often worked to their mutual benefit. For example, victim surveys were originated by criminologists in the 1960s, and became firmly established in the 1980s, as a way of supplementing and testing trends in crime based on the official criminal statistics supplied by the police. They were motivated in part by the claims of some sociologists of deviance that rises in crime based on the police figures were unduly inflated, or even spurious, due to changes in reporting and recording processes. Victim survey data showed, as expected, that much very petty and some quite serious crime went unreported; the upward direction of the trends in the official figures was also confirmed, although at a lesser annual rate of increase (Maguire *et al.*, 1997).

However, despite such overlap, the two approaches remain distinct in principle. Criminologists are mainly preoccupied with highly focused inquiries into particular forms and trends of crime and its control. Sociologists of deviance not only cast their net more widely, but also pursue issues such as how the media selectively portray and convey images of deviance, the connections that may exist between crime, deviance and the political economy and the changing landscape of punishment in institutions and in the community (Cohen, 1985; Garland, 1990).

Sumner (1994) argues that the sociology of deviance came into being to challenge the grounds on which deviance was attributed to some groups rather than others, especially political deviants and other outsiders such as drugtakers. He claims that since that challenge has now been abandoned, the subject can no longer be said to exist. However, this assertion is groundless. The intellectual radicalism of the sociology of deviance resided in asking two sets of questions. First, how are some *behaviours*, and not others, defined as deviant? Second, given those definitions, why and how are some *persons* and not others processed as deviant, and with what consequences? On those two basic issues is built the entire edifice of the field. Since these two fundamental questions remain – and it is difficult to see how they can ever vanish – the sociology of deviance in some form or other will survive and even flourish.

This chapter will focus on how the sociology of deviance has evolved an array of theories to account for crime and delinquency. As these theories stem from intellectual roots which involve conflicting views about human nature and society, it is difficult to see how they can be fused into some overall synthesis. Moreover, 'crime' and 'delinquency' are terms that encompass a vast diversity of behaviours, united only by the common denominator that they are infractions of the criminal law. No one theory can begin to encompass them all. Nevertheless, the justification for attempting to theorize at all is that crime and delinquency are not utterly random and entirely unpredictable phenomena. Insofar as they display certain discernible patterns and forms, they are amenable – at least in principle – to causal explanation and the possibility of understanding the meanings and motivations of those engaged in them. The first section looks at some of these regularities, the following sections look at the main theoretical approaches to deviance and the final section outlines some of the current issues in the field.

Some Regularities That Any Theory Must Fit

1. Crime rates have risen strikingly since the mid-1950s in virtually all societies. In Britain, there has been a tenfold increase in the crime rates over the past 40 years, although they levelled out in the 1980s, and fell in the USA in the 1990s. After 1981 victim surveys also showed a lesser but still marked rate of increase. This rise and rise of crime has not only presented the criminal justice system with immense logistical problems, it also confounded the simple belief that greater prosperity and welfare provision would *reduce* crime, which social reformers had argued was mainly due to mass poverty.

2. Offending behaviour is far more common among some groups than others. Males commit several times more crime than females and the young more than the old. Socio-economic deprivation is also an important risk factor for offending and anti-social behaviour. However, low family income, poor housing and large family size are better measures and

produce more reliable results than low occupational prestige (Farrington, 1997). As a result, offending is heavily skewed, some 6–7 per cent of males committing 60–70 per cent of officially recorded offences. Victimization is also heavily skewed, with 1 per cent of the population suffering some 25–40 per cent of household property crimes. Crime is a form of regressive taxation levied disproportionately, although not exclusively, by the poor on the poor.

3. Much crime is relatively hidden – being generally unreported and therefore unrecorded and investigated by the police – and its exposure would modify standard images of deviance. Domestic violence is also regressive but occupational crimes by employees and employers, and corporate crime by companies and businesses redress the balance. Poor people are hardly in a position to commit major frauds, insider dealing on the Stock Exchange or compel employees to work in dangerous conditions. However, the general fear of crime is greatest in relation to the non-hidden offences of burglary, robbery, crimes of violence and car-related crime.

4. Only a relatively small proportion of offences, perhaps as low as 2 per cent a year, result in the conviction of offenders. If the hidden volume of offending was added to the total which we know about from police figures and victim surveys, that percentage would shrink to even more negligible proportions. Yet – except in the worst-hit communities – crime remains a manageable problem. Some people, especially among the better off, sail through life without ever being victimized. The dynamics of crime seem to differ from those of punishment. Texas imprisons ten times as many offenders as Britain, but its murder rate remains several times higher (Hood, 1996). If the prospect of imprisonment as a fearsome deterrent was the main reason for keeping within the law, the situation should be the reverse. This suggests that social, cultural and economic factors are far more important in explaining crime than the severity of punishments. It also suggests that, although the situation may be steadily worsening, powerful constraints do operate in society to keep crime in check. The fact that the formal control system captures so few, although in the longer run an appreciable chance of conviction rises, points to *informal* social controls as immensely potent.

Sociological Approaches to Crime and Delinquency

Social theories of crime have proliferated greatly over the past century. No one theory or approach has 'won out' over this period, and no 'knock out blow' has been delivered which would allow us to consign some of them to the sidelines. Nor did they emerge in neat chronological succession, although some are more prominent at some periods than others. They are endlessly adapted, extended, revised and renamed, and numerous attempts have been made to blend two or more into a more ambitious synthesis. There is no master key to making sense of this profusion, but most analytical schemes differentiate them into:

1. *Strain theories*, which stress the malintegration of key social institutions, giving rise to deviant *motivations* on the part of the groups most affected.
2. *Interactionist theories,* which stress the socially constructed nature of identity, and the consequent importance of *labelling* processes for some persons and groups becoming deviant.
3. *Control theories*, which stress the significance of controls against deviance. Control theories have tended to divide into those which primarily stress *social* controls and those which emphasize *situational* factors.
4. *Radical* theories, which stress the fundamentally crime-generating nature of *capitalist* political economy.

Strain Theories

The progenitor of strain theories was Durkheim, whose work was a major influence on what came to be known as functionalism (for further discussion of functionalism see Chapter 3). For Durkheim (1895/1982), the assignment of functionality to an institution involved two criteria. First, was an institution widely prevalent, or even ubiquitous, in human societies? If so, the sociologist was alerted to its likely functionality, since it would be unlikely that an institution, such as the family and kinship, would survive unless it promoted some fundamental social end. Second, however, it was essential to ask the question: in what ways does the institution function to enhance the conditions of social cohesion and group life? Only if the second criterion could be fulfilled could functionality be inferred.

Durkheim's (1893/1984) most surprising demonstration of his claims for the method concerned the functions of deviance. Crime, he argued, is normal, and attempts to extirpate it altogether were doomed not only to failure but to making things worse. His reasons were that crime functions to elicit responses which arouse collective sentiments and mobilize upright consciences, the result of which is to reinforce and clarify the most significant norms and values in society. To eradicate crime, so signal a process of mobilizing consciousness against the most trivial act of deviation would be needed that social stagnation would result from all behaviour becoming excessively over-regulated. Thus, it is a sign of social pathology if the crime rate falls too low just as when it rises too high. Durkheim's theory was considered immoral in its day and in some ways would elicit a similar reaction today. It would take a brave sociologist to endorse the approach to an audience of parents of the children who were massacred in their school in Dunblane in Scotland. Not that such endorsement would be called for: Durkheim would have no doubt regarded such an act as pathological. For while it is clear that he regarded a crime-free society as a contradiction in terms, a sociological impossibility; what remains unclear is what levels of crime are normal, and what are pathological. The only clue that Durkheim gave is that the norm is set by the average rate in societies of comparable development and type. But what if conditions are universally present to produce an unduly high crime rate globally?

That state of affairs is more or less theorized by Durkheim as existing in the transitional stage at which most societies stand in the evolution from mechanical to some future, somewhat utopian organic solidarity. In such societies, the free-market economy produces a predatory, highly competitive war of all against all, a dog-eat-dog world in which greed is good and the strain to anomie is ever present. Economic materialism has outstripped the capacity for moral regulation. In his celebrated study of *Suicide* (1897/1952) Durkheim introduced a major source of variation in suicide rates as stemming from economic boom and slump. In both extreme situations, the suicide rate rises, which he explained as due to the weakening of moral regulation under circumstances of rapid change. Here Durkheim relied on a view of human nature as innately liable to the malady of infinite aspirations. Lacking a moral order which alone can restrain them, people's aspirations rapidly overshoot any possible fulfilment, leading to a state of chronic frustration, bitterness and anger capable of driving them to such ultimate acts as suicide or homicide. In sum, a certain amount of crime is normal in any society, but crime and deviance assume pathological proportions in a state of anomie brought about by unduly turbulent economic change. Intervention in the economy to moderate such extremes was logically called for as a remedy.

Merton (1968, 1938/1993) reformulated Durkheim's theory of anomie in four crucial respects. First, he saw the capacity to aspire 'infinitely' not as a natural human trait but as a propensity which had to be *culturally* nurtured. The unique egalitarianism of the American 'way of life', in which everyone was led to accept the belief that anyone could make it from 'log cabin to White House', and in which advertising matched mass production with mass consumption, was the precursor of a global 'revolution of rising expectations'. Second, the strain to anomie was not, as in Durkheim, released only in exceptional circumstances, but became a routine feature of American life. Third, the causal sequence was reversed: for Durkheim, deregulation led to infinite aspirations; for Merton, infinite aspirations led to deregulation. The end result, however, was in each case the same: high rates of deviation. Fourth, for Durkheim, the strain to anomie was at its height in the upper reaches of society. For Merton, the disparity between aspirations and rewards was at its greatest in the lower depths. As a result, higher rates of crime and deviance were to be expected the lower the position in the social class hierarchy.

In some respects, Merton took not Durkheim but Marx as his inspiration. The most powerful element in Merton's theory is his emphasis on what Marx saw as the engine of capitalism: the fostering of the propensity to consume. Left to themselves, people do not necessarily want super-abundance: but they are goaded into ever-expanding realms of consumption by ceaseless advertising. The capitalist show can only be kept on the road by 'institutionalized dissatisfaction'. The result is at best 'mild economic anomie', the feeling that one has never quite made it until one buys the bigger car, the better holiday, the brighter washing powder. At worst, anomie becomes chronic, or long term, and deviant ways of adapting to it institutionalized: crime organized, fraud rampant, theft routinized and violence normal. Both Durkheim and Merton, in different ways, do address the central criminological problem of the twentieth century: how to explain the rise and rise of crime in the context of rising prosperity. It is not, in their view, prosperity as such which causes rising crime, but the disruptive effects of unplanned economic growth (in Durkheim's case) or the perpetuation of inequalities in the context of rising expectations (in Merton's), which leads to the experience of *relative* deprivation.

Fresh developments in strain theory arose in the attempt to explain the specific phenomenon of gang delinquency. In the post-war period of rising prosperity and limited welfare provision, it had been expected that crime and delinquency would gradually subside. In fact, the reverse occurred, with crime and delinquency both rising and assuming even more florid forms, first becoming manifest in the USA. Youth gangs, of the sort romanticized in the musical *West Side Story*, flourished, yet their bitter 'turf wars' and high death toll did not seem well accounted for by Merton's celebrated but rather mechanistic typology of 'deviant aspirations' to inequality. The goal of 'money-success' which he had taken as the acme of mass American culture, was difficult to link with delinquency which was primarily *expressive* rather than instrumental. They were far more likely to vandalize their school than to rob a bank.

Cohen (1955) argued that gang delinquency amounted to a way of life which was:

1. non-utilitarian, that is, not mainly concerned with economic gain
2. negativistic, in the sense that a certain malice entered into the defiance of authority
3. not simply at odds with respectable society, but lived by rules which ran counter to it
4. celebrated 'short-run hedonism', not only living for the moment, but actively resisting any attempt to plan for the future, was versatile rather than specialized in its delinquency and owed allegiance to the gang alone.

Such a way of life was concentrated in a small section of society, among some male, urban, working-class adolescents. In accounting for this behaviour, Cohen elaborated a theory of *sub-cultures,* that is, cultures within cultures. Sub-cultures emerge when people confront problems which they simply cannot avoid or solve, because they are set up by the way society is structured. In this case, the problem arises precisely because American egalitarianism, operating through the schools, insists upon high levels of achievement and ambition from allcomers. Yet the odds are stacked against working-class children from the outset. School failure therefore presents large numbers of working-class children, boys in particular, with a real problem which Cohen argued they resolve by creating a counter-framework within which they *can* succeed: the delinquent gang. The gang gives them status, a sense of achievement, and a way of hitting back at the system that has labelled them failures. Cloward and Ohlin (1960) supported the concept of the 'delinquent sub-culture' but argued against Cohen that at least three kinds could be distinguished: criminal (for gain); conflict (for turf); and retreatist (for drugs), depending on the character of adult crime. In neighbourhoods where adult rackets were prevalent gang delinquency serves as a kind of apprenticeship for recruitment to the mob. In areas so disorganized that even the rackets avoid them, the conflict gang prevails. Where 'double failure' occurs – the world of crime being no easier to succeed in than the 'straight' world – the retreatist pattern of drug use is likely to be chosen. Moreover, in all this swirl of activity, the school is of no account to downntown boys. What inspires their sense of alienation is not school failure but lack of material success. Well-paid jobs are their goal rather than status in school. Cloward and Ohlin predicted the crisis that would occur when de-industrialization led to the large-scale disappearance of secure and well-paid manual jobs, a development documented vividly by Wilson (1996).

Matza (1969) took a different tack, arguing that the idea of 'delinquent sub-cultures' conjured up a mythical picture of lower-class youth committed to incessant warfare against middle-class adult institutions. In reality, most delinquency was petty and intermittent. By over-predicting delinquency, these theories could not account for its decline in adulthood, nor for the 'techniques of neutralization' deployed in explanation by the young people involved (Sykes and Matza, 1957). Phrases such as 'I didn't mean to do it'; 'They had it coming to them'; 'Everybody does it'; are not just rationalizations but attempts to neutralize a sense of guilt which, if the offenders were so righteously indignant about their social situation, they would not even feel. So what makes delinquency attractive in the first place? Here the stress is placed on what delinquents have in common with the rest of society, rather than on what sets them apart.

They are seen as sharing adherence to 'subterranean values' (Matza and Sykes, 1961) such as the equation of toughness with masculinity, the search for excitement and a disdain for routine work. These are the values of gentlemen of leisure as well as delinquents: delinquents differ, however, in acting them out without respect for time and place. Their accentuation makes for a 'sub-culture of delinquency', in which law breaking is an option not a necessity. Youths may drift into delinquency by a temporary loosening of controls rather than through commitment to a delinquent way of life (Matza, 1964). The more extreme forms of delinquency arise from desperation or 'compulsive' behaviour. In correcting for what he saw as positive defects (the scientific search for causes which override free will), Matza may have under-predicted delinquency yet been obliged to retain a positivist model for its most extreme forms.

How well did these largely American theories, fashioned to account for gang delinquency in the USA, transplant to Britain? (See Tierney, 1996, for an unusually full account of these approaches.) Mays (1954) argued that 'growing up in the city' involved working-class boys almost inevitably in traditions of fighting to display toughness and vandalism and rowdiness to show daring. They would normally grow out of this phase, given decent jobs and education. Mays was also a pioneer of more robust forms of youth work and adventure playgrounds to divert youthful energies from law breaking (Mays, 1959). Morris (1958), in a study of suburban London, found that social planning and public housing recreated problems in certain areas which American sociologists had seen as peculiar to the inner city. Cramming the most turbulent families into a few neighbourhoods intensified their problems, a theme taken up later by Gill (1977) in Liverpool and in Sheffield by Bottoms and Xanthos (1989).

These approaches dealt well with the persistence but not the rise in rates of delinquency in the second half of the twentieth century. Applying sub-cultural theories to delinquency in East London, I inclined to Matza's approach as best capturing the impulse to delinquency in the search for excitement (Downes, 1966). However, Matza played down the class aspects of leisure, into which working-class boys and young men channelled their energies most potently. Out of the expanse of boredom that met rising expectations in the mid-twentieth century came both the creative format of British youth culture and the new styles of delinquency of the Teds and the Mods and Rockers. In these tentative beginnings, the American theories were borne out quite well by the mildness of delinquency in Britain, given the strength of working-class community, full employment and realistically low job aspirations. However, they also pointed to the ways in which this situation might change drastically if those structural guarantees changed.

Interactionist Theories

Interactionist theories raise a fundamentally different set of questions about deviance. Instead of taking conformity for granted, and deviance as so odd that distinct motivations had to be sought to account for it, interactionists asked why some behaviour was defined as deviant in the first place, and why only some groups, and not others, became so labelled. Cohen (1980), in a book which added the phrase 'moral panic' to the English language, was not so interested in why the Mods and Rockers had running fights on the beaches of English seaside towns in the mid-1960s, but why the social reaction to them was so excessive. Youth 'letting off steam' was nothing new, but the media coverage invoked unprecedented forms of youthful deviance. Cohen went on to argue that not only was the reaction wildly exaggerated, it also had the ironical effect of making things worse. Alerted by saturation media coverage to these dramatic events, far more were recruited to the Mods and Rockers ranks than would otherwise have been the case. Labelling such groups as drastically deviant created a 'deviation amplification spiral', in which an ever-hardening minority of deviants increasingly resisted the imposition of authority. Eventually, the deviants may be dragooned back into conformity by the forces of law and order, but only after a bloody, protracted and largely unnecessary sequence of law enforcement.

The seminal work in this approach is Becker's *Outsiders* (1963). Indeed, it was Becker's achievement to recast what had been the 'sociology of social problems', 'social pathology' or criminology into the distinctive shape of the sociology of deviance. He did so by exploring, more purposefully than earlier theorists, the full implications of its social character:

> Social groups create deviance by making the rules whose infraction constitutes deviance, and by applying those rules to particular people and labelling them as outsiders. From this point of view, deviance is not a quality of the act the person commits, but rather a consequence of the application by others of rules and sanctions to an 'offender'. The deviant is one to whom that label has successfully been applied; deviant behaviour is behaviour that people so label. (1963: 9)

Becker's work is exemplified by the skill with which he demonstrated its relevance to an understanding of marihuana use. To Becker, marihuana use is actively learnt behaviour, to be understood only if the sequence of stages through which the learner must pass is grasped. It is not a sudden leap into the unknown, sparked off by social deprivation or anti-social character traits. Moreover, the very status of marihuana use as deviant is problematic originating, in Becker's view, from the 'moral entrepreneurship' of the Federal Bureau of Narcotics, whose case was more of a moral crusade than a scientific demonstration that the drug was more dangerous than alcohol or tobacco. *Outsiders* triggered a momentous chain reaction in the sociology of crime and delinquency. It brought into play as variables the very processes of defining behaviour as deviant, and of labelling some people but not others in that way, which had previously been ignored. Before Becker, the social and legal responses to crime had been little studied, assumed to be a constant, background element in processing offenders through the criminal justice system. Now that system became part of the picture, not simply its frame. Law making, prosecution, policing and sentencing were to be as intensively studied over the next few decades as offending behaviour itself. Moreover, the interaction between the two was now a central concern.

Labelling theory developed from the work of Mead which was discussed in some detail in Chapter 3. For Mead, the self is partly a compound of the social roles we learn to play (both within the family and in the larger worlds of neighbourhood, school and work), which he termed the 'me'; and partly an active, observing 'I', the unique source of one's identity. The result is a 'vital division within consciousness' (Downes and Rock, 1988: 192) which allows for the self-questioning, self-doubting aspects of the self. To a formidable extent, our sense of self is socially derived and sustained, which is not to say that it collapses with the absence or removal of our socially 'significant' others. Once formed, the self may still transform but it may also display astonishing resilience.

The implications of taking this approach seriously proved momentous for theory, method and policy making. If people are taken to retain the capacity for change throughout life, if they are taken to be sensitive to the definitions others make about their conduct and themselves and if they are active agents, rather than passive receptors, in the process, then character and motivation are not to be simply inferred from such attributes as gender, age, ethnicity, class and nationality, or from their wealth, income and education, but can only be known by direct observation. The main implications of the approach theoretically were that if social definitions are consequential for people's sense of self-worth and identity, then formal definitions are of particular significance. They flow from authorities with the power to impose definitions and enforce sanctions that may have enduring implications for those labelled deviant.

Lemert (1967) distinguished between 'primary' and 'secondary' deviation. Primary deviation abounds: many people, perhaps the majority, steal at some time or other. Secondary deviation is where 'the original 'causes' of the (primary) deviation recede and give way to the central importance of the disapproving, degradational, and isolating reactions of society' (Lemert, 1967: 81): a minority become processed as 'thieves', 'thugs', 'perverts' and so on. Lemert argued that research into secondary deviation is in many respects more pertinent, since the symbolic attachment of deviance to persons may fundamentally reconstitute their moral character, whether in the eyes of the wider society, their local networks, family intimates, themselves or a combination of all four. These ideas have also had a powerful influence on sociological explanations of sickness (see Chapter 12). In the work of Goffman (1991), for example, the 'moral career' of the mental patient was analysed in terms of such self-redefinition, and the asylum was seen as a prolonged assault on the psyches of those labelled 'mad'.

Out of this perspective was to come a welter of concern that the stigma-tizing social reactions to deviance were more to do with the public reconsti-tution of moral character than the prevention of crime or the rehabilitation of the mentally ill. Strong policy directions flow from this work: decriminaliza-tion should be preferred wherever possible to the imposition of the criminal sanction; destigmatization should be pursued, for example, in the form of diversion from court proceedings to some pre-trial alternatives: ultimately, decarceration should be prioritized, since imprisonment and mental hospital-ization are profoundly damaging to the self, and in ways which make subse-quent offending or illness more likely. Alternative community sanctions should be preferred wherever possible.

Criticisms of the approach include the view that it is a pendulum swung too far. Social reactions to deviance, and their implications for future deviance, may have been overly neglected in the past, but there are severe limits to decriminalization and diversion. Victims demand redress, or may 'take the law into their own hands', and even 'crimes without victims' may not be perceived that way as, for example, in hostile community responses to drug trafficking and prostitution.

Nevertheless, interactionist insights continue to influence the subject, most recently in the form of 'social constructionist' approaches to the study of the claims and counter-claims that enter into the processes of the making of 'social problems' (Hester and Elgin, 1992).

Control Theories

Control theories come closer to commonsense views of crime and deviance than other approaches. In a sense, we are giving practical expression to control theories of a *social* kind whenever we accompany young children to school or keep tabs on who they are playing with, and of a *situational* kind whenever we lock our doors at night. The nub of control theories is the central importance given to variations in control as the key to trends in crime and deviance. It is a somewhat secondary matter for them to seek to understand what motivates offenders, who are presumed to be rational actors seeking to maximize their pleasures and minimize their pains. Far from looking for some special set of motives to account for crime, or some adverse effect of labelling, they assume we would all be deviant if we dared. What stops most of us most of the time are the losses we would incur if we are caught, and the investment we have made in good reputation that we value highly.

Such notions are not only widely held but have long been so. The idea that each fresh generation is somehow more lacking in discipline than one's own recurs regularly across the centuries (Pearson, 1983). It may be partly for that reason that sociologists were disinclined to take them seriously until recently: theorists tend to abhor the obvious. However, a more likely reason is that such views have tended to be associated with psychological approaches which focused on the individual in the family setting rather than the wider community and society. More tellingly still, the absence or weakness of control was seen as a poor basis for explaining the often non-utilitarian character of deviance. Why should anyone, left to their own devices, want to beat another up or wreck the local youth club?

The first formal attempt to theorize along these lines came from Hirschi (1969). He analysed the social bond linking individuals to society as composed of four main elements: attachment, commitment, involvement and belief. Effective social bonds attach people to key social institutions – the family, school, work – and the stronger their attachments, the more they develop commitments to those concerned – parents, teachers, employers. Such bonding entails involvement in conforming activities: family life, learning, earning, a 'virtuous circle' which encourages belief in abiding by the rules. None of us is immune from deviance, but the stronger our attachments, commitments and so on, the more we will choose to resist its temptations. We simply have too much 'stake in conformity' to risk losing the good opinion others hold of us and our family by violating the law. We have, as it were, built up a certain 'social capital' and become wary of losing it by offending. Hirschi backed up his theory by evidence from a self-report study of delinquency on over 4000 students in California. The variations in self-reported delinquency did not correlate much with differences of class, ethnicity or income – factors stressed heavily by strain and labelling theories – but did match with those associated with social control: for example, children scoring highly on measures of communication and identification with their parents were signally less involved in delinquency than those who scored less well in these respects. Two decades later, Hirschi felt sure enough of this approach to present it, with Gottfredson, as a general theory of crime (Gottfredson and Hirschi, 1990). Low self-control stemming from poor socialization in families and schools – and inconsistent monitoring and punishing of deviance – is viewed as the main common denominator in offending behaviour.

Wilson (1980) and Wilson and Herbert (1978), in a broadly similar study in England, developed a concept of 'chaperonage' to explain differences in delinquency between children from much the same background. In a carefully chosen sample of 56 socially deprived families, all of whom were poor, overcrowded and similarly circumstanced, striking differences in the delinquency of their children correlated strongly with the extent to which the parents monitored their behaviour as, for example, in accompanying them to and from school, setting play and bed times, and vetting children as companions. 'I blame the parents' was not, however, her conclusion, since the emotional costs involved in such chaperonage were too severe. She emphasized instead the priority of ending social deprivation. However, parental supervision, at least of young children, was seen as a 'neglected feature' of delinquency control.

Control theory also emerged well from an important study on the gender gap in offending behaviour. Hagan *et al.* (1979) used Hirschi's methods in Toronto to explore what they termed the 'sexual stratification of social control'. Boys and girls reported strikingly different experiences of parental supervision, encouragement to take risks and involvement in delinquency. In brief, boys were encouraged to take risks far more than girls and were more subject to lax parental controls. They were also far more likely to be involved in delinquency than girls. But these links held *within* as well as *between* genders, suggesting the causal significance of socialization for delinquency regardless of gender. Nevertheless, the major finding was that the informal social control of girls is far more intensive and extensive than that of boys, who as a result are more subject to formal social control by the police and the courts. These findings also confirm the importance of cultural definitions of masculinity in delinquency, which field studies have shown to be most power-fully associated with *machismo*, the overriding stress on the tough, arrogant, combative image of the male. An obvious inference from such findings is that placing delinquent boys and men in prisons, which are veritable *machismo* factories, is somewhat self-defeating.

Another theory in this vein links crime with changes in 'routine activities' (Felson, 1994). Opportunities for 'motivated offenders' to commit crime consist of 'suitable targets' and the absence of 'capable guardians', and the commonplace structures of social life can multiply such opportunities in unforeseen ways. For example, the huge increase in car ownership not only creates millions of fresh opportunities for car-related crime, but also makes it far easier for motivated offenders to travel rapidly and anonymously: the 'quick getaway' on a mass scale. Similarly, the growth of single person house-holds and women working part time expands targets for residential burglary denuded of capable guardians. Such trends arguably increase the supply of motivated offenders, because rational offending is enhanced by easier gains for less risk. The work of Newman (1972) was similarly based on the ways in which mass housing served to reduce informal social control. In such projects, it was often the case that surveillance and monitoring of local space which, as we saw in Chapter 4, leads to greater self-regulation of behaviour, were effectively 'designed out' by their architecture. Lacking 'defensible space', people withdrew into the confines of their own apartments, ignoring what went on outside by way of noise or disturbance, fearful of the empty lift and the deserted stairwell. Over the past decade, a great deal of crime preven-tion has focused on the need to redesign such projects to enhance a sense of symbolic ownership by providing electronic locks for access doors to blocks, for example – and by redesigning estates to provide better sight-lines over neighbouring properties.

Stress on the 'situational' in crime prevention gained prominence in England chiefly through the work of Clarke (1980, 1992) and his colleagues at the Home Office Research and Planning Unit. Clarke argued that criminology had for centuries sought the explanation for crime in 'dispositional' theories of social, psychological or even biological and genetic kinds. Not only had these proved less than adequate as explanations: they also had the drawback of proffering improbable strategies for prevention, notably social or psychological changes of a fundamental character, for example revolution or psychic cure. In all this root-cause explanation, Clarke argued, we have lost sight of the most obvious point of intervention: the crime situation itself. Most offending is opportunistic, and the scope for prevention is greatest at that point: either by 'target hardening' or enhanced surveillance or both. A good example of this is the unanticipated plummeting of the rate of motor-cycle theft after the introduction (for reasons of road safety) of compulsory safety helmets: bike thieves either had to walk around with helmets or drive without helmets and risk arrest. Situational control theorists could cite many examples of successful prevention by such means: rates of phone kiosk vandalism fell with the installation of tougher coin boxes; car thefts in Germany fell after steering locks were made compulsory, rates of domestic burglary halved following the removal of coin slot meters for gas and the 'cocooning' of burglary victims (Forrester *et al.*, 1988). 'Cocooning' meant the heightening of neighbours' awareness by police and agency workers that a particular household had been victimized by burglary, and encouragement for them to be vigilant over the next two weeks – the period of maximum risk of revictimization. Control theorists accept that professional criminals will not be deterred by such measures, but most crime is not committed by sophisticated professionals but by relatively disorganized opportunists.

Support for this approach stems from perhaps the most influential single article on crime prevention ever written: the Wilson and Kelling (1982) theory of 'broken windows', the inspiration for what is now termed (often misleadingly) 'zero-tolerance' policing. The root idea of 'broken windows' is that crime and disorder are intimately connected. Leaving 'broken windows' unrepaired signals community apathy and police indifference to 'incivilities', acts which are not in themselves crimes but which signify something awry about a neighbourhood. Without remedial action, graffiti proliferates, noise levels rise, vandalism burgeons and more windows get broken. The result is to tip a neighbourhood into decline: property values fall, insurance costs rise, respectable families move out (if they can), and deviants – petty criminals, the mentally ill, beggars – move in. The theory recommends repairing the first broken window, if the cycle of deterioration is to be halted: 'zero-tolerance' policing reverses decades of prioritizing only serious crimes and turning a blind eye to petty crime and disorderly behaviour. The results in New York have been claimed to verge on the momentous (Kelling and Coles, 1997). Beginning with a crackdown on subway disorders – 'aggressive' begging and fare dodging – William Britton, the NYPD Chief – extended the strategy to precincts across New York. In a few years, from 1993–96, the crime rate fell not only for standard crimes but for homicide too: a drop of

50 per cent, from some 1927 to 986 murders. Not surprisingly, the results have attracted global attention, and several police forces have adopted comparable methods in Britain. Few theories have seemingly received such dramatic confirmation in hard practice. The view that policing and criminal justice processes make little difference to crime trends – which are mainly responsive to social, economic and cultural causes – finds its credibility at stake in the wake of such developments.

Without belittling what may turn out to be a watershed in policing, some attempt must be made to put such trends and claims into context. First, even at what for New York is a very low figure, 986 murders in that city is still more than the total for the whole of England and Wales, and remains several times higher than the rate for London. *That* major difference still has to be accounted for. The huge disparity in handgun ownership is part of the story, but even the non-gun murder rate is markedly higher in the USA than in the UK. Second, the fall in overall crime in the USA over the past five years as measured by victim surveys is to a lesser extent also the case for Canada, where zero-tolerance policing has not been so intensively pursued. In contrast, crime rates in England, measured by victim surveys, rose steadily over that period, despite major investments in situational crime prevention such as closed circuit television (CCTV). Third, the USA has, over the past 20 years, become the most punitive nation, at least in the western world, with a prison population quadrupling from 400,000 in the mid-1970s to some 1,600,000 today. In some cities, one in three of the most at risk of offending groups, especially young black and hispanic males, is either in prison or under penal disciplines such as probation or parole. It would be surprising if such high levels of incapacitation had no effect on crime rates: but the gains are bought at a terrible price, both economically and socially. Fourth, situational crime prevention differs from social crime control in one key respect. In unashamedly tackling symptoms not causes, it risks displacing or deflecting offences from one site or type to another: the offender deterred from burglary by better security devices may turn to robbery; the offender may avoid well protected areas (the rise of 'gated' communities in the USA is another reflection of the fear of crime there) but home in on poorer and less defended areas: displacement can be by offence, victim, time, place or method. By contrast, insofar as they address the causes appropriately, social forms of crime prevention run no such risk. The bored teenager who steals cars for kicks may be content with a number of schemes for car racing laid on by community youth teams. Employment and training schemes around the country work surprisingly well for some young offenders who lacked elementary skills which denied them even routine work (Downes, 1993). The best crime prevention schemes combine both elements in an overall strategy.

Radical Theories

Radical theories link crime to the political economy of capitalism. Taylor *et al.* (1973), drawing on the insights of the 'New Left' in Britain, applied two master concepts to existing theories. First, how 'fully social' a picture of deviance did they project? Second, how well did they analyse the political economy of crime? Measured against these criteria, all existing theories were found wanting. Labelling theory, although an advance of sorts on previous theories, still pictured the deviant as passive victim, while Marxism still gave too materialistic an image of deviance for a fully social, essentially human agency to be envisaged. However, by wedding the more constructive aspects of prior theories to a neo-Marxist analysis of political economy, a 'new' and 'critical' criminology could be developed. On that basis criminologists could work towards the overthrow of the capitalist system, in alliance with deviants victimized by the capitalist state, with the eventual aim of constructing a crime-free society based on 'social diversity' – a clean break with orthodoxy was envisaged.

A good example of this approach is *Policing the Crisis* (Hall *et al.*, 1978). Their starting point was the length of sentences passed against three youths who had 'mugged' a man for a paltry sum in 1973. The offenders had returned two hours after the attack to inflict further injury, and this in part explained the severe penalties of 20 and 10 years' imprisonment. However, these were exemplary sentences, imposed by the judiciary when the threat of a certain type of offence had reached epidemic proportions. Hall *et al.* argue that a 'moral panic' about robbery had been caused, not by a real increase, but by media reportage, the recent adoption of the term 'mugging' from the USA and a police-led campaign against 'black' muggers in particular. In this case, one youth was half West Indian, another of Cypriot background – the link with race was central to its media coverage. Unlike Cohen, who invented the term, Hall and his colleagues were disinclined to see 'moral panics' as simply arising 'from time to time': more fundamental interests are usually at stake when large investments of media resources become taken up with particular issues, in this case the threat to the capitalist state from the successful sequence of strikes, especially the miners.

In this 'crisis of legitimation' for the British state, the moral panic over 'mugging', especially of whites by blacks, became both a potent symbol of growing lawlessness and disorder and a convenient means for converting the crisis confronting the state at the point of production into a 'war against crime'. Hence, 'policing the crisis' is a metaphor for how the capitalist state was shielded from popular awareness of its critical condition by the deflection of attention to an essentially marginal issue – policing black muggers. The originality in this approach lay in applying neo-Marxist methods to the analysis of deviance, linking its diverse manifestations to the dynamics of capitalist political economy in Britain. In the USA, radical criminologists such as Chambliss (1978) and Platt (1978) had linked capitalism with organized crime and with street crime, but in a sweeping fashion which made little sense of changes over time or differences between societies which shared a capitalist economy.

Cohen (1972) provided a much more sophisticated method for explaining changes in deviance in the light of the dynamics of political economy. He linked the notion that sub-cultures are evolved by some groups to solve problems that the larger culture lands them with to the contradictions of post-war capitalist development. As a result of increasingly right-wing political and economic policies in many developed societies over the last two decades, people are now much more familiar with what such contradictions look like than they were in the early 1970s, for example the tendency of capitalist interests to ride roughshod over the needs of communities if they happen to stand in the way of making profits. Profits come first, unless governments dictate otherwise – and governments have shown an increasing tendency not to do so. However, the main object of Cohen's work was to account for the bewildering proliferation of youthful styles that were created in post-war Britain, styles which were deviant, not illegal, but which became strongly associated with delinquency. The Teddy Boys, the Mods and Rockers, the Skinheads and later the Punks were seen as attempts to resolve, albeit 'magically', a set of contradictions facing working-class youth; in particular the loss of community, family tensions, the breakdown of class solidarity and the failure to gain access to power in a newly 'affluent society'. In this impasse, working-class youth could revolt culturally if not politically. Thus, for example, the Mod style could be seen as an attempt to realize, in an imaginary way, the conditions of existence of the socially mobile white-collar worker (Cohen, 1972). The Mod office boy might be low in power and status but he could out-dress and out-talk the managing director. The Skinhead style symbolized the hard masculinity associated with traditional manual labour under threat from technological change. However, sartorial fashion is not structural change: these were revolts of the powerless, and they ultimately led nowhere. Hence the rise and fall of successive styles, resisting but never capable of resolving structural contradictions. Cohen provided a template that could be applied to diverse movements.

Such movements are a constant reminder that growing up in a class society stifles a huge creative potential which will seek expression in deviant form if conventional outlets are blocked or resented as patronage. As we saw in Chapter 9, Willis (1977) documented the process whereby working-class boys take on working-class jobs, not by forced labour, but by self-schooling into a subordinate culture of masculinity which idealizes physical strength, sexual prowess and verbal wit above educational achievement. The price is high: sexism and racism. But the pay-off for society is a willing cohort of manual labourers, ironically now consigned to the dole since the work for which they have been socialized over the generations has now largely vanished (Wilson, 1996). McRobbie and Garber (1976) similarly argued that 'the lads'... peer group consciousness and pleasure frequently seem to hinge on a collective disregard for women and sexual exploitation of girls'. As a result, 'girls tend to be pushed to the periphery of social activities and much "girl culture" becomes a culture of the bedroom rather than the street' (Newburn, 1997: 621). However, girls' insubordination is just as anti-school as that of boys and 'is as crucial in preparing them for the realities of the labour market as are Willis' lads in pre-shop floor collaboration' (Hobbs, 1997: 811). *Resistance Through Rituals* (Hall and Jefferson 1976) is the common thread linking diverse forms of youthful deviance.

Critics of the radical approach (Smart, 1976; Downes, 1979; Rock, 1979; Cohen, 1980) focused on the dangers of romanticizing motives and the unacceptability for victims, especially women, of impugning authoritative action against crime; on the vagueness of the socialist alternatives on offer; and on the extent to which the imaginative readings of deviance may also be imaginary. The force of such criticisms, some arising from the radicals themselves, led to a split in the approach, some retaining a strong neo-Marxist method, others developing what Young termed 'Left Realism' (Lea and Young, 1984; Matthews and Young, 1986). Its starting point was the reality of the pains of criminal victimization (never in doubt for many outside the Left), especially for working-class communities, and from street crime. They did much to document the extent and character of victimization in the worst-hit areas by pioneering local victim surveys (see Kinsey, 1984; Jones *et al.*, 1986). Their main explanation for rising crime is relative deprivation and social injustice, basically a return to the root-cause approach of strain theories. However, the approach is given a radical inflection by, for example, their emphasis on crimes of the powerful, on political as well as material and status deprivation and marginalization, and by their concern to bring policing more in line with people's needs at the very local level.

Conclusion

The deviance perspective is now integral to sociological theory and is likely to remain so, largely because it provides a framework for the analysis of diverse social problems which are commonly linked by their social definition as warranting social control. The four main approaches to the explanation of distinct forms of crime and delinquency all have their strengths and weaknesses. Strain theories cope quite well with accounting for the 'rise and rise' of crime over the past four decades, largely because the combination of rising expectations in the context of persistent inequalities is central to the approach (for a recent and broader analysis of contemporary ills along similar lines, which also draws heavily on psychological evidence, see James, 1997). They also address the problem of motivation far more directly than other approaches, although they tend to 'over-predict' the scale of deviance in the process, a problem also for control and radical theories. Labelling theory alone lends itself to discounting much of the so-called rise in crime, seeing processes of redefinition as crucially involved. The virtues of labelling theory lie not so much in explaining trends as in questioning the definitions underlying them. As the approaches differ in key respects, for example in their views of the nature of society and the social bond, or of the importance of motivation compared with opportunity, no ready synthesis is likely. It is, of course, eminently possible to clump them together, seeing crime as increasingly due to growing social strains, more punitive labelling, weakening social controls and a context of capitalist greed careering out of control. Such an approach over-predicts the problem far more than any one approach taken alone, as well as glossing over the fundamental conflicts between them philosophically. However, although a neat consensus is not foreseeable, theoretical debate is immensely fruitful, not only for better theory but also for better informed method and policy making. It is as a result of informed uncertainty, rather than any spurious unison, that we have learnt as much as we have about deviance compared with our relative ignorance in the past.

Current Issues

There is no neat list of issues which cover current debates, but the four that follow have immense implications for research and policy making. Discussion of these issues should be linked with the relevant parts of the chapter.

Crime and Inequality

Many developed societies have experienced massive de-industrialization, particularly over the last two decades of the twentieth century, which has been combined with widening inequalities, growing poverty and increasing levels of male unemployment. However, the conclusion that the doubling of the crime rate and the re-emergence of urban riots in Britain, for example, were in any way due to these trends was denied by the government and some criminologists. They could point to counter-instances to refute the critics, such as the far lower crime rates in the 1930s, when the slump had led to even greater unemployment, and the 1960s, when crime rates rose annually despite full employment. In the 1980s, the USA experienced the same trends – vanishing work and growing inequality – but the crime rate hardly changed. In response, it can be said that *relative deprivation* is the key factor: that rising expectations, driven by the consumer society, make people ever more resistant to, and embittered by, joblessness and impoverization.

As for the USA, rates of criminal violence, especially homicide, remain far higher than in Europe, despite the far higher levels of imprisonment, which may have held property crime levels down to some extent, but at a huge cost socially and economically. What kinds of research would assist in clarifying this issue, which is of immense importance if we are to make informed political and policy choices?

Restorative versus Punitive Justice

Politicians often make political capital for themselves by promising to get tough on crime and promising something closer to a US-style punitive sentencing system. Against that view, penal reformers increasingly argue for what has come to be called 'restorative justice', which emphasizes community-based sanctions, such as as probation, community service orders and mediation between victim and offender. These are intended to give offenders greater insight into their offending behaviour and its effects on the victim, and to jolt them into an awareness of the true causes and costs of their crime. Braithwaite (1989) boosted this approach by arguing that societies which practised inclusionary shaming, such as Japan, enjoyed far lower crime (and imprisonment) rates than those which practised punitive, exclusionary policies, such as the USA. Just how far and in which ways such forms of 'restorative' justice may be effectively used is a key question for criminal justice policy making.

Situational versus Social Crime Prevention

The attraction of purely situational measures for governments and citizens is that they can be implemented piecemeal and very quickly without any need to address the underlying causes of crime. For example, CCTV monitoring, the electronic tagging of offenders, 'gated' communities and endless variations on target hardening, such as satellite car tracking (top end of the market) or Rottweiler in the back of the van (bottom end) do not depend on elaborate theories of motivation and meaning. Yet the scope for ever more widespread and sophisticated forms of situational prevention holds the danger that, over time, they lead to a 'fortress' mentality, an increasingly constrained and yet still fearful society, where only designated persons can enter designated zones for designated purposes. It is already the case that in Los Angeles only those holding the right swipe-card can enter the business centre. By contrast, social forms of crime prevention carry no implications of repressive side-effects on the freedom of the streets or civil liberties.

Drug-related Crime

This term encompasses violations of the laws governing illegal substances, that is, their use, possession, production or distribution, and crimes committed as a consequence, such as burglaries to finance an addiction and violence to enforce payment for supply. The whole issue is especially germane for the sociology of deviance, because the criminal definition of certain substances is the key pre-condition for drug-related crime. This has led to arguments for the decriminalization, if not outright legalization, of some 'soft' drugs, especially cannabis, and for the return to a medical model of treatment for heroin addiction to cut out the 'black market' and its organized crime bases. On the other hand, few have argued for the legalization of cocaine which, in the form of 'crack', provides an unusually rapid route to an intense form of addiction. At present, all but a few governments have refused even to discuss the possibility of even very limited forms of decriminalization. The Dutch government is under intense international pressure to end its long-standing policy of limited tolerance of cannabis use in licensed venues. Yet the levels of cannabis and heroin use in the Netherlands are no higher and often lower than in other countries. The Prohibition era in the United States led to the explosive growth of organized crime there. The prohibition of illicit drugs globally seems to be leading to the same result worldwide. Is it possible to devise forms of regulation which neither criminalize nor lead to a commercial 'free-for-all'; which take account of the particular properties of each drug, and which are workable internationally?

Further Reading

Davies, N. *Dark Heart,* London, Chatto & Windus, 1997. An account of an investigative journalist's close-up of some of the most damaging forms of deviance.

Downes, D. and Rock, P. *Understanding Deviance,* 3rd edn, Oxford, Oxford University Press, 1998. Provides detailed coverage of the major theories of deviance.

Maguire, M., Morgan, R. and Reiner, R. (eds) *The Oxford Handbook of Criminology,* 2nd edn, Oxford, Clarendon Press, 1997. A key reference book, containing informative articles on most key topics in the fields of crime, deviance and social control.

Tierney, J. *Criminology: Theory and Context,* London, Prentice Hall/Harvester Wheatsheaf, 1996. Provides a clear and detailed explanation of the history of criminology and its major theories.

12

Health, Illness and Medicine

Steve Taylor

The sociological study of health and illness has much in common with the study of deviance as illness is also a form of unintentional 'rule breaking'. Sociologists have examined both the social causes of diseases and also how the meanings of 'health' and 'illness' are constructed in social processes. There are also connections between the sociological study of medicine and religion. Some sociologists have argued that medicine has taken over some of the social control functions that have traditionally been associated with established religion and that in contemporary societies the religious distinction between good and evil is being increasingly replaced by the medical distinction between healthy and unhealthy. This chapter aims to illustrate how sociologists have examined the social origins of disease and the processes that shape both people's experiences of illness and disability and the medical knowledge and practices around which health care is organized. It should help you to understand:

- What is meant by the biomedical model of health and how it has been questioned in recent years

- How sociologists have tried to measure and explain health inequalities

- The relationship between stress, social support and health

- What is meant by the sick role and how sociologists have tried to illuminate people's experiences of sickness and disability

- How sociologists have explained ideas about health, illness and the human body as social constructions

---

CONCEPTS

epidemiology ■ longitudinal study
materialist and lifestyle theories ■ stress ■ illness behaviour
stigma ■ iatrogenic disease ■ holistic medicine

Introduction

At first sight a *sociology* of health, illness and medicine appears something of a contradiction in terms. After all, in modern societies the study of health and disease and treatment of the sick has been dominated by the biological sciences and, for most of the twentieth century, it has been generally assumed that the battle against disease will be won in the laboratory and the treatment room. In this *biomedical model of health* disease can be defined objectively in terms of recognized symptoms and health is simply the absence of these symptoms. The body is likened to a machine to be restored to health by treatments of one sort or another. The biomedical approach still dominates the training of health professionals, the allocation of resources, and those at the top of health care's pyramid of power have traditionally been the experts in curative treatments.

In modern and modernizing societies health policies are still organized predominantly around the assumption that improvements in health will come largely from new and improved treatments and from the greater availability of medical resources. However, in the last two decades in particular, this view has been increasingly called into question. First, despite some spectacular medical advances in certain areas, the major diseases of modern societies, such as arthritis, cancer and heart disease have for the most part remained stubbornly resistant to effective medical treatment and cure, and the attentions of more health professionals and policy makers has switched to the environmental causes of disease. Second, modern medicine has been criticized for its detached and mechanistic approach to illness, where patients are seen as collections of symptoms rather than people. As the burden of disease in contemporary societies moves increasingly from acute (life threatening) to chronic (long-term) illness and disability, critics argue that more attention should be given to the social and psychological and, more recently, political consequences of illness and disability. Third, modern medicine's claim to be a beneficent and value-free science has been increasingly challenged in a more consumer-orientated and sceptical late modern world.

Sociologists of health and medicine have made significant contributions to each of these debates and this chapter is organized around these issues. The first section examines the social influences on health, the second looks at how people's experiences of illness are shaped by social contexts and the chapter concludes by considering the relationship between medical knowledge and practice and wider social influences.

The Social Bases of Health

Most research within the biomedical model of health involves trying to identify the origins of specific diseases under controlled laboratory conditions with the aim of developing effective treatments which are usually administered in the form of personalized medical care. An alternative *epidemiological* approach involves trying to identify the environmental influences on health by examining their distribution in *populations* over time. This approach has shown that diseases do not strike randomly but are consistently linked to various environmental influences, including social variables, such as region, ethnicity, class, gender, age and culture. This section will illustrate the social influences on health by looking at two of the most important sociological variables, social deprivation and social integration.

Socio-economic Factors and Health

Links between comparative economic deprivation and poor health have been reported in most developed countries, although international comparisons are difficult because so many different measures, or indicators, of socio-economic position have been used. These links are usually measured by calculating standardized mortality and morbidity (that is, illness) rates for different socio-economic groups. A number of studies in Britain, for example, have found a persistent relationship between occupational class and rates of mortality and morbidity (Townsend *et al.*, 1988; Benzeval *et al.*, 1995) (Table 12.1). Four-fifths of all officially recorded causes of death, including heart disease, which is commonly thought to be predominantly a disease of the over-stressed high achieving executive classes, are more prevalent among the manual working classes. It has been estimated that if the death rate of manual workers was the same as that for non-manual, there would be 42,000 fewer deaths each year (Benzeval *et al.*, 1995). The result of this is that people from the manual working classes are more than twice as likely to die before retirement age than people from the professional class and are twice as likely to be suffering from a longstanding illness.

Social class also affects the health of children. Working-class mothers are more likely than middle-class mothers to have complications during pregnancy and have low weight babies. Rates of infant mortality, that is babies dying in the first year of life, also vary between the social classes. On average, for every baby born to professional parents who dies, two die born to skilled manual workers and three die from unskilled manual backgrounds. These inequalities persist into childhood and the mortality rate of children from manual working-class backgrounds is double that of the children of Class I parents.

There has been a great deal of controversy and debate among sociologists and others about the interpretation of the statistics on class and health. One major source of debate concerns whether the statistics provide a comparatively reliable and valid measure of health inequality. Official statistics are not self-evident 'facts' simply waiting to be explained by sociologists. They are socially produced and necessarily reflect the conceptual categories and bureaucratic

Table 12.1   Occupational class and standardized mortality ratios for men aged
16–64, 1981–89: for all men and for unemployed men
seeking work

	All men	*Unemployed men seeking work*
Social class I	60	73
Social class II	80	104
Social class IIIN	90	110
Social class IIIM	97	114
Social class IV	109	136
Social class V	134	172
All men aged 16–64	100	125
Ratio V/I	2.2	2.4

Standardized mortality ratios represent the mortality of sub-groups within a population as a percentage
of the mortality of the population as a whole.
Source: OPCS Longitudinal Survey, reported in Benthume, A. (1996) 'Economic activity and mortality
of the 1981 Census Cohort in the OPCS Longitudinal Survey, *Population Trends*, **83**: 37–42.

procedures in terms of which they are compiled. In this context, a number of
critics have argued that many of the difficulties of 'measuring' social class,
discussed in Chapter 5, apply to research into socio-economic status and health.

First, there have been significant changes in the composition of the respective occupational classes in most developed societies. In Britain, since the
Second World War, Class I has doubled while Class V has halved to around
only 6 per cent of the working population. Thus Illsley (1986), for example,
has argued that drawing general conclusions about the persistence (and sometimes even the worsening) of health inequalities simply by comparing the
health of those in Class I with those in Class V, as many studies have done, is
bound to distort and almost certainly exaggerate the extent of the problem.
Second, the long established method of classifying women in terms of their
husbands' occupation not only makes the statistics to some extent 'gender
blind' (Arber, 1990), but also fails to take into account the significant differences between single and dual earner households. Third, using occupation as
an indicator of socio-economic position is becoming increasingly limited in
an ageing society where most people are living well beyond retirement age
(Klein, 1988).

Some critics argued that the methodological problems just outlined mean
that the existence of widespread (and possibly worsening) health inequality
remains unproven and its persistence in the literature owes more to the political rhetoric of sociologists than established empirical evidence (Green, 1988).
However, most academics working in the area do not take such a dismissive

view of the problem. First, they argue that, in spite of acknowledged deficiencies, the data on occupational class do provide a useful outline of the problem. Second, they argue that some of the criticisms have been answered to some extent by studies using alternative techniques of 'measurement'. For example, an OPCS longitudinal study following a 1 per cent sample of the population using much more comprehensive data from the 1971 Census found that health inequalities persist after retirement age (Fox *et al.*, 1986). Other studies have used more specific indicators of comparative deprivation. For example, studies of different grades of employment within particular occupations and industries have found consistently higher levels of morbidity and mortality among the lower grades (Marmot, 1978; Davey Smith *et al.*, 1994), while specific indicators of material deprivation have been positively linked to poor health (Townsend *et al.*, 1988; Davey Smith *et al.*, 1991).

A second major debate concerns the alleged causes of health inequality. For most sociologists, the major explanations are located in terms of material factors associated with comparative poverty, such as low income, poor housing, the nature of manual work and the lack of it. For example, poor housing can affect health directly by making respiratory and parasitic diseases and childhood accidents more likely and, indirectly, by contributing to stress which can lead to conditions such as anxiety and depression (Eames *et al.*, 1993). It has been estimated that around 2 million people a year suffer from work-related illness. People in manual occupations run a far greater risk than people in non-manual occupations not only from industrial accidents, but also from the greater likelihood of contracting cancer and respiratory disorders. The repetitive nature of industrial work with its close supervision and lack of autonomy also makes the likelihood of stress-related disorders more likely. One study estimated that 20 per cent of the class variation in cancer mortality is due to hazards at work (Fox and Adelstein, 1978). More recently, emerging evidence of the long-term influences on health has led researchers to develop longitudinal models which explore the cumulative influences on health over people's life course. While some early influences on health in later life are probably programmed biologically, it is also likely that they are influenced socially, and sociologists have began to explore the cumulative influences of social disadvantages on health (Bartley *et al.*, 1994). For example, the socio-economic environment of a child's home is likely to influence their attitudes and educational attainments which will then become a determinant of their labour market position which will influence their economic position in middle and old age (Davey Smith *et al.*, 1997). In general, for most researchers, health inequality is to be explained in terms of material influences which are largely outside most people's direct control.

However some critics claim that the materialist theories tend to depict working-class people as essentially passive victims, condemned to comparatively poor health simply by their class position. They argue that such a view negates the importance of human agency; that is, it reduces people to mere puppets of the class system and fails to take into account the choices that people make in how they live their lives. In this context it is argued that a great deal of behaviour commonly known to produce increased risk of ill-health is class related. For example, smoking is one of the major preventable causes of ill-health and premature death, contributing to 100,000 deaths a year and a third of all cancers. However, on average, working-class people have been less receptive to warnings about the dangers of smoking and the proportion of smokers in Social Class V is two and half times that of Social Class I (Office of Population, Censuses and Surveys, 1996) (Table 12.2). Similarly, other well-known health risks such as sedentary lifestyle, high alcohol consumption and a poor diet of refined convenience foods all appear to be more prevalent among the working classes. Some theorists put forward the idea of a sub-culture of ill-health, where poor 'health behaviour' is passed down through the generations. From this point of view health inequality is less an automatic product of material deprivation and more a consequence of lifestyle and behavioural choices and, therefore, policy solutions are seen more in terms of health education rather than economic redistribution favoured by advocates of materialist theories.

Table 12.2   Cigarette smoking by sex and socio-economic group of head of household, persons aged 16 and over, Great Britain, 1974 and 1994 (%)

	1974		1994	
	Male	*Female*	*Male*	*Female*
Professional	29	25	16	12
Employers and managers	46	38	20	20
Intermediate and junior non-manual	45	38	24	23
Skilled manual and own account non-professional	56	46	33	29
Semi-skilled manual and personal service	56	43	38	32
Unskilled manual	61	43	40	34
Total non-manual	45	38	21	21
Total manual	56	45	35	31
All	51	41	28	26

Source: OPCS/ONS (Office of Population, Censuses and Surveys, now Office for National Statistics) (1996): adapted from Table 4.9.

Some sociologists have argued that 'lifestyle' choices cannot be divorced from the material contexts in which they are made. For example, in her work on women and smoking Graham (1987b, 1994) has argued that the higher rates of smoking among working-class women with children, while reflecting 'free' choices, are still influenced by material factors. Caring for small children in difficult circumstances produced high levels of stress for some women, and smoking was a part of a strategy they used to take some 'time out' for themselves. Smoking thus occupied a paradoxical position in these women's lives. On the one hand it was an increased health risk for them and their children, on the other hand a part of a strategy for coping in deprived circumstances. A major task facing sociological research in this context is developing models which combine inherited lifestyle and material influences (Figure 12.1).

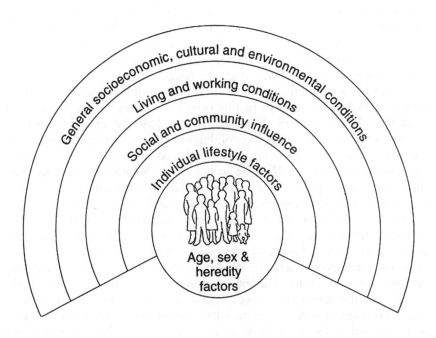

Figure 12.1   The Whitehead/Dahlgren model (Dahlgren and Whitehead, 1991, *Policies and Strategies to Promote Social Equity in Health*, Stockholm, Institute for Future Studies)

Social Integration and Health

An allied approach to the social origins of disease has focused on the relationship between stress, social integration and health. Since the 1960s a number of studies have shown that exposure to stressful life events, such as bereavement, divorce, occupation change, unemployment, migration and social problems, can make people more vulnerable to disease and premature death (Williams and House, 1991).

Researchers are not entirely sure how people's life experiences influence their physical health but there is increasing evidence from the biological sciences that prolonged exposure to events which disrupt people's normal patterns of behaviour and cause psychological stress, such as worry or great sadness, can result in biochemical changes in the body which make the immune system (that is, the body's natural defences) less efficient, leaving the individual more vulnerable to 'non-specific' diseases (Kaplan, 1991). However, while stressful life events are associated with the higher risk of disease, they do not *necessarily* cause it and there has been a great deal of research, particularly in biology and psychology, into factors (such as genetic predisposition or personality type) which influence people's ability to adapt to stress.

Although sociological contributions to this problem are comparatively recent, one of their key ideas had its origins a century ago in the work of Durkheim. In his study of suicide Durkheim (1897/1952) argued that the variations between the suicide rates of different social groups and their consistency over time was a 'social fact' to be explained sociologically. For example, the statistics showed that Catholic areas had consistently lower suicide rates than Protestant areas, people who were married with children had lower suicide rates than the unmarried and childless and societies' suicide rates fell in times of war or political unrest. Durkheim argued that the underlying cause of these variations was the extent to which individuals are integrated, or bonded, into the social groups around them. In modern 'individualized' societies, the more people are integrated into society the more protected they appear to be from suicide. Durkheim's study of suicide has been widely criticized for its theoretical inconsistency and dependence on official suicide rates, but the concept of social integration has become one of the central ideas in sociology and, in the last two decades in particular, has been applied to the study of the relationship between stress and health. Sociologists have also used the concept of social support which refers to the extent and quality of a person's social relationships (Eurelings-Bontekoe *et al.*, 1995). Social integration and social support are clearly closely related and, while the terms are sometimes used interchangeably, social integration is usually used to refer to a characteristic of *populations*, while social support usually means a resource of *individuals* (Figure 12.2).

Studies of social support tend to use the longitudinal method of studying groups of individuals over time. For example, in one of the best-known studies, Berkman and Syme (1979) 'followed' a sample of 5000 adults aged 30–70 over a nine-year period. A social network score was calculated for each person using the indictors of marriage, regular contact with friends, church membership and membership of voluntary organizations. After controlling for health status and health behaviour the authors found that the mortality rates of those with low

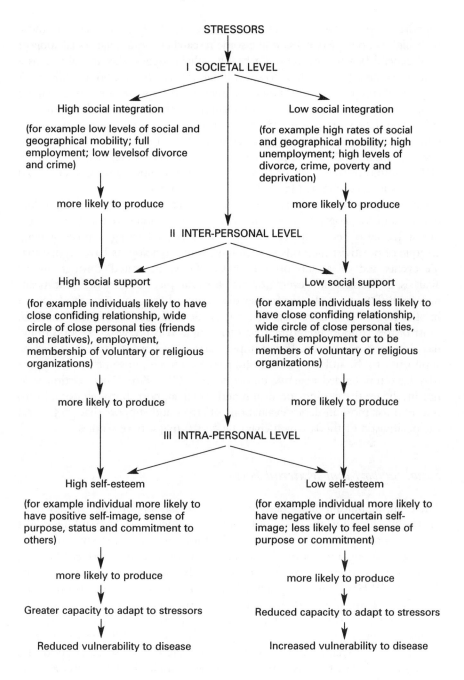

Figure 12.2 The social context of stress and health (Taylor S., 1997, 'Social Integration, Social Support and Health' in Taylor S. and Field D. eds *Sociology of Health and Health Care*, 2nd edn, Oxford, Blackwell)

support network scores were between two and three times higher than those with high support networks. While some researchers argue that social support is of general benefit in promoting health, others suggest that its value is as a 'buffer', helping people adjust to stressful life experiences, including illnesses. A number of studies have also shown the importance of social support in helping people adapt to a range of diseases including various cancers, heart disease, stroke and depression (Ell, 1996). For example, in a study of 44 patients recovering from a first stroke, Glass and Maddox (1992) found positive correlations between high levels of support and good recovery, while Fitzpatrick *et al.* (1991) found higher levels of psychological deterioration among rheumatoid arthritis sufferers who had lower levels of social support.

The study of social support and health has become one of the most productive areas in sociology, linking social with biological and psychological factors, but it has also been subject to criticism. First, reflecting a more general critique of positivist methods in sociology, some sociologists have argued that life events and social support cannot simply be 'measured' through survey analysis, as the same life 'event', divorce for example, can have different meanings for different people (for further discussion of the general methodological implications of this issue, see Chapter 2). Second, the assumption made in most of the 'support literature' that social support is *necessarily* a 'good thing' has also been questioned. For example, caring for a sick person may well be supportive to the sufferer but stressful to the carer and, in some cases, support may have unintended negative consequences (Ell, 1996). These critiques do not invalidate the findings on health and social support, but they do point to the need for more in-depth evaluations of stress and support that go beyond the positivistic methods which characterize the majority of studies.

Social Support and Material Factors

There are significant links between stress, social support and the material factors considered in the study of health inequalities. First, stressful life events such as unemployment, marital difficulties and bereavement are more common among the more disadvantaged socio-economic groups. Second, lower socio-economic status is associated with lower levels of social support. (Whelan, 1993). Third, the potential of social support to buffer people from the effects of stressful life events is influenced by material factors. For example, a family's ability to provide support for a sick person is also influenced by its ability to obtain external support from social services (Ell, 1996). A good example of the relationship between stressful life events, social support and class is provided by the classic study of Brown and Harris (1978) on the social origins of depression in women. Brown and Harris found a clear relationship between adverse life events, which were subjectively perceived by the women in the sample to have long-term implications, and the onset of depression.

However, whether the women then became depressed was influenced by four vulnerability factors: lack of paid employment outside the home, having three or more dependent children living at home, loss of the mother before the age of 11 and, most important, lack of close confiding relationship. The greater the number of vulnerability factors the greater the likelihood of depression. Working-class women were more vulnerable to depression than middle-class women because they were more likely to experience both stressful life events and greater vulnerability factors. As these precipitating factors arose out of social situations, Brown and Harris argued that although depression is a biological condition, its origins are essentially social.

Sociological Approaches to Sickness and Disability

As societies modernize, and more people reach middle and old age, the proportion of the population suffering from chronic, or long-term, illnesses increases. While medicine is able to treat more of these conditions, such as heart disease and arthritis, it cannot cure most of them and thus living with illness becomes a way of life for an increasing number of people. It has now become common in the sociology of sickness to distinguish between impairment and disability. *Impairment* refers to some abnormality in the structure and function of the body, through disease or injury, while *disability* refers to restrictions of activities of daily living which may result directly from impairment but may also be social, such as negative reactions from others, lack of resources and restricted opportunities in work and leisure.

Estimates of the prevalence of disability vary due to the different 'measures' that have been used. In Britain, for example, a number of surveys carried out by the Office of Population, Censuses and Surveys between 1985 and 1988 – combining the judgements of researchers, professionals and people with disabilities – estimated that there were around 6 million adults with disabilities in Britain, almost 70 per cent of whom were over 60, with women outnumbering men (Martin *et al.*, 1988). Sociologists have been interested in examining the social consequences of illness and disability as well as its distribution. They have theorized about the relationship between sickness and social structures and explored people's experiences of illness and disability, particularly how their 'disruptive' effects are 'managed' in daily social life.

Sick Role and Social Structure

Parsons (1951) was one of the first sociologists to conceptualize sickness as a social state. For Parsons, sickness was a form of deviance which posed a threat to the functioning of the social system as people were not complying with the work-orientated norms of modern industrial societies. Allocating people a distinct sick role helped the social system manage the potential threat posed by sickness to social and moral order.

The sick role consists of privileges and obligations. Sick people are exempted from their normal social roles and from responsibility for their illness. However, they are expected to be motivated to get better and they must seek professional medical help and comply with medical advice in the treatment of their illness. Failure to comply with the obligations may result in a loss of the privileges. Parsons also identified a corresponding medical role of privileges and obligations. While doctors had privileged access to the patient's body and confidential information, they were obligated to adhere to professional standards, remain objective, confine their interest to the patient's condition, and always act in the best interests of the patient. For Parsons, doctors not only served the interests of their individual patients, they also served the interests of wider society by acting as gatekeepers of the sick role in defining who was (and was not) legitimately sick.

Parsons did very little empirical research on illness himself but the concept of the sick role – with its recognition of sickness as a change in *social,* as well as biological, status – opened the door to a range of sociological questions about professional power, social control and the ways in which meanings are attributed to physical states. The concept can still provide insight into a number of contemporary issues, such as the distinction health professionals sometimes make between 'deserving' and 'undeserving' patients. Jeffrey (1979) found that casualty staff distinguish between 'good cases', such as head injuries or cardiac arrests, and what they called the 'rubbish', such as drunks and repeated overdosers. What characterized the 'rubbish' was that, like the unrepentant smokers who are pushed to the back of the waiting lists for cardiac surgery, they were seen to have been largely responsible for their condition and therefore not 'legitimately' sick.

The concept of the sick role has been subjected to a battery of empirical criticisms. First, it has been widely argued that Parsons' model cannot be applied to many chronic illnesses, such as arthritic conditions, where the patient cannot get better and leave the sick role. However, Gerhardt (1987) has argued that this critique is the result of 'a too literal reading of Parsons' and, as Parsons (1978) himself observed on a number of occasions, sometimes using the example of his own diabetes, people with chronic illness are still expected to comply with medical advice to control and minimize symptoms in a way that mirrors recovery in acute illnesses.

Second, it has been shown that access to the sick role is rather more problematic than Parsons' model assumes. Studies of illness behaviour, that is, the processes by which people come to define themselves as ill, have shown that only a minority of symptoms are brought to medical attention (Scambler *et al.*, 1984) and that a decision to consult a doctor is often the result of a long process of help seeking, influenced by a range of social and cultural factors. In this context it is argued that what Parsons is really talking about is a *patient role* rather than a sick role (Turner, 1995). A third criticism of the sick role focuses on the consensus it assumes in the doctor–patient relationship. A number of sociological studies of doctor–patient interaction have shown that consultations were rarely as smooth as Parsons' model supposes and that there was frequent negotiation and sometimes conflict over diagnosis and treatment (Tuckett *et al.*, 1985).

General criticisms of Parsons' structural functionalist theory for its overemphasis on both consensus and structure (see Chapter 3) are also reflected in specific critiques of the sick role. Like Parsons, Marxists also see medicine's management of the sick role in terms of social control. However, while Parsons saw this control being exercised for the benefit of the social system, or society as a whole, Marxists argue that it operates largely in the interests of the ruling class (Navarro, 1978). By conceiving sickness in 'individualistic' terms, as the result of biological predisposition or unhealthy lifestyle for example, medicine is performing an important ideological function by 'de-politicizing' the effects of capitalism and deflecting attention from the environmental and predominantly economic origins of disease. It has also been suggested that capitalism's preoccupation with production, profitability and 'materialist' values contributes to a process of excluding and devaluing people who are not 'productive', such as the mentally ill (Scull, 1993), elderly (Phillipson, 1982) and long-term sick and disabled (Oliver, 1996). The recent tendency for health economists and policy makers to talk grimly about the 'costs', and even the 'burden', of continuing to provide health and social care for the increasing number of elderly and long-term sick into the next century suggests that this idea is not without some foundation.

For social action theorists a major shortcoming of Parsons' formulation of the sick role is that it conceives sickness only in terms of its relationship to social structures. In contrast to Parsons, action theorists have developed concepts which help to illuminate the micro-social contexts of sickness, in particular the relationship between individuals' experiences of sickness and disability and the specific organizational contexts that shape those experiences.

Experiences of Sickness and Disability

Despite the valid critique of Parsons' sick role, it is generally seen as a seminal contribution to the sociology of health and illness for its recognition that sickness is a social state where the sick person is surrounded by a new set of social and cultural expectations. Sociologists have been particularly interested in exploring how these expectations impute meaning to sickness and disability and shape people's experiences of them (Gerhardt, 1989). A great deal of this work has been influenced by symbolic interactionist theory developed from the work of Mead, Becker's (1963) ideas on social groups creating deviance by labelling some people as outsiders and Goffman's (1969) work on the presentation and protection of the self in everyday life. Like Parsons, the interactionist approach sees sickness and disability in terms of deviance. However, whereas Parsons is asking how the social system copes with sickness, interactionists are more interested in how sick and disabled individuals cope with society. In this context the distinction made by Lemert between primary and secondary deviance, described in the previous chapter, has been particularly helpful. The labelling of a person as sick or disabled constitutes a form of primary deviance, while secondary deviance refers to the adaptations a person makes in response to such labelling. In their analysis of sickness, interactionists have been interested in both the characteristics of societal reactions to sickness and their consequences for individuals.

Sickness labels can easily become a dominant status; that is, the impairment (especially if it is easily visible) comes to be seen by others (and sometimes by the person themselves) as a major source of identity, even if the person has a high profile in other areas they may still be seen as a *disabled* writer or a *diabetic* footballer for example. There is also a tendency to interpret a person's behaviour (past as well as present) in terms of the sickness label. For example, in his classic study of an American mental hospital Goffman (1991) observed how patients' resistance to their diagnosis would be interpreted by staff as further confirmation of their 'illness'.

Sickness and disabling conditions are often stigmatizing. People are socially stigmatized when they are seen to be in some way unacceptable or inferior and are thus denied full social acceptance (Goffman, 1968). There is thus a discrepancy between what Goffman calls their 'virtual social identity (the way they should be if they were 'normal') and the 'actual social identity' (the way they are). Those who are stigmatized are confronted with a series of decisions about the management of spoiled identity both in terms of their interaction with others and their own self-concept. People are more likely to experience stigmatized reaction from others when their impairment is highly visible. In Goffman's terms, they are 'discredited' and this may lead to a greater withdrawal from social participation, especially in public areas. When the condition is not visible, as in epilepsy or HIV for example, and the person is potentially 'discreditable', they have to decide whether to be open about their condition or try to 'pass' as 'normal'. Thus the implications of stigma go beyond public reaction. For example, Scambler and Hopkins (1986) found that comparatively few of the epileptics they interviewed had actually experienced a stigmatizing reaction from others (enacted stigma). However, the shame of being epileptic (felt stigma) led most of them to conceal their condition even from those close to them. For example, two-thirds of those experiencing epilepsy at the time of their marriage concealed it from their partners, while three-quarters had not disclosed their condition to their employers. The authors found that, paradoxically, felt stigma was more disruptive to people's lives than enacted stigma.

However, being officially diagnosed and labelled as sick is not *necessarily* stigmatizing in itself. Sometimes it can have the opposite effect. For example, some illnesses such as Parkinson's disease and multiple sclerosis can develop very slowly and there may be a long time between initial experiences of symptoms and medical diagnosis. In such circumstances diagnosis can be a relief in that it both legitimizes the patient's complaints and confirms the reality of their symptoms (Robinson, 1988), while the failure to obtain a diagnostic label can be stigmatizing. In her study of myalgic encephalomyelitis (ME) Cooper (1997) found a great deal of conflict between patients who felt ill and their doctors who could find no evidence of disease. Consequently, many were not allowed access to the sick role and, as result, 'their social position was to some extent eroded, their social identity devalued and stigmatised, and they found it difficult to obtain legitimate absence from work or disability benefit' (1997: 203).

Interactionists' interest in people's capacity to 'take the role of the other' and see themselves as they believe others see them has led them to explore the effects of societal reaction to sickness and disability for the individual's self-concept. A number of the earlier studies focused on the effects of the 'crisis' brought about by a person's comparatively sudden status transition from 'health' to 'sickness'. Some of these studies have gone as far as suggesting that the societal reaction creates the conditions of a self-fulfilling prophecy where, through a process of socialization, the person's identity comes to correspond with the images *others* have of the condition.

A good example of this approach is Scott's (1969) classical study of blindness. Scott argues that there is nothing in the condition of blindness itself which produces the stereotyped view of the 'blind personality' as passive, docile and compliant. From his observations of interaction between experts and their newly blind clients, Scott argues that the blind personality is a product of a process of socialization in which experts emphasize to clients the importance of coming to terms with blindness by defining themselves as blind. These expectations constitute a 'putative identity' which is gradually internalized by the clients as a basis for their own identity. Thus Scott argues that blindness is 'a learned social role' whereby the blind agencies create for blind people the experience of being blind.

Higgins (1980) presented a rather different view of socialization in his study of the long-term deaf. Although the deaf people he studied were 'discredited' in wider society and were vulnerable to public stereotypes of deaf people as slow and dim witted, these reactions did not tend to form part of their self-concept. They were confronted with spoiled *interaction* rather than spoiled identity. Higgins argues that this was because a major source of socialization for the deaf he studied – most of whom had been deaf since childhood – came largely from the deaf community which acted as an alternative sub-culture within which members felt no stigma. Although they may play the deaf role in public, sometimes mockingly or for strategic reasons, they were usually able to distance themselves from it subjectively.

Labelling theory is taken a stage further in studies of mental illness. Whereas studies of physical disabilities examine the way in which meanings are imputed to various conditions through societal reactions, some interactionists have argued that mental illnesses are *entirely* a product of societal reaction. In the best known of these studies Scheff (1966) argued that unusual, crazy or bizarre behaviour is widespread in society. It is only when this behaviour can no longer be accommodated within the individual's social situation that psychiatric intervention is sought. Thus it is the societal reaction rather than any objective clinical evidence that determines whether or not a person becomes the subject of psychiatric intervention. However, once a person is defined as 'mentally ill' – a definition which can, if necessary, be enforced with legal powers of detention and compulsory treatment – there is then pressure on the person to play the stereotyped 'mentally ill role'. In mental hospitals, for example, patients are socialized into their role by being rewarded for conforming to staff views and punished for deviating from them (Goffman, 1991).

The labelling theory of mental illness has been criticized for its failure to explain primary deviance and for its assertion, rather than its demonstration, of the effects of labelling. Pilgrim and Rogers (1993) suggest that the labelling theory of mental illness 'has now fallen out fashion'. However, such an obituary is rather premature as some of its key ideas, admittedly developed in a more sophisticated way, continue to influence contemporary work. For example, Prior (1998) has shown that the definition of certain behaviour as a 'psychiatric case' is determined by organizational requirements rather than 'intrinsic' evidence of psychiatric symptoms.

In more recent interactionist work on sickness and disability the focus has moved from 'crisis' to looking at illness more in terms of a series of gradual transformations of identity and experience. This shift in emphasis arose partly from a dissatisfaction with the rather mechanistic approach of the 'crisis model' and partly from sociologists' increased interest in chronic illness. Many chronic illnesses, such as arthritis, multiple sclerosis and Parkinson's disease are not characterized by a sudden 'event' which precipitates the individual into the sick role or a 'deviant identity'. On the contrary, they usually develop slowly and often inconsistently and, for many people, becoming ill is experienced as a series of status transitions. New ways of life and changes of self-concept have to be negotiated and re-negotiated as the disease progresses and sufferers reorientate their relationship to things like work, leisure and personal commitments. Thus illness is seen as 'adaptation rather than adoption of a deviant identity' (Bury, 1997).

Adaptations to illness, even the 'same' illness, can take a number of different forms. For example, in his study of colitis, Kelly (1992) has shown that some people adapt much more easily than others to the potentially stigmatizing consequences of the disease. While some are prepared to incorporate the condition into their self-concept, others make a rigid distinction between self and disease. However, underlying particular adaptations to illness is the recurring theme of people struggling to maintain a sense of order and coherence in the face of the difficulties brought about by illness. Adaptation involves managing both physical and biographical processes (Corbin and Strauss, 1991). The management of physical processes often involves the development of new skills, such as operating machinery, administering medication and building it into daily routines. People suffering from the disfiguring skin condition of psoriasis, for example, have to conform to a strict programme of bathing, scrubbing, putting on oils and creams which may take several hours a day (Jobling, 1988). Sufferers from physically debilitating conditions, such as respiratory disorders, have to learn very quickly what can be achieved in the day before chronic fatigue sets in and plan their days accordingly (Williams, 1993). The management of physical symptoms tends to be public in character and, rather like Parsons' sick role, often contains an element of 'performance', of being seen to be conforming to the 'obligations' involved in being ill.

Biographical adaptation, in contrast, tends to be more private and subjective and refers to the ways in which people with chronic illnesses try to make sense of what Bury (1982) has called the 'biographical disruption' to their lives and identities caused by illness. Part of this process involves developing 'explanations' for the illness and its progression. Williams (1984) and Williams *et al.* (1996) observed how many people with rheumatoid arthritis engage in a process of 'narrative reconstruction' in which their biography is reorganized in order to make sense of the onset of the illness. Similarly, people may construct narratives to explain the uncertainty and sudden fluctuations in symptoms that characterize many chronic illnesses in terms of preceding events, such as 'overdoing it' the day before or going out in the cold (Locker, 1983). While these 'lay theories' may have little clinical validity they are crucial in helping people try to restore some sense of order and meaning to their lives. In recent years, as a result of sociological work, health professionals have become more interested in lay theories of illness as they give important insight into the world of patients and can act as a bridge to aid professional–patient communication.

Like all approaches in sociology, interpretive studies of experiences of illness and disability have their limitations. One of the most important of these, reflecting a more general debate in sociology between macro- and micro-sociology described in Chapter 3, concerns the comparative lack of attention to the relationship between individual experiences of illness and social institutions. While many studies make vague references to 'wider society', its nature is rarely explored and, as such, it remains elusive and ephemeral, little more than a blank canvass on which micro-social contexts are etched.

A second issue involves relating people's experiences of illness to the changing, and increasingly fragmented, nature of late or postmodern, societies. In this context Kelly and Field (1998) have questioned sociologists' conceptualizations of illness and disability as processes necessarily involving the disruption of normality and consequent re-establishment of certainty with the development of illness identities. Not only is the 'normality' from which illness is a supposed 'deviation' increasingly difficult to identify with any certainty, but the idea of illness as a 'dominant and all-pervasive identity' is open to question as it implies a stability in the world of sickness which is less and less apparent elsewhere. Kelly and Field suggest that new conceptualizations of illness may be required which take account of the more fragmented and 'open' structuring of everyday life and the greater variety of ways in which chronic illness may be experienced. It may be that chronic illness is 'just one more uncertainty in a continually changing and uncertain world' (Kelly and Field, 1998: 15).

Medicine and Society

Increasing interest in the social aspects of health and sickness in the last quarter of the twentieth century has been accompanied by a growing scepticism of modern medicine. Not only has medicine failed to find a cure for most of the major diseases of contemporary society, but research has also suggested that improvements in health in the past probably owed far more to social and behavioural changes than to clinical intervention (McKeown, 1979). Sociologists have contributed to this scepticism with their examination of the social nature of medicine, particularly the ways in which medical knowledge and practices both reinforce and reflect the social orders from they emerge. This section illustrates this general theme by looking first, at sociological interpretations of the consequences of medical intervention, particularly increasing medical intervention, in people's lives, and second, at the ways in which modern medical knowledge is shaped by social and cultural influences.

Medicalization

Parsons (1951) argued that doctors perform an important social control function for society as a whole by restricting access to the sick role and by regulating the conduct of the sick. However, a later generation of sociologists went further, arguing that the medical profession does more than define *who* is (and is not) legitimately sick. It also has the power to decide *what* sickness is and has used this power to extend its professional dominance by bringing more areas of life under medical authority (Freidson, 1970). From the 1970s sociologists became increasingly critical of what was described as the 'medicalization' of modern societies; that is, the processes where experiences once seen as 'normal', such as pregnancy, childbirth, misbehaviour, feeling unhappy, growing old and dying, become seen as 'illnesses' requiring medical supervision and control.

Illich (1976) claimed that 'medical colonization' of societies has produced a dependency on medical expertise and treatment that is taking from people their capacity to cope with the pain and suffering that are an inevitable part of the human condition. He argued that medicine's monopolistic domination over health needs to be broken and that people should be encouraged to take more responsibility for their own lives rather than demanding a pill for every ill. 'Medicalization', for Illich, is just one aspect of a more general process in modern societies by which individual autonomy is crushed by the control of scientific and bureaucratic élites and, in this sense, it has similarities to Weber's pessimism about the 'iron cage' of industrialism.

For Navarro (1975), adopting a Marxist perspective, the explanation of medicalization is to be found not in industrialism as such, but in the political economy of industrial capitalism. It is the transnational pharmaceutical companies, the manufacturers of medical equipment and private hospital complexes that have most to gain from persuading doctors that medical treatments can be applied to an ever widening area of social life. Navarro disagrees with Illich's view that the medical profession causes medicalization; rather it merely administers it on behalf of capitalist organizations who gain from it directly in terms of greater profits and, indirectly, from extending control over the work force.

Feminists have argued that the medicine has had a powerful influence in defining femininity and legitimizing patriarchal control over women. Medieval systems of medical knowledge, derived from the 'classical medicine' of ancient Greece, tended to depict women as both biologically and morally inferior to men (James, 1994). Some feminists have argued that the medicalization of modern societies has reinforced patriarchal control. Medicalization of pregnancy and childbirth, for example, gave a predominantly male medical profession the power, once exercised by organized religion, to regulate women's bodies by controlling their sexuality and reproductive capacity (Oakley, 1984). The supervision of contraception, ante-natal care, delivery and abortion by medicine also plays an important part in defining and reinforcing women's sense of dependence on 'masculine' science and technology.

The medicalization thesis, although remaining popular, has been increasingly questioned in contemporary sociology. Empirically, it has been argued that the extent of medicalization has been exaggerated, and people's capacity to resist medical control underestimated (Williams and Calnan, 1996). There is also evidence of some 'demedicalization' in contemporary societies; for example in pregnancy and childbirth and mental health problems. Ethically, it has been argued that the effects of medicalization are not *necessarily* as negative as critics like Illich suggest. For example, the recognition of things such as battle fatigue, addiction and nervous shock as illnesses can be experienced by people as welcome relief from personal blame and possible punishment

(Seale, 1994). Theoretically, while the medicalization thesis is very critical of the *consequences* of some forms of medical intervention, especially those that produce *iatrogenic* (that is, doctor caused) complications, it does not challenge the *idea* of objective medical knowledge. Indeed, one of the most common criticisms of labelling things like life problems, deviance, eating and alcohol problems as 'diseases' is that these conditions do not meet the *objective* criteria needed for defining something as a disease. Thus the critical thrust of the medicalization thesis comes from comparing the 'illegitimate' with the 'legitimate' application of disease labels and ironically reinforces, rather than undermines, the ontological status of 'real' medical knowledge. For this reason it should be distinguished theoretically from an alternative *social constructionist* approach to medicine which questions the idea of *any* objective medical knowledge and any criteria for establishing its effectiveness. This approach is grounded in a radical philosophical idealism which holds that all knowledge, including scientific medical knowledge, cannot be divorced from the varying cultural contexts that produce it.

Social Constructionism

The theoretical ideas underlying social constructionism are almost the opposite of the empiricist ideas that inform most medical sociology. In empiricism, a real world is described with theoretical (that is, fictional) concepts. For example, real inequalities in health are described through concepts such as 'class' or 'deprivation'. However, social constructionists argue that there are no 'real facts' which exist independently of systems of ideas or discourses. From this point of view nature is collapsed into culture. For example, the body and bodily processes are not natural phenomena whose reality has been uncovered by the progress of medical science. Rather they are cultural constructions that have no meaning outside the ideas and practices that surround them. Social constructionists put questions of the progress and benefits (or otherwise) of medical science to one side and focus instead on how some systems of knowledge and practice come to dominate health care at particular times.

For example, the emergence of the dominant modern biomedical views of the body and disease coincided with the growth and reorganization of hospitals in western Europe, especially Paris, towards the end of the eighteenth century. The new hospitals became centres for medical training and, for the first time, the bodies of a large number of relatively compliant and defenceless patients were brought under the inquiring eye of doctors and this changed the focus of medical knowledge. Whereas most doctors in the eighteenth century had taken a more holistic approach, seeing diseases in very general terms as symptoms of some disturbance within the whole *person*, the observation, dissection and systematic classification of patients gave rise to a new form of clinical medicine where diseases were located in specific parts of the human *anatomy*, such as the heart or liver. For social constructionists, this development was not the result of some progressive enlightenment, where the truth about the body was 'revealed' through clinical examination, but simply a different way of constructing, or 'reading', the body. As Armstrong, one of the leading social constructionists, puts it:

> The fact that the body became legible does not imply that some invariant biological reality was finally revealed to medical inquiry. The body was only legible in that there existed in the new clinical techniques a language by which it could be read. (1983: 2)

For Foucault (1973), the modern hospitals and the new anatomy that developed within them were manifestations of wider social and political changes, especially changes in the way in which power is exercised over citizens. He argued that in modern societies 'governmental' power is characterized less by visible demonstrations of physical force and more by invisible observation of people's actions, which has the effect of producing self-discipline in those observed. This disciplinary power was not just evident in the hospital, where bodies were laid open for inspection, but in the school, the asylum, army barracks and in punishment where surveillance of criminals increasingly replaced more public forms of punishment, such as pillorying and public floggings (Foucault, 1979). It was only when the body came to be seen as something essentially docile which could be surveilled, transformed and improved that a new medical approach, focused on the inspection of the body, could develop and flourish.

Foucault has been the major influence on social constructionism. Medical sociologists have used a Foucauldian approach to examine not only the consolidation of the biomedical model, but also new developments in health care arising largely from critiques of biomedicine. For example, in the later part of the twentieth century health professionals have become interested once more in the environmental causes of disease. The focus of their inquiries now extends beyond the sick to the monitoring of entire populations for evidence of risk of disease and this has resulted in mass screenings and programmes of health education and health promotion. Another comparatively recent development in medicine and medical education has been to encourage doctors and nurses to adopt a more holistic approach, taking notes on their patients' lives as well as their symptoms (Armstrong, 1995).

For social constructionists, these developments are not so much 'progress' towards creating a more socially conscious and person-centred medical profession but rather, an extension of disciplinary power where people are encouraged to be sentries of own bodies. As a major policy document outlining government strategy for health in England put it:

The way in which people live and the lifestyles they adopt can have profound effects on subsequent health. Health education initiatives should continue to ensure that individuals are able to exercise informed choice when selecting the lifestyles which they adopt. An increasing number of screening programmes are being implemented, such as those for breast and cervical cancer. The promotion of high uptake rates through effective health education is essential to the success of these programmes. (HMSO, 1992: 11)

From a Foucauldian perspective, this preventative strategy is a good example of what Helliwell and Hindess in their discussion of power in Chapter 4 called 'government at a distance', where free individuals regulate their behaviour in line with government norms.

Social constructionism has become one of the most creative and productive approaches in medical sociology. One of its major contributions has been to make problematic things sociology has tended to take for granted. For example, prior to social constructionism, most sociologists merely assumed that the human body was a given; a comparatively unchanging entity which was galvanized into action by relatively autonomous agents and constrained by social structures. Social constructionists, in contrast, have shown that medicine came before 'the body'; that is, the very idea of the body as an invariant *biological* structure which can become diseased and cured, is a product of medical discourses.

However, certainly in its more radical forms, social constructionists have suggested that the body is nothing *other* than a social construction (Lupton, 1994). There is thus nothing to be said about the body other than the systems of ideas that surround it. As Armstrong explains:

> To answer a question about the nature of the body with reference to what is seen simply sidesteps the problem because seeing is a form of perception. The body is what it is perceived to be; it could be otherwise if perception were different. The question is not therefore concerned with the nature of the body but with the perceiving process which allows the body's nature to be apprehended. (1987: 66)

Much of the plausibility of this kind of *relativist* stance comes from simply contrasting it with a crude *realism* where 'facts' – in this case 'facts' about the body – are assumed to 'speak for themselves'. As Pawson showed in his discussion of methodology in Chapter 2, the sociologist does not have to take one or other of these options. The fact that knowledge is culturally constructed need not rule out objective knowledge. The purpose of generating data in research, as Pawson argued, is to evaluate theories and help choose between them. Thus the fact that the modern treatment of prescribing penicillin for meningitis is a product of culturally relative medical discourses would not necessarily prevent even the most radical of social constructionists from taking the tablets if they contracted the disease, as available evidence has shown that, at present, this treatment represents the best hope for survival.

It seems that in quite rightly criticizing sociologists' long acceptance of a view of the body that reduces it to its biological components, social constructionists have substituted a view that reduces it to the cultural ideas in terms of which it is described. As Bury observes in his critique of the latter position:

> If the body is to be invoked in sociological inquiry, and especially in medical sociology, then the place of the biological sciences... have to be more clearly appreciated. (1997: 199)

It seems that the major task facing the emerging sociology of the body is synthesis of the biological and the cultural rather than giving precedence to one and eliminating the other (Osborne, 1997).

Conclusion

It has become a topic of concern to a growing number of sociologists that many of the concepts which have long been cornerstones of sociological inquiry, such as class, gender and ethnicity, are becoming increasingly less stable bases of identity and behaviour. Some of the same concerns are beginning to be felt in medical sociology. As we have seen, a great deal of sociological work in this area – quite properly – involves making *comparisons* in one way or another between states of health and states of illness. For example, why does one social group stay healthier longer than another? Or, how do social contexts shape people's transition from health to sickness. However, a problem for sociologists is that these states of 'health' and 'illness' and the boundaries between them are becoming more difficult to identify. A consequence of changing cultural expectations and medical establishments now monitoring whole populations for risk factors is that symptoms are inevitably discovered everywhere and good health recedes. In a humorous article, Meador argues that well people are disappearing:

> I began to realise what was happening a year ago, at a dinner party. Everyone there had something. Several had high cholesterol levels. One had 'borderline' anaemia. Another had a suspicious Pap smear. Two others had abnormal treadmill-test results, and several were concerned about co-dependency. There were no well people. (1994, cited in Davey *et al.*, 1995: 423)

Of course, such developments are of little concern to the advocates of various branches of *relativism* in the sociology of health and medicine, such as social constructionists and postmodernists, whose aim is simply to explore varying discourses about 'health' and 'illness'. However, those sociologists who still wish to follow 'modernist' ambitions, such as exploring things like social influences on disease or people's experiences of illness, and engage in critical analysis, are faced with the challenge of securing the ontological reality of their key concepts, such as health, disease and sickness, in an increasingly fluid and fragmented social world.

Further Reading

Bury, M. *Health and Illness in a Changing Society,* London, Routledge, 1997. An excellent, well-balanced general text which focuses on the impact of social change on experiences of health and illness.

Field , D. and Taylor, S. (eds) *Sociological Perspectives on Health, Illness and Health Care,* Oxford, Blackwell Science, 1998. A collection of original essays by leading medical sociologists on researching the sociology of health, social divisions and health and the provision of health care.

Taylor, S. and Field, D. *Sociology of Health and Health Care,* 2nd edn, Oxford, Blackwell Science, 1997. A clear introductory text for those new to the area.

Turner, B. *Medical Power and Social Knowledge,* 2nd edn, London, Sage, 1995. A general text which focuses on different theoretical explanations of health, disease and medical practice.

13

Religion

Grace Davie

The sociological study of religion is about furthering the understanding of the role of religion in society, analysing its significance in human history and understanding the social influences that in turn shape religion. The key assumption is that the sociologist is interested in the relationship between religion and its social context. This chapter aims to explore some of the ways in which classical and contemporary sociologists have approached these questions. It should help you to understand:

■ The different ways in which sociologists have defined religion and theorized its relation to wider society

■ What is meant by secularization and the concept of a civil religion

■ Sociological interest in new religious movements

■ The difficulties of defining religious fundamentalism and explaining the rise of fundamentalist religious movements in contemporary societies

■ The continuing significance of religion in everyday life

CONCEPTS

alienation ■ sacred ■ cult ■ sect
new religious movements ■ ideal type

Introduction

The principle task of the sociologist of religion concerns the subtle and elusive connections between religion and wider society (Hamilton, 1994). It is this relational quality that distinguishes the sociological approach from a variety of other disciplines that have interests in the area. However, the field remains a wide one, for both religions and societies vary enormously. Two preliminary points are important in this connection. The first is methodological and reflects the role of sociologists. Whatever their views in terms of their commitment (or otherwise) to religious belief and practice, as sociologists, they must remain agnostic. It is not sociologists' task to evaluate the relative truth claims of the religions that form the focus of their inquiry. The second point is substantive and opens up the question of definition, for it is by no means self-evident what should or should not be included within the category of religion. Decisions in this area are, moreover, of crucial significance, for once made they will lead the writer forward in a particular direction. Ultimately, therefore, choices about definition have theoretical as well as substantive importance.

This chapter starts by considering sociological definitions of religion and looking at the development of sociological understanding in the field of religion, from the earliest days of sociology onwards. It then examines a range of contemporary debates, and concludes by presenting some of the current dilemmas facing those working in this area. An important thread runs through all the sections. Sociologists of religion work in very varied contexts; their frames of reference are – at least in part – conditioned by the surrounding circumstances, whether these be defined in economic, social, intellectual or religious terms. It follows that debates that resonate in one part of the world may not resonate in another, a point that becomes increasingly significant as global, rather than western, perspectives begin to dominate the sociological agenda.

Definitions of Religion

There are two ways of defining religion in terms of its relationship to society. The first is *substantive:* it is concerned with what religion *is*. Religion involves beliefs and practices which assume the existence of supernatural beings. The second approach is *functional:* it is concerned with what religion *does* and how it affects the society of which it is part. For example, religion offers answers to otherwise unanswerable questions (what happens when we die), or it binds people together in distinctive forms of collective action. The tension between the two types of definition has existed from the first days of sociology. As we shall see in the following section, Weber worked from a substantive point of view, while Durkheim developed a functional perspective.

Each standpoint has advantages and disadvantages. Substantive definitions limit the field to beliefs or activities which involve supernatural entities or beings. Such a limitation is helpful in that the boundaries are easier to discern, but even a preliminary survey will reveal the amazing diversity of forms that the supernatural can take in human society. More particularly, non-western forms of the supernatural often sit uneasily within frames of reference which derive from western culture. These are practical difficulties. The sharpest critique of substantive definitions comes, however, from those sociologists who maintain that the presence of the supernatural (however described) should not be the defining feature of religion. Such an emphasis is likely to exclude a whole range of activities or behaviour which – to the participants at least – take on the character of 'sacred' even if the supernatural as such is not involved. Any ideology, for instance, which addresses the ultimate problems of existence, such as an ecological or green movement, could be thought of as a religion, whether or not it makes reference to the supernatural. Also included should be certain forms of nationalism which undoubtedly provide collective frames of meaning and powerful inspiration for the populations involved, even if the goals remain firmly of this world rather than the next.

Where, though, can the line be drawn once the need for a supernatural element within the definition of religion has been discarded? This is the crucial problem with functional definitions and it remains for the most part unresolved. Once the gold standard, in the form of the supernatural, has been abandoned, it is very difficult to draw any precise or undisputed boundary about what should or should not be included in the sociological study of religion.

Sociological Approaches

Beginnings

The sociology of religion is inseparable from the beginnings of sociology as a distinctive discipline. Its early and distinguished practitioners were the founders of sociology itself: Marx, Weber and Durkheim. It is important to contextualize the writing of these scholars. As we have seen in earlier chapters, each of them was reacting to the economic and social upheavals of the late nineteenth and early twentieth century, prompted more often than not by the devastating consequences that rapid industrialization had inflicted on the populations of which they were part. The study of religion could hardly be avoided in this framework for religion was seen as an integral part of the society that appeared to be mutating beyond recognition.

There are two essential elements in the Marxist perspective on religion: the first is descriptive, the second evaluative. Marx *described* religion as a dependent variable; in other words its form and nature were dependent on social and above all economic relations. It was the economic order and the most fundamental relationship of all, that of the capitalist or worker to the means of production, that formed the bedrock of human society. The second aspect of Marxist thinking about religion pursues this line of thinking but contains an additional, *evaluative* element. Religion is a form of alienation; it is a symptom of social malformation which disguises the exploitative nature of capitalist society. The point is nicely illustrated in the lines of the Victorian hymn:

> The rich man in his castle, the poor man at his gate
> He made them high and lowly, each in their own estate.

Religion persuaded people that such relationships were natural and, therefore, acceptable. The real causes of social distress could not be tackled until the religious element in society had been stripped away to reveal the injustices of the capitalist system; everything else was a distraction.

Subsequent debates concerning Marx's approach to religion have to be approached with care. It has become increasingly difficult to distinguish between:

- Marx's own analysis of religious phenomena
- a subsequent school of Marxism as a form of sociological thinking
- what has occurred in the twentieth century in the name of Marxism as a political ideology.

The essential and enduring point to grasp from Marx himself is that religion cannot be understood apart from the world of which it is part. However, this crucial sociological insight needs to be distinguished from an over-deterministic interpretation of Marx which postulates the dependence of religion on economic forces in mechanical terms. The final point is more political. Marx was correct to point out that one function of religion is to mitigate the very evident hardships of this world and so disguise them. Nowhere, however, does Marx legitimate the destructive doctrines of those 'Marxist' regimes which maintained that the only way to reveal the true injustices of society was to destroy – sometimes with hideous consequences – the religious element of society. Marx himself took a longer-term view, claiming that religion would disappear of its own accord given the advent of the classless society: quite simply it would no longer be necessary.

Weber's contribution to the sociology of religion spread into every corner of the discipline. Central to his understanding is the conviction that religion can be constituted as something other than, or separate from, society. Three points follow from this (Beckford, 1989: 32). First, the relationship between religion and 'the world' is contingent and variable; how a particular religion relates to the surrounding context will vary over time and in different places. Second, this relationship can only be examined in its historical and cultural specificity. Documenting the details of these relationships becomes, therefore, the central task of the sociologist of religion. Third, the relationship tends to develop in a determinate direction; a statement which indicates that the distance between the two spheres, religion and society, is being steadily eroded in modern societies. This erosion, to the point where the religious factor ceases to be an effective force in society, lies at the heart of the process known as secularization.

These three assumptions underpin Weber's *magnum opus* in the field, *The Sociology of Religion* (Weber, 1922/1963), his comparative study of the major world faiths and their impact on everyday behaviour in different parts of the world. Everyday behaviour, moreover, becomes cumulative as people adapt and change their lifestyles; hence the social consequences of religious decisions. It is at this point that the question of definition begins to resonate, for it is clear that, *de facto* at least, Weber is working with a substantive definition of religion. He is concerned with the way that the *content* (or substance) of a particular religion, or more precisely religious ethic, influences the way that people behave. In other words different types of belief have different outcomes. Weber goes on to elaborate this theme: the relationship between ethic and behaviour not only exists, it is socially patterned and contextually varied. Central to his understanding in this respect is the complex relationship between a set of religious beliefs and the particular social stratum which becomes the principal carrier of such beliefs in any given society. Not everyone has to be convinced by the content of religious teaching for the influence of the associated ethic to be widespread. The sociologist's task is to use comparative analysis to identify the crucial social stratum at the key moment in history.

The questions, moreover, can be posed in ways that are pertinent to contemporary societies. For example, why is it that women seem to be more preoccupied by religion than men? Will the disproportionate influence of women as the principal carriers of the religious tradition in modern western societies have an effect on the content of the tradition itself, or will a male view continue to dominate despite the preponderance of women in our churches? What is the relationship between lifestyle and belief in such societies when the roles of men and women are mutating so rapidly? Such questions are just a beginning, but they build on the work of Weber; the approach, once established, can be taken in any number of directions. Inquiries could also be made, for example, about minority groups, especially in societies which are both racially and religiously diverse; for example, it is likely that majorities and minorities will maintain their traditions in different ways?

Durkheim began from a very different position. Working outwards from his study of totemic religion among Australian Aborigines, he became convinced above all of the binding qualities of religion: 'religion celebrates, and thereby reinforces, the fact that people can form societies' (Beckford, 1989: 25). In other words, his perspective is a functional one. Durkheim is concerned above all with what religion does: it binds people together. As we saw in Chapter 3, Durkheim was interested in what would happen when time-honoured forms of society begin to mutate so rapidly that traditional forms of religion inevitably collapse. How will the essential functions of religion be fulfilled? Durkheim responded as follows: the religious aspects of society should be allowed to evolve alongside everything else, in order that the symbols of solidarity appropriate to the developing social order (in this case incipient industrial society) may emerge. The theoretical position follows on: religion as such will always be present for it performs a necessary *function*. However, the precise nature of that religion will differ between one society and another and between different periods of time in order to achieve an appropriate 'fit' between religion and the prevailing social order.

Of the early sociologists, Durkheim was the only one to provide his own definition of religion. It has two elements:

> A religion is a unified system of beliefs and practices relative to sacred things, that is to say, things which are set apart and forbidden – beliefs and practices which unite into one single moral community called a Church, all those who adhere to them. (Durkheim, 1976: 47)

First, there is the celebrated distinction between the sacred (the set apart) and the profane (everything else) which includes an element of substantive definition. The sacred, however, possesses a *functional* quality not possessed by the profane; by its very nature it has the capacity to bind, for it unites the collectivity in a set of beliefs and practices which are focused on the sacred object. Acting collectively in a moral community, following Durkheim, is of greater sociological importance than the object of such actions.

Subsequent Developments: the United States and Europe

What happened next in the sociology of religion depends very largely on where you look, for developments of each side of the Atlantic were very different. Each situation, moreover, reflects the prevalent cultural influences. In the United States where religious institutions remained relatively buoyant and where religious practice continued to grow, sociologists of religion in the early twentieth century were, very largely, motivated by and concerned with the social gospel. Christianity, rather like sociology itself, could be harnessed for the good of society. A second, rather less positive, theme ran parallel; one in which religion became increasingly associated with the social divisions of American society and their relationship to denominational boundaries (Demerath, 1965).

By the mid-1950s and 1960s, however, the principal focus of American sociology lay in the normative functionalism of Parsons, who stressed above everything the integrative role of religion (once again what religion does). Religion, a functional prerequisite (a necessary part of society), was central to the complex models of social systems and social action elaborated by Parsons and discussed in Chapter 3. His influence was lasting; it can be seen in the work of subsequent generations of scholars, both in America (Bellah, 1967 – see later) and elsewhere. The relationship with American society is also important. The functionalism of Parsons emerged from a social order entirely different from the turbulence that motivated the thinking of the early Europeans. Post-war America symbolized a settled period of industrialism in which consensus appeared not only desirable but possible. The assumption that religious (indeed Christian) values provided the natural underpinning of the social order was widespread.

Such optimism did not last. As the 1960s gave way to a far less confident decade, American sociology of religion shifted once again, this time to the social construction of meaning systems epitomized by the work of Berger and Luckmann (1967). Here the Parsonian model is inverted; social order (or social structure) indeed exists but it is constructed from below, not imposed from above. It is the product rather than the cause of social interaction and derives from the cumulative effect of individual actors or agents. The earlier consensus did not return: the later 1970s merge into the contemporary period, a world in which religion has become increasingly contentious. Conflict, including religious conflict, rather than consensus dominates the sociological agenda.

The sociology of religion had already taken a rather different turn in western Europe. Religious institutions on the European side of the Atlantic, unlike their American equivalents, were far from buoyant, and a growing group within French Catholicism were increasingly worried by the weakening position of the Catholic Church in French society (Godin and Daniel, 1943). Anxiety proved, however, a powerful motivator. In order that the situation might be remedied, accurate information was essential. A series of empirical inquiries were carried out under the direction of Gabriel Le Bras with the intention of discovering what exactly characterized the religion of the French people, or 'lived religion' as it became known.

Themes and Perspectives

Secularization

Secularization involves the assumption, now increasingly challenged, that religion is necessarily losing its significance in modern societies. With this in mind, it is hardly surprising that the debate about secularization and its relationship to other social processes dominates a large section of the literature within the sociology of religion. Wallis and Bruce (1989), for example, use this theme as a pivot for their review of the British contribution to the field. The first point to grasp is the close links between definitions of religion and the ongoing debate about secularization. Those who see religion primarily in substantive terms are more likely to argue that western society is becoming increasingly secular, for what they perceive as religion is diminishing in a way that can be convincingly measured (for example in the marked decline in regular churchgoing in almost all western European countries in the post-war period). Dobbelaere (1981), Wilson (1982) and Bruce (1996) are persuasive exponents of this approach. Those who see religion in functional terms, however, will be less convinced, for they will want to include within the definition a set of phenomena that at the very least meet the Durkheimian description of the sacred. These are phenomena which show considerable persistence even in contemporary societies.

Hervieu-Léger (1986, 1993) has generated an alternative approach to the secularization debate that steers between the extremes on either side. It is true that modern societies are destructive of certain forms of religious life (regular attendance at Mass, for example, or the unquestioning acceptance of Christian teaching), but it is also the case that modern societies create their own need for and forms of religion. Twentieth-century individuals are encouraged to seek answers, to find solutions, to make progress and to move forwards and, as contemporary societies evolve, such aspirations become an increasingly normal part of the human experience. Their realization, however, is – and must remain – problematic, for the goal will always recede. There is a permanent gap between the experiences of everyday life and the expectations that lie on or beyond the horizon. It is this utopian space that generates the need for the religious in Hervieu-Léger's analysis, but in forms compatible with modernity. The process of secularization becomes, therefore, not so much the disappearance of religion altogether, but an ongoing process of reorganization in the nature and forms of religion into configurations which are compatible with modern living. The two examples cited by Hervieu-Léger are the supportive emotional communities that can be discovered both inside and outside the mainline churches of western society (these are frequently charismatic in nature) and the types of religion which provide firm indicators of identity (both ethnic and doctrinal) in the flux of modern life. This point connects with the discussion of fundamentalism examined later in this chapter.

Another innovative contribution in the ongoing debate about secularization can be found in the work of Casanova (1994). Casanova builds on the work of Martin (1978) who has always been more ambivalent about the concept of secularization than many of his contemporaries (Martin, 1991). For Martin, using a Weberian framework, secularization may or may not occur and, if it does, the process will always be influenced by a wide range of contingent variables. Careful comparative analysis is necessary to discern both the nature of such influences and their effects. What emerges in Martin's work is a typology of possibilities in which different countries, or groups of countries, provide different 'versions' of secularization, or different versions of resistance. One of the most obvious contrasts lies in the opposing patterns of Europe and the United States. Why is it that the country with the most advanced economy in the world, a country which possesses a carefully worded constitution eliminating religion from privilege within the public sphere, turns out to be one of the most religiously active societies in the western world?

Casanova, to some extent following Dobbelaere (1981) in discerning different dimensions of religiosity, develops this theme by separating out three distinct strands within the concept of secularization:

> Secularization as differentiation of the secular spheres from religious institutions and norms, secularization as decline of religious beliefs and practices, and secularization as marginalization of religion to a privatized sphere... the fruitless secularization debate can end only when sociologists of religion begin to examine and test the validity of each of the three propositions independently of each other. (1994: 211)

The comparison between Europe and the United States illustrates this point very clearly.

American society has a strict separation of spheres but a high level of religious activity. European societies, with certain important exceptions, reveal closer connections between church and state and markedly lower levels of religious activity. The innovative emphasis in the work of Casanova lies, however, in the third strand within the concept of secularization. It is simply not the case, he argues, that privatization of religion is a modern structural trend. Privatization may well have occurred in some western societies – usually in those which display a parallel degree of religious decline – but this is a historical option, not a necessary feature of modern society. A glance at global politics at the turn of the millennium indicates that Casanova is right: whether we look at the New World (North and South America), the Pacific Rim or the rapidly modernizing societies in parts of the Islamic world, religion is playing an major part in the formation of both *social* structure and *public* policy.

A further point follows on: the secularization debate as it has been traditionally conceived is essentially a western, if not a European, debate. It has frequently embodied the crucial but dangerous assumption that what western Europeans do today in terms of their religious life, the rest of the world will do tomorrow. Secularization is seen as a necessary part of industrialization and as the world industrializes, it will secularize. This is simply not the case. Sociologists of religion must catch up with events. Martin (1996), for example – building on to his studies of Pentecostalism in Latin America (Martin, 1990) – is beginning to rethink the argument:

Initially, about a quarter of a century ago, I asked myself why the voluntary denominations of Anglo-American culture had not taken off in Latin America as they had
in the USA, and concluded that Latin America must be too similar to Latin Europe
for that to happen. But now I am inclined to reverse the question and ask why the
burgeoning denominations of Latin America have not taken off in Latin Europe.
(1996: 41; citation taken from the English original)

The essence of Martin's argument lies in the observation that the factors that
encouraged European secularization in the first place – a fortress Catholicism, buttressed by political power, and opposed by militant secularity – are
themselves beginning to erode. There is no reason, therefore, why the
patterns of the New World (based on voluntary membership rather than a
state church) should not transplant to the Old. It follows that the moderately
advanced secularization of western Europe, explainable by contingent and
time-limited features, may in the long term turn out to be the exception
rather than the rule.

In western Europe itself, the discussion relating to the dimensions of religiosity takes a slightly different form. Here the principal features of the late
twentieth century are the persistence of the softer indicators of religious life
(that is, those concerned with feelings, experience and the less specific religious beliefs) alongside the undeniable and at times dramatic drop in the hard
indicators (those which measure religious orthodoxy, ritual participation and
institutional attachment). These are the findings of the European Values
Study, an invaluable source of empirical information for a growing number of
European (and other) societies (Barker *et al.*, 1993). Bearing this perspective
in mind, sociologists vary in their interpretations of Britain as one illustration
of a European society. Bruce (1995), for example, sees Britain as a secular
society in which religion plays its part, but in forms – notably the denomina-
tion and the cult – which are compatible with modernization and rationalization (for Bruce the two are necessarily linked). Davie (1994), in contrast,
pays considerably more attention to the persistence of belief in modern
Britain despite the undeniable fall in religious practice since 1945. British
society is characterized by the phrase 'believing without belonging'; it is a
society in which belief has drifted away from the norms of Christian orthodoxy but has by no means disappeared.

Both the process of secularization itself and the debate that surrounds it are
far from straightforward. The impact of modernization is neither clear cut nor
consistent and it influences different societies in different ways. What has
happened in western Europe (that is, a marked decline in religious practice
and in some aspects of religious belief) has not happened elsewhere in the
world and, even in western Europe, religion remains a significant, if somewhat altered, feature of post-industrial life.

Civil Religion

Another way into the comparative debate is through the concept of 'civil religion', a term associated above all with the work of Bellah, whose 'Civil religion in America' (1967) became a seminal article in the literature, drawing attention to the peculiar mix of transcendental religion and national preoccupations that characterized the belief systems of modern Americans. We have already seen that religion is eliminated from the public sphere of American society in terms of institutional privilege or church/state connections. Other forms of religion and religious language are nonetheless pervasive. Their nature can be summarized as follows:

> The widespread acceptance by a people of perceived religio-political traits regarding their nation's history and destiny. It relates their society to the realm of absolute meaning, enables them to look at their political community in a special sense, and provides the vision which ties the nation together as an integrated whole. (Piérard and Linder, 1988: 22–3)

Americans have evolved a whole series of rituals associated with the machinery of state, with the school system (swearing allegiance to the American flag) and with public holidays (Memorial Day, Thanksgiving and so on). American presidents reinforce the connections using carefully chosen vocabulary in high-profile speeches. There is considerable empirical evidence for the concept of civil religion in its American forms.

However, the concept of civil religion can be adapted to other contexts. The British equivalent is well described by Wolffe (1993). It is epitomized first of all in the sacredness that surrounds the royal family in Britain and the rituals associated with the monarch as head of state. The most obvious examples can be found in the coronation ceremony and associated jubilee celebrations, but powerful echoes exist in royal weddings, services of remembrance and national thanksgivings (in which the royal family plays – and is expected to play – a major role). Royal divorces are, however, more problematic and there can be little doubt that the sacredness evoked in the immediate post-war period (notably by the coronation) has become more than a little tarnished by the activities of the younger royals in recent years. There is an additional problem in the case of Britain or, to be more accurate, the United Kingdom. Strictly speaking, not one but four distinct civil religions co-exist within the United Kingdom as each national identity in the Union asserts its specificity. Up to a point, the royal family works to overcome these differences (the Celtic countries are carefully included in the titles, activities and venues of the royal family), but the position of the Church of England (with the monarch as Supreme Governor) does not. The Church of England is just what its name implies: it is the privileged church of one part of the United Kingdom only.

Its privileged constitutional status cannot, in many ways, be anything but excluding to the Scots, Welsh and the Northern Irish.

The debate about 'establishment' (the legal connection between the Church of England and the state) raises other issues in a society in which fewer and fewer British people attend their churches with any regularity, and only a minority of these attend the Church of England itself. Such issues are compounded by the arrival of numerically small, yet sociologically significant, other faith communities into Britain in the post-war period. The debate, however, is complex, for there is a considerable body of opinion within the other faith communities which supports the privileged position of the Church of England. It is regarded as an institution which protects the interests of anyone in the population who takes faith seriously, whether that faith be Anglican, other Christian or non-Christian (Modood, 1994). It seems that a numerically weak and relatively marginalized established church can operate as an *inclusive* institution, in a way that its historically stronger, somewhat intolerant, antecedents could not.

A third form of civil religion can be found in France. Here a coherent secular world-view or ideology has replaced the transcendent element still to be found in the United States and in Britain. Public life in twentieth-century France is dominated by the concept of *laïcité*, an idea best described as the creation of *neutral* space in public life. This is an areligious space in which no religion is privileged and all religions compete as equals. The transfer of power from one French president to another, for example, is a strictly godless ceremony. The tomb of the unknown warrior in Paris lies under the Arc de Triomphe, not in consecrated ground, while the British equivalent, in contrast, can be found just inside the door of Westminster Abbey. Unlike most European countries, the teaching of religion in state schools is not permitted in France; suggestions that this might change arouse extremely strong reactions.

An interesting development within the field of civil religion can be found in the debates surrounding the evolution of European identity. If the European Union is to function effectively, it will – it can be argued – require its own civil religion, complete with flag, anthem and belief system. Conversely the fact that such symbols of commonality have barely emerged since the early days of the European Community, and that attempts to create them resonate so little in popular consciousness may indicate the lack of viability in the idea of Europe as a socio-political entity. Only time will tell. Bearing this in mind, it is all the more paradoxical that a continent which has, very largely, ceased to practise its historic faith appeals so frequently to its Christian heritage in order to define and protect its borders.

New Religious Movements and the New Age

There remains a persistent paradox within the material available to the sociology of religion. We know, sociologically at least, considerably more about new religious movements than we do about the beliefs and practices of the great majority within many western populations. Or to put the same point in a more positive way, there is an important and growing body of sociological material on sects, cults and new religious movements, which has been carried out by some of the most distinguished scholars in the field. Writers such as Barker, Beckford, Dobbelaere, Richardson, Wallis and Wilson have contributed substantially to our knowledge in this area.

What, then, is covered by the term 'new religious movement'? The best introduction to this field in the British context can be found in Barker's (1995) *New Religious Movements: A Practical Introduction,* which provides in a readily accessible form a large amount of practical as well as sociological material in this area. Included in the text is an extensive glossary of the new religious movements most likely to be encountered in Britain, giving a pen portrait of the group's history together with its principal beliefs. These range from the London Church of Christ (with beliefs that are relatively close to conservative evangelicals), through the groups that were especially well known in the 1960s and 70s (such as ISKCON or the Unification Church) to movements which are less easily assumed within the category 'religious' (such as the Human Potential Movements or Scientology). Indeed the first point to grasp is that new religious movements cannot just be lumped together as they are enormously varied both in their structures and in their belief systems. However, it *is* possible to establish categories – those for example of world-affirming or world-rejecting movements, plus those in-between which accommodate and adapt to the surrounding society – but such typologies are essentially heuristic devices (they help us to see patterns and contrasts), they are not absolute terms.

Bearing such diversity in mind, Barker (1995) suggests that some hundreds of thousands of British people may have had passing contact with new religious movements in the past 25 years. *Very* few of these, however, will have developed any sustained commitment to the groups in question. The main reason for new religious movements catching the attention of sociologists lies elsewhere, that is, in what they tell us about the nature of contemporary society. By looking at new religious movements and the controversies that they generate, we can discover a great deal about ourselves. What, for example, is regarded as normal or abnormal, as acceptable or unacceptable, as tolerable or intolerable in the name of religion and how does this vary from place to place or time to time? The answer lies in careful empirical analysis, which includes a comparative element. A good example can be found in the work of Richardson (1995) who looks at the workings of the emergent pan-European institutions with respect to minority religions and basic human rights in the European Union. This is an excellent study of social change. Change in this context should be understood in two ways: first in terms of institutions as a pan-European socio-legal framework begins to emerge and second, in terms of religious evolution as the notion of 'European religion' gives way to an increasing diversity of religions in Europe. New religious movements are one element in this diversity, the growing other faith communities are another. The legal aspect of this study gives it an admirably specific focus.

One form of new religious life at the turn of the millennium has acquired the title New Age. New Age religion (Heelas, 1996) is even harder to define than new religious movements, for it constitutes a rich amalgam of philosophies and practice from both eastern and western traditions. Like new religious movements, it can take myriad forms and can be discovered in a diversity of social contexts. Its influence can be felt, for example, in alternative medicine (in healing therapies), in the ecological debate (the Gaia principle), in the publishing world (scores of titles are published in this area every year) and in the world of management science. The overlap between the New Age and new forms of capitalism provides much food for thought for the sociologist. Is this a form of religion particularly suited to late capitalist development? Heelas (1996) explores this theme in some detail, looking at the New Age from two contrasting angles. At one and the same time the New Age is both a continuation of the key aspects of capitalism (global communication being an obvious illustration), and a rejection of these (preferring, for example, an altogether simpler and more human scale of living). In some ways it affirms the cultural trends of modernity, appealing more often than not to the successful or professional classes; in other ways it retains a counter-cultural element, a more or less explicit rejection of the societal aspirations, epitomized in the middle-class lifestyle. Broadly speaking, however, the real significance of the New Age in modern western societies lies in its affirmation of the sacred but in far from conventional forms. Whether or not it endures in the new millennium, the New Age itself remains a question for the next generation of sociological enquiry.

Fundamentalisms in the Contemporary World

The emergence of fundamentalisms worldwide has, quite rightly, demanded both public and sociological attention. The general public was bewildered by the vehemence of religious expression in, for example, the Iranian Revolution and its repercussions in Britain at the time over Rushdie's *Satanic Verses*. Many Europeans feel equally uneasy about the televangelism in Northern America. Sociologists, however, were also ill-prepared for such a phenomenon: the appearance on a large scale and across several continents of the type of religion normally associated with the word 'fundamentalist' was not anticipated as the twentieth century came to a end. It upset established patterns. One commentator puts this as follows:

> Around 1975 the whole process went into reverse. A new religious approach took shape, aimed no longer at adapting to secular values but at recovering a sacred foundation for the organisation of society – by changing society if necessary. Expressed in a multitude of ways, this approach advocated moving on from a modernism that had failed, attributing its setbacks and dead ends to separation from God. The theme was no longer aggiornamento but a 'second evangelisation of Europe': the aim was no longer to modernise Islam but to 'Islamicise modernity'. Since that date, the phenomenon has spread all over the world. (Kepel, 1994: 2)

It is this phenomenon which is known by the term fundamentalism; its rise has both astonished and bewildered its observers.

It is, however, a term which is notoriously difficult to define. The following offers a starting point: 'Fundamentalism can be described as a world-view that highlights specific essential "truths" of traditional faiths and applies them with earnestness and fervour to twentieth-century realities' (Kaplan, 1988: 5). Two crucial points are present: the existence of essential truths and their application to twentieth-century realities. Both elements need to be there, for the word fundamentalism should not normally be used to describe the traditional elements of religion that have been left undisturbed by the modern world, nor does it mean the creation of new ideas. It evokes, in contrast, the reaffirming of essential truths within a situation that has been profoundly disturbed by the pressures of an expanding global economy and the effects that this has had on social, political or ideological life.

The word 'fundamentalist' itself emerges from the debates among American Protestants in the years immediately following the First World War. The focus lay on re-establishing what were felt to be the traditional truths of Protestant teaching; beliefs that had been threatened by more liberal interpretations of scripture. The 'fundamentals' were set down once and for all and included a strong emphasis on the literal truth of the Bible. An important question follows from this: is it possible to transfer this kind of thinking – developed in a markedly western, not to say Protestant culture – to other world faiths which embody entirely different thought processes? Answers to this question vary but, whatever the case, the study of fundamentalisms requires understanding and empathy from the sociologist: what does it feel like to be in a situation in which patterns of belief and practice established for centuries are under attack? It demands in addition considerable sensitivity to and empathy with world-views that may be very different from the sociologist's own.

One of the most constructive ways forward has been to make use of an ideal-type analysis – that is a 'pure' type of fundamentalism is constructed against which empirical examples can be measured. There are various examples of this kind of approach (Caplan, 1987; Marty, 1989; Hunter, 1991) and the introductions to the enormous volumes produced by the Fundamentalist Project, directed by Marty and Appleby in the University of Chicago. (The sheer scale of this project gives some indication of the seriousness with which American academics regard this question. Five volumes now cover not only diverse aspects of fundamentalism itself, but detailed empirical studies from every world faith and almost every corner of the globe.) The ideal type elaborated in the following paragraph is also by Marty (1988) and is entitled, aptly enough, the 'Fundamentals of Fundamentalism':

> Fundamentalisms usually occur on the soil of traditional cultures which have been relatively protected from disturbance either from within or from outside. The seeds of fundamentalism are sown when such a situation is challenged or disturbed. A vague sense of threat, however, requires articulation; hence the crucial importance of the leader in the emergent fundamentalist group. From which situation the *reac*tion begins to set in: *re*action, *counter*action or *revanchist* action – these are the characteristics of fundamentalisms. They almost always make use of selective retrieval from the past, for which particular authority is sought. Such authority is very often discovered in the form of a sacred text or book. Subsequent actions aim to draw attention to the group in question. They are, quite frequently, aggressive actions, calculated to shock and indeed to intimidate. The 'us and them' mentality which emerges supplies a further characteristic of fundamentalisms; it is constructed quite deliberately to create and to maintain an impenetrable boundary between the group in question and the surrounding context.

A further point is crucial. In order to achieve such aims, fundamentalists make maximum use of modern technology. Hence the paradox in which groups that perceive themselves very largely as resistors to modernity, however this is experienced in each individual case, make optimal use of the products of the system which they regard as threatening to their very existence. The final step of the argument follows naturally enough: that fundamentalisms are themselves products of modernity in that they are born out of the clash between modernity and traditional cultures. Such a statement needs immediate qualification for not all such encounters end in a fundamentalist reaction; they seem, nonetheless, to constitute a necessary, if not sufficient, condition for the emergence of fundamentalist groups.

An important question concludes this section: should the word 'fundamentalism' be used in the singular or the plural? Is it possible, in other words, to find sufficient common elements between a wide diversity of movements to regard each of them as variations on a single theme? Commentators vary. It is probably more accurate to use the word in the plural, indicating a greater emphasis on difference rather than commonality; the ideal-type approach, in contrast, implies at least a degree of common themes or a family resemblance to use a different metaphor. Whatever the case, this is an additional area where careful comparative analysis is essential to the successful sociological task.

Religion and the Everyday: Aspects of Embodiment

An alternative and more recent focus draws from a different line of socio-logical thinking. It concerns the significance of religion in everyday life, not least its impact on the basics of human existence and the relationships of humanity to the environment. All religions have something to say about the body and about nature: diet, sex, sexuality, health, healing, death, even martyrdom (to name but some features of this debate) all lie within the remit of religious control and religious teaching. It should be remembered, however, that social anthropologists have never stopped making connections between the everyday and religion. The work of Mary Douglas on purity and pollution, for example, is required reading for sociologists in this area (Douglas, 1973, 1978).

An interesting sub-theme within this section concerns the relationship between religion and gender (Walter and Davie, 1998). In modern western societies it is almost always the case that women are more religious than men: they practise more, they believe more and what they believe in is noticeably different from their male counterparts. Why should this be so? This is a ques-tion that opens up the debate between nature and nurture. One school of thought finds the explanation primarily in the roles that women have been, and to some extent still are, obliged to fulfil in western societies. It follows that as these roles gradually evolve to become more like those of men (in terms, that is, of entry into the labour market and increasingly shared family commitments) so, too, will the religious predilections of women alter. This view is well documented in the work of Steggarda (1993). An alternative argument, however, emphasizes the physiological differences between men and women and the implications of such differences for the most sacred moments in life: those of birth and death. This school of thought argues that it is women that give birth and this experience leads them to see 'life' differ-ently from men. Despite the very evident changes in the medical conditions in which most women give birth, this experience remains a pivotal moment in the lives of most women. It is also the case that women tend, even in late modern societies, to be closer to death than men; the caring roles are more often ascribed to women (even within institutions) and women frequently outlive their partners.

Indeed a second illustration of religion and the everyday can be found in the burgeoning studies of death in modern societies. After decades of silence, comparable to the Victorian distaste for talking about sex, both society and sociologists have become increasingly preoccupied with the greatest mystery of all: what happens to us when we die. Offering solutions to this mystery is, undoubtedly, one of the traditional functions of religion. What happens then when the time-honoured explanations are no longer considered valid but death remains as unavoidable as ever. All that can be said about modern societies is that death can be put off for longer and that we die in greater comfort than in previous generations, but we still die.

The work of Walter (1990, 1994, 1996) is central in this area. He describes the evolution of death from traditional, through modern to neo-modern societies. Parts of the story are by now commonplace: death has evolved from being primarily a public event embedded in community, to being a private affair discussed in medical rather than religious terms. Antibiotics are of greater use for most of our ailments than cycles of prayer. This is not the end of the story, however. As dissatisfaction with the modern way of death increases, there is pressure for further change. Following Walter (1994) there are two possibilities. On the one hand, 'late-modern' revivalists assert the right of individuals to know that they are dying and to express how they feel, insisting (perhaps too strongly) that there is a need for such expressiveness. The 'postmodern' revivalist, on the other hand, is both more radical and more conservative. Individuals must be allowed to choose: to know that they are dying, or not to know; to grieve in an expressive manner, or not to do so. Whatever works for the individual in question is right.

Beneath these questions, however, lies a powerful subtext: both the dying and the grieving individual must be considered as a person, not simply a bundle of symptoms or sorrows. Walter drives the argument to a provocative conclusion: he maintains that holistic care has entered the mainstream of medicine largely as a response to the needs of dying people. The issues that he raises go, therefore, far beyond the immediate subject matter of his book. Among other things, they challenge very directly both the institutional arrangements of modern societies and the theoretical implications of some aspects of the secularization theory. Increasing specialization – an essential tenet of this theory – is obliged to give way, as 'holy' and 'whole' re-acquire their common root. The set apart, or the sacred, becomes once again integral to the well-being of both individual and collective life. Religion is rediscovered in the everyday.

Current Dilemmas

Imbalances

Imbalances prosper within the sociology of religion. Sociologists know far more about the exotic edges of religious life than they do about the beliefs of ordinary people. Or to put the same point in a different way, the edges of the religious jigsaw are far more adequately explored than the middle, which remains – at times – alarmingly blurred. Nobody would deny that the edges throw up interesting questions, maybe the most interesting, but the lack of information about the centre is hardly reassuring. Explanations for this lack derive, at least in part, from a preoccupation with secularization. Sociologists have assumed that the picture in the middle is blurred because it is fading away. It is true that certain aspects of religious life show a marked decline in western societies and we need to know why this is so. However other aspects do not, and why not is an equally important question. Non-western societies, moreover, demonstrate markedly different religious evolutions.

The imbalance needs, therefore, to be tackled in two ways. On the one hand, there is a need to refocus attention on the middle of the western picture: on the beliefs and practices of ordinary people and the effects that these do, or do not, have on everyday behaviour. On the other hand, the sub-discipline needs to escape from the assumption that the west – and more particularly western Europe – is necessarily leading the way. Martin's studies of Pentecostalism in Latin America, for example, suggest that new spaces are being cleared in European societies which may permit forms of religion that come from the New World into the Old, rather than the other way round.

Isolation and Insulation from Mainstream Sociology

Beckford (1989) has underlined both the insulation and the isolation of the sociology of religion from the parent discipline of sociology as it is tradition-ally conceived. This has proved a persistent weakness. For decades sociologists of religion have pursued their own interests, using their own frameworks of understanding, with relatively little reference to what has been going on else-where in sociology. Both partners have been impoverished as a result. The sociology of religion has lost the stimulus of theoretical developments within sociology itself; mainline (more especially European) sociologists continue to assume that religion is of marginal interest in contemporary society. Is it possible to escape from this dilemma? The following are tentative sugges-tions, which draw on the themes and perspectives of previous sections.

First, the sociology of religion – and especially the discussion about secu-larization – needs to escape from the discussions which concern the shift from pre-industrial to post-industrial societies (the shift which stimulated the early sociologists). The debate needs to move on if it is to get to grips with the characteristics of late-modern societies. Hervieu-Léger (1986) has made a significant start in this area, recognizing that the nature and forms of religion at the turn of a new century depend significantly on the nature of modern societies themselves. Contemporary religion is a product of, not a reaction to, modernity. At the same time Casanova has encouraged us to recognize the *public* nature of religion in the modern world; he does this by exploring case studies on both sides of the Atlantic.

A third possibility pursues an idea suggested by Beckford himself (1989): the proposition that religion should be seen as a cultural resource rather than a social institution, a focus that reflects a shift from structure to culture within sociology itself. Beckford sees the deregulation of religion as an unintended consequence of the secularization process. As religion frees itself from institutional control it changes its nature. It does not, however, disappear. Following Beckford, religion can become a highly significant cultural resource for a whole range of groups and individuals anxious to legitimate their point of view in an increasingly complex, and at times bewildering, society.

Finally, it is important to relate the evolutions in religious life to the changes taking place in secular society. It is true that religious institutions have declined since the Second World War and especially in western Europe. However, and the point cannot be emphasised too strongly, there have been similar changes in secular institutions; in, for example, political parties, trades unions and a wide range of leisure activities. To be more precise, the divergence between believing and belonging (already recognized in religious activities) can be seen in economic, political and cultural life as well (Davie, 1994 especially Chapter 10). Bearing this in mind, might it not be the case that explanations for at least some of these mutations lie in societal evolutions rather than religious ones? Or, to put the same point more provocatively, other areas of society appear to have been subject to some aspects of the process known as secularization.

Whatever the case, a demanding agenda awaits the sociologist of religion as the twentieth century gives way to the twenty-first. They must rise to the challenge, and religion must become once more an integral part of the discipline of sociology.

Further Reading

Barker, E. *New Religious Movements: A Practical Introduction,* London, HMSO, 1995. An excellent introduction to new religious movements.

Bruce, S. *Religion in the Modern World: from Cathedrals to Cults,* Oxford, Oxford University Press, 1996. A robust defence of the secularization thesis.

Davie, G. *Religion in Britain Since 1945,* Oxford, Blackwell, 1994, and Bruce, S. *Religion in Modern Britain,* Oxford, Oxford University Press, 1995. Both offer empirical material and contrasting perspectives on the evolution of religion in modern Britain.

Hamilton, M. *The Sociology of Religion,* London, Routledge, 1994. A useful and accessible introductory text to the sociology of religion.

Heelas, P. *The New Age Movement,* Oxford, Blackwell, 1996. A comprehensive introduction to New Age movements.

14

Mass Media

Natalie Fenton

The mass media refers to institutions concerned with the large-scale production and diffusion of communication. In contemporary societies most of the information through which we understand the world around us is constructed from media images of one sort or another. The media are thus relevant to all areas of social research and media saturation of societies raises important issues for the key sociological questions of social order, social change and the relationship between the individual and society. The information explosion is also central to questions of globalization which are examined in the last chapter. This chapter aims to introduce you to some of the ways in which sociologists have examined the production, content and effects of media representations. It should help you to understand:

■ Issues surrounding the relationship between the media and dominant ideologies

■ The significance of ownership and control and professional practices in the production of media representations

■ The interpretations of media texts provided by semiology, content analysis and postmodernism

■ Differing sociological views on how media representations are understood by audiences

■ The importance of linking the analysis of production, texts, and audience reception in understanding media

---

CONCEPTS

culture industry ■ ideology ■ hegemony
discourses ■ hyperreality ■ text ■ genre ■ code

Introduction: Why Study the Media?

The mass media are part of the 'cultural industries'. These industries contain public communications systems that differ from other areas of production by virtue of the goods they manufacture – newspapers, television programmes, advertisements, films and so on that play a pivotal role in organizing the images and discourses through which people make sense of the world. The ability of the media to construct meaning is debated widely. Do the mass media tell us how to think or do people create their own meanings through their experiences of life outside of the media? Does the type of media, whether it is radio, television, newspapers and so on effect the meaning we take from it? Does the context of reception matter; that is, where we happen to be, who we are with and the social and cultural issues that may arise from a viewing, listening or reading situation? How does the economic organization of these industries impinge on the production and circulation of meaning? These questions and others like them indicate that there are many different approaches to studying the mass media. However, their reasons for attending to the area of the mass media are remarkably similar – they all believe that mass communication has implications for freedom and control, consensus and the power structure of society. These issues are fundamental to sociology's quest to understand society.

A sociological approach to the media does not start with the media and say what they do to us. Rather it looks at the media as part of a set of institutions interconnected to other institutions within the wider context of society. Within this societal context it takes into account the production processes (standardized, routinized, controlled) and economic base of the media industries (types of ownership and uniform type), the content itself (narrative structure, genre), the audience (dependent, passive, organized, small, large) and what the sum effect of all this may be. This chapter gives a brief introduction to the study of media production, media content and media reception which is then situated in wider recent debates concerning globalization and new communication technologies.

The Media and Ideology

Access to a full range of debate, ideas, political policies and the like gives us the possibility of making informed choices about how society is run and to pass judgement on events and their causes. These choices are controlled and limited by the array of information the mass media choose to represent. With the majority of mass media being market led; that is, operating for profit rather than the public good, it is argued that the choice available to the general public is constrained largely to that which is both popular and cheap. Hence the predominance of quiz shows, soap operas and chat shows.

This is only one way in which the ongoing manipulation of public information and imagery takes place. It is useful to think of this as macro-manipulation via global political economic systems that limit the range of media products available to us. Such control over cultural production is said to construct an ideology which, it is argued, helps to sustain the material and cultural interests of its creators. An ideology is a system of ideas about society which has normally been simplified and manipulated in order to obtain popular support for certain actions. The mass media have established a leadership in the production and transmission of a particular type of culture in contemporary society. Fabricators of such dominant ideologies become 'information elites'. Their power or dominance stems directly from their ability publicly to articulate their preferred ideas. Socio-economic élites are able to saturate society with their preferred ideological agenda because they control the institutions that disseminate symbolic forms of communication such as the mass media. Viewed in this way it is easy to understand why Gerbner (1969) said that the ultimate purpose of the study of mass communication is to 'illuminate the complex web of power roles that govern the collective image making of a culture'. This perspective is born of classical Marxist theory that stresses economic position as the strongest predictor of social differences.

Economic disparities still underlie and help reproduce social inequalities in industrialized societies. Technological developments in the twentieth century have made the manner of social domination more and more complex. Social class differences in today's world are not determined solely or directly by economic factors. Ideological influence is crucial in the exercise of power. As we saw in Chapter 3, Gramsci – to whom the term hegemony is attributed – broadened Marxist theory of the dominant ideology. Gramsci emphasized society's 'super structure', its ideology producing institutions, which were in constant struggles over meaning and power (for example Gramsci, 1971, 1978). A shift in critical theory was thus made away from a preoccupation with capitalist society's 'base' (its economic foundation) and towards its dominant dispensaries of ideas (Lull, 1995). Attention was given to the structuring of authority and dependence in symbolic environments that correspond to, but are not the same as, economically determined class-based structures and processes of industrial production. According to Gramsci's theory of ideological hegemony, mass media are tools that ruling élites use to perpetuate their power, wealth and status by popularizing their own philosophy, culture and morality. The mass media uniquely 'introduce elements into individual consciousness that would not otherwise appear there, but will not be rejected by consciousness because they are so commonly shared in the cultural community' (Nordenstreng, 1977: 226).

Elliot suggested that the most potent effect of mass media is how they subtly influence their audiences to perceive social roles and routine personal activities; the controlling economic forces in society use the mass media to provide 'a rhetoric [through] which these [concepts] are labelled, evaluated and explained' (1974: 262). Television commercials for example, encourage audiences to think of themselves as 'markets rather than as a public, as consumers rather than as citizens' (Gitlin, 1979: 255). Hegemony implies a willing agreement by people to be governed by principles, rules and laws they believe operate in their best interests, even though in actual practice they may not. So, control is exercised by social consent and not by coercion. The study of mass communications is an attempt to uncover and unravel the complex mechanisms by which the production, distribution and consumption of ideological content is managed without recourse to the coercive use of state power in capitalist society.

In reality, dominant ideologies are not unified codes. Media imagery contains variety and contradiction. Furthermore, the effects of ideological representation and technological mediations cannot be easily predicted. There is no uniform social response to the perspectives put forward by the mass media. While dominant ideologies are cultivated hegemonically and contribute to the formation of mainstream consciousness, human beings – as individuals, family members, workers, students and so on – interpret and use mass media in ways that do not always coincide with the message senders' intentions. Hegemony is fragile. It requires renewal and modification through the assertion and reassertion of power. Hegemony has to be actively won and secured in a process that often involves struggles over meaning and conflict of views. The concept of hegemony allows for social change originating both from those who hold power in society and also from those who do not, because, crucially, hegemonic struggles can be lost (Hall, 1977).

This struggle over meaning takes place between the process of production and the act of reception, both of which are determined by their place in a wider social, political, economic and cultural context. Both are subject to constraints. Choices made by the audience must be looked at within the social context of their daily life and the content itself must be interpreted according to the social and political circumstances of its production. So, rather than just looking at how the mass media may exert an ideological effect on the behaviour and attitudes of individuals, it is crucial to consider the functioning of the mass media within the larger sociological perspective of culture, social structure and social groups. To understand the role of the mass media in society we need to consider it in its social entirety from inception to reception. No one part is distinct from the other; neither is the making of meaning a straightforward linear process. Nonetheless, we still need a detailed understanding of the parts to appreciate the whole – and so to media production.

Media Production – Encoding Meaning

The study of media production has developed in two main directions (Deacon *et al.*, 1999). The first considers how political and economic forces structurally delimit news production. This has focused largely on patterns of ownership in media industries and state regulation and the subsequent control exerted over the news creation process (for example Golding and Murdock, 1991). The second is more related to mainstream sociology with the study of media organizations and the sociology of occupations, the impact of professional practices, occupational routines and cultural values of journalists (for example Tunstall, 1971). Unlike the standard political economy perspective it takes the central problem for understanding journalism in liberal societies to be the journalists' professed autonomy and decision making power. The tensions between the traditions rest on the differing emphasis each gives to internal and external factors as the main determinants of news production.

Ownership and Control

Ownership of private media is now largely in the hands of multinational corporations (Golding and Murdock, 1991). The power conferred by ownership to influence the ethos, editorial direction and market definition of commercial media – principally through the hiring and firing of staff, the setting of organizational policy and the allocation of rewards within media organizations – is mostly vested in one corporate sector. The increasing amount of cultural production accounted for by large corporations has long been a source of concern to theorists of democracy. These theorists saw a fundamental contradiction between the ideal that public media should operate largely in the public interest and the reality of concentrated private ownership. They feared that proprietors would use their property rights to restrict the flow of information and debate on which the vitality of democracy depended. These fears were fuelled by the rise of the great press barons at the turn of the century who had no qualms about using their large circulations to promote their pet political causes or to denigrate people they disagreed with. Since then, we are faced with multimedia conglomerates with significant stakes across a range of central communications sectors. The most well-known example is Rupert Murdoch's media empire (Figure 14.1).

Place	Media ownership
London	News International (*The Times*, the *Sun*, *Today*, *News of the World*, *The Sunday Times*), BSkyB (with over 20 satellite channels reaching over 4 million homes), HarperCollins UK, News Datacom
Hong Kong	Star TV and related satellite services
Australia	News Corporation, related newspaper interests, airlines
Germany	50 per cent interest in Vox
South America	An interest in Canal Fox, joint ventures with the Globo organization
United States	Newspaper and magazine interests as well as control of Fox Television Stations

Figure 14.1   Rupert Murdoch's global media empire

The rise of communications conglomerates facilitated by privatization, deregulation and the vast development of global media markets adds a new element to an old debate about potential abuses of owner power. Not only are there problems of proprietor power influencing editorials and the firing of staff who do not share their political philosophies, but different parts of the media industry have come together in support of each other to exploit the overlaps between the company's different media interests. The company's newspapers may give free publicity to their television stations or the record and book divisions may launch products related to a new movie released by the film division. The effect is to reduce the diversity of cultural goods in circulation. Growing concentration of ownership has increased the potential for centralized control over the media. Its dangers were illustrated in Italy's 1994 election when the Fininvest TV channel (with a 40 per cent market share) gave ill-disguised support to its controller and right-wing businessman, Silvio Berlusconi, who was thrust into the premiership without ever having held office before (Curran, 1996).

The production of communications, however, is not merely a reflection of the controlling interests of those who own or control the broad range of capital and equipment which make up the means by which cultural goods are made and distributed. It is also subject to those who produce the words and images on a daily basis – the media professionals.

Professional Practices: the Sociology of News Production

News is the product of organizational processes and human interaction. It is shaped by the methods used in the news-gathering process which is in turn affected by the information sources available, and the organizational requirements, resources and policies of particular institutions. For example, the need of news organizations to secure regular and usable copy means that certain journalists are assigned to specific beats – such as Westminster or the law courts. This encourages fuller reporting of these areas. It also places journalists close to key sources where information is often traded for publicity (Gandy, 1982). With several newspapers covering the same beats, it has also been said to encourage a pack mentality in which journalists on the same beat form collective news judgements (Tunstall, 1971).

News relies on the sources journalists feed on for information. Sources can be anyone who can provide information of any sort, from the person in the street to a government minister or an 'expert'. The role of sources and their relationship to journalists and the production of news has contributed to a more recent third approach to the study of news production, which McNair (1994) labels the 'culturalist approach'. It differs from other approaches in its insistence that the production of news 'is not simply a function of ownership, nor of journalistic practices and rituals, but of the interaction between news organisations, the sources of their output, and other social institutions' (McNair, 1994: 48, cited in Deacon, 1996: 174). News creation is seen as a constant struggle between different players, each attempting to present their own version of reality. However, opportunities to access the news-making process are not the same for all. Those in positions of power are given the added advantage of speaking as an authority on a topic and asserting the primary definition of an issue to which all other interpretations must respond. This focus on news sources rather than the media organization *per se* has generated more interest in the specific dynamics of news creation. It has also led to criticisms of earlier accounts of news production for being excessively deterministic, and for exaggerating the ability of social and political élites to manage hegemonic power via the mass media.

On the whole the news may work hegemonically to reflect prevailing views, opinions, and values, but this hegemony is neither faultless nor all encompassing. Not all reporters support the dominant ideology in their writing. Rather, news reflects a continual struggle for renewal and renegotiation for a ruling bloc to maintain its position (Fenton *et al.*, 1995). From this perspective, the power of 'primary definition' (the initial interpretation of reality by those in positions of authority) is not a precise expression of the social structure, but an achievement gained through successful strategic action (Schlesinger, 1990). Although agencies of the state and other powerful élites enjoy many advantages in getting their messages across, their ability to define the news is not absolute. Tensions within political systems, investigative journalism, inter-governmental conflict, and political interventions by non-official sources who have gained credibility within the media, can and do open up media debate on certain issues (Deacon and Golding, 1994).

Approaching news production from the position of news sources brings social action and agency to the fore and dismisses earlier research based on reproductionist accounts of ideology. 'The concept of active production challenges the view that the media are just a passive conduit by which the powerful instruct the powerless what to think and feel. However, at the same time, most proponents... are sensitive to the dangers of overstating the diversity and plurality that this resistance is capable of creating' (Deacon *et al.*, 1999). The autonomy of the moments of production must also take account of the limits to this freedom.

One way of analysing how the media may present limitations to freedom is to look at the output of the cultural industries to gauge the type of imagery and information in circulation that we take for granted.

Media Content

In a society saturated with mass media the images they produce are ever more responsible for the construction and consumption of social knowledge and represent a bank of available meanings which people draw on in their attempts to make sense of their situation and find ways of acting within and against it. The media select items for attention and provide rankings of what is and is not important – they set an agenda for public opinion. The way the media choose themes, structure dialogue and control debate is a crucial consideration in any discussion on representations.

Representations should be viewed as just that – accounts of the world that are incomplete interpretations rather than unmediated descriptions of the 'really real' (Rakow, 1992). Reality cannot be assimilated unproblematically into a representation that is merely descriptive because representation also entails delegation and construction.

Semiology

One way of studying media representation is through semiology. Semiology is the study of signification, or meaning production. It treats language as a system of codes and signs which construct meaning. Semiology argues that material reality can never be taken for granted, imposing its meanings upon human beings. Reality is always constructed and made intelligible by culturally specific systems of meaning. This meaning is never innocent but rather has a particular purpose behind it which semiology can uncover. In Barthes (1957/1973) seminal work, *Mythologies*, he suggested that meanings are produced through the codes at work in representations, and that while meanings might appear to be natural and obvious they are in fact constructed. To enable us to understand this constructedness Barthes treated each sign as a combination of thing (material object) and interpretation (concept).

In semiology a sign is anything that stands for something else. For example, a bunch of red roses stands for passion. Signs also acquire meaning from the things that they fail to stand for – we know that it is a bunch of red roses because it is not a bunch of weeds – as well as from their position in social myths and conventions which shape the way we perceive ourselves; in our particular culture red roses may stand for passion, in another culture they may mean something entirely different. A bunch of red roses is in essence a load of flowers which have no significant meaning outside the systems of rules and conventions which constituted it as signifying passion. Barthes breaks the bunch of roses down analytically into a signifier, the roses (or form), a signified, passion (or concept), with the combination of the signified and the signifier together making the sign (the act of signification). This attribution of meaning – that the roses signify passion and not anger – cannot be understood simply in terms of the system of signs, but must be located in the context of social relationships in which the meaning making occurs.

The ideas of semiology go further than signifier+signified=sign to consider the concept of myth. The use of the mythic dimension in the analysis of texts allows us to pass from semiology to ideology. In Barthes' words the principle of myth 'transforms history into nature':

> What allows the reader to consume myth innocently is that he does not see it as a semiological system but as an inductive one... the signifier and the signified have, in his eyes, a natural relationship... any semiological system is a system of values; now the myth-consumer takes the signification for a system of facts: myth is read as a factual system, whereas it is but a semiological system. (Barthes, 1953/1967: 142)

An example given by Barthes is that the presentation of women in many media texts makes the role of women as mothers appear natural and inevitable. In his later work Barthes introduces two new concepts of denotation and connotation. Denotation is the literal, taken-for-granted meaning, a bunch of red roses, a white dress, a pair of running shoes. But the task of semiology is to go beyond these denotations to get at the connotations of the sign – respectively passion, purity and fitness. This reveals how myth works through particular signs. In this way the constructed, manufactured and historical location of the myth can be discovered. This may appear to be a bunch of roses but it connotes passion; this may appear to be just a picture of a woman in a white dress but it connotes purity and so on. Thus the methods of semiology reveal the ideologies contained in cultural myths (Strinati, 1995). Connotation or 'second order signification' concerns the latent cultural beliefs and values expressed by a sign or a sign system. A recognition and understanding of the various codes and conventions underlying the particular articulation of signs is necessary for second order signification to work; that is, one needs to have a thorough knowledge of the culture a sign system originates from.

A much-quoted semiological study of a girls' magazine called *Jackie* was undertaken by McRobbie in 1982. *Jackie* is conceived of as system of signs that work to 'position' the female readers for their later roles as wives and mothers by means of the ideology of teenage femininity it cultivates. The magazine addresses a young female audience on the basis of a consumerism and culture which defines female adolescence and which hides differences such as race or class. McRobbie uses semiology to reveal the codes which form the ideology of adolescent femininity. This methodology allows McRobbie to uncover the 'culture of femininity' which, as 'part of the dominant ideology', 'has saturated' the lives of the young girls, 'colouring the way they dress, the way they act and the way they talk to each other' (McRobbie, 1991: 93). Semiological analysis is used to discover codes in *Jackie* which define its ideology of teenage femininity, which McRobbie then argues acts as a powerful force on the lives of its readers. The main codes include the code of romance, which involves searching for (heterosexual) romance, finding the right boy and thus placing yourself in a competitive relationship with your girl friends; the code of personal life, which includes personal difficulties and concerns usually raised in the problem pages with the replies reinforcing the ideology of adolescent femininity found elsewhere in the magazine; the code of fashion and beauty which instructs readers on how to dress and look in order to be able to meet the demands of this ideology; and finally the code of pop music that involves stars and fans. Her analysis of these codes leads McRobbie to the following conclusion:

> *Jackie* sets up, defines and focuses exclusively on the 'personal', locating it as the sphere of prime importance to the teenage girl. This world of the personal and of the emotions is an all-embracing totality, and by implication all else is of secondary interest. Romance, problems, fashion, beauty and pop all mark out the limits of the girl's feminine sphere. Jackie presents 'romantic individualism' as the ethos *par excellence* of the teenage girl... This is a double edged kind of individualism since in relation to her boyfriend... she has to be willing to give in to his demands, including his plans for the evening, and by implication, his plans for the rest of their lives. (McRobbie, 1991: 131)

The main criticism of semiological analyses is that ultimately the conclusions it reaches are arbitrary. Depending on the views and opinions of the researchers the analysis of the representation will change. The 'meanings' taken from the text are implied meanings that rest on connotative interpretation. Semiological analysis is based on three main assumptions: first, that in the process of analysis the researcher can uncover the latent meaning that will match the understanding of every reader; second, that covert meanings have more impact on one's consciousness than overt or denotative meanings; and third, that the researcher is able to resist all manner of ideological influence.

Content Analysis

Not all research on media texts has drawn on semiotic analysis – much of it has turned to content analysis. Content analysis is often used to assess the dominant characteristics of large quantities of media output. Content analysis is defined as 'a research technique for the objective, systematic and quantitative description of the manifest content of communication' (Berelson, 1952). Simplified greatly, the basic premise of content analysis is to count things like the amount of women characters, the roles they are presented in and the themes that accompany their representation. Studies that adopt this methodology have discovered that males greatly outnumber females in prime-time TV, in advertisements women stereotypically clean, launder and cook while men give the orders and eat the meals (Tuchman *et al.*, 1978; van Zoonen, 1994). This methodology has the advantage of being able to handle large quantities of data, such as months of newspaper coverage or broadcast material and offer an audit of the types of information and entertainment available to us. It has been criticized because it does not go beyond the manifest content and delve into the deeper connotative or latent meanings in a text. This limitation can be construed as an advantage, since it enables a methodology that fulfils traditional scientific requirements of objectivity with results that are reliable and able to be tested statistically for their significance. A focus on manifest content should ensure that a replication of the same project will produce roughly similar results. In practice the more sophisticated content analysis that accounts for thematic prevalence does demand some degree of qualitative evaluation. In these cases definitions of categories must be as tight as possible to ensure continuity and validity of the final figures.

Putting Postmodernism in the Picture

Since the mid-1980s an approach which has been labelled 'postmodernism' has emerged that has impacted on the way we think about media content. Postmodern thinking has abandoned traditional sociological reasoning based on determinist models of social structure replacing it with how discourses comprising words and statements and other representational forms actively produce social realities as we know them. The term 'discourse' refers to specific meanings and values which are articulated in language in specific ways describing and delimiting what it is possible to say and not to say.

Those who go under the banner of postmodernism approach society as an ensemble of fragmented individual consumers swimming in a sea of images, from which they construct their own meanings about the world. There are no overarching narratives about how the world works. Reality is fragmented. The consequences of this are to conceptualize power as highly dispersed rather than concentrated in identifiable places or groups. In media studies this shift has been seen in a move away from the political economy of cultural production to a concern with words, texts and representations (or discursive constructions).

Postmodern theorists claim that contemporary communication practices are non-representational and non-referential. In other words, they have no purchase outside the text, they have no separate external domain. Rather, they are self-reflexive and self-referential. Contemporary culture becomes no more than a constant recycling of images previously created by the media. The recognition of media implosion has caused many postmodern theorists to question the practices of mass communication in terms of the relationship of an event and its media representation. It is claimed that the proliferation of new media technologies makes it difficult, if not impossible, to discern the difference between images and reality. Moreover, postmodernists point out that many media images are hyperreal; that is, more real than real. As Poster (1990: 63) explains, 'a communication is enacted... which is not found in the context of daily life. An unreal is made real... The end result is a sensational image that is more real than real and has no referent in reality.' Thus the notion of representation becomes problematic. Contemporary media do not represent reality, they constitute it.

Postmodernism asserts that popular culture signs and media images increasingly dominate our sense of reality, and the way we define ourselves and the world around us. In a media-saturated society it is no longer a question of the media distorting reality, rather the media have become reality – the only reality we have (Strinati, 1995). So, there is little point in studying the content of the mass media to see how they may affect our everyday lives; little point in counting instances of racism or sexism and arguing against them; little point even in studying how people understand the media since 'one interpretation is not by definition better or more valid than another' (van Zoonen, 1996: 48). There is little point because the media are reality, are inescapable. As McRobbie says:

> We do not exist in social unreality while we watch TV or read the newspaper nor are we transported back to reality when we turn the TV off to wash the dishes or discard the paper and go to bed. Indeed perhaps there is no pure social reality outside the world of representation. Reality is relayed to us through the world of language, communication and imagery. Social meanings are inevitably representations and selections. Thus when the sociologists calls for an account which tells how life really is, and which deals with the real issues rather than the spectacular and

exaggerated ones which then contribute to the moral panic, the point is that their account of reality would also be a representation, a set of meanings about what they perceive as the real issues. (1994: 217)

The idea that the mass media take over reality has been criticized for exaggerating their importance. The notion that reality has imploded inside the media such that they can only be defined by the media has also been questioned. Most people would probably still be able to distinguish between the reality created by the media and that which exists elsewhere. As Strinati (1995: 239) states, if reality has really imploded into the media how would we know it has happened? The only response is that we know it has happened because there are those who are all knowing and have seen it.

The world according to postmodernists is a world of surface appearances. No one experiences anything directly, there is only mediated reality resulting in a complete absence of lived experience. Issues of truth are treated as out of date in favour of speculation about the possible meanings of texts. However, whereas we may recognize the description of reality as disorderly and fragmented it also shows patterns of inequality. If the media are literally our reality we effectively deny that material inequalities do exist. This is insulting to all who suffer them. As Kitzinger and Kitzinger argue:

Feminists struggled for decades to name 'sexism' and 'anti-lesbianism'. We said that particular images of women – bound and gagged in pornography magazines, draped over cars in advertisements, caricatured as mothers-in-law or nagging wives in sitcoms – were oppressive and degrading. The deconstructionist insistence that texts have no inherent meanings, leaves us unable to make such claims. This denial of oppressive meanings is, in effect, a refusal to engage with the conditions under which texts are produced, and the uses to which they are put in the dominant culture. (1993: 15)

Ultimately, any work that focuses on texts, form and images alone at the expense of power and the structural constraints of class, income, culture and history is limiting and partial. For example, when studying gender in the media, an exploration of the concept of power in relation to female authority, influence, coercion, and manipulation inside media organizations as well as the public performance and record of high visibility women in economic and political élites is crucial to communications research on imaging and empowerment.

Similarly, any work that dismisses the role of the audience in the process of mass communication cannot account for differences or similarities in interpretation and runs the risk of reductionism whereby we all become either enslaved by ideology or free-floating discourses. In recognition of this, research has emerged that prioritizes the role of the audience in meaning making rather than seeing the audience as constructed or subsumed by the text:

If we are concerned with the meaning and significance of popular culture in contemporary society, and how cultural forms work ideologically or politically, then we need to understand cultural products as they are understood by audiences. (Lewis, 1991: 47)

Media Reception – Decoding Meaning

The role of the audience, or consumer, in the construction of meaning has been subject to differing analytical perspectives. Each tackles in its own way the tension between audiences' constructive capabilities and the constraining potential of culture and ideology (expressed through the mass media). Media theorists in this area agree on the importance of media in our daily lives. Yet the majority disagree on most of the major dimensions of audience analysis: in their conception of the audience (is it active or passive, vulnerable or resistant?); of the programme (as a resource for diverse motivations or a normative pressure on all of us, as comprised of literal or hidden meanings); of the processes of effects (either by audience selectivity or by media imposition); of the nature of effects (ideological, symbolic, belief-based or behavioural); of the level of effects (individual, familial, social mainstreaming or political); and of the appropriate methods for study (ethnography, survey, experiment, text analysis, or social commentary) (Livingstone, 1991).

For the sake of simplicity, two intertwined strands can be distinguished. The first emphasizes the capacity of texts to position readers, thus ensuring that the limitations of response are provided by the texts themselves. Readers are thus 'held in ideology' (Tudor, 1995) by their textual placement. This audience positioning has led to texts being described as having 'inscribed readers'. The main thrust of this analysis was to see texts as instruments of ideology primarily in their capacity to situate the reader. The second strand shifts emphasis from the power of texts to confer meaning to the interpretative power of the audience.

Media Effects – The Audience as Powerless

Media effects research has most commonly been associated with a stimulus–response learning theory. This suggests that mass media texts are very powerful and that their messages are more or less irresistible; the media are seen to behave like a hypodermic needle, injecting audiences with their messages. Throughout the 1950s and 60s this perspective recurred around two themes – could violence in the mass media induce violent behaviour in the audience; and what effect did the mass media have on people's political attitudes? In the case of media and violence many proponents of early effects studies argued that horrible images on the media will make us horrible, not horrified; that terrifying things will make us terrifying, not terrified; and to see something aggressive makes us feel aggressive, not aggressed against (Barker and Petley, 1997).

Media effects theory was widely criticized as textual determinism which robbed readers of their social context and critical agency leaving no room for interpretative manoeuvre. In the extreme this translated the audience into cultural dupes, blank slates waiting to be written on. Media effects research is also criticized for only studying one type of effect – that which is more or less immediate, behavioural and measurable. The effects measured are confined to those intended by the sender thus lacking a critique of the production of messages from within the power relations of society. Media effects research is said to take messages as neutral and non-problematic givens and to be overly simplistic in dimensions of messages selected for study. Ironically media effects research is criticized most of all for being unable to understand the effects of the mass media because it fails to take account of cumulative, delayed, long-term and unintended effects including those which stabilize the status quo (Golding and Murdock, 1978). For example, political coverage in the mass media may not change the way we actually vote, but it may influence the way we think politically. Similarly, the fact that violence in the media does not appear to generate homicidal tendencies in most who consume it does not mean that it is of no consequence (Lewis, 1991).

The downfall of 'effects' research lead theories of communication away from sender–receiver objectivist models to subjectivist theories which start from the premise that reality is socially constructed. In other words, theorists rejected the idea that 'reality' somehow exists 'out there' and all that the media do is act as a mirror to reflect it; to a more sophisticated understanding of 'reality' as something that is constantly changing, constructed and manipulated by all social players. The notion of a reality that the media pass on more or less truthfully and unproblematically is far too simplistic: media production is not just a matter of reflection but entails a complex process of negotiation, processing and reconstruction; media audiences do not simply take in or reject media messages, but use and interpret them according to their own social, cultural and individual circumstances – the audience is involved in making sense of the images they see; media are not only authorized to reflect reality but to represent our collective hopes, fears and fantasies (for example, in films which seek to challenge sexual stereotyping) – the message does not have the total monopoly on meaning. Of course, the power to set the media agenda may not be evenly spread as already discussed; neither may the ability to manipulate and interpret information be equal for everyone.

Media Reception – The Audience as Powerful

As an antidote to a life condemned to ideological slavery came the second analytic strand – the active audience. Active audience theorists have stressed that audiences are capable of arriving at their own decisions about the meaning of a media text and that the text themselves were *polysemic* (for example Radway, 1984; Ang, 1985). Polysemy refers to the potential for multiple meanings to be taken from one text, thus allowing ambiguity and interpretative freedom.

Active audience research is most often associated with the work of the Centre for Contemporary Cultural Studies (CCCS) at the University of Birmingham from the late 1970s onwards. Hall (1980) the director of the centre argued that a text contains a 'preferred reading' – the meaning intended by the person who produced it – but that reading may be undermined when it is 'decoded' by the audience. A 'negotiated reading' may be generated in which audiences modify the text's meaning in the context of their own experiences, or an 'oppositional reading' may occur in which the meaning of the text is undermined by the audience.

Early empirical support for these ideas came in the form of research on audience interpretations of *Nationwide,* an early evening news programme in Britain in the 1970s. Morley (1980) showed recordings of the programme to groups which were made up of students, trade unionists, managers or apprentices. He found that managers and apprentices were most likely to interpret the texts in ways that were consistent with the preferred readings; teacher training and art students were most likely to construct negotiated readings; and groups of trade unionists tended to come up with oppositional readings. This research was seen to offer confirmation of the ability of certain segments of the audience to interpret certain texts differently from the meaning intended by the author or producer and from other audience groups. This stimulated further examinations of the role of the active audience in relation to (among others) television programmes (Ang, 1985; Corner *et al.*, 1990), romantic fiction (Radway, 1984) and comics (Barker, 1993). It also stimulated a tradition of what is often called 'ethnographic' research on audiences in which members are either interviewed about a text or invited to write about their consumption. The audience was no longer conceptualized as a collection of passive spectators but as a group of individuals who can see the hidden text of a cultural product for what it is and is not. The corollary of this was that as individuals have the capacity to undermine the intended meaning of texts, they can therefore subvert the relations of power within which they are located (Fenton *et al.*, 1998).

Postmodernism takes this theorizing one step further, insisting that we are all forever actively resisting that which is reality. We do this, it is claimed, through our knowledge of images and their construction. In other words we know we cannot escape mainstream imaging, we know that it is as real as our material existence but we also know that it is constructed and that we can play a part in the meanings given to it. The idea is that we play with the notion of constructedness and take what we want from the bits and pieces at our disposal. In most of this work audiences are seen as actively constructing meaning so that texts which appear on the face of it to be reactionary can be subverted. The subversion comes through the pleasures that are gained from it. For example, following postmodern ideas Ang argues that the world of fantasy is the 'place of excess where the unimaginable can be imagined' (1996: 106) and this is interpreted by Ang as liberatory. Based on the assumption that discourse is reality and there are always multiple discourses to choose from the individual becomes a self-made jigsaw of bits and pieces who recognizes, enjoys and plays with the constructedness of their own existence. This ignores the fact that someone made the jigsaw pieces in the first place, drew particular configurations on them and gave them to us in particular packaging designed to appeal and to sell. Postmodern perspectives suffer from an under-theorizing of the social conditions and foundations for creating meaning and communication or what Jameson (1991) has called a lack of historicity: they fail to situate their analyses within larger historical and structural contexts. There is also a huge contradiction in postmodernism which asserts both that representation constitutes reality and that the audience is powerful and able to resist media messages. Put simply, if the media are everywhere, inescapable, reality itself, then how can we resist them, avoid them, see through them and recognize their constructedness?

If the active audience theories are taken to the extreme they translate into an interpretative free-for-all in which the audience possesses an unlimited potential to read any meaning at will from a given text. There are many problems with studies that adopt such an extreme approach. Morley has criticized the neglect in most active audience research of 'the economic, political and ideological forces acting on the construction of texts' (1993: 15). By drawing attention away from the media and texts generally as instruments of power, they have been accused of a lack of appreciation of wider political factors and hence of political quietism (Corner, 1991) and ideological desertion. The same criticism can be directed at postmodern accounts.

The very notion of 'active' has been equated with powerful. This has caused several critics to question the extent to which audiences genuinely exert power over the text. Condit (1989), for example, argued that the common finding that audiences derive their own pleasures from texts should not be taken to imply that they are in fact deriving their own interpretation and therefore undermining the inscribed messages of those texts. She suggests through an examination of points made by two people about an episode of *Cagney and Lacey,* an American detective show, that 'they shared a basic construction of the denotations of the text' (1989: 107), in spite of holding very different views about the central focus of the episode (abortion). Thus, while audiences are active in their consumption of texts they are not necessarily critical of its denotation; nor do they derive alternative views about it (Fenton *et al.*, 1998). A further criticism is that the active audience approach fails to give adequate recognition to the fact that authors of texts are able to frame issues and messages. They do this through what is actually present in the text and through what is absent – the silences in texts are just as significant as the messages within the texts themselves in terms of the capacity of audiences to derive alternative interpretations (Bryman, 1995).

What is clear is that how we think about the audience depends on our theoretical framework. As a result of a growing awareness of the framing power of texts and an understanding that the text must be viewed in relation to hegemonic culture, more circumscribed accounts of audience activity have emerged. As the earlier example illustrates, these tend to recognize that differently located audiences may derive particular interpretations of texts, but that the text itself is rarely subverted. In other words, the essential power of authors to frame audience reception is accepted; audiences do engage in interpretation but that interpretation is marginal to the denotative structure of the text. In this manner ideology remains a crucial reference point. Examples of research which reveals this orientation include Kitzinger's (1993) research on AIDS in the media, Corner *et al.*'s (1990) study of the representation of the nuclear energy industry and Fenton *et al.*'s (1998) study of the representation of social science in the media. In the latter, the researchers analysed responses to newspaper, television and radio news reports of social scientific research to reveal a marked consistency between intended meaning at the point of production and audience understanding and interpretation of the text. This is not to say that audience members passively deferred to the text – on the contrary, they found substantial evidence of independent thought and scepticism. However, the 'distinctiveness of decoding' occurred when evaluating the text rather than at the point of interpretation. Resistance to the message did not lead to a renegotiation of it. It was interrogated but not expanded. Two reasons are given for this interpretative closure. The first relates to the genre of the text being analysed. Hard news reporting is governed by a range of mechanistic, narrative conventions that are intended to generate a denotative transparency to inhibit potential readings. For example, it is a genre where prominence and frequency of appearance are reliable indications of significance *and* signification. Most news consumers are conversant with the rules of this presentational game and construct their readings according to them. As such news is a peculiarly 'closed' form of actuality, coverage whose polysemic potential is circumscribed. There is none of the *interpretative* room to manoeuvre that is such an evident and essential facet of other forms of fictional and factual genres.

The second reason for this interpretative closure relates to the nature of the subject matter being reported. For example, one of the news reports under study is about a remote and esoteric issue (false memory) which, although its broader implications resonate with the audience, remains beyond their direct personal and professional experiences. This, it is argued, is a situation where we find the most acceptance of media definitions and the power of the audience is at its most limited (Fenton *et al.*, 1998).

In these analyses the reader can effect the reading process, can resist the 'preferred reading' (that is, that which appears dominant in the text) up to a point and to that end is an active agent. Yet agency is limited by structure. As Tudor (1995: 104) says:

> The remarkable capacity of human beings to construct diverse meanings and take a variety of pleasures from texts is matched only by the equally remarkable degree to which those meanings and pleasures are common to large numbers of people.

Understanding the Mass Media

What this holistic approach to the sociology of the mass media reveals is that when we think about the role of the media in society we must include the location of the medium in economic structures (commercial or public media), their specific characteristics (print or broadcast), the particular genres (news or soap opera and so on), and the audiences they appeal to. Individually the elements of production, texts and reception of media make no sense; they are intrinsically linked in the process of meaning production (van Zoonen, 1994). The production of media texts is full of tensions and contradictions resulting from conflicting organizational and professional discourses. As a result of the tensions in the production or 'encoding' process (Hall, 1980), media texts do not constitute a closed ideological system, but reflect the contradictions of production. In this way media texts carry multiple meanings and are open to a range of interpretations. However, the range of meanings a text offers is not infinite. The encoded structures of meaning are brought back into the practices of audiences by their decoding process.

These largely theoretical debates on the mass media in society can be related to almost any development in the mass cultural industries. The processes of mass communication from production, text, to reception are fundamental to all forms of media. However, every so often new forms of media are developed that force us to reconsider the way we look at mass media and society. New communication technologies have resulted in a shrinking of time and space. Think of the birth of television that enabled us to watch images of starving children in another continent as we eat our evening meal; that enabled people all over the world simultaneously to watch live sporting events or worldwide fundraising initiatives. New communication technologies such as the video recorder and the portable video camera have also increased the potential for official and unofficial surveillance. For example, hand-held video footage of a racial assault by police on an Afro-Caribbean man, Rodney King, was filmed by a bystander and shown on television prompting outrage in the Los Angeles community that led to social unrest; in the UK surveillance cameras filmed a child, Jamie Bulger, with two young boys who were then accused and later found guilty of his murder. Most recently, the information superhighway, otherwise known as the Internet, has opened up debates on the democratic potential of communication technologies to provide everyone with access to a full range of information. Alongside and directly related to the development of new communication technologies the globalization of the cultural industries has taken place. Any sociology of the mass media must locate itself within this changing political economic context – it is to these two contemporary issues that this chapter now briefly turns.

Contemporary Issues

Globalization

Many media groups are increasingly operating internationally or globally. The term 'globalization', discussed in more detail in Chapter 15, refers to 'the intensification of worldwide social relations which link distant locations in such ways that local happenings are shaped by events occurring many miles away and vice versa' (Giddens, 1991a: 64). The increasing trend towards globalization of the mass media can be divided into three main areas. First, as noted earlier, the media industries are part of communication conglomerates which are increasingly transnational in terms of the range of their operations and activities. This is a process that has been spurred on by large-scale mergers and take-overs among the communication conglomerates. One example among many is the Japanese electronics giant Sony's take-over of the US-based CBS record label in 1987; the international record industry is now largely owned by five labels – Sony-CBS, RCA, Warner, Thorn-EMI and Poly-gram – each of which is owned by a multinational corporation. Another obvious example is Rupert Murdoch's media empire (Figure 14.1) with control over media industries around the world.

The second aspect of globalization refers to the increasing role of exports and the production of media goods for an international market. In the case of television the sale of programmes in foreign markets is becoming an important source of revenue. The BBC now sells it programmes to over 100 countries (Thompson, 1990). Programme producers, advertising agencies, as well as the companies that manufacture consumer products are owned in advanced capitalist societies. International film and television sales are largely dominated by American companies. In 1981 American films accounted for 94 per cent of foreign films broadcast on British television, 80 per cent of those broadcast on French television and 54 per cent of those broadcast on West German television. In western Europe as a whole in 1983 approximately 30 per cent of television broadcasting time was filled with imported programmes; American imports representing 75 per cent of all imports. The share represented by US-originated programming in other parts of the world is even greater. These media products depict western (often idealized) lifestyles. This *cultural imperialism* is transnational. More recently, there is some debate about whether US dominance is slipping in world television markets. American television programmes are facing increased competition at regional, national and local levels. However, what has happened to replace American programming in a number of countries is a local adaptation of the American commercial model and American television programme formats. In the process the American model has been generalized and adapted in a global model for commercial media (Straubhaar, 1997). This development illustrates that the process of globalization is not complete and those who argue the all-pervasive threat of globalization should also bear in mind:

> The slippery nature of the linguistic terms used in international communications analysis: that 'global' rarely means 'universal' and often implies only the actors of the North; that 'local' is often really 'national' which can be oppressive of the 'local'; that 'indigenous' culture is often already 'contaminated' through older cultural contacts and exists as a political claim rather than a clear analytic construct. (Sreberny-Mohammadi, 1991: 134)

A third aspect of globalization stems from the deployment of new communication technologies. We now have a mass media system that can dissolve and permeate boundaries between localities and between political entities allowing the transmission of cultural products to take place at an increasingly rapid rate.

Partly as a response to the changing technological make-up of the media industries, many western governments have sought to deregulate the activities of media organizations and to remove legislation that was perceived as restrictive. The trend towards deregulation has been particularly pronounced in the field of broadcasting. With the deployment of cable and satellite systems of transmission, the traditional arguments about the limited number of channels or restriction to a single-state organization on the basis that this would preserve the public interest and prevent commercialism and the potentially harmful and disruptive consequences of uncontrolled broadcasting began to appear less plausible. While deregulation (the removal of legislation that restricted unduly the pursuit of commercial interests) was welcomed by many as a necessary antidote to an overly regulated media sector, it has been criticized by others as an avenue for the acceleration of concentration in the media industries. This, it is argued, increases the dominant role of the conglomerates in the new global economy of information and communication.

New Communication Technologies and the Social Order

The development of new communication technology is linked directly to globalization. New communication technologies have profoundly affected the activities of the media industries from newspaper printing and desk-top publishing to the reproduction of music on tape and compact disc, from computerized systems of information recall to digital broadcasting. The more developed nations have been able to use modern communications technology to conduct business and represent their economic interests and cultural values worldwide. Schiller claims that 'what is now happening is the creation and global extension of a near total corporate informational-cultural environment' (1989: 128). As the United States still authors most internationally consumed messages, American cultural commodities have 'overwhelmed a good part of the world' by 'smothering the senses' with a 'consumerist virus' (Schiller, 1991).

However, this media/cultural imperialism thesis assumes that institutional infrastructure and technology work together in a uniform way to benefit only their owners and managers. In reality mass media institutions and technology often do the opposite; they stimulate ideological and cultural diversity, sometimes precisely by contradicting their owners and managers intentions. It is important to remember lessons learnt from political economic studies of the media that have gone before and even studies of media reception that introduced the active audience – institutions are constituted by human beings and whatever ideological preferences institutions confer they are neither static nor automatically perceived according to authorial intentions.

Worldwide hegemony of corporate ideology, speech and activity is, according to Schiller and his sympathisers, made possible by communications technology interacting with the enormous expansion of scientific and technical information, computerization and the pre-eminence of the transnational corporation. The immediate benefactors of new communication technologies are those who can gain the most materially by an increased capacity to gather, store, manage and send information. Transnational corporations quickly took control of everything from satellite channels and multimedia configurations to car phones and voice mail systems. Capitalizing on communications also falls not only to rich countries but to rich individuals and rich people in poor countries who enjoy far greater access to technology allowing them to watch international television via satellite or conduct business with a cellular phone.

One example brings these debates into sharp focus – the information superhighway. The information superhighway or Internet is an international network of direct links between computers. The Internet is global in its reach but not total in its coverage. In 1995 Waters stated that the Internet had 15 million users, growing at a rate of 20–30 per cent every three months. Hypermedia software such as World Wide Web and Global Network Navigator act as agents for the user, independently searching the network, finding bits of information, combining them and presenting them back to the user. As with the introduction of other new communication technologies the Internet has been claimed to offer radical potential for increased democracy by providing open access to a wide range of information. There have been claims that the information superhighway will connect people to people and people to information giving everyone access to the information they need when and where they want it – at an affordable price.

However, the historical development of new communication technologies is determined by social and political factors. In the rich industrialized countries new communication technologies are central to the integration of business activities as well as to the production of commercial culture. Their increased use and development depends largely on private investment and competition. These rarely go hand in hand with open access and universal service. In 1984 the rich industrialized countries (US, Canada, western Europe, Japan and Australia) owned 96 per cent of the world's computer hardware; of the world's 700 million telephones, 75 per cent can be found in the 9 richest countries; in 39 countries there are no newspapers, while in 30 others there is only 1, Japan has 125 dailies and the US has 168; the world average for television set ownership is 137 per 1000 – in rich countries this is 447 per 1000, in poor countries this drops dramatically to 36 per 1000 (UNESCO, 1989). Inequalities also exist within countries: in the UK in the mid-1990s 52 per cent of professional households had a home computer and 98 per cent had a telephone – compared to 21 per cent of unskilled households with a computer and 73 per cent with a telephone. Similarly a much higher proportion of professionals than the most unskilled owned more advanced new communication technologies such as a CD-ROM, Internet link, mobile phone, or satellite or cable link (Office of Science and Technology, 1995).

The free flow of information and communications is essential to a democratic society and requires that powerful instruments of information and communication be accessible to all. Without a free flow of information, citizens cannot be adequately informed and without access to forums of public discussion and debate they are excluded from that which enables them to participate in society. In general there is a growing gap between the potential of new technology to give people better control over their lives and the drive by others to use it for profit and centralizing control. It is difficult to conclude that the introduction of such technology into a consumerist world controlled by capital can result in progress.

Conclusion

This chapter began by asserting that the questions about who controls the media and debates over the public's access to media, media accountability and responsibility, media funding and regulation, and implications for individual freedom, democracy and collective well-being have been central to media sociologists over the years. If we believe that the mass media has implications for the reorganization of life on all its levels – from the economic to the experiential, from world trade to cognition then these questions will become ever more vital in the future. As Kellner has said 'the proliferation of media culture and technologies focuses attention on the importance of media politics and the need for public intervention in debates over the future of media culture and communications in the information highways and entertainment byways of the future' (Kellner, 1995: 337). Without an understanding of how the larger social forces, such as the nature of the mass cultural industries, pervade and create changes in culture, leisure activity and everyday life it is difficult to envisage how such a public intervention will take place. Without an understanding of the processes of production and reception and the nature of media output we will never know what shape such an intervention could take.

Further Reading

Ang, I. *Living Room Wars: Rethinking Media Audiences for a Post-modern World,* London, Routledge, 1996. An analysis of contemporary debates around the audience.

Golding, P. *Beyond Cultural Imperialism: Globalization, Communication and the New International Order,* London, Sage, 1996. Discusses the implications for inequality, power and control of global media culture and politics.

McQuail, D. *Mass Communication Theory: An Introduction,* 2nd edn, London, Sage, 1994. A non-technical introduction to the range of approaches to understanding mass communications related to the understanding of society as a whole.

Strinati, D. *An Introduction to Theories of Popular Culture,* London, Routledge, 1995. A clear and accessible guide to major theories of popular culture.

15

Globalization

Leslie Sklair

Globalization refers to the growing interdependence of different parts of the world. Globalization theories involve looking beyond nation states and the relations between them to social processes which result from social interaction on a world scale, such as the development of an increasingly integrated global economy and the explosion of worldwide telecommunications. The aim of this chapter is to explain some of the different ways in which sociologists have approached globalization and illustrate some of the major topics in globalization research. It should help you to understand:

- What sociologists mean by globalization

- What is meant by world-systems theory

- The ideas of a global culture and a global society

- The contribution of global capitalism theory

- Some of the main issues in globalization research

CONCEPTS

nation state ■ transnational corporations
newly industrializing countries ■ 'Third World'
reflexive modernization ■ consumerism
export-processing enclaves ■ feminization of poverty
human development index

Introduction

Globalization is a relatively new idea in the social sciences although people who work in and write about the mass media, transnational corporations and international business have been using it for some time. Jacques Maison-rouge, former President of IBM World Trade, was an early exponent of the view that the future lies with global corporations which operate as if the world had no real borders rather than organizations tied to a particular country. The influential US magazine, *Business Week* (May, 1990) summed this view up in the evocative phrase: 'The Stateless Corporation'.

The central feature of the idea of globalization is that many contemporary social issues cannot be adequately studied at the level of nation states; that is, in terms of each country and its inter-national relations, but need to be seen in terms of transnational processes, beyond the level of particular countries. Some globalists have even gone so far as to predict that global forces, by which they usually mean global economic institutions, global culture or globalizing belief systems/ideologies of various types are becoming so powerful that the continuing existence of the nation state is in serious doubt (Ohmae, 1990). This is not a necessary consequence of most theories of globalization, although many argue that the significance of the nation state is declining (even if the ideology of nationalism is still strong in some places). This chapter will begin by looking at what sociologists mean by globalization; it will then look at some of the main approaches that sociologists have adopted to study globalization and some of the problem areas that have attracted special attention in the globalization literature; the chapter concludes by looking at globalization and everyday life and resistances to globalization.

Globalization

There is no single agreed definition of globalization and some argue that its significance has been much exaggerated but, as the ever-increasing number of books and articles discussing different aspects of it suggests, it appears to be an idea whose time has come in sociology in particular and in the social sciences in general (Robertson, 1992; Waters, 1995; Albrow, 1996). Globalization is important for sociology precisely because it challenges established ideas of society and nation state that are the basis of the theories and research of most contemporary writers (Holton, 1998). Most sociological research is rather narrow in focus and most research projects are restricted to one country, usually understood as a single society. Globalization theorists argue that more and more social relations and social structures can only be explained by looking beyond the boundaries of a single country, or society, as an increasing number of forces influencing social relations and moulding social structures are now global. These global forces are not bound to a single place, but are detached from what we normally understand by national origins and local culture.

This idea is very difficult for many people to accept, although the founders of sociology put forward ideas that have been developed in a global direction. Marx's analysis of capitalism has had an important influence on many ideas about the global economy and the forces that have dominated it for centuries (see Frobel *et al.*, 1980; Chase-Dunn, 1989; Ross and Trachte, 1990; Sklair, 1995), while Weber's influence has been most marked on those who have tried to analyse the idea of cultural globalization (see Robertson, 1992; Albrow, 1996).

One problem in understanding much of the globalization literature is that not all those who use the term distinguish it clearly enough from inter-nationalization, and some writers appear to use the two terms interchange-ably. In this chapter a clear distinction will be drawn between the inter-national and the global. The hyphen in inter-national is to signify that this conception of globalization is founded on the existing – even if changing – system of nation states, while the global signifies the emergence of processes and a system of social relations not founded on the system of nation states.

This difficulty is compounded by the fact that most theory and research in sociology is based on concepts of society that identify the unit of analysis with a particular country, sub-systems within countries or comparisons between single countries and groups of them. For example, the data on patterns of health inequalities discussed in Chapter 12 are based on national data sets and explanations developed in terms of factors *within* those soci-eties, such as income distribution and lifestyle choices. This general approach, usually called state-centrism, is still useful in many respects and there are clearly good reasons for it, particularly the fact that most historical and contemporary sociological data sets have been collected on particular coun-tries. However, most globalization theorists argue that the nation state is no longer the only important unit of analysis and some argue that it is now less important in some fundamental respects than global forces, such as the mass media and the corporations that own and control them, transnational corpo-rations (some of which are richer than the majority of nation states in the world today) and social movements that spread ideas such as universal human rights, global environmental responsibility and the worldwide call for democracy and human dignity.

Yearley (1996) identifies two main obstacles to making sociological sense of globalization: first, 'the tight connection between the discipline of sociology and the nation state' (1995: 9) and second, the fact that countries differ significantly in their geographies. Despite these difficulties, he argues that the increasing focus on the environment encourages us to 'work down to the global' (1995: 17) from the universal, a necessary corrective to state-centrist conceptions which work up to the global from the nation state or even, as we shall see, from individualistic notions of 'global consciousness'. The point of this distinction is that 'the global' is a distinctive level of analysis, separate from universal (values or biological characteristics, for example), international (relations between states) and individual phenomena (like people's awareness of the global). For this to make sense, sociologists have to be able to identify and study *global* forces and institutions as I attempt to do in a later section, for example, when discussing my own contribution to globalization theory and research – the global capitalism approach.

The study of globalization in sociology revolves primarily around two main classes of phenomena which have become increasingly significant in the last few decades. These are the emergence of a *globalized economy* which, as we saw in Chapter 10, is based on new systems of production, finance and consumption, and the idea of *'global culture'*. While not all globalization researchers entirely accept the existence of a global economy or a global culture, most accept that local, national and regional economies are undergoing important changes as a result of processes of globalization (Scott, 1997). In this context, researchers on globalization have focused on two phenomena which have become increasingly significant in the last few decades. First, they have looked at the ways in which transnational corporations (TNCs) have facilitated the globalization of capital and production (Dunning, 1993; Barnet and Cavanagh, 1994; Dicken, 1998). Second, they have been interested in transformations in the global scope of particular types of TNCs, those who own and control the mass media, notably television channels and the transnational advertising agencies. This is often connected with the spread of particular patterns of consumption and a culture and ideology of consumerism at the global level, which will be discussed below (Featherstone, 1990; Sklair, 1995).

Transnational corporations are firms that have operations outside their countries of origin. They range from a small company that has one factory across the border in the next country to massive corporations that operate all over the world, such as Unilever, Mitsubishi or General Motors. The largest TNCs have assets and annual sales far in excess of the gross national products of most of the countries in the world. The World Bank annual publication *World Development Report* for 1996 reports that only about 70 countries out a total of around 200 for which there is data had GNPs of more than ten billion US dollars. By contrast, the 1996 *Fortune Global 500* list of the biggest TNCs by turnover reports that over 400 TNCs had annual sales greater than $10 billion. Thus, in this important sense, such well-known names as General Motors, Shell, Toyota, Unilever, Volkswagen, Nestlé, Sony, Pepsico, Coca-Cola, Kodak, Xerox and the huge Japanese trading houses have more economic power at their disposal than the majority of the countries in the world. These figures indicate the *gigantism* of TNCs relative to most countries. Figure 15.1 is a graphic illustration of these comparisons.

Figure 15.1 *Fortune Global 500* by revenues

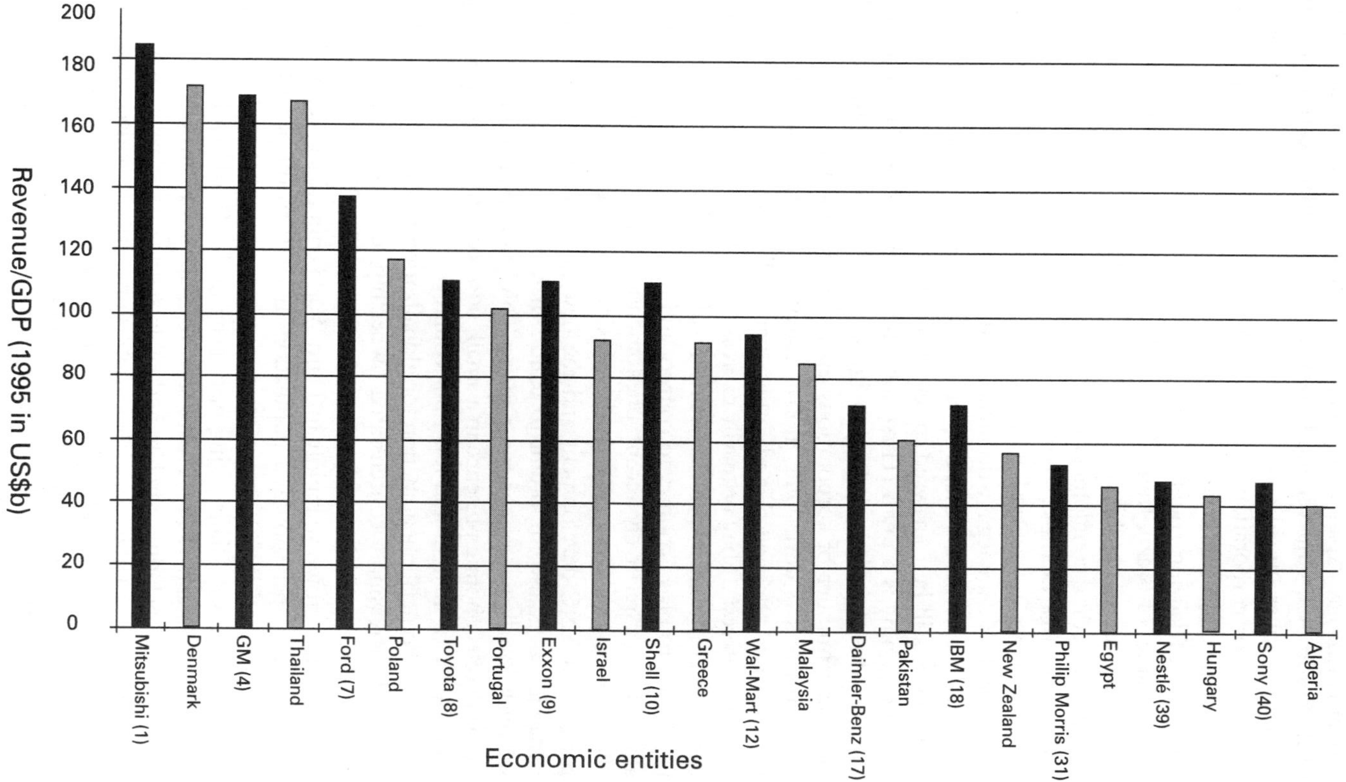

Not only have TNCs grown enormously in size in recent decades but their 'global reach' has expanded dramatically. TNCs such as Colgate–Palmolive, IBM, Nestlé, ICI, Unilever and Dow Chemicals regularly earn more than half of their revenues outside the countries in which they are legally domiciled. Not all major corporations are based in the First World, some come from what is conventionally called the Third World or that part of it known as the newly industrializing countries (NICs). Examples of these are the 'national' oil companies of Brazil, India, Mexico, Taiwan and Venezuela, banks in Brazil and China, an automobile company from Turkey, and the Korean manufacturing and trading conglomerates, a few of which have attained global brand-name status (for example, Hyundai and Samsung).

Writers who are sceptical about economic globalization argue that the fact that most TNCs are legally domiciled in the USA, Japan and Europe and that they trade and invest mainly between themselves means that the world economy is still best analysed in terms of *national* corporations and that the global economy is a myth (Hirst and Thompson, 1996). However, to globalization theorists, this deduction ignores the well-established fact that an increasing number of corporations operating outside their 'home' countries see themselves as developing global strategies. It cannot simply be assumed that all 'US', 'Japanese' and other 'national' TNCs somehow express a 'national interest'. They primarily express the interests of those who own and control them, even if historical patterns of TNC development have differed from place to place, country to country and region to region. Analysing globalization as a relatively recent phenomenon, originating from the 1960s, allows us to see more clearly the tensions between traditional 'national' patterns of TNC development and the new global corporate structures and dynamics. It is also important to realize that, even in state-centrist terms, a relatively small investment for a major TNC can result in a relatively large measure of economic presence in a small, poor country or in a poor region or community of a larger and less poor country.

A second crucial phenomenon for globalization theorists is the global diffusion and increasingly concentrated ownership and control of the electronic mass media, particularly television (Barker, 1997). The number of TV sets per capita has grown so rapidly in Third World countries in recent years (from fewer than 10 per thousand population in 1970 to 60 per 1,000 in 1993, according to UNESCO) that many researchers argue that a 'globalizing effect' due to the mass media is taking place even in the Third World (Sussman and Lent, 1991; Sklair, 1995). As we saw in Chapter 14, ownership and control of television, including satellite and cable systems, and associated media like newspaper, magazine and book publishing, films, video, records/tapes/ compact discs, and a wide variety of other marketing media, are concentrated in relatively few very large TNCs. The predominance of US-based corporations is being challenged by Japanese, European and Australian groups globally, and even by 'Third World' corporations like the Brazilian media empire of TV Globo (Nordenstreng and Schiller, 1993). The following section examines some of the different ways in which sociologists have tried to make sense of globalization.

Main Approaches to Globalization

There are several ways to categorize theory and research on globalization. One approach is to compare mono-causal with multi-causal explanations of the phenomenon (see McGrew, 1992). This is a useful way of looking at the problem, but it can end up putting thinkers with entirely different types of explanations, for example those who see globalization as a consequence of *material-technological* forces and those who see it as a consequence of *ideological and/or cultural* forces, in the same bag. A second approach is to compare the disciplinary focus of globalization studies. This is certainly an interesting and fruitful avenue to explore: contributions from anthropology, geography and international political economy are commonly borrowed by sociologists of globalization, and vice versa, and this will be reflected in my own categorization.

I have chosen to categorize globalization in sociology on the basis of four theory and research clusters in which groups of scholars are working on similar research problems, either in direct contact with each other or, more commonly, in rather indirect contact. Accordingly, I identify the following four sources of globalization research in contemporary sociology which cover what is currently being produced in the field:

- the world-systems approach
- the global culture approach
- the global society approach
- the global capitalism approach.

World-systems Model

World systems as a model in social science research, inspired by the work of Wallerstein, has been developed in a large and continually expanding body of literature since the 1970s (see Wallerstein, 1979 and Shannon, 1989 for a good overview). The world-systems approach is not only a collection of academic writings but, like the Frankfurt School discussed in Chapter 3, it is also a highly institutionalized academic enterprise, based at the Braudel Center for the Study of Economies, Historical Systems and Civilization at the State University of New York, where Wallerstein has been Director since its foundation. Although the work of the world-systems theorists cannot be said to be fully part of the globalization literature as such (see King, 1991), it undoubtedly prepared the ground for globalization in the social sciences.

The world-systems approach is based on the distinction between core, semi-peripheral and peripheral countries in terms of their changing roles in the international division of labour dominated by the capitalist world system. The central idea is that the 'core' capitalist countries, like those of western Europe and the USA, have historically exploited the poor 'peripheral' countries of Africa, Asia and Latin America by extracting their raw materials cheaply and turning them into much more expensive manufactured goods, some of which they sell back to people in these poor countries. When manufacturing wages rise in the core countries, capitalists move some of their factories to the 'semi-periphery' countries in Latin America and east Asia for example, and people in these countries, while still being exploited, do better than raw material producers in the periphery. In their turn, when wages rise in the semi-periphery, some factories are shifted to countries in the periphery.

In some senses, Wallerstein and his school could rightly claim to have been 'global' all along – after all, what could be more global than the 'world system'? However, there is no specific concept of the 'global' in most world-systems literature. Reference to the 'global' comes mainly from critics who, reflecting a more general criticism of theories in sociology which give the 'economic' precedence over the 'cultural', argue that there is a world system of 'global culture' (see later) which cannot be 'reduced' to the economic processes of capitalism (see Featherstone, 1990). Chase-Dunn (1989) does try to take the argument a stage further by arguing for a dual-logic approach to economy and polity. At the economic level, he argues, a global logic of the world economy prevails whereas at the level of politics a state-centred logic of the world-system prevails. However, as the world economy is basically still explicable only in terms of national economies (countries of the core, semi-periphery and periphery), Chase-Dunn's formulation largely reproduces the problems of Wallerstein's state-centrist analysis.

There is, therefore, no distinctively 'global' dimension in the world-systems model apart from the international focus that it has always emphasized. Wallerstein himself rarely if ever uses the word 'globalization'. For him, the *economics* of the model rests on the international division of labour that distinguishes core, semi-periphery and periphery countries. The *politics* are mostly bound up with anti-systemic movements and 'superpower struggles' and the *cultural*, insofar as it is dealt with at all, covers debates about the 'national' and the 'universal' and the concept of 'civilization(s)' in the social sciences. Many critics are not convinced that the world-systems model, usually considered to be 'economistic' (that is, locked into economic factors), can deal with cultural issues adequately. Wolff tellingly comments on the way in which the concept of 'culture' has been inserted into Wallerstein's world-system model: 'An economism which gallantly switches its attentions to the operations of culture is still economism' (in King, 1991: 168). Wallerstein's attempts to theorize 'race', nationality and ethnicity in terms of what he refers to as different types of 'peoplehood' in the world system (Wallerstein, 1991) might be seen as a move in the right direction but few would argue that cultural factors are an important part of the analysis.

Global Culture Model

A second model of globalization derives specifically from research on the 'globalization of culture'. The global culture approach focuses on the problems that a homogenizing mass media-based culture poses for national identities. As we shall see later, this is complementary to the global society approach, which focuses more on ideas of an emerging global consciousness and their implications for global community, governance and security. Although global culture researchers cannot be identified as a school in the same way as world-system researchers, their works do constitute a relatively coherent whole (see Featherstone, 1990). First, they tend to prioritize the cultural over the political and/or the economic. Second, there is a common interest in the question of how individual and/or national identity can survive in the face of an emerging 'global culture'.

A distinctive feature of this model is that it poses the existence of 'global culture' as a reality, a possibility or a fantasy. A major influence on the idea of a global culture is the very rapid growth that has taken place over the last few decades in the scale of the mass media of communication and the emergence of what McLuhan (1964) famously called 'the global village'. The basic idea is that the spread of the mass media, especially television, means that everyone in the world can be exposed to the same images, almost instantaneously. This, the argument goes, turns the whole world into a sort of 'global village'.

While globalization has brought about an increased cultural homogeneity where people all across the world can drink Coca-Cola, eat McDonald's and watch the same Hollywood films, it has also produced increasing differentiation. Increasingly different cultural traditions exist alongside each, other competing for people's attention. For postmodernists, such as Baudrillard (1988), the explosion of information technologies has produced cultural diversity and fragmentation rather than unity. As we saw in Chapter 14, Baudrillard and other postmodernists argue the 'electronic reality' created by the media has produced a state of hyperreality, where the distinction between the 'real' world and the media image is eroded. He argues that the hyperreal is becoming a condition of the whole of the contemporary world: reality is broken down and people's identities and lifestyles are no longer anchored in social structures but are rather constructed through the mass of media images of the lifestyle options available to them. In many cases old identities have been replaced by 'hybrid' identities (Hall *et al.*, 1992: 310).

An apparently paradoxical consequence of globalization has been to make people more aware of cultural and national differences. There has been an upsurge of regionalism and nationalism, particularly among groups which have been incorporated into larger units, such as those which once formed part of the former Soviet Union. In this context Friedman, a Swedish anthropologist, has argued that:

> Ethnic and cultural fragmentation and modernist homogenization are not two arguments, two opposing views of what is happening in the world today, but two constitutive trends of global reality. The dualist centralised world of the double East–West hegemony is fragmenting, politically, and culturally, but the homogeneity of capitalism remains as intact and a systematic as ever'. (Friedman, 1990: 311)

While not all would agree either that capitalism remains intact and systematic or that it is, in fact, the framework of globalization, the fragmentation of the control once exercised by eastern and western power blocs is beyond doubt. With the collapse of the Soviet Union and the declining influence of the hegemony of the United States, many old national and ethnic loyalties have reasserted themselves, sometimes resulting in political instability and war.

In this context a compilation of articles by edited by Albrow and King (1990) raises several central issues relevant to the ideas of global sociology, global society and globalization as new problem areas in the social sciences. One important emphasis has been the 'globalization' of sociology itself as a discipline; that is, the extent to which each society, or community, requires its own sociology. While the classical sociological theorists, notably Marx, Weber and Durkheim, all tried to generalize about how societies changed and tried to establish some universal features of social organization, none of them saw the need to theorize on the global level. This connects in some important ways with the debate about the integrity of national cultures in a globalizing world, and particularly the influence of 'western' economic, political, military and cultural forms on non-western societies. For example, there is a tendency to reduce globalization to 'westernization', or even 'Americanization', but this can distort the nature of genuinely global forces and mystify the relationship between globalization and capitalism. The more 'global' and less 'nationalistic' sociology becomes, the less likely this is to happen.

Globalization is not simply about the 'disembedding' of the 'local' by the 'global', it is rather about the creation of a new global–local nexus, about exploring the new relations between global and local spaces. These questions have been explored most fully in a sub-set of the global culture approach, known as *globo-localism*. Writers such as Alger (1988) and Mlinar (1992) have focused on the question of what happens to *territorial identities* (within and across countries) in a globalizing world. The apparent contradiction between globalization as a force for homogenization, and the disintegration of countries in central and eastern Europe, for example the former Yugoslavia, and in other parts of the world (notably Africa), and the so-called revival of nation-alisms do present challenges to the more extreme versions of globalization.

The main research question in this context is the autonomy of local cultures in the face of an advancing 'global culture'. Competing claims of local cultures against the forces of 'globalization' have forced themselves onto the sociological, cultural and political agendas all over the world. This is largely continuous with the focus of the third globalization model, based on the idea of global society, which focuses more on ideas of emerging global consciousness and their implications for global community, gover-nance and security.

Global Society Models

Inspiration for this general conception of globalization is often located in the pictures of planet earth sent back by space explorers. A classic statement of this was the report of Apollo XIV astronaut Edgar Mitchell in 1971:

> It was a beautiful, harmonious, peaceful-looking planet, blue with white clouds, and one that gave you a deep sense... of home, of being, of identity. It is what I prefer to call instant global consciousness.

Had astronaut Mitchell penetrated a little through the clouds he would also have seen horrific wars in Vietnam and other parts of Asia, bloody repression by various dictatorial regimes in Africa and Latin America, dead and maimed bodies as a result of sectarian terrorism in Britain and Ireland, as well as a terrible toll of human misery from hunger, disease, drug abuse and carnage on roads all round the world as automobile cultures intensified their own peculiar structures of globalization.

Nevertheless, some leading globalization theorists, for example Giddens (1991) and Robertson (1992), do attribute great significance to ideas such as 'global awareness' and 'planetary consciousness'. Global society theorists argue that the concept of world, or global, society has become a believable idea only in the modern age and, in particular, science, technology, industry and universal values are increasingly creating a contemporary world that is different from any past age. The globalization literature is full of discussions of the decreasing power and significance of the nation state and the increasing significance (if not actually power) of supra-national and global institutions and systems of belief.

Globalization brings some of the 'foundational concepts' of sociology, such as nation state and society, into question (McGrew, 1992: 64). As we have seen from the previous chapters of this book, most empirical research in sociology is focused on a particular society, which is usually a nation state and its citizens. Global sociologists argue that this view is increasingly difficult to sustain as relations between individuals, institutions and states are being transformed by social processes which are worldwide. Global transportation and communications allow more and more people to overcome what used to be seen as insurmountable boundaries of time and space. Harvey (1989: 241) uses the term time–space compression to describe how processes of global-ization compress, stretch and deepen space time for people all over the world thus creating the conditions for a global society.

Giddens (1991), in particular, has developed these themes in his analysis of the relations between globalization and modernity. He defines globalization in terms of four dimensions, the nation state system, the world military order, the international division of labour and the world capitalist economy, and explains it as a consequence of modernity itself. He characterizes the trans-formation of key social relations in terms of the relation between *globalizing tendencies* of modernity and *localized events* in daily life. More and more people live in circumstances where their relationships with others and with social institutions have become 'disembedded' from their local contexts. For Giddens, globalization is best conceptualized as 'reflexive modernization', by which he means that 'social practices are constantly examined and reformed in the light of incoming information about those very practices, thus consti-tutively altering their character' (Giddens, 1990b: 38). The global society thrust of Giddens' concept of globalization is clear from his reference to 'emergent forms of world interdependence and planetary consciousness'.

Spybey (1996) contrasts Giddens' view that 'modernity is inherently global-izing (1991: 63) with Robertson's (1992) view that globalization predates modernity with aspects going back 2,000 years. There is thus a debate in sociology about whether globalization is a new name for a relatively old phenomenon (which appears to be the argument of Robertson), or whether it is relatively new, a largely twentieth-century phenomenon (the argument of Giddens), or whether it is very new and primarily a consequence of post-1960s' capitalism (the argument of Sklair, discussed later in this chapter). Why does this matter? It matters because if we want to understand our own lives and the lives of those around us, in our families, communities, local regions, countries, supra-national regions and, ultimately how we relate to the global, then it is absolutely fundamental that we are clear about the extent to which the many different structures within which we live are much the same as they have been or are different.

The idea of globalization is itself a contested concept. Hirst and Thompson, in their attempt to demonstrate that globalization is a myth because the global economy does not really exist, argue that there is 'no fundamental difference between the international submarine telegraph cable method of financial trans-actions [of the early twentieth century] and contemporary electronic systems' (Hirst and Thompson, 1996: 197). However, to globalization theorists, the fundamental difference is, precisely, in the way that the electronics revolution (a post-1960s phenomenon) has transformed the quantitative possibilities of transferring cash and money capital into qualitatively new forms of corporate and personal financing, entrepreneurship and, crucially, the system of credit on which the global culture and ideology of consumerism largely rests. Some globalization theorists argue forcefully that these phenomena are all new and fundamental for understanding not only what is happening in the rich countries, but in social groups anywhere who have a part to play in this global system. In this sense, the idea of a global society is a very provocative one but, as I shall go on to discuss in the section 'Globalization in Everyday Life', while it is relatively easy to establish empirically the objective dimensions of globalization as they involve the large majority of the world's population, the idea of a global society based on *subjective* relationships to globalization, planetary consciousness and the like remains highly speculative.

For many writers the possibility of a global society is an important idea. As McGrew (1992) shows, this theme is elaborated by scholars grappling with the apparent contradictions between globalization and local disruption and strife based on ethnic and other particularistic loyalties. Perlmutter (1991), for example, argues that humankind is on 'the rocky road to the first global civilization' and, while others are more sceptical of the progress that we have made to this goal, it is safe to predict that the idea of a global society will be increasingly discussed in the social sciences. It is in this type of approach, in particular, that a growing appreciation of the ethical problems of globalization is to be found. The reason for this is simple: now that humankind has the capacity to destroy itself through war and toxic accidents of various types, a democratic and just human society on the global level, however utopian, seems to be the best long-term guarantee of the continued survival of humanity (Held, 1995).

Global Capitalism Model

A fourth model of globalization locates the dominant global forces in the structures of an ever-more globalizing capitalism (for example, Ross and Trachte, 1990; Sklair, 1995; McMichael, 1996; Robinson, 1998). While all of these writers and others who could be identified with this approach develop their own specific analyses of globalization, they all strive towards a concept of the 'global' that involves more than the relations between nation states and state-centrist explanations of national economies competing against each other.

Ross and Trachte (1990) focus specifically on capitalism as a social system which is best analysed on three levels: the level of the internal logic of the system, that is, theories of how capitalism works (inspired by Marx and Adam Smith), how it changes over time and how capitalist societies differ from each other. They explain both the deindustrialization of some of the heartland regions of capitalism, for example the decline in the automobile industry around Detroit in the USA, and the transformations of what we still call the

'Third World', for example the rise of substantial manufacturing industries such as textiles, footwear and shipbuilding in these terms. They argue that the globalization of the capitalist system is deeply connected to the capitalist crises in the 1970s, brought about by rising oil prices, increasing unemployment and growing insecurity as the rich countries experienced problems in paying for their welfare states. This leads them to conclude that: 'We are only at the beginning of the global era' (Ross and Trachte, 1990: 230). Capitalism has not stopped changing and its future, in global perspective, will undoubtedly continue to hold surprises, such as the unexpected crisis in Asian economies in the late 1990s.

Sklair (1995) proposes a more explicit model of the global system based on the concept of *transnational practices*, practices that originate with non-state actors and cross state borders. They are analytically distinguished in three spheres: economic, political and cultural-ideological. Each of these practices is primarily, but not exclusively, characterized by a major institution. The *transnational corporation* (TNC) is the most important institution for economic transnational practices; the *transnational capitalist class* (TCC) for political transnational practices; and the *culture ideology of consumerism* for transnational cultural-ideological practices (Sklair, 1995). The research agenda of this theory is concerned with how TNCs, transnational capitalist classes and the culture ideology of consumerism operate to transform the world in terms of the global capitalist project.

This approach is really an attempt to limit the scope of globalization by focusing on the extent to which capitalism has been successful in extending its reach globally. The point here is that as globalization can cover so many things in the social world, the focus on the global *capitalist* system restricts the scope of application of the concept to its most characteristic economic institution (the TNC), its most characteristic political institution (the TCC) and its most characteristic cultural-ideological driving force (consumerism). This focus, however, should not lead to the conclusion that capitalism is the only global force even if, in the view of many theorists, it is the dominant force in the contemporary world.

The massive presence of transnational corporations has already been discussed. The transnational capitalist class is made up of four groups: those who own and control these corporations, their allies in the state (globalizing bureaucrats) and in political parties and professions (globalizing politicians and professionals) and consumerist élites. While this approach is developed from Marx's analysis of the revolutionary nature of modern capitalism, it differs from Marxism in several ways. First, it does not restrict membership of the capitalist class exclusively to those who own the means of production but extends it to those who directly serve the interests of capital. Second, it argues that the relative autonomy of the state to dominate the capitalist class is much reduced in global capitalism and that globalizing bureaucrats are the main representatives of the state in the interests of capital. Third, it explains how the system works in terms of the intimate connections between the TNCs, transnational capitalist class and the culture ideology of consumerism, the rationale of the system. While, as Scott (1997: 312) argues, there is little evidence as yet to establish firmly the existence of an 'integrated global capitalist class', there are indications that such a class is emerging. Table 15.1 suggests the structure (economic base, political organization and culture ideology) of the four groups in the transnational capitalist class and how their material, political and cultural interests interlock.

Table 15.1 The global ruling class

Transnational practices	Leading institutions	Integrating agents
Economic sphere	*Economic forces*	Global business élite
Transnational capital	Global TNCs	
International capital	World Bank, IMF, BIS	
State capital	State TNCs	
Political sphere	*Political forces*	Global political élite
TNC executives	Global business organization	
Globalizing bureaucrats	Open-door agencies, WTO,	
Politicians and professionals	parties and lobbies	
Regional blocs	EU, NAFTA, ASEAN	
Emerging transnational states	UN, NGOs	
Culture-ideology sphere	*Culture-ideology forces*	Global cultural élite
Consumerism	Shops, media	
Transnational	Think tanks, élite social	
Neo-liberalism	movements	

The culture ideology of consumerism prioritizes the exceptional place of consumption and consumerism in contemporary capitalism, increasing consumption expectations and aspirations without necessarily ensuring the income to buy. The extent to which economic and environmental constraints on the private accumulation of capital challenge the global capitalist project in general and its culture ideology of consumerism in particular is a central issue for the global capitalist system approach (Sklair, 1994b; see also Durning, 1992).

McMichael (1996) focuses on the issue of Third World development and provides both theoretical and empirical support for the thesis that globalization is a qualitatively new phenomenon and not simply a quantitative expansion of older trends. He contrasts two periods. First, the 'Development Project' (late 1940s to early 1970s), when all countries tried to develop their national economies with the help of international development agencies and institutions. The second period he labels the 'Globalization Project' (1980s onwards), when development is pursued through attempts to integrate economies into a globalized world market, and the process is directed by a public–private coalition of 'Global Managers'. He explains:

> As parts of national economies became embedded more deeply in global enterprise through commodity chains, they weakened as national units and strengthened the reach of the global economy. This situation was not unique to the 1980s, but the mechanisms of the debt regime institutionalised the power and authority of global management within states' very organisation and procedures. This was the turning point in the story of development. (McMichael, 1996: 135)

To these writers on globalization and capitalism we can add other Marxist and Marx-inspired scholars who see capitalism as a global system, but do not have any specific concepts of globalization. The most important of these is the geographer, Harvey, whose Marxist analysis of modernity and post-modernity is significant for the attempt to build a bridge between the debates around economic and cultural globalization. For Harvey (1989), the shrinking of space, brought about by global capitalism that brings diverse communities into competition with each other, can lead to an increased awareness of locality and the development of specialized areas of production, such as the ceramics, knitwear and textile regions in Italy which were described in Chapter 10. This rehabilitation of locality and specialization is very different from the uniformity and economies of scale typically associated with global capitalism and is celebrated as further evidence of cultural diversity by postmodernists. However, for Harvey, this interpretation misses the underlying forces that lie behind this process; local self-assertion remains tied to globalism, particularly the requirements of a more developed, global capitalism.

Summing-up the Approaches

Each of the four approaches to globalization has its own distinctive strengths and weaknesses. The world-system model tends to be economistic (minimizing the importance of political and cultural factors) but, as globalization is often interpreted in terms of economic actors and economic institutions, it still seems the most realistic approach to many. The globalization of culture model, on the other hand, tends to be culturalist (minimizing economic factors) but, as much of the criticism of globalization comes from those who focus on the negative effects of homogenizing mass media and marketing on local and indigenous cultures, the culturalist approach has many adherents. The world society model tends to be both optimistic and all-inclusive, an excellent combination for the production of world-views, but less satisfactory for social science research programmes. Finally, the global capitalism model, by prioritizing the global capitalist system and paying less attention to other global forces, runs the risk of appearing one-sided. However, the question remains: how important is that 'one side' (global capitalism)?

Concrete Problems in Globalization Research

Among the most important substantive issues, widely discussed by globalization researchers inside and outside the four approaches discussed in the previous section, are global environmental change, gender and globalization, global cities, globalization and regionalization. Some of the main dimensions of these problems will now be outlined.

Global Environmental Change

While the literature on all aspects of globalization has been expanding very rapidly in the last decade, it is probably no exaggeration to say that the literature on global environmental change has led the way. This is due to:

1. The enormous political, academic and popular interest in a series of high-profile international meetings throughout the 1970s and 80s, culminating in the United Nations Conference on Environment and Development in Rio in 1992.
2. Growing disquiet about daily environmental degradation (notably the destruction of the ozone layer, the greenhouse effect, decreasing bio-diversity, worsening land, air and water pollution in many places) and sudden environmental catastrophes such as the disaster at Chernobyl where a nuclear reactor exploded in 1986.
3. The rise of the global environmental movement.

These three forces have combined to provide a framework for the study of global environmental change in the context of 'sustainable development' (see World Resources Institute, 1994). Under this rubric the United Nations has established several bodies to manage environmental change at the global level and while many well-informed scientists and activists fear a variety of existing environmental crises and predict others, some notable advances have been made, for example in the control of CFC gases and the stewardship of the atmosphere, the oceans, forests, and other natural resources, the so-called 'global commons' (Yearley, 1996).

While many TNCs (some of the largest Fortune 500 companies as well as smaller consumer-sensitive companies) have begun to institutionalize in-house mechanisms for dealing with resource and pollution issues, of continuing concern is the laxity of other TNCs, their subcontracting partners and local firms in observing environmental good practice in production and waste disposal, even where required to do so by law. More generally, the role of the TNCs in promoting unsustainable patterns of consumption with little thought for the environmental consequences has been critically scrutinized (Durning, 1992; Sklair, 1994a). This latter issue raises fundamental questions about the capitalist global project and the central place of consumption for both economic growth and ideological credibility. While environmental concerns move up and down the agendas of social groups, the media, and governments all over the world, it is likely that they will continue to be one of the main areas of globalization theory and research for the foreseeable future. Yearley (1996: 24) is correct in his assertion that very few globalization theorists have grappled with the environment as a research site, but his work and that of others (see Redclift and Benton, 1994) should show more of them what a rich site it is.

Gender and Globalization

Gender plays a particularly important role for many writers on globalization for two main reasons. First, much of the debate about globalization originates from the version of the new international division of labour (NIDL) – formulated by Frobel *et al.* (1980) to describe the relocation of TNCs to Third World countries with low labour costs – particularly research that emphasized the role of young women working for TNCs in export-processing enclaves of various types (Nash and Fernandez-Kelly, 1983; Mitter, 1986). While many have questioned the economic significance of these new patterns of employment, there is no doubt as to their symbolic importance in publicizing, not only in academic circles but also through the mass media, the changing patterns of the global economy and their social, political and cultural consequences.

Second, the 'feminization of poverty' thesis (see Tinker, 1990) has drawn attention to the adverse consequences for both urban and rural women and their families of the process of development in general, and global structural adjustment policies in particular, in the 1980s and 90s. These policies have been imposed by transnational financial and aid institutions through national governments in many poor countries. This is one sphere in which the local consequences of global economic and social policies have been comprehensively researched and there appears to be a growing consensus that the processes of globalization may affect men and women differently. In addition, an increasing body of evidence suggests that such programmes tend to create more burdens for women and more opportunities for men (Beneria and Feldman, 1992). Mies (1998) argues that the position of women in the new international division of labour can be theoretically linked with the feminization of poverty. 'Women, defined as housewives and sex objects, are the optimal labour force for global capital' (Mies, 1994: 113). While not a direct contribution to the globalization literature, Mies provides both empirical evidence and conceptual insights of relevance for research in gender and globalization.

Global Cities

With the tremendous growth of urbanization in the last few decades, particularly in the Third World, many scholars have begun to study the global as well as the national significance of cities, leading to the idea of world or global cities which are largely independent of national control. In the most influential formulation of this idea, Friedmann (1995) maintained that these can be identified in terms of the extent to which a city is a major financial centre, has global or regional TNCs and international institution headquarters, has rapid growth of business services, is an important manufacturing centre and is a major transport node. On the basis of these criteria, Friedmann constructs a 'world-city hierarchy' with primary and secondary cities in the core and semi-periphery countries. His formulation has been criticized on several counts, mainly because it appears to reproduce the problems of world-system analysis, but it remains an excellent starting point for this aspect of global studies. Subsequent research on global cities focuses on the global role of particular cities (London, New York, Los Angeles and Tokyo having attracted most attention), and the interconnections between the global economy, regions, cities and communities (Sassen, 1994).

'Global cities', however, are not located exclusively in the First World of rich countries. Processes of globalization have also been identified in the rapid growth of what have been conveniently if sometimes misleadingly labelled 'Third World' cities. Many researchers have noted the paradoxical phenomenon of cities like Kuala Lumpur, Manila, Bangkok, Calcutta and Shanghai in Asia; Mexico City and Buenos Aires in Latin America; Nairobi and Lagos in Africa; Cairo and Amman in the Middle East; and many others where world-class telecommunications and the skyscrapers that accommodate the global or regional headquarters of TNCs are in close proximity to shanty towns lacking basic amenities of sewerage, clean running water and a dependable electricity supply, not to speak of adequate schools and medical services (for data, see World Resources Institute, 1994). Globalization in the form of the increased coverage of the mass media, particularly access to television, is widely held to have added to the longstanding magnetic pull of the cities for the poorer strata of rural dwellers, many of whose livelihoods have been threatened or actually destroyed by global agribusiness (McMichael, 1996).

The sectoral composition of the labour force has not changed a great deal in many poor countries, particularly those with large populations, mainly because the absolute numbers of village dwellers tends to hide large increases in absolute numbers of industrial and service workers in the cities. Despite this, in more or less every country, the proportion of service workers in the labour force has increased in the last few decades (service workers include police and armed forces). Many of these service workers labour in the 'informal' sector, defined as all those people not in the formal waged economy. As we saw in Chapter 10, looking at inequalities in the contemporary world, a considerable literature has grown on the subject of such workers, and how they interact with those in the 'formal' economy in the local context and relate to the global economy. There are many conflicting interpretations of the informal sector, but the structural approach is of most interest to globalization theorists. Structuralists see the informal sector as an integral part of the capitalist economy, locally and globally, in the First World as well as the Third World. So the informal sector is theorized not as a more 'primitive form' of economic life, but as that part of a capitalist economy unregulated by the state, with its own structures of wealth and exploitation (see Portes and Castells, 1989). TNCs, for example, commonly use 'informal' (unregulated) producers and service-providers as part of their direct and indirect global production and distribution chains.

Globalization and Regionalization

Many scholars who accept the declining significance of the nation state, particularly in economic affairs and mass culture, are uncertain about the existence of a truly global system. For them regionalization, that is, the comparison between different geographical zones, appears to be a more satisfactory answer than globalization to the 'sociological question' of social change. This thinking is clearly linked to ideas about the hegemony of the superpowers which have dominated analysis of the international system for centuries. In the 1970s there emerged a rather new mode of thinking which has come to be known as 'Trilateralism'; this is the view that the anti-communist powers, the USA, western Europe and Japan, each have their own 'natural spheres of interest' and that world peace and prosperity depended on these three regional powers being able to work out their differences peacefully and, eventually, destroy the global advance of communism. Since the demise of the Soviet empire and the 'opening up' of China, the trilateralism argument has been developed in a variety of directions. 'Regional responses' to globalization are, by the nature of the case, very varied. Most commentators argue that while much of western Europe, Japan and East Asia and North America has been able to take advantage of globalization and increase prosperity, most of the rest of the world has not been able to do so and that many communities have suffered from globalization. Brecher and Costello (1994) put forward the radical argument that globalization involves a 'race to the bottom' as corporations and governments scramble to reduce living standards for vulnerable groups of workers and citizens in order to compete 'successfully' in the global economy.

However, while much of the research on the relationship between the global and the regional provides very useful empirical examples and counter-examples for sociologists to consider, it remains difficult to conceptualize and research empirically global forces that drive certain kinds of development. Part of the problem is that regionalization itself relies on data in terms of national economies and societies (an idea that is very difficult to abandon but sometimes misleading when you want to study globalization). A global sociology requires more research comparisons between communities, cities, industrial districts, sub-national and supra-national regions to be made.

The little data on such comparisons that do exist yield quite surprising results. For example, the United Nations Development Programme (UNDP) *Human Development Report* (1993), although largely based on country-by-country rankings on a human development index (HDI), has started to disaggregate some of its findings. This reveals that the HDI for whites in the USA is slightly above the average for people in Japan as a whole, while the HDI for blacks in the USA is about the same as for people in Trinidad and Tobago. For hispanics in the USA the average is even lower, about the same as the average for the population of Estonia. Disaggregating on gender reveals similarly striking results. White females in the USA rank higher than any other group, anywhere, while black females rank well below, about the same as the Greek average. Black males in the USA rank slightly above the Bulgarian average (UNDP, 1993: 18). So, while country-level data will obviously continue to be usefully collected for the foreseeable future, it is just as obvious that such disaggregated data comparing the conditions of groups on other criteria across national borders are necessary if theories of globalization are to have adequate empirical foundations.

Globalization and Everyday Life

The study of globalization appears much more abstract and much less obviously part of our daily lives than the other substantive topics considered in this book, such as gender, education or work. This is not surprising and, indeed, is a fundamental part of the problem and salience of globalization for an understanding of some of the determining circumstances under which we live out our daily lives. This is the reason why it is important to think about both the subjective, as well as the objective, side of globalization. These are not two separate issues, but merely two ways of looking at the same phenomenon. The subjective side looks at globalization from the point of view of the individual whose life is affected by globalization and whose own decisions (for example, media use, job preferences, voting behaviour, consumption choices) in their turn play a part in affecting the structures of globalization. The objective side starts from the forces of globalization themselves (mass media corporations, global economic forces, institutions that structure politics, global marketing) and how they create and condition opportunities for individual choices for different groups of people. Theories of globalization obviously have to consider both. However, as we saw in Chapter 3, linking structure and action raises a number of theoretical issues in sociology in general and which apply to globalization research in particular.

Many people who are sympathetic to the idea of globalization find most accounts of it excessively structuralist and abstract, focusing on impersonal global forces against which the individual has no say. This is exemplified in the declining influence of Wallerstein's world-system theory, with its obvious 'globalizing' tendencies from the outside, and the current popularity of more reflexive approaches to globalization, encapsulated in the idea of globalization as 'reflexive modernity'. However, Giddens' (1991: 175) view of globalization involving 'emergent forms of world interdependence and planetary consciousness' is misconceived for most of the world's people. Watching CNN or *Friends* or the World Cup on TV in a village, shanty town or global city does not necessarily mean that all viewers share the same experience let alone planetary consciousness, whatever that is (Dowmunt, 1993). What it does mean, however, is that if and when the viewer actually starts to become conscious of and to desire the global prestige of the lifestyles these products embody and eventually buys the products, then an objective relationship to the global corporations whose existence depends on the profits from these purchases is established. Whether or not any given individual or group has planetary consciousness, or consciousness of the global whole, is an open *empirical* question, although not one which any theorist of globalization has actually studied empirically, so far. The findings of studies on this question would help to evaluate the validity of the culturalist approach discussed earlier. Perhaps some people would recognize and confirm such consciousness in some contexts and on some occasions (perhaps when the media are full of some 'global' issue) but not in other contexts and at other times. This would be very interesting to research and would, of course, tell us much about the subjective side of globalization. But we cannot assume the existence of such consciousness and we certainly cannot assume it exists just because millions of people watch similar TV programmes and adverts, idealize the same stars and buy the same products all over the world. These 'objective' facts on media use, name recognition of celebrities and global sales are in the public record. These are what the objective side of global-ization is about, and they do not depend for their validity on anyone's 'global consciousness'.

Resistances to Globalization

Globalization is often seen in terms of impersonal forces wreaking havoc on the lives of ordinary defenceless people and communities. It is not coinci-dental that interest in globalization over the last two decades has been accom-panied by an upsurge in what has come to be known as New Social Movements (NSM) research (Ray, 1993; Spybey, 1996). NSM theorists, despite their substantial differences, argue that the traditional response of the labour movement to global capitalism, based on class politics, has generally failed and that a new analysis based on identity politics (notably of gender, sexuality, ethnicity, age, community, belief systems) is necessary to mount effective resistance to sexism, racism, environmental damage, warmongering, capitalist exploitation and other forms of injustice.

The globalization of identity politics involves the establishment of global networks of people – made easier by the development of new means of communication such as the Internet – with similar identities and interests outside the control of international, state and local authorities. There is a substantial volume of research and documentation on such developments in the women's, peace and environmental movements, some of it in direct response to governmental initiatives, but most theorists and activists tend to operate under the slogan: think global, act local (Ekins, 1992).

The main challenges to global capitalism in the economic sphere have also come from those who 'think global and act local'. This normally involves disrupting the capacity of TNCs and global financial institutions to accu-mulate private profits at the expense of their workforces, their consumers and the communities which are affected by their activities. An important part of economic globalization today is the increasing dispersal of the manu-facturing process into many discrete phases carried out in many different places. Being no longer so dependent on the production of one factory and one workforce gives capital a distinct advantage, particularly against the strike weapon which once gave tremendous negative power to the working class. Global production chains can be disrupted by strategically planned stoppages, but this generally acts more as inconveniences than as real weapons of labour against capital. The international division of labour builds flexibility into the system so that not only can capital migrate anywhere in the world to find the cheapest reliable productive sources of labour but also few workforces can any longer decisively 'hold capital to ransom' by withdrawing their labour. At the level of the production process globalizing capital has all but defeated labour. In this respect, the global organization of the TNCs and allied institutions like globalizing government agencies and the World Bank have, so far, proved too powerful for the local organization of labour and communities.

Nevertheless, the global capitalists, if we are to believe their own propaganda, are continuously beset by opposition, boycott, legal challenge and moral outrage from the consumers of their products and by disruptions from their workers. There are also many ways to be ambivalent or hostile about cultures and ideologies of consumerism, some of which the 'Green' movement has successfully exploited (see Mander and Goldsmith, 1996).

The issue of democracy is central to the advance of the forces of globalization and the practices and the prospects of social movements that oppose them, local and global. The rule of law, freedom of association and expression, freely contested elections, as minimum conditions and however imperfectly sustained, are as necessary in the long run for mass market-based global consumerist capitalism as they are for alternative social systems.

Conclusion

This account of globalization has focused on what distinguishes *global* (transnational) from *inter-national* forces, processes and institutions and some of the models which have been developed to explain it. It is based almost exclusively on the European and North American literature, but this does not preclude the possibility of other and quite different conceptions of globalization being developed elsewhere. Despite the view, particularly evident in the accounts of 'global culture' theorists that globalization is more or less the same as westernization or Americanization or McDonaldization (Ritzer, 1995), more critics, especially from Africa and Asia, are beginning to question this one-way traffic bias in the globalization literature (see Albrow and King, 1990; Sklair, 1994b; Jameson and Miyoshi, 1998). It is very likely that an introduction to the sociology of globalization written ten years from now will reflect non-western perspectives much more strongly. Nevertheless, although of quite recent vintage, it is undeniable that globalization as a theoretical issue and an object of research, is now firmly on the agenda of the social sciences.

Further Reading

Albrow, M. *The Global Age,* Cambridge, Polity Press, 1996. A 'Weberian' attempt to interpret globalization in terms of the transition to the global age.

McMichael, P. *Development and Social Change: A Global Perspective,* Thousand Oaks, Pine Forge Press, 1996. The first sociology of development textbook written from an explicitly global perspective.

Sklair, L. *Sociology of the Global System,* 2nd edn, Baltimore, Johns Hopkins University Press, 1995. A critical discussion of how global capitalism structures the world in terms of the transnational practices of transnational corporations, the transnational capitalist class and the culture ideology of consumerism.

Yearly, S. *Sociology, Environmentalism, Globalization: Reinventing the Globe,* London, Sage, 1996. One of the few books on environmental sociology that assesses issues of globalization.

Glossary

Agency In sociology the term agent is sometimes simply used to mean individual. However, agency does have a rather more specific meaning. It refers to *purposeful* human action, that is, the choices people make to act in certain ways. There is a long-standing debate in sociology (and other social sciences) about the extent to which people are 'free agents'. Some theoretical perspectives, such as interactionism and ethnomethodology, place great stress on human agency. Others, such as Marxism and structural functionalism, focus more on the ways in which people's behaviour is influenced by processes in wider society.

Alienation This means estrangement or separation. Marx argued that the organization of production for private profit meant that most workers were denied the opportunity to realise their inherent creative capacities and were thus alienated from their true, or essential, selves. For Marx, religious belief was simply an expression of this alienation.

Anomie Literally a state of normlessness where the rules structuring social interaction have broken down or become meaningless to the individual. Durkheim linked anomie to a condition of **modernity** where the institutionalization of socially approved dissatisfaction was producing a situation where more individuals experienced an imbalance between their wants and the means of achieving them, making them vulnerable to, among other things, suicidal impulses.

Bureaucracy A system of administration associated with the complex organizations of modern societies based on formal rules, specialized occupational tasks, hierarchical structures and impersonality. For Weber, the growth of bureaucratic organizations was an inevitable consequence of the increasing rationality of modern societies, where calculation and efficiency replaced sentiment and tradition. However, sociologists have also documented the inefficiencies and irrationalities of bureaucracy.

Childhood The idea of childhood as a distinct social category separate from adults began to develop in European societies with the children of the nobility and spread throughout **modern** societies in the nineteenth century with the passing of legislation to protect children from exploitation in the work place and make some education compulsory.

Citizenship The political and economic rights entailed in being a member of a political community. The extension of the principle of citizenship from a narrow élite to the majority of the population is seen as one of the defining characteristics of the process of **modernization**.

Class conflict Political action arising from recognition of the different interests of social classes. Marx believed that class conflict would lead to the overthrow of the capitalist system and its replacement by socialism. Some sociologists writing in the middle years of the twentieth century, such as Dahrendorf, argued that **class consciousness** had become 'institutionalized in western societies; that is, rather than seeking to overthrow capitalism, working-class organizations and political parties pursued their interests within the capitalist system. In contemporary societies manifestations of class consciousness are much less apparent and the idea of class itself has become a contested concept.

Class consciousness Processes by which members of a social class become increasingly aware of their common interests. Marx predicted that working-class consciousness would grow under capitalism. However, this would not happen 'automatically'. Working-class sense of injustice had to be channelled into appropriate political action. Some sociologists argued that the growth of **culture industries** played a major part in inhibiting working-class consciousness, others point to the increasing diversity and fragmentation of the relatively homogenous working class of early capitalism.

Code This means the rules that govern a system of signs.

Coercion This usually describes situations where people feel compelled to do something through force, or threat of force, when they do not recognise the **legitimacy** of the controlling agency to have power over them.

Colonialism A process by which a nation state imposes its control over other territories. Colonialism usually refers to rule by western states over distant territories involving longstanding patterns of settlement and the separation of foreign and indigenous populations.

Consensus and conflict Consensus theories argue that the basis of **social order** in any society comes from people's common interests and shared values. Comte, Durkheim and Parsons tended to take this view. In Parsons' structural functionalist theory, for example, social stability is seen as the 'normal' condition of society, while conflict is 'pathological', rather like a disease in a part of the body. Consensus theorists are interested in questions of power and social control but, as Helliwell and Hindess argue in Chapter 4, they see them as general resources in society which are exercised by some, like the government and police for example, for the benefit of society as a whole. Conflict theorists, in contrast, take the view that all societies are divided into groups which are in competition over scarce resources, power and opportunity. They argue that social order is the result of some groups holding power over others. Marxists, for example, argue that there is always a conflict of interest between those who own the means of economic production (ruling class) and those who have only their labour power to sell (subordinate classes). Feminist sociologists also see societies in terms of conflicts of interest between women and men.

Consumerism The idea that **modern** societies are increasingly characterized by the promotion and acquisition of consumer goods.

Critical criminology Theoretical approaches which attempt to locate the origins of crime and the societal reaction to it in terms of a critical analysis of the political economy of capitalism.

Cult A term loosely applied to religious organizations and groups whose practices and beliefs are seen to be individualistic, esoteric and somewhat divorced from the cultural traditions of the society in which they are practised. However, globalization and the fragmentation of cultural boundaries are making such a distinction difficult to establish empirically.

Cultural reproduction The processes by which the values of the dominant culture are explicitly and implicitly reproduced in educational institutions.

Culture/culture industries In everyday language, culture is usually used to refer to 'highbrow' things, such as classical music, art or literature. However, in sociology, culture has a much wider meaning and describes the ideas, values and customs of a social group. There is a debate in sociology about the relationship between culture and other aspects of society. **Materialist** theories argue that culture is shaped largely by the productive forces of society, while **idealist** theories argue that culture exerts an independent influence on societies. **Postmodern theory** takes this argument much further, arguing that, in the media saturated contemporary world, society has become 'collapsed' into culture; that is, there is no independent standpoint outside media images of one sort or another. Culture industry refers to institutions and organizations that produce and disseminate 'popular culture', through newspapers, magazines and television for example. Criticism of culture industries is associated with, but not confined to, Marxist theory. While Marx himself and most Marxist writers have adopted an essentially **materialist** view of society, other Marxists adopted a more idealist view. Writers of the Frankfurt School, Adorno and Marcuse for example, argued that culture industries played an important and independent role in maintaining capitalism by helping to produce a largely passive, uncritical, consumer-orientated public. Other sociologists have criticised this view, arguing that it underestimates the importance of human **agency**. People are not simply the 'passive' recipients of culture industries, but rather 'actively' select and interpret what they want from it.

Culture of deprivation The idea that aspects of working-class disadvantage, such as the comparatively poor educational performance of working-class children and the relatively poor health of working-class people, can be explained to some extent by the fact that the working-class home and neighbourhood provide less motivation and linguistic skills and a more fatalistic attitude to life.

De-skilling Processes by which occupations become downgraded. In the 1970s Braverman argued that many manual and white-collar occupations were becoming de-skilled. In opposition to this view, it has been argued that technical developments in production and an increase in service occupations has generally produced higher and more flexible levels of skill in the working population. Debates about de-skilling are complicated by problems in defining and 'measuring' skill levels and the fact that contradictory processes may be operating. For example, an occupation may be officially upgraded yet be less demanding in practice. Alternatively, an occupation may require more technical skills but may be undertaken under conditions of increased supervision and control. For example, teaching has become more demanding but, as Burgess and Parker show in Chapter 9, it is now carried out under much greater **surveillance** which reduces teachers scope for autonomous decision making.

Delinquent sub-cultures Social groups – usually, but not necessarily, comprised of young males – organized around practices and values which, in some respects, are opposed to dominant social norms and values.

Discourses Systems of language, ideas and practices around which the understanding of some aspect of social reality is established. The analysis of discourses is associated most commonly with post-structural theories. Foucault, for example, analysed the ways in which the control of madness had been informed by a number of different discourses.

Discrimination Practices of individuals and groups that systematically and adversely effect the **life chances** of others. Discrimination may arise from prejudice and active hostility to others, but it may also occur unintentionally even when people may be actively trying not to be prejudiced.

Division of labour The process of increasing specialization of production which can be used at the societal level to describe increased differentiation of sectors and functions and at the level of organizations to describe the specialization and fragmentation of occupational tasks. The division of labour is generally seen as an essential element in the process of industrialization and central to the increased productive capacity of modern societies.

Domestic labour The work involved in running a household, such as cleaning, shopping and child care, which is undertaken largely by women without remuneration.

Domestic violence Violent conduct perpetrated by one member of household against another.

Epidemiology The study of the distribution of health and disease in populations.

Epistemology Epistemological questions in philosophy are concerned with theories of knowledge, or *how* questions: how do we know something is true? In sociology, epistemological questions are related to methodological issues: how is the information the sociologist is putting forward justified?

Ethnicity An awareness of belonging to a social group sharing a common cultural identity and heritage.

Export-processing enclaves A spatially circumscribed area in which products are asssembled, usually for re-export, from economies where wages are lower and conditions of production are less restrictive, to economies where wages are higher and conditions of production more restricted.

False consciousness In its most general sense this term simply means an individual or social group having a distorted view of the 'truth'. It is most specifically associated with Marxist theory's description of the *working-class* people's continued compliance with the capitalist system instead of pursuing their own 'true' interests.

Feminism A generic name for a variety of movements and doctrines concerned with promoting the rights and interests of women.

Feminization of poverty The argument that development policies, particularly programmes imposed by financial institutions such as The World Bank and the IMF as a condition for development funds, tend to have more severe impacts on low-income women and their children than on other groups in poorer countries.

Fordism A label used loosely to describe the promotion of mass production, scientific management and an intense division of labour in industrial economies.

Gender blind Theories and research studies that fail to take into account gender differences.

Genre A text whose content is structured around a distinct and recognizable form such as 'sitcom', 'soap opera' or 'thriller'.

Global commodity chain This refers to the sequence of activities a commodity passes through before it is sold on the **market**. Commodity chain analysis looks particularly at two elements: first, how it is co-ordinated and second, the spacial distribution of the transformation. Commodity chain analysis is used increasingly to understand how transnational (or multinational) corporations organize their global production systems.

Government This describes the processes by which a society is regulated by some legally constituted authority. For many sociologists government not only involves the 'visible' exercise of authority, such as elections or the passing of laws, it also involves the 'invisible' authority where people are indirectly influenced to behave in various ways. From this perspective, educational, health and welfare organizations, for example, act as instruments of government.

Hegemony This word was originally used to describe the domination of one state by another. Gramsci adapted this idea to explain the continuing dominance of the ruling class in capitalist society through political and **ideological** dominance (Chapter 4). He argued that the ruling class did not, and could not, simply control society through active force but had actively to obtain the consent of the subordinate classes. In this context he was particularly interested in the role of cultural institutions, such as family, education and media, in helping to obtain this consent.

Holistic medicine Medical practices based on the idea that disease, rather than being localised in a specific part of the body, such as the heart or the liver, is a symptom of a disturbance of the whole person.

Household An individual, or group of people, sharing the same accommodation for a period of time. Many sociologists now use the term household in preference to 'the family' because they feel that the former, with its assumption of a married couple and children, fails to reflect the diversity of domestic arrangements in contemporary societies.

Human development index A general measure of how countries compare on different criteria of development, the most widely used of which is the United Nations development programme which combines measures of longevity (life expectancy at birth), knowledge (adult literacy and mean years of schooling) and income (real income per capita).

Hyperreality An idea advanced by some **postmodern** theorists, particularly Baudrillard, claiming that the media-saturated contemporary world increasingly involves the consumption of images that have no purchase in 'reality'; thus the boundaries between what is 'real' and what is 'illusory' become increasingly blurred.

Hypothesis This refers to an idea or a theory which has been developed in such a way that it can be 'tested' with relevant evidence.

Iatrogenic disease Disease resulting from medical treatment.

Ideal type A model describing the essential characteristics of an organization, institution or pattern of behaviour.

Ideology The concept of ideology is widely used in a number of different ways in sociology. In its most general sense ideology refers to the shared ideas, beliefs and values which are held by social groups and justify their action. Sociologists tend to see ideologies negatively and are particularly interested in the ways in which they help to justify social inequalities and reinforce the power of dominant groups in societies. For example, Marxists argue that the class that rules economically has the power to disseminate ideologies throughout society legitimizing its control. Similarly, feminists have examined the part played by **patriarchal** ideologies in the subordination of women. Some sociologists have argued that ideologies can create a '**false consciousness**' of conformity among the oppressed who remain unaware of their 'real' interests. However, this raises the question of defining what those 'real' interests are, which can lead to the circularity of comparing ideological beliefs and preferences (see Chapter 4).

Illness behaviour A term used to describe the study of how people come to define themselves as sick and the factors influencing a decision to seek professional help.

Industrialization The development of mechanized technology and large-scale productive processes, seen most clearly in the factory system. Industrialization was a major source of the transformation of pre-modern to modern society. Sociology began as an attempt to make sense of industrial society.

Interviews: structured and unstructured In the structured, or 'closed', interview, respondents are asked a set of identical questions in more or less the same way and choose from a limited range of answers. Structured interviews enable the researcher to collect a large amount of data in a relatively short time and the results can be quantified. In the unstructured, or 'open', interview there is no set format and the interview is more like a conversation. There is comparatively little input from the researcher and respondents answer in their own words. Unstructured interviews tend to give richer, more detailed data.

Kinship Social relations deriving from blood ties. As societies modernise kinship becomes a less important basis for both social organization and determining an individual's position within institutions and organizations.

Legitimacy The belief of people that the power exercised over them is just because, for example, a leader was born to rule or a government has been democratically elected. While some sociologists, following Weber, have simply focused on *how* legitimacy is established, others, following Marx, have adopted a more critical stance by questioning *whether* or not belief in legitimacy is justified. However, as Helliwell and Hindess observe in Chapter 4, this latter approach can result in comparing one set of value judgements with another.

Liberalism A political doctrine which stresses the importance of the state guaranteeing the rights of free individuals by, for example, being freely elected, accountable and acting within the law. Liberalism is associated with modern western societies and the liberal tradition is usually compared favourably with other forms of **government**, such as traditional authority or the totalitarian **government** of the former Soviet Union. However, many sociologists have criticized western liberal democracies for the economic inequalities they produce, both within and between societies, and for failing to attain their democratic **ideology** in practice. Other sociologists have been more interested in exploring how liberal democracies work. For Foucault, as Helliwell and Hindess explain in Chapter 4, liberalism is a means by which **government** can be effected in increasingly complex and diverse societies.

Life chances The idea that an individual's prospects of attaining material rewards and high **status** in a society are profoundly influenced by '*structural* factors', such as their class position, gender or ethnic group.

Lifestyles Differences in the patterns of consumption of goods, services and culture which have been explained largely as a reflection of different class positions. In British sociology, in particular, there was a long-running debate focusing on the consequences of increasing numbers of more affluent working-class people adopting 'middle-class' lifestyles. For many sociologists, particularly those who argue that we are now living in a **postmodern** society, people's sense of identity is shaped more by what they consume than what they produce.

Longitudinal study Obtaining data from the same sample at regular intervals over a long period of time.

Macro- and micro-theories Macro-theories focus on larger social changes, such as broad historical changes and comparisons between societies and social institutions, and are usually associated with structural theories in sociology. Micro-theories are more likely to focus on face-to-face interactions of relatively small numbers of people and are usually associated with **social action theories**. While many studies in sociology are either macro or micro, others try to combine aspects of both. For example, in *Learning to Labour*, which is cited in several chapters in this book, Willis linked a detailed micro-analysis of the experiences of a small group of boys to macro-educational and industrial processes.

Markets Arenas within which buyers and sellers meet in order to exchange goods and money. In economics, the price of goods emerge from this interaction as expressions of the aggregated results of the preferences of individuals. This then feeds into production and consumption decisions. **Liberalism** holds that the market is the foundation of freedom in modern societies as it is based on choice, while Marxists argue that as people enter the market unequal it merely reproduces inequality. Economic sociologists are increasingly interested in how markets are socially constructed both inside and outside the exchange process.

Marketization The spread of market economics, especially in institutions concerned with things like education and health care which had largely been taken out of the market place by the expansion of social welfare policies.

Marriage A *social institution* which legally sanctions the union of partners. In the later part of the twentieth century marriage has become less important with an increasing proportion of the population choosing to cohabit outside marriage.

Materialism and idealism Materialism describes theories, such as Marxism, which hold that economic institutions are the major influence on how societies work and change. Idealist theories, in contrast, place more emphasis on the part played by culture, values and ideas.

Materialist and lifestyle theories Examining health inequalities, materialist theories argue that people's health is influenced primarily by their economic circumstances while lifestyle theories focus more on the choices people make, such as whether or not to smoke. Some sociologists have tried to synthesize the theories by exploring the extent to which people's lifestyle 'choices' are shaped by their material circumstances.

Meta-narratives This term, which is sometimes used interchangeably with grand narratives, describes general, encompassing ideas and beliefs about how the world works, such as religious or scientific doctrines. In sociology, general sociological perspectives, such as Marxism, functionalism or **feminism**, are sometimes described as meta-narratives, or grand-narratives. **Postmodernists**, in particular, are critical of meta, or grand, narratives for failing to recognize the diversity of the social world and for trying to tell people *how* they should think about the world.

Methodological individualism The view that sociological explanation has to be based on individual characteristics of one sort or another. Society should not be theorized as something 'over and above' individuals as such abstraction is not justified.

Modernity This is a very general descriptive term which is usually taken to mean two things. First, it refers to the emergence of modern societies based around things such as industrial production, urban living, science, technology, political democracy, rational planning and the growth of the state. Second, modernity is characterized by a particular outlook on the world which sets itself against tradition, superstition and religious interpretations. It celebrates the power of rational understanding, and science in particular, to understand how the world works. Sociology is closely tied to modernity. Not only did it begin in the nineteenth century as an attempt to understand the 'new' modern societies that were developing in western Europe, it was itself a product of modernity. That is, the idea of understanding how societies work with a view to improving them is a distinctly modern idea. Some theorists now argue that the modern era is ending and we are now moving to a new form of **postmodern** society.

Moral panic A term used to describe a media-fuelled over-reaction to a social group, form of behaviour or social problem. A characteristic of moral panic is that the specific issue is depicted as a symptom of a much more general breakdown of **social order** and values.

Nation state A state, characteristic of **modernity** and the rise of **nationalism**, where a government claims legitimate authority over a specific territory.

Nationalism An **ideology** founded on the belief that people living in the same national community share common interests that separate them from other nations.

New racism Racist **ideologies** based on cultural and religious identities rather than supposed biological differences.

New religious movements A term used to describe the growth of unorthodox religious beliefs and practices in contemporary societies.

New Right This loosely describes political and economic theories developed in the 1970s and 80s which celebrated the liberal tradition of free-market economies and opposed the continued expansion of welfare states on economic and moral grounds. New Right ideas were associated with the governmental policies of Margaret Thatcher in Britain and Ronald Regan in the USA in the 1980s.

Nuclear family A husband, wife and dependent children living in the same household. The term was used to contrast the smaller and relatively more isolated families of modern societies with what were taken to be the much larger extended families of pre-industrial societies. However, more recent research has suggested that such a distinction is oversimplified as extended family structures were not characteristics of all pre-modern societies and persist to some extent in modern societies.

Objective knowledge This is knowledge which is supposed to be free from bias, opinion, personal values and prejudices and is most commonly associated with scientific data that is generated under experimental conditions. While some sociologists argue that sociology is about producing objective knowledge of societies, others argue that this is an impossible ambition as the researchers' own subjective ideas and values will necessarily influence what is discovered and presented to others. Another point of view, put forward by Pawson in Chapter 2, is that sociologists should strive towards *greater* objectivity even though *total* objectivity is impossible in practice.

Ontology Ontological questions in philosophy are concerned with the nature of the things: *what* they are. In sociology, ontological questions are about what societies are. For example, are societies best conceptualised as interdependent institutions shaping individual lives (*structural theory*) or as the outcome of individual actions (*action theory*)?

Paradigm This describes a set of general ideas and practices around which specific areas of research are organised. In sociology there are several different paradigms, with their own theories and research strategies, and there are disputes between them about the 'right' way to do sociological research.

Patriarchy This originally means the rule of the father. Feminist sociologists use it much more generally to describe the **ideological** and **material** structures of power by which men dominate and control women.

Phenomenology Phenomenological sociology tries to avoid making preconceived judgements and hypotheses and focuses instead on people's subjective understanding of everyday life. Phenomenologists are critical of the idea of a 'scientific' sociology which tries to attribute causality to social phenomena. For example, a great deal of sociological research has tried to uncover some of the social causes of things like crime, suicide and educational failure. For phenomenologists, the fluctuating and subjective nature of social life makes this ambition impossible, the most sociology can do is employ in-depth, qualitative methods to explore how certain things come to be 'seen' by people as 'crimes', 'suicides' or 'educational failure'. Phenomenology has been very influential in sociology, but has been criticized for being both trivial and neglecting the importance of wider social influences on people's lives.

Polarization A concept used by Marx to describe a hardening of the divisions between the capitalist and working classes.

Positivism A philosophical doctrine holding that scientific knowledge can only deal with observable entities which then prove, or disprove, theories. In sociology positivism is associated with the idea that sociology should follow the principles of the natural sciences and produce objective knowledge through methods of research which are reliable, quantifiable and value neutral. Positivism has been heavily criticized in social theory by those, such as **realists**, who have different views of what science is, and by those, such as **phenomenologists**, who argue that scientific methods cannot be applied to the study of societies.

Post-Fordism A very general and contested term used to describe a transition from mass industrial production epitomised by the factory production line developed by Henry Ford's motor company, to more diverse and flexible systems of production, associated with information technology enterprises, for example. The term has also been used more generally to describe a transition from 'organised' state regulated capitalism to a more 'disorganised' and less regulated capitalism.

Postmodernity and Postmodernism These are very general terms which are sometimes used in a different ways by different writers. Postmodernity is usually used to describe a situation where developments such as de-industrialization, globalization of the economy, media saturation of societies and the collapse of grand ideologies, such as communism and socialism, are bringing about a new social condition which is different from **modernity**. Postmodernism usually describes a set of social and cultural beliefs, values and ways of behaving which result from living in modernity. Some sociologists, such as Lyotard and Baudrillard, argue that a consequence of these changes has been to fragment what sociologists previously understood as 'society', and that a new postmodern sociology is now needed to make sense of these developments. Others, such as Bauman, argue for a sociology *of* postmodernity while others, such as Giddens, believe that these radical changes have simply transformed, rather than ended, modernity.

Post-structuralism This describes a form of analysis which has much in common with **postmodern** theory. Post-structuralists argue that as social reality is only made intelligible through language, the focus of social inquiry should be on the various lilnguistic forms, or **texts**, through which the world is described. Texts can only be compared to each other as there is no independent 'reality' against which they can be evaluated. Post-structuralists are thus **relativists**.

Power élite Elites are groups who have power, influence and high social **status** in societies or social organizations. In sociology, 'élite theorists' have argued that both Marxist hopes for a 'classless society' and western notions of **liberal democracies** are impossible in practice as the major institutions of societies would always be controlled by élites who would inevitably use the power they hold over others for their own interests. Most famously, C. Wright Mills argued that despite its **ideology** of being open, accountable and democratic **government**, the United States was ruled by a relatively *integrated* and perpetuating power élite who controlled its political, economic and military institutions.

'Race relations' The study of racist ideologies, the structures that give rise to them and the consequences for people's **life chances**.

Realism In its most general sense realism means that societies are real in the sense of having certain invariant properties which then allow generalizations to be made. More specifically, realism describes a philosophical approach which argues, in opposition to positivism, that scientific, and social scientific, explanations involve uncovering the unobservable, but real, mechanisms that generate relations between observable phenomena. In the last twenty years 'new realism' has become increasingly influential in sociology. However, elements of social realism can be found much earlier in the work of Marx and Durkheim, for example. In his realist theory of suicide, Durkheim attempted to demonstrate that consistent relationships between suicide and other social factors, such as religion and family, were generated by invisible but real moral forces which had their origins in collective social life.

Relativism Relativists argue that as the knowledge that sociologists use to develop and test their theories is necessarily 'constructed' in terms of ideas and values which are variable and constantly changing, there are no independent and fixed criteria by which they can be evaluated. Therefore, sociological explanation cannot transcend the particular and offers only partial and temporary interpretations rather than general truths. **Phenomenological theory** (see Chapter 2), interactionist theories of deviance (see Chapter 11) and social constructionist approaches to medicine and the body (see Chapter 12) are all examples of relativist approaches in sociology.

Sacred That which is special, awe inspiring and set apart from the ordinary and everyday. The distinction between the sacred and the profane was the cornerstone of Durkheim's definition of religion.

Secondary deviance Behaviour which follows being identified and labelled as deviant which may, or may not include further rule breaking.

Sect A religious group which is formed by breaking away from an established religious organization.

Sex and gender Sex differences are typically seen as natural and biological while gender divisions are shaped by social values and vary between societies and within societies over time. However some sociologists dispute this distinction, arguing that even the apparently 'fixed' and stable anatomical reality of the human body is a cultural construction the meaning of which is given by social values and practices (see Chapter 12).

Sexual division of labour The argument that access to economic resources and opportunities is gendered.

Sexual harassment Sexual advances by one person to another, or others, which persist in spite of the recipient making it clear that they are not welcome.

Social action theory Social action theories in sociology start from the idea that human behaviour has meaning and intention; that is people do not just respond to things, they actively interpret the world around them and have reasons for what they do. Action theorists usually begin by exploring how individuals interpret the situations in which they find themselves. Action theories are often contrasted to **structural theories** which focus more on wider social and organizational processes. A major question for action theory is how, if individuals are 'free', creative agents, do we explain **social order**? The relationship between action and structure is examined in Chapter 3.

Social integration A concept which describes the different ways in which people are tied, or bonded, to each other through joint membership of social institutions, such as the family, work and religious organizations. It was used most famously by Durkheim in his study of suicide, in which he argued that the more people in modern societies were integrated into *social institutions*, the less vulnerable they were to suicide. However, it has been widely developed in more contemporary sociology. For example, a great deal of research has shown that levels of social integration can profoundly influence people's mental and physical health.

Social mobility This describes the movement of people between social positions – usually occupational, or class categories. Intragenerational mobility compares an individual's position over a lifetime, while intergenerational mobility compares a person's present position with that of their origin. Rates of social mobility are often taken as indicators of the openness, or fairness, of a society.

Social order The description and explanation of social order is one of the key problems of sociological theory. Structural theorists tend to conceptualize order arising from the ways in which individuals' behaviour is constrained by the institutional organization of societies. Action theorists, in contrast, focus on the ways in which social order is produced from agents' identification and realization of goals.

Social stratification The hierarchical ranking of different social groups in terms of unequal access to wealth, income, **status** and power. For most sociologists, social stratification is structured, that is, it is a consequence of forms of social organization that produce systematic differences in the **life chances** of members of different social groups. For example, the average educational attainment of children from professional backgrounds is consistently higher than that of children from manual working-class backgrounds.

Social structure The idea of social structure is one of the ways in which sociologists have tried to conceptualize the relationship between the individual and society. It focuses on societies as enduring systems of organization which are larger than the individual and shape the individual's life in various ways. Sociologists have different interpretations of social structure. For some, such as Marx, societies are defined in terms of their economic structure, that is, the ways in which the production of goods and services is organised. For others, such as Durkheim, social structures are defined more in terms of the cultural ideas that help bind individuals to social groups. A common criticism of all 'structural' theories is that they do not attach enough importance to the part individuals play in actively shaping their own lives. Sociologists' attempts to bring together ideas of social structure and individual actions are discussed at some length by Swingewood in Chapter 3.

Socialization A term used to describe the processes by which people become aware of social norms and values and learn what is expected of them in given situations. Socialization begins in infancy but continues through adult life and sociologists have used the concept to explore how people 'learn' gender, occupational or deviant roles, for example.

Status This describes the social standing or prestige of an individual or group with a society or social organization. Many sociologists have followed Weber in seeing status differences, arising from religion or **ethnicity** for example, as distinct sources of inequality which are in important respects independent of class or economic position. Status groups are often characterised by distinct **lifestyles** and values and can act an important source of identity for individuals.

Stigma People are socially stigmatized when they are discredited in some way and denied full social acceptance. Sociologists are interested in the processes by which individuals and groups become stigmatized and the effects this has on their identities and social behaviour.

Stress A theoretical concept used to describe the relationship of an organism to its environment; an organism is said to be stressed when the demands placed on it tax its adaptive capabilities. Sociologists and psychologists of health are interested in the ways in which 'stressful' life experiences which people find difficult to cope with make disease more likely.

Surveillance This means monitoring people's behaviour. Some sociologists describe the contemporary world as the surveillance society since people's behaviour is increasing being surveilled, directly by things such as security cameras and indirectly by the amount of information about them that is now stored by public and private institutions.

Symmetrical family This describes an idea that in late modern societies the domestic division of labour is becoming more flexible, with women taking on more paid employment outside the home and men becoming more involved in household responsibilities. While there is a great deal of evidence of the former, there is little to support the latter.

Text In its most general sense a text is a written or visual document. However, in **post-structural** analysis, it is used more specifically to refer to the ideas through which the world is made intelligible. Social analysis is the analysis of texts.

Theory-dependence Doing social research necessarily involves using general, or theoretical, ideas through which the information, or data, is gathered and interpreted. The data are thus shaped by the theory and there is no such thing as 'pure' knowledge. Facts never speak for themselves.

Third World A very general term used loosely to describe societies which are less developed economically.

Transnational corporation Technically, this describes any business corporation located in more than one country. However, it more commonly refers to very large corporations with interests in many countries whose activities are aimed at world markets.

Victim survey Victim surveys attempt to get round the official underreporting of crime by interviewing representative samples of the general population to find out how many of them have been victims of crime in a given period.

Welfare state State provision of a range of services and economic benefits, such as education and pensions, to try and guarantee basic living standards for all citizens.

Zero sum view of power The view that there is only so much power in a given social situation and that one group therefore holds it at the expense of others.

References

Abbott, P. and Wallace, C. (1996) *An Introduction to Sociology: Feminist Perspectives,* 2nd edn, London, Routledge

Abraham, J. (1995) *Divide and School: Gender and Class Dynamics in Comprehensive Education,* London, Falmer Press

Acker, S. (1994) *Gendered Education,* Buckingham, Open University Press

Adonis, A. and Pollard, S. (1997) *A Class Act,* London, Hamish Hamilton

Afshar, H. (1989) 'Gender roles and the "moral economy of kin" among Pakistani women in West Yorkshire', *New Community,* **15**(2): 211–25

Agenda for Action, London, King's Fund

Albrow, M. (1996) *The Global Age,* Cambridge, Polity

Albrow, M. and King, E. (eds) (1990) *Globalization, Knowledge and Society,* London, Sage

Alger, C. (1988) 'Perceiving, analysing and coping with the local-global nexus', *International Social Science Journal,* **117**: 321–40

Althusser, L. (1972) 'Ideology and ideological state apparatus: notes towards an investigation', in B. Cosin (ed.) *Education, Structure and Society,* Penguin/Open University Press, Harmondsworth

Amin, A. (1994) *Post-Fordism,* Oxford, Blackwell

Amin, A. and Thrift, N. (1995) *Globalization, Institutions and Regional Development in Europe,* Oxford, Oxford University Press

Anderson, B. (1983) *Imagined Communities: Reflections on the Origin and Spread of Nationalism,* London, Verso

Anderson, M. (1980) *Approaches to the History of the Western Family 1500–1914,* London, Macmillan

Ang, I. (1985) *Watching Dallas: Soap Opera and the Melodramatic Imagination,* London, Methuen

Ang, I. (1996) *Living Room Wars: Rethinking Media Audiences for a Post-modern World,* London, Routledge

Anthias, F. and Yuval-Davis, N. (1989) 'Introduction', in N. Yuval-Davis and F. Anthias (eds), *Woman-Nation-State,* London, Macmillan

Anthias, F. and Yuval-Davis, N. (1992) *Racialized Boundaries,* London, Routledge

Arber, S. (1990) 'Opening the black box: inequalities in women's health', in P. Abbott and G. Payne (eds) *New Directions in the Sociology of Health,* Basingstoke, Falmer

Arber, S. and Ginn, J. (eds) (1995) *Connecting Gender and Ageing,* Buckingham, Open University Press

Archer, M. (1979) *The Social Origins of Educational Systems,* London, Sage

Armstrong, D. (1983) *The Political Anatomy of the Body,* Cambridge, Cambridge University Press

Armstrong, D. (1987) 'Bodies of knowledge: Foucault and the problem of human anatomy', in G. Scambler (ed.) *Sociological Theory and Medical Sociology,* London, Tavistock

Armstrong, D. (1995) 'The problem of the whole person in holistic medicine', in B. Davey, A. Gray and C. Seale (eds) *Health and Disease: A Reader,* Buckingham, Open University Press

Arnot, M., David, M. and Weiner, G. (1996) *Educational Reforms and Gender Equality in Schools,* Manchester, Equal Opportunities Commission

Arnot M., Gray J., James M., Rudduck J. with Dunveen, G. (1998) *Recent Research on Gender and Educational Performance*, OFSTED

Babbie, E. (1989) *The Practice of Social Research*, 5th edn, Belmont, Wadsworth

Bachrach, P. and Baratz, M.S. (1969) 'Two faces of power' and 'Decisions and nondecisions', in R. Bell *et al.* (eds), *Political Power: A Reader in Theory and Research*, pp. 94–9, New York, Free Press

Balibar, E. and Wallerstein, I. (1991) *Race, Nation and Class: Ambiguous Identities*, London, Verso

Ball, S. J .(1981) *Beachside Comprehensive*, Cambridge, Cambridge University Press

Ball, S. J. (1990) *Politics and Policy-Making in Education*, London, Routledge

Ball, S. J. (1994) *Educational Reform: A Critical and Post-structural Approach*, Buckingham, Open University Press

Banks, M., Bates, I., Breakwell, G. *et al.* (1992) *Careers and Identities*, Milton Keynes, Open University Press

Banton, M. (1967) *Race Relations*, London, Tavistock

Banton, M. (1983) *Racial and Ethnic Competition*, Cambridge, Cambridge University Press

Barker, C. (1997) *Global Television*, Oxford, Blackwell

Barker, D., Halman, L. and Vloet, A. (1993) *The European Values Study 1981–1990*. Summary Report, London/Tilburg, European Values Study

Barker, E. (1995) *New Religious Movements: A Practical Introduction*, London, HMSO

Barker, M. (1981) *The New Racism*, London, Junction Books

Barker, M. (1993) 'Seeing how far you can see: on being a fan of *2000 AD*', in D. Buckingham (ed.), *Reading Audiences: Young People and the Media*, Manchester, University of Manchester Press

Barker, M. and Petley, J. (eds) (1997) *Ill Effects: the Media /Violence Debate*, London, Routledge

Barker, M. and Petley, J. (eds) (1998) *Ill Effects: the Media /Violence Debate*, 2nd edn, London, Routledge

Barnet, R. and Cavanagh, J. (1994) *Global Dreams*, New York, Simon & Schuster

Barrett, M. (1980/1988) *Women's Oppression Today*, London, Verso

Barrett, M. and McIntosh, M. (1982) *The Anti-Social Family*, London, Verso

Barthes, R. (1953/1967) *Writing Degree Zero*, London, Cape

Barthes, R. (1957/1973) *Mythologies*, London, Paladin

Bartley, M., Power, C., Blane, D., Davey-Smith, G. and Shipley, M. (1994) 'Birth weight and later socio-economic disadvantage: evidence from the 1958 British cohort study', *British Medical Journal*, **309**: 1475–8

Baudrillard, J. (1983) *Simulations*, New York, Semiotext

Baudrillard, J. (1988) *Selected Writings* (M. Poster, ed.), Cambridge, Polity

Bauman, Z. (1992) *Intimations of Postmodernity*, London, Routledge

Beck, U. (1992) *Risk Society*, London, Sage

Becker, H. (1963) *Outsiders: Studies in The Sociology of Deviance,* Basingstoke, Macmillan

Beckford, J. (1985) *Cult Controversies*, London, Tavistock

Beckford, J. (1989) *Religion and Advanced Industrial Society*, London, Unwin Hyman

Bell, C. and Newby, H. (1976) 'Husbands and wives: the dynamics of the deferential dialectic', in D. Leonard Barker and S. Allen (eds), *Dependence and Exploitation in Work and Marriage,* London, Hutchinson

Bellah, R. (1967) 'Civil religion in America', *Daedalus*, **96**: 1–21

Beneria, L. and Feldman, S. (eds) (1992) *Unequal Burden*, Boulder, CO, Westview

Ben-Tovim, G., Gabriel, J., Law, I. and Stredder, K. (1986) *The Local Politics of Race*, London, Macmillan

Bendix, R. (1956) *Work and Authority in Industry,* New York, Wiley & Sons

Bendix, R. and Lipset, S.M. (1967) 'Karl Marx's theory of social classes', in R. Bendix and S. Lipset (eds), *Class, Status and Power*, London, Routledge

Benzeval, M., Judge, K. and Whitehead, M. (eds) (1995) *Tackling Inequalities in Health: An Agenda for Action*, London, King's Fund

Berelson, B. (1952) *Content Analysis in Communication Research*, New York, Free Press

Berger, P. and Kellner, H. (1964) 'Marriage and the construction of reality', *Diogenes*, 46(1): 1–23; reprinted in B. Cosin *et al.* (1971), *School and Society*, Open University Course Reader, London, Routledge & Kegan Paul

Berger, P. and Luckman, T (1967) *The Social Construction of Reality*, London, Penguin

Berkman, L. and Syme, S. (1979) 'Social networks and host resistance and mortality: a nine year follow-up of Almeda residents', *American Journal of Epidemiology*, 109: 186–204

Berliner, L. (1990) 'Domestic violence: a humanist or feminist issue?', *Journal of Interpersonal Violence*, 50: 128–9

Bernard, J. (1972) *The Future of Marriage*, Harmondsworth: Penguin

Bernard, J. (1982) *The Future of Marriage*, 2nd edn, Newhaven, CN, Yale University Press

Bernardes, J. (1997) *Family Studies: An Introduction*, London, Routledge

Bernstein, B. (1975) *Class, Codes and Control*, Vols 1–3, London, Routledge

Beynon, J. (1985) *Initial Encounters in the Secondary School*, London, Falmer Press

Beynon, J. and Atkinson, P. (1984) 'Pupils as data gatherers: mucking and sussing' in S. Delamont (ed.) *Readings on Interaction in the Classroom*, pp. 255–72, London, Methuen

Blaikie, N. (1993) *Approaches to Social Inquiry*, London, Polity

Blau, P. and Duncan, O. (1967) *The American Occupational Structure*, New York, Wiley

Blood, R. and Woolfe, D. (1960) *Husbands and Wives*, New York, Free Press

Blumer, H. (1967) *Symbolic Interactionism*, New York, Prentice Hall

Bogatz, G. and Ball, S. (1971) *The Second Year of Sesame Street: A Continuing Evaluation*, Princeton, Educational Testing Service

Bonal, X. (1995) 'Curriculum change as a form of educational policy legitimation: the case of Spain: international studies in sociology of education', 5(2): 203–20

Bott, E. (1971) *Family and Social Network*, London, Tavistock

Bottoms, A. and Xanthos, P. (1989) 'A tale of two estates', in D. Downes (ed.), *Crime and the City*, London, Macmillan

Bourdieu, P. (1990) *In Other Words*, Cambridge, Polity

Bowe, R. and Ball, S. with Gold, A. (1992) *Reforming Education and Changing Schools*, London, Routledge

Bowles, S. and Gintis, H. (1976) *Schooling in Capitalist America*, London, Routledge & Kegan Paul

Boyer, R. and Drache, D. (1996) *States Against Markets*, London, Routledge

Boyer, R. and Durand, J. (1997) *After Fordism*, London, Macmillan

Bradley, H. (1996) *Fractured Identities*, Cambridge, Polity

Brah, A. (1992) 'Difference, diversity and differentiation' in J. Donald and A. Rattansi (eds) *Culture and Difference*, London, Sage

Brah, A. (1994) '"Race" and "culture" in the gendering of labour markets: South Asian young women and the labour market', in H. Afshar and M. Maynard (eds), *The Dynamics of Race and Gender: Some Feminist Implications*, London, Taylor & Francis

Brah, A. (1996) *Cartographies of Diaspora, Contesting Identities*, London and New York, Routledge

Braithwaite, J. (1989) *Crime, Shame and Integration*, Cambridge, Cambridge University Press

Brannen, J. (1995) 'Young people and their contribution to household work', *Sociology*, 29(2): 317–38

Brannen, J. (ed.) (1992) *Mixing Methods: Qualitative and Quantitative Research*, Aldershot, Gower

Brannen, J. and Moss, P. (1991) *Managing Mothers*. London, Unwin Hyman

Brannen, J. and O'Brien, M. (eds) (1994) *Children in Families*, London, Falmer

Brannen, J. and Wilson, G. (eds) (1987) *Give and Take in Families: Studies in Resource Distribution*, London, Allen & Unwin

Braverman, H. (1974) *Labor and Monopoly Capital*, New York, Monthly Review Press

Brecher, J. and Costello, T. (1994) *Global Village or Global Pillage: Economic Reconstruction from the Bottom Up*, Boston, South End Press

Broadfoot, P. (1996) *Education, Assessment and Society*, Buckingham, Open University Press

Brown, C. (1984) *Black and White Britain. The Third PSI Survey*, London, Heinemann Educational

Brown, C. (1992) '"Same difference": the persistence of racial disadvantage in the British employment market', in P. Braham, A. Rattansi and R. Skellington (eds), *Racism and Antiracism. Inequalities, Opportunities and Policies*, pp. 46–63, London and Newbury Park, Sage

Brown, C. and Gay, P. (1985) *Racial Discrimination: 17 Years After the Act*, London, Policy Studies Institute

Brown, G. and Harris, T. (1978) *The Social Origins of Depression*, London, Tavistock

Brown, P. (1989) 'Schooling for inequality', in B. Cosin, M. Flude and M. Hales (eds) *School, Work and Equality*, London, Hodder & Stoughton

Brown, P. and Lauder, H. (1991) 'Education, economy and social change', *International Studies in Sociology of Education*, 1: 3–23

Brown, P., Halsey, A., Lauder, H. and Stuart-Wells, A. (1997) 'The transformation of education and society: an introduction', in A. Halsey, H. Lauder, P. Brown and A. Stuart-Wells (eds) *Education: Culture, Economy, Society*, pp. 1–44, Oxford, Oxford University Press

Bruce, S. (1995) *Religion in Modern Britain*, Oxford, Oxford University Press

Bruce, S. (1996) *Religion in the Modern World: From Cathedrals to Cults*, Oxford, Oxford University Press

Bryan, B., Dadzie, S. and Scafe, S. (1985) *The Heart of the Race*, London: Virago

Bryman, A. (1995) *Disney and His Worlds*, London, Routledge

Buckley, M. (1989) *Women and Ideology in the Soviet Union*, Hemel Hempstead, Harvester Wheatsheaf

Burgess, R. (1998) Postgraduate education in Europe, Special Issue, *European Journal of Education*, (June)

Bury, M. (1982) 'Chronic illness as biographical disruption', *Sociology of Health and Illness*, 4: 167–82

Bury, M. (1997) *Health and Illness in a Changing Society*, London, Routledge

Butler, J. (1990) *Gender Trouble: Feminism and the Subversion of Identity*, London, Routledge

Butler, T. and Savage, M. (eds) (1996) *Social Change and the Middle Classes*, London, University College London Press

Calnan, M. and Williams, S. (1992) 'Images of scientific medicine', *Sociology of Health and Illness*, 14: 233–54

Caplan, L. (ed.) (1987) *Studies in Religious Fundamentalism*, London, Macmillan

Casanova, J. (1994) *Public Religions in the Modern World*, Chicago, University of Chicago Press

Castells, M. (1996) *The Rise of Network Society*, Oxford, Blackwell

Castells, M. (1997) *The Power of Identity*, Oxford, Blackwell

Castells, M. (1998) *End of the Millennium*, Oxford, Blackwell

Central Statistical Office (1993) *Social Trends*, 23, London, HMSO

Central Statistical Office (1994) *Social Focus on Children*, London, HMSO

Central Statistical Office (1995) *Social Trends*, **25**, London, HMSO

Centre for Contemporary Cultural Studies (1982) *The Empire Strikes Back. Race and Racism in 70s' Britain*, London, Hutchinson

Chambers, D. (1986) 'The constraints of work and domestic schedules on women's leisure', *Leisure Studies*, **5**: 309–25

Chambliss, W. (1978) *On the Take: From Petty Crooks to Presidents*, Bloomington, Indiana University Press

Chase-Dunn, C. (1989) *Global Formation*, Oxford, Blackwell

Cheney, D. (1996) 'Those whom the immigration law has kept apart – let no one join together: a view on immigration incantation', in D. Jarrett-Macauley (ed.), *Reconstructing Womanhood, Reconstructing Feminism*, London and New York, Routledge

Clark, T. and Lipset, S. (1991) 'Are social classes dying?', *International Sociology*, **6**(4): 397–410

Clarke, R. (1980) 'Situational crime prevention: theory and practice', *British Journal of Criminology*, **20**(2): 136–47

Clarke, R. (1992) *Situational Crime Prevention: Successful Case Studies*, New York, Harvard & Heston

Cloward, R. and Ohlin, L. (1960) *Delinquency and Opportunity*, London, Collier Macmillan

Cockburn, C. (1983) *Brothers: Male Dominance and Technological Change*, London, Pluto Press

Cohen, A. (1955) *Delinquent Boys*, London, Free Press

Cohen, P. (1972) 'Subcultural conflict in working class community', *Working Papers in Cultural Studies* No. 2, Centre for Contemporary Cultural Studies, University of Birmingham

Cohen, P. (1997) *Rethinking the Youth Question*, Basingstoke, Macmillan

Cohen, R. (1997) *Global Diasporas*, London, UCL Press

Cohen, S. (1980) *Folk Devils and Moral Panics*, 2nd edn, Oxford, Martin Robertson

Cohen, S. (1985) *Visions of Social Control*, Cambridge, Polity

Coleman, D. (1988) 'Population', in A.H. Halsey (ed.), *British Social Trends Since 1900*, Basingstoke, Macmillan

Collins, P. (1990) *Black Feminist Thought*, London, Routledge

Comte, A. (1896) *The Positive Philosophy*, London, Bell and Sons

Condit, C. (1989) 'The rhetorical limits of polysemy', *Critical Studies in Mass Communications*, **6**: 103–22

Connell, R. (1995) *Masculinities*, Cambridge, Polity

Cooper, L. (1997) 'Myalgic encephalomyelitis and the medical encounter', *Sociology of Health and Illness*, **19**: 186–207

Corbin, J. and Strauss, A. (1991) 'Comeback; the process of overcoming disability', in G. Albrecht and J. Levy (eds), *Advances in Medical Sociology*, Vol. 2, Greenwich, JAI Press

Corbridge, S., Thrift, N. and Martin, R. (eds) (1995) *Money, Space, Power*, Oxford, Blackwell

Corner, J. (1991) 'Meaning, genre, context: the problematics of public knowledge in the new audience studies', in J. Curran and M. Gurevitch (eds), *Mass Media and Society*, London, Edward Arnold

Corner, J., Richardson, K. and Fenton, N. (1990) *Nuclear Reactions: Form and Response in Public Issue Television*, London, John Libbey

Corrigan, P. (1979) *Schooling the Smash Street Kids*, London, Macmillan

Coser, L. (1967) *Continuities in the Study of Social Conflict*, New York, Free Press

Crompton, R. (1993/1998) *Class and Stratification*, Cambridge, Polity

Crompton, R. (1996) ' The fragmentation of class analysis', *British Journal of Sociology*, 47(1): 56–67

Crompton, R. and Gubbay, J. (1977) *Economy and Class Structure*, Basingstoke, Macmillan

Crompton, R. and Jones, G. (1984) *White-Collar Proletariat: Deskilling and Gender in the Clerical Labour Process*, Basingstoke, Macmillan

Crompton, R., Gallie, D. and Purcell, K. (eds) (1996) *Changing Forms of Employment*, London, Routledge

Crouch, C. and Streeck, W. (eds) (1997) *Political Economy of Modern Capitalism*, London, Sage

Curran, J. (1996) 'Rethinking mass communications', in J. Curran, D. Morley and V. Walkerdine (eds), *Cultural Studies and Communications*, London, Arnold

Dahl, R. (1957) 'The concept of power', *Behavioural Scientist*, 2: 201–5

Dahl, R. (1958) 'A critique of the ruling élite model', *American Political Science Review*, 52: 463–9

Dahl, R. (1961) *Who Governs? Democracy and Power in an American City*, New Haven and London, Yale University Press

Dahrendorf, R. (1969) *Class and Class Conflict in the Industrial Societies*, London, Routledge

Davey, B., Gray, A. and Seale, C. (eds) (1995) *Health and Disease: A Reader*, Buckingham, Open University Press

Davey Smith, G., Bartely, M. and Blane, D. (1991) 'Black on class and health: a reply to Strong', *Journal of Health and Medicine*, 13: 350–57

Davey Smith, G., Blane, D. and Bartley, M. (1994) 'Explanations for socio-economic differentials in mortality; evidence from Britain and elsewhere', *European Journal of Public Health*, 4: 131–44

Davey Smith, G., Hart C., Blane D. and Hawthorne, V. (1997) 'Lifetime socioeconomic position and mortality: prospective observational study', *British Medical Journal*, 314: 547–52

David, M. (1991) 'Comparisons of "educational reform" in Britain and the USA: a new era?', *International Studies in Sociology of Education*, 1: 87–109

Davie, G. (1994) *Religion in Britain Since 1945*, Oxford, Blackwell

Davie, G. (1995) 'Competing fundamentalisms', *Sociology Review*, 4(4)

Davie, G. (1996) 'Religion and modernity: the work of Danièle Hervieu-Léger', in K. Flanagan and P. Jupp (eds), *Postmodernity, Sociology and Religion*, pp. 101–17, London, Macmillan

Davis, K., Leijenaar, M. and Oldersma, J. (eds) (1991) *The Gender of Power*, London, Sage

Deacon, D. (1996) 'Voluntary activity in a changing communication environment', *European Journal of Communication*, 11(2): 173–98

Deacon, D., Fenton, N. and Bryman, A. (1999) 'From inception to reception: the natural history of a news item', *Media, Culture and Society*, 21(1): 5–31

Deacon, D. and Golding, P. (1994) *Taxation and Representation: The Media, Political Communication and the Poll Tax*, London, John Libbey

Dean, M. (1998) 'Administering asceticism: reworking the ethical life of the unemployed citizen', in M. Dean and B. Hindess (eds), *Governing Australia. Studies in Contemporary Rationalities of Government*, pp. 87–107, Cambridge and Melbourne, Cambridge University Press

Delamont, S. (1981) 'All too familiar? A decade of classroom research', *Educational Analysis*, 3(1): 69–83

Delamont, S. (1986) 'Beyond Flanders: the relationship of subject matter and individuality to classroom style', in M. Stubbs and S. Delamont (eds) *Explorations in Classroom Observation*, Chichester, Wiley

Delphy, C. (1994) 'Changing women in a changing Europe: is "difference" the future for feminism?', *Women's Studies International Forum,* **17**(2/3): 187–201

Delphy, C. and Leonard, D. (1992) *Familiar Exploitation: A New Analysis of Marriage in Contemporary Western Societies*, Oxford, Polity

Demerath, N. (1965) *Social Class in American Protestantism*, Chicago, Rand-McNally

Denscombe, M. (1994) *Sociology Update 1994*, Leicester, Olympus Books

Derrida, J. (1982) *Margins of Philosophy,* Chicago, University of Chicago Press

DfEE (1997) *DfEE News,* 26 June, London, DfEE

DfEE (1998) *Teaching: High Status, High Standards*, London, DfEE

Dicken, P. (1998) *Global Shift: Transforming the World Economy,* 3rd edn, London, Paul Chapman

Diesing, P. (1971) *Patterns of Discovery in the Social Sciences*, London, Routledge

Dobash, R. and Dobash, R. (1980) *Violence Against Wives,* Shepton Mallet, Open Books

Dobash, R.and Dobash, R. (1992) *Women, Violence and Social Change,* London, Routledge

Dobbelaere, K. (1981) 'Secularization: a multi-dimensional concept', *Current Sociology,* **29**(2)

Douglas, J. (1964) *The Home and the School*, London, MacGibbon & Kee

Douglas, J. (1977) *The Nude Beach,* Beverley Hills, Sage

Douglas, M. (1973) *Natural Symbols,* London, Barrie & Jenkins

Douglas, M. (1978) *Purity and Danger*, London, Routledge & Kegan Paul

Dowmunt, T. (ed.) (1993) *Channels of Resistance: Global Television and Local Empowerment*, BFI/Channel Four

Downes, D. (1966) *The Delinquent Solution*, London, Routledge & Kegan Paul

Downes, D. (1979) 'Praxis makes perfect: a critique of radical criminology', in D. Downes and P. Rock (eds), *Deviant Interpretations,* Oxford, Martin Robertson

Downes, D. (1993) *Employment Opportunities for Offenders,* London, Home Office

Downes, D. and Rock, P. (1988) *Understanding Deviance*, 2nd edn, Oxford, Oxford University Press

Drew, E., Emerek, R. and Mahon, E. (eds) (1998) *Women, Work and the Family in Europe,* London, Routledge

Duncan, S. and Edwards, R. (eds) (1997) *Single Mothers in an International Context: Mothers or Workers?* London, UCL Press

Duncombe, J. and Marsden, D. (1993) 'Love and intimacy: the gender division of emotion and "emotion work"', *Sociology,* **27**(2): 221–41

Dunne, G. (1997) 'Women are doing it for themselves: new models for the organization of work in partnerships'. Paper presented to the British Sociological Association Annual Conference, University of York

Dunning, J. (1993) *Multinational Enterprises and the Global Economy*, Wokingham, Addison-Wesley

Durkheim, E. (1893/1984) *The Division of Labour in Society,* Basingstoke, Macmillan

Durkheim, E. (1895/1982) *The Rules of Sociological Method,* Basingstoke, Macmillan

Durkheim, E. (1897/1952) *Suicide: A Study in Sociology,* London, Routledge & Kegan Paul

Durkheim, E. (1912/1976) *The Elementary Forms of Religious Life,* London, Allen & Unwin

Durkheim, E. (1956) *Education and Sociology*, New York, Free Press

Durning, A. (1992) *How Much is Enough?*, London, Earthscan

Dworkin, A. (1981) *Pornography,* London, Women's Press

Eames, N., Ben-Shlomo, Y. and Marmot, M. (1993) 'Social deprivation and premature mortality: regional comparison across England', *British Medical Journal,* **307**: 1097–102

Economist (1992) 19 December: 21–2

Edgell, S. (1980) *Middle Class Couples*, London, Allen & Unwin

Edgell, S. and Duke, V. (1991) *A Measure of Thatcherism*, London, HarperCollins Academic

Edholm, F. (1982) 'The unnatural family', in E. Whitelegg, M. Arnot, E. Bartels, V. Beechey and L. Birke (eds), *The Changing Experience of Women*, Oxford, Martin Robertson

Edwards, R. (1993) 'The inevitable future: post-Fordism in work and learning', in R. Edwards, S. Sieminski and D. Zeldin (eds) *Adult Learners, Education and Training*, Buckingham, Open University Press

Ekins, P. (1992) *A New World Order: Grassroots Movements for Global Change*, London, Routledge

Ell, K. (1996) 'Social networks, social support and coping with serious illness: the family connection', *Social Science and Medicine*, **42**: 173–83

Elliott, B. and Maclennan, D. (1994) 'Education, modernity and neo-conservative school reform in Canada, Britain and the US', *British Journal of Sociology of Education*, **15**(2): 165–85

Elliott, P. (1974) 'Uses and gratifications research: a critique and a sociological alternative', in J. Blumler and E. Katz (eds), *The Uses of Mass Communications: Current Perspectives on Gratifications Research*, London, Sage

Elman, R. (ed.) (1996) *Sexual Politics and the European Union*, Ford, Berghahn Books

Emmison, M. (1991) 'Wright and Goldthorpe: Constructing the agenda of class analysis', in J. Baxter, M. Emmison and J. Western, *Class Analysis and Contemporary Australia*, Basingstoke and Sydney, Macmillan

Emmison, M. and Western, M. (1990) 'Social class and social identity', *Sociology*, **24**: 241–54

Engels, F. (1940) *The Origins of the Family, Private Property, and the State*, London, Lawrence & Wishart

Epstein, D. (ed) (1994) *Challenging Gay and Lesbian Inequalities In Education*, Buckingham, Open University Press

Erikson, R. and Goldthorpe, J. (1988) 'Women at class crossroads', *Sociology*, **22**: 545–53

Erikson, R. and Goldthorpe, J. (1992) *The Constant Flux*, Oxford, Clarendon Press

Esping-Andersen, G. (ed.) (1997) *Welfare States in Transition*, London, Sage

Eurelings-Bontekoe, E., Diekstra, R. and Verschuur, M. (1995) 'Psychological distress, social support and support seeking: a prospective study among primary mental health care patients', *Social Science and Medicine*, **40**:1083–9

Farrington, D. (1997) 'Human development and criminal careers', in M. Maguire, R. Morgan and R. Reiner (eds), *The Oxford Handbook of Criminology*, 2nd edn, pp. 361–408, Oxford, Clarendon Press

Featherstone, M. (ed.) (1990) *Global Culture: Nationalism, Globalization and Identity*, London, Sage

Fekete, L. and Webber, F. (1994) *Inside Racist Europe*, London, Institute of Race Relations

Felson, M. (1994) *Crimes and Everyday Life*, Thousand Oaks, Pine Forge

Fenton, N., Bryman, A. and Deacon, D. with Birmingham, P. (1998) *Mediating Social Science*, London, Sage

Fenton, N., Deacon, D., Bryman, A. and Birmingham, P. (1995) *Social Science the Media and the Public Sphere*. Paper presented at the European Sociological Association Conference, Budapest

Ferlie, E., Ashburner, L., Fitzgerald, L. and Pettigrew, A. (1996) *The New Public Management in Action*, Oxford, Oxford University Press

Finch, J. (1983) *Married to the Job: Wives' Incorporation into Men's Work*, London, George Allen & Unwin

Finch, J. and Mason, J. (1993) *Negotiating Family Responsibilities*, London, Routledge

Fiske, J. and Hartley, J. (1978) *Reading Television*, London, Methuen

Fitzpatrick, R., Newman, S., Archer, R. and Shipley, M. (1991) 'Social support, disability and depression: a longitudinal study of rheumatoid arthritis', *Social Science and Medicine*, **33**: 605–11

Floud, J. and Halsey, A. (1961) *Education, Economy and Society: A Reader in the Sociology of Education*, Milton Keynes, Open University Press

Foddy, W. (1993) *Constructing Questions for Interviews and Questionnaires*, Cambridge, Cambridge University Press.

Foreman-Peck, J. (1995) *A History of the World Economy: International Economic Relations since 1850*, 2nd edn, London, Harvester Wheatsheaf

Forrester, D., Chatterton, M. and Pease, K. (1988) *The Kirkholt Burglary Prevention Demonstration Project*, London, Home Office

Foster, P. (1992) 'Teacher attitudes and Afro/Caribbean educational attainment', *Oxford Review of Education*, **8**(3)

Foster, P., Gomm, R. and Hammersley, M. (1996) *Constructing Educational Inequality*, London, Falmer Press

Foucault, M. (1973) *The Birth of the Clinic,* London, Tavistock

Foucault, M. (1979) *Discipline and Punish*, Harmondsworth, Penguin

Foucault, M. (1980) *Power/Knowledge*, Brighton, Harvester

Foucault, M. (1982) 'The subject and power', in H. Dreyfus and P. Rabinow (eds), *Michel Foucault: Beyond Structuralism and Hermeneutics*, pp. 208–26, Brighton, Harvester

Foucault, M. (1984) *The Foucault Reader* (P. Rabinow, ed.), London, Penguin

Foucault, M. (1986) *The Birth of the Clinic*, London, Routledge

Foucault, M. (1988) 'The ethic of care for the self as a practice of freedom', in J. Bernauer and D. Rasmussen (eds), *The Final Foucault*, pp. 1–20, Boston, MA, MIT Press

Foucault, M. (1991) 'Governmentality', in G. Burchell, C. Gordon and P. Miller (eds), *The Foucault Effect*, pp. 87–104, Hemel Hempstead, Harvester Wheatsheaf

Foucault, M. (1997) *Ethics: Subjectivity and Truth*, (P. Rabinow, ed.), New York, New Press

Fox, A. (1985) *History and Heritage: The Social Origins of the British Industrial Relations System*, London, Allen & Unwin

Fox, A. and Adelstein, A. (1978) 'Occupational mortality: work or way of life?', *Journal of Epidemiology and Community Health*, **32**: 73–8

Fox, A., Goldblatt, P. and Jones, D. (1986) 'Social class mortality differentials: artefact, selection or life circumstances', in R. Wilkinson (ed.), *Class and Health: Research and Longitudinal Data*, London, Tavistock

Fraser, N. (1989) 'Foucault on modern power: empirical insights and normative confusions', in N. Fraser, *Unruly Practices: Power, Discourse and Gender in Contemporary Social Theory*, pp. 17–34, Cambridge, Polity

Freidson, E. (1970) *Profession of Medicine: A Study of the Sociology of Applied Knowledge,* Chicago, University of Chicago Press

Friedan, B. (1965) *The Feminine Mystique*, Harmondsworth, Penguin

Friedman, J. (1990) 'Being in the world: globalization and localization.' in M. Featherstone (ed.) op. cit.: 311–28

Friedman, J. (1995) 'Where we stand: a decade of world city research' in P. Knox and P. Taylor (eds) *World Cities in A World System*, Cambridge, Cambridge University Press

Frobel, F., Heinrichs, J. and Kreye, O. (1980) *The New International Division of Labour*, Cambridge, Cambridge University Press

Fryer, P. (1984) *Staying Power: The History of Black People in Britain*, London, Pluto

Fuller, M. (1983) 'Qualified criticism, critical qualifications', in L. Barton and S. Walker (eds) *Race, Class and Education*, Beckenham, Croom Helm

Gabriel, J. (1994) *Racism, Culture, Markets,* London and New York, Routledge

Gallie, D. (1994) 'Are the unemployed an underclass?', *Sociology*, **26**: 737–57

Galton, M. and Delamont, S. (1980) 'The first weeks of middle school', in A. Hargreaves and L. Tickle (eds) *Middle Schools: Origins, Ideology and Practice*, pp. 207–27, London, Harper & Row

Gandy, O. (1982) *Beyond Agenda Setting: Information Subsidies and Public Policy*, Norwood, NJ, Ablex

Garfinkel, H. (1984) *Studies in Ethnomethodology,* Cambridge, Polity

Garland, D. (1990) *Punishment and Modern Society*: *A Study in Social Theory,* Oxford, Oxford University Press

Gavron, H. (1966) *The Captive Wife*, Harmondsworth, Penguin

Gerbner, G. (1969) 'Toward "cultural indicators": the analysis of mass mediated public message systems', W.H. Allen (ed.), *AV Communication Review,* 17(2): 137–48

Gereffi, G. (1995) 'Global production systems and Third World development', in B. Stallings (ed.), *Global Change, Regional Response*, pp. 100–42, Cambridge, Cambridge University Press

Gereffi, G. and Korzeniewicz, M. (eds) (1994) *Commodity Chains and Global Capitalism,* Westport, CT: Praeger

Gerhardt, U. (1987) 'Parsons, role theory and health interaction', in G. Scambler (ed.), *Sociological Theory and Medical Sociology,* London, Tavistock

Gerhardt, U. (1989) *Ideas about Illness,* Basingstoke, Macmillan

Gibson-Graham, J. (1996) *The End of Capitalism (as we knew it): A Feminist Critique of Political Economy*, Oxford, Blackwell

Giddens, A. (1971) *Capitalism and Modern Social Theory,* Cambridge, Cambridge University Press

Giddens, A. (1973/1981) *The Class Structure of the Advanced Societies,* London, Hutchinson

Giddens, A. (1976) *New Rules of Sociological Method*, London, Hutchinson

Giddens, A. (1984) *The Constitution of Society,* Cambridge, Polity

Giddens, A. (1990a) 'Structuration theory and social analysis', in J. Clark, C. Mogdil and S. Mogdil (eds), *Anthony Giddens: Consensus and Controversy,* Basingstoke, Falmer

Giddens, A. (1990b) *The Consequences of Modernity*, Cambridge, Polity

Giddens, A. (1991a) 'Structuration theory: past, present and future', in G. Bryant, G. Jary and D. Jary (eds), *Giddens' Theory of Structuration,* London, Routledge

Giddens, A. (1991b) *Modernity and Self Identity: Self and Society in the Late Modern Age*, Cambridge, Polity

Giddens, A. (1992) *The Transformation of Intimacy*, Cambridge, Polity

Giddens, A. and Turner, J. (eds) (1987) *Social Theory Today,* Cambridge, Polity

Gill, O. (1977) *Luke Street: Housing Policy, Conflict and the Creation of Deliquent Areas,* London, Macmillan

Gillborn, D. (1990) *'Race', Ethnicity and Education*, London, Unwin Hyman

Gilroy, P. (1987) *There Ain't No Black In the Union Jack. The Cultural Politics of Race and Nation*, London, Hutchinson

Gilroy, P. (1992) 'The end of antiracism', in J. Donald and A. Rattansi (eds) *Race, Culture and Difference*, London, Sage

Gitlin, T. (1979) 'Prime-time ideology: the hegemonic process in television entertainment', *Social Problems*, **26**: 251–66

Glass, D. (ed) (1954) *Social Mobility in Britain*, London, Routledge & Kegan Paul

Glass, T. and Maddox, G. (1992) 'The quality and quantity of social support: stroke recovery as a psycho-social transition', *Social Science and Medicine*, **34**: 1249–61

Godin, H. and Daniel, Y. (1943) *La France, Pays de Mission*, Paris, Cerf

Goffman, E. (1968) *Stigma: Notes on the Management of Spoiled Identity*, London, Penguin

Goffman, E. (1969) *The Presentation of the Self in Everyday Life*, London, Penguin

Goffman, E. (1972) *Interaction Ritual*, London, Penguin

Goffman, E. (1983) 'The interaction order', *American Sociological Review*, **48**

Goffman, E. (1991) *Asylums: Essays on the Social Situation of Mental Patients and Other Inmates*, London, Penguin

Golding, P. and Murdock, G. (1978) 'Theories of communication and theories of society', *Communication Research*, **5**(3): 390–456

Golding, P. and Murdock, G. (1991) 'Culture, communications and political economy', in J. Curran and M. Gurevitch (eds), *Mass Media and Society*, London, Edward Arnold

Goldthorpe, J. (1982) 'On the service class: its formation and future', in *Classes and the Division of Labour*, A. Giddens and G. Mackenzie (eds), Cambridge, Cambridge University Press

Goldthorpe, J. (1983) 'Women and class analysis: in defence of the conventional view', *Sociology*, **17**(4): 465–78

Goldthorpe, J. (1987) *Social Mobility and Class Structure in Modern Britain*, 2nd edn, Oxford, Clarendon Press

Goldthorpe, J. (1996) 'The service class revisited', in T. Butler and M. Savage (eds), *Social Change and the Middle Classes*, London, University College London Press

Goldthorpe, J. and Marshall, G. (1992) 'The promising future of class analysis', *Sociology*, **26**(3): 381–400

Goldthorpe, J., Lockwood, D., Bechhofer, F. and Platt, J. (1968) *The Affluent Worker: Industrial Attitudes and Behaviour*, Cambridge, Cambridge University Press

Goldthorpe, J., Lockwood, D., Bechhofer, F. and Platt, J. (1969) *The Affluent Worker in the Class Structure*, Cambridge, Cambridge University Press

Goldthorpe, J. with Llewellyn, C. and Payne, C. (1980/1987) *Social Mobility and Class Structure in Great Britain*, Oxford, Clarendon Press

Goode, W. and Hatt, P. (1952) *Methods in Social Research*, New York, McGraw-Hill

Goodman, A., Johnson, P. and Webb, S. (1997) *Inequality in the UK*, Oxford, Oxford University Press

Gordon, S. (1992) *History and Philosophy of Social Science*, London, Routledge

Gorz, A. (1982) *Farewell to the Working Class*, London, Pluto

Gottfredson, M. and Hirschi, T. (1990) *A General Theory of Crime*, Stamford, Stamford University Press

Grace, G. (1991) 'Welfare Labourism versus the New Right: the struggle in New Zealand's education policy', *International Studies in Sociology of Education*, 1: 25–41

Graham, H. (1987a) 'Women's poverty and caring', in C. Glendinning and J. Millar (eds), *Women and Poverty in Britain*, Brighton, Wheatsheaf

Graham, H. (1987b) 'Women's smoking and family health', *Social Science and Medicine*, **25**: 47–57

Graham, H. (1994) 'Gender and class as dimensions of smoking behaviour in Britain: insights from a survey of mothers', *Social Science and Medicine*, **38**: 691–8

Gramsci, A. (1971) *Selections from the Prison Notebooks*, London, Lawrence & Wishart

Gramsci, A. (1978) *Selections from Cultural Writings*, Cambridge, MA, Harvard University Press

Gray, A. (1992) *Video Playtime*, London, Routledge

Green, A. (1997) 'Educational achievement in centralised and decentralised systems' in A. Halsey, H. Lauder, P. Brown and A. Stuart-Wells (eds) *Education: Culture, Economy, Society*, pp. 283–98, Oxford, Oxford University Press

Green, D. (ed.) (1988) *Acceptable Inequalities? Essays on the Pursuit of Equality*, London, Institute of Economic Affairs

Gregson, N. and Lowe, M. (1994) 'Waged domestic labour and the renegotiation of the domestic division of labour within dual career households', *Sociology*, **28**(1): 55–78

Habermas, J. (1989) *The Theory of Communicative Action:* Volume 2, Cambridge, Polity

Hagan, J., Simpson, J. and Gillis, A. (1979) 'The sexual stratification of social control: a gender based perspective on crime and delinquency', *British Journal of Criminology*, **30**

Hall, C. (1992) *White, Male and Middle Class: Explorations in Feminism and History*, Oxford, Polity

Hall, S. (1997) 'The work of representation' in S. Hall (ed.) *Representation: Cultural Representations and Signifying Practices*, London, Sage/Open University

Hall, S., Critcher, C., Jefferson, T., Clarke, J. and Roberts, B. (1978) *Policing the Crisis: Mugging, The State and Law and Order*, London, Hutchinson

Hall, S. (1977) 'Culture, media and the "ideological effect"', in J. Curran, M. Gurevitch and J. Woolacott (eds), *Mass Communication and Society*, London, Edward Arnold

Hall, S. (1980) 'Encoding/decoding', in S. Hall, D. Hobson, A. Lowe, and P. Willis (eds), *Culture, Media, Language*, London, Hutchinson

Hall, S. and du Gay, P. (eds) (1996) *Questions of Cultural Identity*, London, Sage

Hall, S., Held, D. and McGrew, T. (eds) (1992) *Modernity and its Futures*, Cambridge, Polity

Hall, S. and Jaques, M. (eds) (1989) *New Times*, London, Lawrence & Wishart

Hall, S. and Jefferson, T. (eds) (1976) *Resistance Through Rituals: Youth Subcultures in Post-war Britain*, London, Hutchinson

Halsey, A. (1977) 'Towards meritocracy? The case of Britain', in J. Karabel and A. Halsey (eds), *Power and Ideology in Education*, New York, Oxford University Press

Halsey, A., Health, A. and Ridge, J. (1980) *Origins and Destinations: Family, Class and Education in Modern Britain*, Oxford, Clarendon Press

Halsey, A., Lauder, H., Brown, P. and Stuart-Wells, A. (eds) (1997) *Education: Culture, Economy, Society*, Oxford, Oxford University Press

Halson, J. (1989) 'The sexual harassment of young women', in L. Holly (ed.), *Girls and Sexuality*, Milton Keynes, Open University Press

Hamilton, M. (1994) *The Sociology of Religion*, London, Routledge

Hammersley, M. (1990) *Reading Ethnographic Research*, Harlow, Longman

Hammersley, M. (1992) *What's Wrong With Ethnography?* London, Routledge

Hanmer, J. (1990) 'Men, power and the exploitation of women', in J. Hearn and D. Morgan (eds), *Men, Masculinities and Social Theory*, London, Unwin Hyman

Hanmer, J., Radford, J. and Stanko, E. (eds) (1989) *Women, Policing and Male Violence*, London, Routledge

Hannaford, I. (1996) *Race. The History of an Idea in the West*, Baltimore and London, The Johns Hopkins University Press

Hargreaves, A. (1994) *Changing Teachers, Changing Times: Teachers' Work and Culture in the Postmodern Age*, London, Cassell

Hargreaves, D. (1967) *Social Relations in a Secondary School*, London, Routledge & Kegan Paul

Harris, C. (1990) *Kinship*, London, Routledge

Harris, N. (1996) *The New Untouchables: Immigration and the New World Worker*, London, Penguin

Hartmann, H. (1976) 'Capitalism, patriarchy and job segregation by sex', *Signs*, **1**: 137–68

Hartmann, P. and Husband, C. (1973) 'The mass media and racial conflict', in S. Cohen and J. Young (eds), *The Manufacture of News*, London, Constable

Harvey, D. (1989) *The Condition of Postmodernity*, Oxford, Blackwell

Haywood, C. and Mac an Ghaill, M. (1996) 'Schooling masculinities', in M. Mac an Ghaill (ed.) *Understanding Masculinities: Social Relations and Cultural Arenas*, pp. 50–60, Buckingham, Open University Press

Heaphy, B., Donovan, C. and Weeks, J. (1997) 'Sex, money and the kitchen sink: power in same sex couple relationships'. Paper presented to the British Sociological Association Annual Conference, University of York

Hearn, J. (1992) *Men in the Public Eye,* London, Routledge

Hearn, J. (1996) 'Men's violence to known women: men's accounts and men's policy developments', in B. Fawcett, B. Featherstone, J. Hearn and C. Toft (eds), *Violence and Gender Relations,* London, Sage

Heath, A. (1981) *Social Mobility*, London, Fontana

Heath, A. and Britten, N. (1984) 'Women's jobs do make a difference', *Sociology*, 18(4): 475–90

Heath, A. and Clifford, P. (1996) 'Class inequalities and educational reform in twentieth-century Britain', in D. Lee and B. Turner (eds) *Conflict about Class: Debating Inequality in Late Industrialism*, pp. 209–24, London, Longman

Heath, A., Curtice, J., Jowell, R., Evans, G., Field, J. and Witherspoon, S. (1991) *Understanding Political Change,* Oxford, Pergamon

Heelas, P. (1996) *The New Age Movement*, Oxford, Blackwell

Held, D. (1995) 'Democracy, the nation state and the global system' in D. Held (ed.) *Political Theory Today*, Cambridge, Polity

Herman, E. and Chesney, R. (1997) *The Global Media: The New Missionaries of Corporate Capitalism*, London, Cassell

Hervieu-Léger, D. (1986) *Vers un Nouveau Christianisme*. Paris, Cerf

Hervieu-Léger, D. (1993) *La Religion pour Mémoire*, Paris, Cerf

Hesse, B., Rai, D., Bennett, C. and McGilchrist, P. (1992) *Beneath the Surface: Racial Harassment*, Aldershot, Avebury

Hester, M., Kelly, L. and Radford, J. (eds) (1996) *Women, Violence and Male Power,* Buckingham, Open University Press

Hester, S. and Elgin, P. (1992) *A Sociology of Crime*, London, Routledge

Higgins, P. (1980) *Outsiders in a Hearing World: A Sociology of Deafness,* London, Sage

Hillman, M., Adams, J. and Whitelegg, J. (1990) *One False Move: A Study of Children's Independent Mobility,* London, Policy Studies Institute

Hindess, B. (1987) *Politics and Class Analysis,* Oxford, Blackwell

Hindess, B. (1995) *Discourses of Power: From Hobbes to Foucault*, Oxford, Blackwell

Hindess, B. (1996), 'Liberalism, socialism and democracy: variations on a governmental theme', in A. Barry, T. Osborne and N. Rose (eds), *Foucault and Political Reason: Liberalism, New-liberalism and Rationalities of Government*, pp. 65–80, London, University College London Press

Hirschi, T. (1969) *Causes of Delinquency,* Berkley, University of California Press

Hirst, P. and Thompson, G. (1996) *Globalization in Question: The International Economy and the Possibilities of Governance*, Cambridge, Polity

Hobbs, D. (1997) 'Criminal collaboration', in M. Maguire, R. Morgan and R. Reiner (eds), *The Oxford Handbook of Criminology,* Oxford, Clarendon Press

Hochschild, A. (1989) *The Second Shift*, London, Piatkus

Hollingsworth, J. and Boyer, R. (1997) *Contemporary Capitalism: The Embeddedness of Institutions,* Cambridge, Cambridge University Press

Holmes, C. (1988) *John Bull's Island: Immigration and British Society,* London, Macmillan

Holmes, C. (ed.) (1978) *Immigrants and Minorities in British Society*, London, Allen & Unwin

Holton, R. (1998) *Globalization and the Nation State,* London, Mcmillan

Hood, R. (1996) *The Death Penalty,* 2nd edn, Oxford, Oxford University Press

Hovland, C. (1959) 'Reconciling conflicting results derived from experimental and survey studies of attitude change', *The American Psychologist*, **14**

Hunter, I. (1988) *Culture and Government. The Emergence of Literary Education*, Basingstoke, Macmillan

Hunter, I. (1994) *Rethinking the School*, Sydney, Allen & Unwin

Hunter, J. (1991) 'Fundamentalism and social science', *Religion and Social Order*, 1: 149–63

Hyman, R. (1975) *Industrial Relations: A Marxist Introduction*, London, Macmillan

Illich, I. (1976) *Limits to Medicine: Medical Nemesis: the Expropriation of Health*, London, Calder & Boyars

Illsley, R. (1986) 'Occupational class, selection and the production of inequalities in health', *Quarterly Journal of Social Affairs*, 2: 151–65

International Sociology (1993) *The Debate on Class*, 8(3): 1

Jackson, B. and Marsden, D. (1962) *Education and the Working Class*, London, Routledge & Kegan Paul

Jackson, S. (1992) 'Towards a historical sociology of housework: a materialist feminist analysis', *Women's Studies International Forum*, 15(2): 153–72

Jackson, S. (1997) 'Women and the family', in D. Richardson and V. Robinson (eds), *Introducing Women's Studies*, 2nd edn, London, Macmillan

Jackson, S. (1998) 'Theorizing gender and sexuality', in S. Jackson and J. Jones (eds), *Contemporary Feminist Theories*, Edinburgh, Edinburgh University Press

Jackson, S. and Moores, S. (eds) (1995) *The Politics of Domestic Consumption: Critical Readings*, Hemel Hempstead, Prentice Hall/Harvester Wheatsheaf

James, M. (1994) 'Hysteria', in C. Seale and S. Pattison (eds) *Medical Knowledge: Doubt and Certainty*, Buckingham, Open University Press

James, O. (1997) *Britain on the Couch*, London, Hutchinson

Jameson, F. (1991) *Postmodernism, or, the Cultural Logic of Late Capitalism*, London, Verso

Jameson, F. and Miyoshi, M. (eds) (1998) *The Cultures of Globalization*, Durham, Duke University Press

Jasinski, J., Williams, L. and Finkelhor, D. (eds) (1998) *Partner Violence. A Comprehensive Review of 20 Years of Research*, London, Sage

Jeffrey, R. (1979) 'Normal rubbish: deviant patients in casualty departments', *Sociology of Health and Illness*, 1: 90–108

Jensen, K. (1990) 'The politics of polysemy: television news, everyday consciousness and political action', *Media, Culture and Society*, 12: 57–77

Jessop, B. (1994) 'Post-Fordism and the state', in A. Amin (ed.) *Post-Fordism*, pp. 251–79, Oxford, Blackwell

Jobling, R. (1988) 'The experience of psoriasis under treatment', in M. Bury and R. Anderson (eds), *Living with Chronic Illness: the Experience of Patients and their Families*, London, Unwin Hyman

Jobson, R., Bingham, G., Whitehouse, J. *et al.* (1996) 'Crowcroft Park Primary School' in National Commission on Education (eds) *Success Against the Odds*, pp. 43–68, London, Routledge

Johnson, C. (1982) *MITI and the Japanese Miracle*, Stanford, Stanford University Press

Joly, D. and Cohen, R. (eds) (1989) *Reluctant Hosts: Europe and its Refugees*, Aldershot, Avebury

Jones, A. (1993) 'Becoming a "girl": post-structuralist suggestions for educational research', *Gender and Education*, 5(2)

Jones, T. (1993) *Britain's Ethnic Minorities*, London, Policy Studies Institute

Jones, T., Maclean, B. and Young, J. (1986) *The Islington Crime Survey*, Aldershot, Gower

Joseph Rowntree Foundation (1995) *Income and Wealth: Report of the Joseph Rowntree Foundation Inquiry Group*, Vol. 1 and 2, York, Joseph Rowntree Foundation

Joyce, P. (ed.) (1995) *Class*, Oxford, Oxford University Press

Kaplan, H. (1991) 'Social psychology of the immune system: a conceptual framework and review of the literature', *Social Science and Medicine*, **33**: 909–23

Kaplan, L. (ed.) (1988) *Fundamentalism in a Comparative Perspective*, Amherst, University of Massachusetts Press

Kapstein, E. (1994) *Governing the Global Economy*, Cambridge, MA, Harvard University Press

Kay, D. and Miles, R. (1992) *Refugees or Migrant Workers? The Recruitment of Displaced Persons for British Industry, 1946–1951*, London, Routledge

Keddie, N. (1971) 'Classroom knowledge', in M. Young (ed.) *Knowledge and Control*, London, Collier Macmillan

Kelling, G. and Coles, C. (1997) *Fixing Broken Windows*, New York, Free Press

Kellner, D. (1995) *Media Culture*, London, Routledge

Kelly, L. (1988) *Surviving Sexual Violence*, Oxford, Polity

Kelly, M. (1992) *Colitis*, London, Tavistock/Routledge

Kelly, M. and Field, D. (1998) 'Conceptualising chronic illness', in D. Field and S. Taylor (eds), *Sociological Perspectives on Health, Illness and Health Care*, Oxford, Blackwell Science

Kennedy Bergen, R. (ed.) (1998) *Issues in Intimate Violence*, London, Sage

Kenway, J. (1993) 'Marketing education in the postmodern age', *Journal of Education Policy*, **8**(2): 105–22

Kepel, G. (1994) *The Revenge of God*, Cambridge, Polity

Kerr, C., Dunlop, J., Harbison, G. and Myers, C. (1973) *Industrialism and Industrial Man*, London, Penguin

Kiernan, K. and Wicks, M. (1990) *Family Change and Future Policy*, London, Family Policy Studies Centre

King, A. (ed.) (1991) *Culture, Globalization and the World-System*, London, Macmillan

Kinsey, R. (1984) *The Merseyside Crime Survey: First Report*, Liverpool, Merseyside County Council

Kitzinger, J. (1993) 'Understanding AIDS: researching audience perceptions of Acquired Immune Deficiency Syndrome', in J. Eldridge (ed.), *Getting the Message: News, Truth and Power*, London, Routledge

Kitzinger, J. and Kitzinger, C. (1993) '"Doing it": representations of lesbian sex', in G. Griffin (ed.), *Outwrite: Lesbianism and Popular Culture*, London, Pluto

Klein, R. (1988) 'Acceptable inequalities?', in D. Green (ed.), *Acceptable Inequalities? Essays on the Pursuit of Equality*, London, Institute of Economic Affairs

Komarovsky, M. (1962) *Blue-Collar Marriage*, New York, Random House

Komter, A. (1989) 'Hidden power in marriage', *Gender and Society*, **3**(2): 187–216

Kuhn, T. (1970) *The Structure of Scientific Revolutions*, Chicago, Chicago University Press

Kunda, G. (1992) *Engineering Culture: Control and Commitment in a High-Tech Corporation*, Philadelphia, Temple University Press

Lacey, C. (1970) *Hightown Grammar*, Manchester, Manchester University Press

Laing, R. (1971) *The Politics of the Family and Other Essays*, London, Tavistock

Lambert, A. (1976) 'The sisterhood', in M. Hammersley and P. Woods (eds) *The Process of Schooling*, pp. 152–9, London, Routledge & Kegan Paul

Lane, C. (1989) *Management and Labour in Europe*, Aldershot, Edward Elgar

Langford, W. (1998) *The Subject of Love*, London, Routledge

Langlois, R. and Robertson, P. (1995) *Firms, Markets and Economic Change*, London, Routledge

Lash, S. and Urry, J. (1987) *The End of Organized Capitalism*, Cambridge, Polity

Laslett, P. (1965) *The World We Have Lost*, London, Methuen

Laws, S. (1994) 'Undervalued families: standing up for single mothers', *Trouble and Strife*, **28**: 5–11

Layder, D. (1994) *Understanding Social Theory,* London, Sage

Lea, J. and Young, J. (1984) *What Is To Be Done About Law and Order?,* London, Penguin

Leach, E. (1967) *A Runaway World?,* London, BBC Publications

Lee, D. and Turner, B. (1996) *Conflicts over Class,* London, Longman

Lees, S. (1997) *Ruling Passions,* Buckingham, Open University Press

Lemert, E. (1961) *Social Pathology,* New York, McGraw-Hill

Lemert, E. (1967) *Human Deviance: Social Problems and Social Control,* Englewood Cliffs, Prentice Hall

Leonard, D. (1990) 'Persons in their own right: children and sociology in the UK', in L. Chisholm, P. Buchner, H.-H. Kruger and P. Brown (eds), *Childhood, Youth and Social Change: A Comparative Perspective*, London, Falmer

Lepkowska, D. (1999) 'Extra prep for boys who cannot write', Daily Express, 13 February

Lewis, C. (1995) 'What opportunities are open to fathers?', in P. Moss (ed.), *Father Figures: Fathers in the Families of the 1990s,* London, HMSO

Lewis, J. (1991) *The Ideological Octopus: An Exploration of Television and its Audience*, London, Routledge

Lister, R. (1998) *Citizenship. Feminist Perspectives,* London, Macmillan

Livingstone, S. (1991) 'Audience reception: the role of the viewer in retelling romantic drama', in J. Curran and M. Gurevitch (eds), *Mass Media and Society*, London, Edward Arnold

Locker, D. (1983) *Disability and Disadvantage,* London, Tavistock

Lockwood, D. (1956) 'Some remarks on "the social system"', *British Journal of Sociology,* 7(2): 134–46

Lockwood, D. (1958/1989) *The Black Coated Worker,* London, Allen & Unwin, Oxford, Oxford University Press

Lockwood, D. (1988) 'The weakest link in the chain', in D. Rose (ed.), *Social Stratification and Economic Change,* London, Unwin Hyman

Lukes, S. (1973) *Emile Durkheim: His Life and Work,* London, Penguin

Lukes, S. (1974) *Power: A Radical View*, London, Macmillan

Lukes, S. (ed.) (1986) *Power,* Oxford, Blackwell

Lull, J.(1995) *Media, Communication, Culture: A Global Approach*, Cambridge, Polity

Lupton, D. (1994) *Medicine as Culture,* London, Sage

Lyotard, J. (1984) *The Postmodern Condition,* Minneapolis, University of Minnesota Press

Mac an Ghaill, M. (1988) *Young, Gifted and Black*, Milton Keynes, Open University Press

Mac an Ghaill, M. (1994) *The Making of Men: Masculinities, Sexualities and Schooling*, Buckingham, Open University Press

Mac an Ghaill, M. (1996) 'Sociology of education, state schooling and social class: beyond critiques of the new right hegemony', *British Journal of Sociology of Education,* 17(2): 163–76

McCarthy, T. (1992), 'The critique of impure reason: Foucault and the Frankfurt School', in T. Wartenberg (ed.), *Rethinking Power,* pp. 121–48, Albany, State University of New York Press

McCruddon, C., Smith, D. and Brown, C. (1991) *Racial Justice at Work,* London, Policy Studies Institute

MacDonald, R. (ed.) (1997) *Youth, the 'Underclass' and Social Exclusion,* London, Routledge

McGrew, T. (1992) 'A global society?', in S. Hall, *et al.* (eds) op. cit.: Chapter 2

McKeown, T. (1979) *The Role of Medicine,* Oxford, Blackwell

McLennan, G. (1992) 'The Enlightenment project re-visited', in S. Hall, D. Held and T. McGrew (eds), *Modernity and Its Futures,* Cambridge, Polity

Mcleod, J., Kosicki, G. and Pan, Z. (1991) 'On understanding and misunderstanding media effects', in J. Curran and M. Gurevitch (eds), *Mass Media and Society*, London, Edward Arnold

McLuhan, M. (1964) *Understanding Media*, London, Routledge & Kegan Paul

McMichael, P. (1996) *Development and Social Change: A Global Perspective*, Thousand Oaks, Pine Forge Press

McNair, B. (1994) *News and Journalism in the UK*, London, Routledge

McNamara, D. (1980) 'The outsider's arrogance: the failure of participant observation to understand classroom events', *British Education Research Journal*, 6: 113–25

McRobbie, A. (1982) 'Jackie: an ideology of adolescent femininity', in B. Waites, T. Bennet and G. Martin (eds), *Popular Culture: Past and Present*, London, Croom Helm

McRobbie, A. (1991) *Feminism and Youth Culture*, Basingstoke, Macmillan

McRobbie, A. (1994) *Postmodernism and Popular Culture*, London, Routledge

McRobbie, A. and Garber, J. (1976) 'Girls and subcultures: an exploration', in S. Hall and T. Jefferson (eds), *Resistance Through Rituals*, London, Hutchinson

Malseed, J. (1987) 'Straw-men: a note on Ann Oakley's treatment of text-book prescriptions for interviewing', *Sociology*, 21: 99–108

Mama, A. (1992) 'Black women and the British state: race, class and gender analysis for the 1990s', in P. Braham, A. Rattansi and R. Skellington (eds), *Racism and Anti-Racism*, Buckingham, Open University Press

Mander, J. and Goldsmith, E. (eds) (1996) *The Case Against the Global Economy*, San Francisco, Sierra Club Books

Mann, M. (1986), *The Sources of Social Power.* Vol. 1. *A History of Power to A.D. 1760*, Cambridge, Cambridge University Press

Mann, M. (1993) *The Sources of Social Power. Vol. II. The Rise of Classes and Nation-States, 1760–1914,* Cambridge, Cambridge University Press

Mansfield, P. and Collard, J. (1988) *The Beginning of the Rest of Your Life: A Portrait of Newly-Wed Marriage*, London, Macmillan

Marcuse, H. (1972) *One Dimensional Man*, London, Abacus

Marmot, M., Rose, G., Shipley, M. and Hamilton, P. (1978) 'Employment grade and coronary heart disease in British civil servants', *Journal of Epidemiology and Community Health,* 32: 659–74

Marsh, C. (1986) 'Social class and occupation', in R. Burgess (ed.), *Key Variables in Social Investigation*, London, Routledge

Marshall, G. (1988a) 'Classes in Britain', *European Sociological Review,* 4: 141–54

Marshall, G. (1988b) 'Some remarks on the study of working-class consciousness', in D. Rose (ed.), *Social Stratification and Economic Change,* London, Unwin Hyman

Marshall, G., Newby, H., Rose, D. and Vogler, C. (1988) *Social Class in Modern Britain*, London, Hutchinson

Marshall, G., Roberts, R. and Burgoyne, C. (1996) 'Social class and underclass in Britain and the USA', *British Journal of Sociology,* 47(1): 22–67

Marshall, G., Swift, A. and Roberts, S. (1997) *Against the Odds?,* Oxford, Clarendon Press

Marshall, T. (1950) *Citizenship and Social Class,* Cambridge, Cambridge University Press

Martin, D. (1978) *A General Theory of Secularization*, Oxford, Blackwell

Martin, D. (1990) *Tongues of Fire*, Oxford, Blackwell

Martin, D. (1991) 'The secularization issue. Prospect and retrospect', *British Journal of Sociology*, 42(3): 465–74

Martin, D. (1996) 'Remise en question de la théorie de la sécularisation', in G. Davie and D. Hervieu-Léger, *Identités Religieuses en Europe*, Paris, La Découverte

Martin, J., Meltzer, H. and Elliott, D. (1988) *The Prevalence of Disability Among Adults*, London, HMSO

Marty, M. (1988) 'Fundamentals of Fundamentalism', in L. Kaplan (ed.), *Fundamentalism in a Comparative Perspective*, Amherst, University of Massachussetts Press

Marty, M. (1989) 'Fundamentalisms compared', *The Charles Strong Memorial Lecture 1989*, published for the Charles Strong Trust by the Australian Association for the Study of Religion

Marx, K. (1957/1970) *Capital*. Vol. 1, London, Lawrence & Wishart

Marx, K. (1962) 'The 18th Brumaire of Louis Bonaparte' in K. Marx and F. Engels *Selected Works*, Moscow, Foreign Languages Publishing House

Marx, K. (1971) *A Contribution to a Critique of Political Economy*, London, Lawrence & Wishart

Marx, K. and Engels, F. (1962a) *Manifesto of the Communist Party in Selected Works*, Vol. 1, Moscow, Foreign Languages Publishing House

Marx, K. and Engels, F. (1962b) *Selected Works*. Vol. 1, London, Lawrence & Wishart

Marx, K. and Engels, F. (1964) *The German Ideology*, London, Lawrence & Wishart

Matthews, R. and Young, J. (eds) (1986) *Confronting Crime*, London, Sage

Matza, D. (1964) *Delinquency and Drift*, New York, Wiley

Matza, D. (1969) *Becoming Deviant*, Englewood Cliffs, Prentice Hall

Matza, D. and Sykes, G. (1961) 'Juvenile delinquency and subterranean values', *American Sociological Review*, 26: 712–19

Maynard, M. (1990) 'The re-shaping of sociology? Trends in the study of gender', *Sociology*, 24(2): 269–90

Maynard, M. (1995) 'Beyond the "Big Three": the development of feminist theory into the 1990s', *Women's History Review*, 4(30): 259–82

Maynard, M. and Winn, J. (1997) 'Women, violence and male power', in D. Richardson and V. Robinson (eds), *Introducing Women's Studies*, 2nd edn, London, Macmillan

Mays, J. (1954) *Growing Up in the City*, Liverpool, Liverpool University Press

Mays, J. (1959) *On the Threshold of Delinquency*, Liverpool, Liverpool University Press

Mead, H. (1934) *Mind, Self and Society*, Chicago, University of Chicago Press

Meador, C. (1994) 'The last well person', *The New England Journal of Medicine*, 330: 440–1

Measor, L. and Woods, P. (1984) *Changing Schools: Pupil Perspectives on Transfer to a Comprehensive*, Milton Keynes, Open University Press

Menter, I., Muschamp, Y., Nicholls, P., Ozga, J. and Pollard, A. (1997) *Work and Identity in the Primary School: A Post-Fordist Analysis*, Buckingham, Open University Press

Merton, R. (1938/1993) 'Social structure and anomie', in C. Lemert (ed.), *Social Theory: The Multicultural Readings*, Boulder, Westview Press

Merton, R. (1968) *Social Theory and Social Structure*, New York, Free Press

Meyer, M. (1984) 'Measuring performance in economic organizations', in N. Smelser and R. Swedberg (eds), *The Handbook of Economic Sociology*, pp. 556–78, Princeton, NJ, Princeton University Press

Michie, J. and Smith, J. (eds) (1995) *Managing the Global Economy*, Oxford, Oxford University Press

Mies, M. (1998) *Patriarchy and Accumulation on a World Scale: Women in the International Division of Labour*, London, Zed Press

Mies, M. (1994) ' "Gender" and global capitalism', in L. Sklair (ed.) *Capitalism and Development*, Chapter 6, London, Routledge

Miles, R. (1982) *Racism and Migrant Labour: A Critical Text*, London, Routledge

Miles, R. (1987) *Capitalism and Unfree Labour: Anomaly or Necessity?*, London, Tavistock

Miles, R. (1989) *Racism*, London and New York, Routledge

Miles, R. (1993) *Racism After 'Race Relations'*, London, Routledge

Miles, R. and Phizacklea, A. (1984) *White Man's Country: Racism in British Politics*, London, Pluto Press

Miles, R. and Thranhardt, D. (eds) (1995) *Migration and European Integration: the Dynamics of Inclusion and Exclusion*, London, Pinter

Miles, R. and Torres, R. (1996) 'Does "race" matter? Transatlantic perspectives on racism after "race relations"', in V. Amit-Talai and C. Knowles (eds), *Re-Situating Identities: The Politics of Race, Ethnicity and Culture*, Peterborough, Broadview Press

Miles, S. and Middleton, S.(1988) 'Girls education in the balance', in M. Flude and M. Hammer (eds) *The Education Reform Act: Its Origins and Destinations*, London, Falmer Press

Millar, J. (1994) 'State, family and personal responsibility: the changing balance for lone mothers in the United Kingdom', *Feminist Review*, **48**: 24–39

Mills, C. (1959) *The Power Elite*, New York, Oxford University Press

Mitter, S. (1986) *Common Fate, Common Bond*, London, Pluto Press

Mitter, S. (1991) 'Computer-aided manufacturing and women's employment: a global critique of post-Fordism', in I. Eriksson, B. Kitchenham and K. Tijdens (eds), *Women, Work and Computerization*, Amsterdam, North Holland

Mlinar, Z. (ed.) (1992) *Globalization and Territorial Identities*, Aldershot, Avebury

Modood, T. (1992) *Not Easy Being British: Colour, Culture and Citizenship*, London, Runnymede Trust and Trentham Books

Modood, T. (1994) 'Ethno-religious minorities, secularism and the British state', *British Political Quarterly*, **65**: 53–73

Moore, B. (1966) *The Social Origins of Dictatorship and Democracy* London: Penguin

Moores, S. (1990) 'Texts, readers and contexts of reading: developments in the study of media audiences', *Media, Culture and Society*, **12**(1): 9–30

Morgan, D. (1996) *Family Connections: An Introduction to Family Studies*, Cambridge, Polity

Morgan, G. (1997) 'The global context of financial services: national systems and the international political economy', in G. Morgan and D. Knights, *Regulation and Deregulation in European Financial Services*, pp. 14–51, London, Macmillan

Morgan, G. and Engwall, L. (eds) (1999) *Regulation and Organizations*, London, Routledge

Morgan, G. and Knights, D. (eds) (1997) *Regulation and Deregulation in European Financial Services*, London, Macmillan

Morgan, G. and Quack, S. (1999) 'Confidence and confidentiality: the social construction of performance standards in German and British banking', in S. Quack, G. Morgan and R. Whitley (eds), *National Capitalisms, Global Competition and Economic Performance*, Berlin, De Gruyter

Morley, D. (1980) *The Nationwide Audience: Structure and Decoding*, London, British Film Institute

Morley, D. (1986) *Family Television*, London, Comedia/Routledge

Morley, D. (1993) 'Active audience theory: pendulums and pitfalls', *Journal of Communication*, **43**: 13–19

Morris, L. (1990) *The Workings of the Household*, Cambridge, Polity

Morris, L. (1995) *Social Divisions*, London, University College London Press

Morris, T. (1957) *The Criminal Area: A Study in Social Ecology*, London, Routledge & Kegan Paul

Morrow, V. (1994) 'Responsible children? Aspects of children's work and employment ourside school in contemporary UK', in B. Mayal (ed.), *Children's Childhoods: Observed and Experienced*, London, Falmer

Mortimore, P. and Whitty, G. (1997) 'Can school improvement overcome the effects of disadvantage?' Institute of Education

Mouzelis, N. (1991) *Back to Sociological Theory*, Basingstoke, Macmillan

Mouzelis, N. (1995) *Sociological Theory: What Went Wrong?*, London, Routledge
Mullins, P. (1991) 'The identification of social forces in development', *International Journal of Urban and Regional Research*, **15**(1): 119–26
Murray, C. (1990) *The Emerging British Underclass*, London, IEA Health and Welfare Unit
Myrdal, A. and Klein, V. (1956) *Women's Two Roles: Home and Work*, London, Routledge & Kegan Paul
Nash, J. and Fernandez-Kelly, M. (eds) (1983) *Women, Men, and the International Division of Labor*, Albany, NY: SUNY Press
National Commission on Education (eds) (1996) *Success Against the Odds*, London, Routledge
Navarro, V. (1975) 'The industrialisation of fetishism and the fetishism of industrialisation: a critique of Ivan Illich', *International Journal of Health Services*, **5**: 351–71
Navarro, V. (1978) *Class Struggle, the State and Medicine: An Historical and Contemporary Analysis of the Medical Sector in Great Britain*, London, Martin Robertson
Nazroo, J. (1995) 'Uncovering gender differences in the use of marital violence: the effects of methodology', *Sociology*, **29**(3): 475–94
Neale, B. and Smart, C. (1997) 'Experiments with parenthood?', *Sociology*, **31**(2): 201–20
Negrine, R. (1996) *The Communication of Politics*, London, Sage
Newburn, T. (1997) 'Youth, crime and justice', in R. Maguire, R. Morgan and R. Reiner (eds), *The Oxford Handbook of Criminology*, Oxford, Clarendon
Newman, O. (1972) *Defensible Space*, London, Architectural Press
Niebuhr, R. and Linder, R. (1988) *Civil Religion and the Presidency*, Grand Rapids, Zondervan
Nordenstreng, K. (1977) 'From mass media to mass consciousness', in G. Gerbner (ed.), *Mass Media Policies in Changing Cultures*, New York, Wiley
Nordenstreng, K. and Schiller, H. (eds) (1993) *Beyond National Sovereignty: International Communications in the 1990s*, Norwood, Ablex
Oakley, A. (1974) *The Sociology of Housework*, Oxford, Martin Robertson
Oakley, A. (1981) 'Interviewing women: a contradiction in terms', in H. Roberts (ed.), *Doing Feminist Research*, London, Routledge
Oakley, A. (1984) *The Sociology of Housework*, 2nd edn, Oxford, Blackwell
Oakley, A. (1984) *The Captured Womb: A History of the Medical Care of Pregnant Women*, Oxford, Blackwell
Offe, C. (1985) 'Work – a central sociological category?', in C. Offe (ed.), *Disorganized Capitalism*, Cambridge, Polity
Office for National Statistics (1997) *Social Trends*, 27, London, The Stationery Office
Office of Population, Censuses and Surveys (1996) *Living in Britain: Results from the General Household Survey*, London, HMSO
Office of Science and Technology (1995) *Technology Foresight Panel 14: Progress through Partnership – Leisure and Learning*, London, HMSO
Oliver, M. (1996) *Understanding Disability: From Theory to Practice*, London, Macmillan
Orru, M., Biggart, N. and Hamilton, G. (1997) *The Economic Organisation of East Asian Capitalism*, London, Sage
Osborne, T. (1997) 'Medicine and the body', in D. Owen (ed.) *Sociology after Postmodernism*, London, Sage
Owen, D. (1994) 'Black people in Great Britain: social and economic circumstances', *National Ethnic Minority Data Archive*, Centre for Research in Ethnic Relations, **1**
Pahl, J. (1989) *Money and Marriage*, London, Macmillan
Pahl, R. (1989) 'Is the Emperor naked?', *International Journal of Urban and Regional Research*, **13**(4): 711–20

Pahl, R. (ed.) (1988) *On Work: Historical, Comparative and Theoretical Approaches,* Oxford, Blackwell

Pakulski, J. (1993) 'The dying of class or of Marxist class theory?', *International Sociology,* **8**(3): 279–92

Panic, M. (1995) 'The Bretton Woods system: concept and practice', in J. Michie and J. Smith (eds), *Managing the Global Economy,* pp. 37–54, Oxford, Oxford University Press

Parker, A. (1996) 'The construction of masculinity within boys' physical education', *Gender and Education,* **8**(2): 141–57

Parker, H. (1974) *The View From The Boys,* Newton Abbott, David & Charles

Parry, O. (1996) 'Equality, gender and the Caribbean classroom', *21st Century Policy Review Special Issue: Institutional Development in the Caribbean*

Parsons, T. (1951) *The Social System,* New York, Free Press

Parsons, T. (1954) 'Social classes and class conflict in the light of recent sociological theory', in T. Parsons, (ed.), *Essays in Sociological Theory,* New York, Free Press

Parsons, T. (1961) 'The school class as a social system: some of its functions in American society', in A. Halsey, P. Broadfoot, P. Croll, M. Osborn and D. Abbott (eds) *Education, Economy, and Society,* pp. 434–55, London, Collier Macmillan

Parsons, T. (1967) *Sociological Theory and Modern Society,* New York, Free Press

Parsons, T. (1969a) 'The distribution of power in American society', in T. Parsons (ed.), *Politics and Social Structure,* pp. 185–203, New York, The Free Press

Parsons, T. (1969b) 'On the concept of political power', in T. Parsons (ed.), *Politics and Social Structure,* pp. 352–404, New York, The Free Press

Parsons, T. (1971) *The System of Modern Societies,* New York, Prentice Hall

Parsons, T. (1978) 'The sick role and the role of the physician reconsidered', in T. Parsons (ed.), *Action Theory and the Human Condition,* New York, Free Press

Parsons, T. and Bales, R. (1956) *Family: Socialization and Interaction Process,* London, Routledge & Kegan Paul

Parsons, T. and Shils, E. (1962) *Towards a General Theory of Action,* New York, Harper & Row

Pawson, R. (1993) 'Social mobility', in D. Morgan and L. Stanley (eds), *Debates in Sociology,* Manchester, Manchester University Press

Pawson, R. (1996) 'Theorizing the interview', *British Journal of Sociology,* **47**: 295–314

Pawson, R. and Tilley, N. (1996) *Realistic Evaluation,* London, Sage

Peach, C. (1968) 'West Indian migration to Britain: the economic factor', *Race,* 7(1): 31–47

Pearson, G. (1983) *Hooligan: A History of Respectable Fears,* Basingstoke, Macmillan

Perlmutter, H. (1991) 'On the rocky road to the first gloabl civilization', *Human Relations,* **44**(9): 897–1010

Phillipson, C. (1982) *Capitalism and the Construction of Old Age,* London, Methuin

Phizacklea, A. and Wolkowitz, C. (1995) *Homeworking Women,* London, Sage

Phoenix, A. (1990) *Young Mothers?,* Cambridge, Polity

Piérard, R. and Linder, R. (1988) *Civil Religion and the Presidency,* Grand Rapids, Zondervan

Pilgrim, A. and Rogers, A. (1993) *A Sociology of Mental Health and Illness,* Buckingham, Open University Press

Piore, M. and Sabel, C. (1984) *The Second Industrial Divide,* New York, Basic Books

Platt, A. (1978) 'Street crime: a view from the left', *Crime and Social Justice,* 9

Pollard, A., Broadfoot, P., Croll, P., Osborn, M. and Abbott, D. (1994) *Changing English Primary Schools,* London, Cassell

Pollert, A. (1981) *Girls, Wives, Factory Lives,* London, Macmillan

Polsby, N. (1963) *Community Power and Political Theory,* New Haven and London, Yale University Press

Polsby, N. (1980) *Community Power and Political Theory: A Further Look at Problems of Evidence and Inference*, New Haven and London, Yale University Press

Portes, A. and Castells, M. (eds) (1989) *The Informal Sector*, Baltimore, Johns Hopkins University Press

Poster, M. (1990) *The Mode of Information: Poststructuralism and Social Context*, Chicago, University of Chicago Press

Poulantzas, N. (1975) *Classes in Contemporary Capitalism*, London, New Left Books

Prior, L. (1998) 'The identification of cases in psychiatry', in D. Field and S. Taylor, *Sociological Perspectives on Health, Illness and Health Care*, Oxford, Blackwell Science

Qualifications and Curriculum Authority (1998) *Maintaining Breadth and Balance at Key Stages 1 and 2*, London, QCA

Quack, S., Morgan G. and Whitley, R. (eds) (1999) *National Capitalisms, Global Competition and Economic Performance*, Berlin, De Gruyter

Rabinow, P. (1989) *French Modern: Norms and Forms of the Social Environment*, Cambridge, MA, MIT Press

Radway, J. (1984) *Reading the Romance: Women, Patriarchy and Popular Literature*, Chapel Hill, University of North Carolina Press

Rahman, M. and Jackson, S. (1997) 'Liberty, equality and sexuality: essentialism and the discourse of rights', *Journal of Gender Studies*, 6(2): 117–29

Rakow, L. (ed.) (1992) *Women Making Meaning: New Feminist Directions In Communication*, London, Routledge

Ramazanoglu, C. (1989) *Feminism and the Contradictions of Oppression*, London, Routledge

Ramazanoglu, C. (1995) 'Back to basics: heterosexuality, biology and why men stay on top', in M. Maynard and J. Purvis (eds), *(Hetero)sexual Politics*, London, Taylor & Francis

Randall, G. (1987) 'Gender differences in pupil–teacher interaction in workshops and laboratories', in G. Weiner and M. Arnot (eds) *Gender and the Politics of Schooling*, London, Hutchinson

Randall, V. and Waylen, G. (eds) (1998) *Gender, Politics and the State*, London, Routledge

Rattansi, A. (1982) *Marx and the Division of Labour*, London, Macmillan

Rattansi, A. and Westwood, S. (eds) (1994) *Racism, Modernity and Identity on the Western Front*, Cambridge, Polity

Ray, L. (1993) *Rethinking Critical Theory: Emancipation in the Age of Global Social Movements*, London, Sage

Redclift, M. and Benton, T. (eds) (1994) *Social Theory and the Global Environment*, London, Routledge

Rees, T. (1992) *Women and the Labour Market*, London, Routledge

Rees, T. (1998) *Mainstreaming Equality in the European Union*, London, Routledge

Rex, J. (1970) *Race Relations in Sociological Theory*, London, Weidenfeld & Nicolson

Rich, A. (1980) 'Compulsory heterosexuality and lesbian existence', *Signs*, 5(4), 631–60

Richardson, D. (1993) *Women, Motherhood and Childrearing*, Basingstoke, Macmillan

Richardson, D. (ed.) (1996) *Theorising Heterosexuality: Telling it Straight*, Buckingham, Open University Press

Richardson, J. (1995) 'Minority religions, religious freedom and the new Pan-European political and judicial institutions', *Journal of Church and State*, 37(1): 40–59

Riddell, S. (1992) *Gender and the Politics of the Curriculum*, London, Routledge

Riley, K. (1994) *Quality and Equality: Promoting Opportunities in Schools*, London, Cassell

Ritzer, G. (1995) *The McDonaldization of Society*, 2nd edn, Thousand Oaks, Pine Forge Press

Robbins, D. (1987) 'Sport, hegemony and the middle class', *Theory, Culture and Society*, 4(4): 579–602

Robertson Elliot, F. (1996) *Gender, Family and Society*, London, Macmillan

Robertson, R. (1992) *Globalization: Social Theory and Global Culture*, London, Sage

Robinson, I. (1988) 'Reconstructing lives: negotiating the meaning of multiple sclerosis', in M. Bury and R. Anderson (eds), *Living with Chronic Illness: The Experiences of Patients and Their Families,* London, Unwin Hyman

Robinson, W. (1996) 'Globalisation: nine theses on our epoch', *Race and Class* 38(2): 13–31

Robinson, W. (1998) '(Mal)development in Central America: globalization and social change' *Development and Change,* 29: 467–97

Rock, P. (1979) 'The sociology of crime, symbolic interactionism and some problematic qualities of radical criminology', in D. Downes and P. Rock (eds), *Deviant Interpretations,* Oxford, Martin Robertson

Rock, P. (1990) *Helping Victims of Crime,* Oxford, Clarendon Press

Roediger, D. (1996) *Towards the Abolition of Whiteness*, London, Verso

Roethliberger, F. and Dickson, W. (1939) *Management and the Worker*, Cambridge, Harvard University Press

Rose, N. (1990) *Governing the Soul: the Shaping of the Private Self*, London, Routledge

Rose, N. (1995) 'Towards a critical sociology of freedom', in P. Joyce (ed.), *Class*, pp. 213–24, Oxford, Oxford University Press

Rose, N. (1996) 'Governing "advanced" liberal democracies', in A. Barry, T. Osborne and N. Rose (eds), *Foucault and Political Reason. Liberalism, Neo-liberalism and Rationalities of Government*, pp. 37–64, Chicago, University of Chicago Press

Rose, N. and Miller, P. (1992) 'Political power beyond the State: problematics of government', *British Journal of Sociology*, 43(2): 173–205

Ross, R. and Trachte, K. (1990) *Global Capitalism: The New Leviathan*, Albany, NY, State University of New York Press

Ruigrok, W. and Van Tulder, R. (1995) *The Logic of International Restructuring,* London, Routledge

Russell, D. (1982) *Rape in Marriage,* New York, Macmillan

Russell, D. (1984) *Sexual Exploitation,* Newbury Park, Sage

Sabel, C. and Zeitlin, J. (1997) *Worlds of Possibility: Flexibility and Mass Production in Western Industrialization,* Cambridge, Cambridge University Press

Sainsbury, D. (ed.) (1994) *Gendering Welfare States*, London, Sage

Sako, M. and Sato, H. (eds) (1997) *Japanese Labour and Management in Transition,* London, Routledge

Sarup, M. (1993) *An Introductory Guide to Post-Structuralism and Postmodernism*, London, Harvester/Wheatsheaf

Sassen, S. (1994) *Cities in a World Economy*, Thousand Oaks, CA, Pine Forge Press

Saunders, P. (1987) *Social Theory and the Urban Question,* London, Unwin Hyman

Savage, M. (1996) 'Class analysis and social research', in T. Butler and M. Savage (eds), *Social Change and the Middle Classes,* London, UCL Press

Savage, M., Barlow, J., Dickens, A. and Fielding, T. (1992) *Property, Bureaucracy, and Culture,* London, Routledge

Scambler, G. and Hopkins, A. (1986) 'Being epileptic: coming to terms with illness', *Sociology of Health and Illness,* 8: 26–43

Scambler, G., Scambler, A. and Craig, D. (1984) 'Kinship and friendship networks and women's demand for primary care', *Journal of the Royal College of General Practitioners,* 26: 746–50

Scheff, T. (1966) *Being Mentally Ill: A Sociological Theory,* Chicago, Aldine

Schiller, H. (1989) *Culture Inc.: The Corporate Takeover of Public Expression*, London, Oxford University Press

Schiller, H. (1991) 'Not yet the post-imperialist era', *Critical Studies in Mass Communication*, **8**: 13–28

Schlesinger, P. (1990) 'Rethinking the sociology of journalism: source strategies and the limits of media centrism', in M. Ferguson (ed.), *Public Communication: The New Imperatives – Future Directions for Media Research*, pp. 84–100, London, Sage

Schutz, A. (1972) *Phenomenology of the Social World*, London, Heinemann

Schutz, A. and Luckmann, T. (1974) *The Structures of the Life World*, London, Heinemann

Scott, A. (ed.) (1997) *The Limits of Globalization*, London, Routledge

Scott, J. (1982) *The Upper Classes*, Cambridge, Polity

Scott, J. (1991) *Who Rules Britain?*, Cambridge, Polity

Scott, J. (1995) *Sociological Theory: Contemporary Debates*, London, Edward Elgar

Scott, J. (1997) *Corporate Business and Capitalist Classes*, Oxford, Oxford University Press

Scott, J. and Morris, L. (1996) 'The attenuation of class analysis', *British Journal of Sociology*, 7(2): 134–46

Scott, R. (1969) *The Making of Blind Men*, Hartford, Russell Sage

Scott, S., Jackson, S. and Backett-Milburn, K. (1998) 'Swings and roundabouts: risk, anxiety and the everyday worlds of children', *Sociology*, **32**(4)

Scull, A. (1993) *The Most Solitary of Afflictions: Madness and Society in Britain, 1700–1900*, New Haven, Yale University Press

Seale, C. (1994) 'Medicalisation and surveillance', in C. Seale and S. Pattinson (eds), *Medical Knowledge: Doubt and Certainty*, Buckingham, Open University Press

Secretary of State for Health and Social Services (1992) *The Health of The Nation: A Strategy for Health in England*, London, HMSO

Sevenhuijsen, S. (1998) *Citizenship and the Ethics of Care*, London, Routledge

Sewell, T. (1997) *Black Masculinities and Schooling: How Black Boys Survive Modern Schooling*, Stoke-on-Trent, Trentham Books

Shannon, T. (1989) *An Introduction to the World-System Perspective*, Boulder, Westview

Sharpe, S. (1994) *Just Like a Girl'. How Girls Learn to be Women: From the Seventies to the Nineties*, London, Penguin

Siltanen, J. (1994) *Locating Gender: Occupational Segregation, Wages and Domestic Responsibilities*, London, UCL Press

Silverman, D. (1985) *Qualitative Method and Sociology*, Aldershot, Gower

Sivanandan, A. (1990) *Communities of Resistance. Writings on Black Struggles for Socialism*, London and New York, Verso

Skelton, C. (1997) 'Women and education', in D. Richardson and V. Robinson (eds), *Introducing Women's Studies*, 2nd edn, London, Macmillan

Sklair, L. (1991) *Sociology of the Global System*, London, Harvester/Wheatsheaf

Sklair, L. (1994a) 'Global sociology and global environmental change', in M. Redclift and T. Benton, op. cit., Chapter 10

Sklair, L. (ed.) (1994b) *Capitalism and Development*, London, Routledge

Sklair, L. (1995) *Sociology of the Global System*, 2nd edn, Prentice Hall and Baltimore, Johns Hopkins University Press

Sleegers, P. and Wesselingh, A. (1993) 'Decentralisation in education: a Dutch study', *International Studies in Sociology of Education*, 3(1): 49–67

Small, S. (1994) *Racialised Barriers: The Black Experience in the United States and England*, New York and London, Routledge

Smart, C. (1976) *Women, Crime and Criminology: A Feminist Critique*, London, Routledge & Kegan Paul

Smart, C. (1989a) 'Power and the politics of child custody', in C. Smart and S. Sevenhuijsen, *Child Custody and the Politics of Gender*, London, Routledge

Smart, C. (1989b) *Feminism and the Power of the Law*, London, Routledge

Smelser, N. and Swedberg, R. (eds) (1994) *The Handbook of Economic Sociology,* Princeton, NJ, Princeton University Press

Smith, C. (1990) *Auctions: The Social Construction of Value,* Berkeley, University of California Press

Smith, C. and Meiskins, P. (1995) 'System, society and dominance effects in cross-national organizational analysis', *Work, Employment and Society,* **9**(2): 241–67

Smith, D. and Gray, J. (1987) *Police and People in London,* Aldershot, Gower

Smith, J. (1995) 'The first intruder: fatherhood, a historical perspective', in P. Moss (ed.), *Father Figures: Fathers in the Families of the 1990s,* London, HMSO

Solomos, J. and Back, L. (1995) *Race, Politics and Social Change,* London and New York, Routledge

Song, M. (1996) '"Helping out": children's participation in Chinese take-away businesses in Britain', in J. Brannen and M. O'Brien (eds), *Children in Families,* London, Falmer

Spender, D. (1983) *Invisible Women: the Schooling Scandle,* London, Women's Press

Spender, D. (1995) *Nattering on the Net: Women, Power and Cyberspace,* Melbourne, Spinifex

Spybey, T. (1996) *Globalization and World Society,* Cambridge, Polity

Sreberny-Mohammadi, A. (1991) 'The global and the local in international communications', in J. Curran and M. Gurevitch (eds), *Mass Media and Society,* London, Edward Arnold

Stacey, M. (ed.) (1992) *Changing Human Reproduction,* London, Sage

Stallings, B. (ed.) (1995) *Global Change, Regional Response,* Cambridge, Cambridge University Press

Stanley, L. and Wise, S. (1990) 'Method, methodology and epistemology in feminist research', in L. Stanley (ed.), *Feminist Praxis,* London, Routledge

Stanworth, M. (1983) *Gender and Schooling,* London, Hutchinson

Stanworth, M. (1984) 'Women and class analysis', *Sociology,* **18**(2): 159–70

Star, S. (1996) 'From Hestia to home page: feminism and the concept of home in cyberspace', in N. Lykke and R. Braidotti (eds), *Between Monsters, Goddesses and Cyborgs: Feminist Confrontations With Science, Medicine and Cyberspace,* London, Zed

Steggarda (1993) 'Religion and the social positions of women and men', *Social Compass,* **40**(1): 65–73

Stobart, G., Elwood J. and Quinlan M. (1992) 'Gender bias in exams: how equal are the opportunities?', *British Education Research Journal,* **18**(3): 261–76

Storey, J. (1993) *An Introductory Guide to Cultural Theory and Popular Culture,* London, Wheatsheaf

Storey, J., Edwards, P. and Sisson, K. (1997) *Managers in the Making: Careers, Development and Control in Corporate Britain and Japan,* London, Sage

Strange, S. (1986) *Casino Capitalism,* Oxford, Blackwell

Strange, S. (1995) 'From Bretton Woods to the Casino Economy', in S. Corbridge, N. Thrift and R. Martin (eds), *Money, Space, Power,* pp. 49–62, Oxford, Blackwell

Strathern, M. (1992) *Reproducing the Future: Anthropology, Kinship and the New Reproductive Technologies,* Manchester, Manchester University Press

Straubhaar, J. (1997) 'Distinguishing the global, regional and national levels of world television', in A. Sreberny-Mohammadi, D. Winseck, J. McKenna and O. Boyd-Barrett (eds), *Media in Global Context: A Reader,* London, Arnold

Streeck, W. (1992) *Social Institutions and Economic Performance,* London, Sage

Strinati, D. (1995) *An Introduction to Theories of Popular Culture,* London, Routledge

Stubbs, R. and Underhill, G. (eds) (1994) *Political Economy and the Changing Global Order,* London, Macmillan

Sudbury, J. (1997) Other Kinds of Dreams: Black Women's Organisations and the Politics of Transformation. Unpublished PhD in Sociology, University of Warwick

Sullivan, O. (1997) 'Time waits for no (wo)man: an investigation into the gendered experience of domestic time', *Sociology*, **31**(2): 221–40

Sumner, C. (1994) *The Sociology of Deviance: An Obituary*, Buckingham, Open University Press

Sussman, G. and Lent, J. (eds) (1991) *Transnational Communications: Wiring the Third World*, London, Sage

Swatos, W. (ed.) (1993) *A Future for Religion*, London, Sage

Swedberg, R. (1994) 'Markets as social structures', in N. Smelser and R. Swedberg (eds), *The Handbook of Economic Sociology*, pp. 255–82, Princeton, NJ, Princeton University Press

Sykes, G. and Matza, D. (1957) 'Techniques of neutralisation: a theory of delinquency', *American Sociological Review*, **22**: 664–70

Sztompka, P. (1994) *The Sociology of Social Change*, Oxford, Blackwell

Taylor, C. (1986) 'Foucault on freedom and truth', in D. Hoy (ed.), *Foucault: a Critical Reader*, pp. 69–102, Oxford, Blackwell

Taylor, I., Walton P. and Young, J. (1973) *The New Criminology: For a Social Theory of Deviance*, London, Routledge & Kegan Paul

Thomas, W. (1976) 'The definition of the situation', in L. Coser and B. Rosenberg, *Sociological Theory*, 4th edn, New York, Macmillan

Thompson, E. (1968) *The Making of the English Working Class*, London, Penguin

Thompson, J. (1990) *Ideology and Modern Culture*, Cambridge, Polity

Thorne, B. (1987) 'Revisioning women and social change: where are the children?' *Gender and Society*, **1**(1): 85–109

Thorogood, N. (1987) 'Race, class and gender: the politics of housework', in J. Brannen and G. Wilson (eds), *Give and Take in Families: Studies in Resource Distribution*, London, Allen & Unwin

Tinker, I. (ed.) (1990) *Persistent Inequalities: Women and World Development*, New York, Oxford University Press

Torrance, H. (1997) 'Assessment, accountability and standards: using assessment to control the reform of schooling', in A. Halsey, H. Lauder, P. Brown. and A. Stuart-Wells (eds) *Education: Culture, Economy, Society*, pp. 320–31, Oxford, Oxford University Press

Touraine, A. (1981) *The Voice and the Eye: An Analysis of Social Movements*, Cambridge, Cambridge University Press

Townsend, P., Davidson, N. and Whitehead, M. (1988) *Inequalities in Health: The Black Report/The Health Divide*, London, Penguin

Townsend, P., Phillimore, P. and Beattie, A. (1988) *Health and Deprivation: Inequality and the North*, London, Croom Helm

Troyna, B. (1993) *Racism and Education*, Buckingham, Open University Press

Troyna, B. and Hatcher, R. (1992) *Racism in Children's Lives: A Study of Mainly-white Primary Schools*, London, Routledge

Tuchman, G., Kaplan Daniels, A. and Benet, J. (1978) *Hearth and Home: Images of Women and the Media*, Oxford, Oxford University Press

Tuckett, D., Boulton, M., Olson, C. and Williams, A. (1985) *Meetings Between Experts*, London, Tavistock

Tudor, A. (1995) 'Culture, mass communication and social agency', *Theory, Culture and Society*, **12**: 81–107

Tunstall, J. (1971) *Journalists at Work*, London, Constable

Turner, B. (1995) *Medical Power and Social Knowledge*, 2nd edn, London, Sage

Underhill, G. (ed.) (1997) *The New World Order in International Finance*, London, Macmillan

UNESCO (1989) *World Communication Report*, Paris, UNESCO

Ungerson, C. and Kember, M. (eds) (1997) *Women and Social Policy*, 2nd edn, London, Macmillan

United Nations (1993) *World Investment Report*, New York, UNCTAD

United Nations Development Programme (1993) *Human Development Report 1993*, Oxford, Oxford University Press

Urry, J. (1996) 'A middle-class countryside?', in T. Butler and M. Savage (eds), *Social Change and the Middle Classes*, London, University College London Press

Usher, R. and Edwards, R. (1994) *Postmodernism and Education*, London, Routledge

Van der Wee, H. (1991) *Prosperity and Upheaval in the World Economy 1945–1980*, London, Penguin

Van Every, J. (1995) *Heterosexual Women Changing the Family: Refusing to be a 'Wife'!*, London, Taylor & Francis

van Zoonen, L. (1994) *Feminist Media Studies*, London, Sage

van Zoonen L. (1996) 'Feminist perspectives on the media', in J. Curran and M. Gurevitch (eds), *Mass Media and Society*, London, Arnold

Wade, R. (1990) *Governing the Market*, Princeton, NJ, Princeton University Press

Walby, S. (1986) *Patriarchy at Work*, Cambridge, Polity

Walby, S. (1990) *Theorizing Patriarchy*, Oxford, Blackwell

Walby, S. (1997) *Gendered Transformations*, London, Routledge

Wallerstein, I. (1979) *The Capitalist World-Economy*, Cambridge, Cambridge University Press

Wallerstein, I. (1991) 'The construction of peoplehood: racism,nationalism, ethnicity', in E. Balibar and I. Wallerstein (eds) *'Race', Nation, Class*, London, Verso

Wallis, R. and Bruce, S. (1989) 'Religion: the British contribution', *British Journal of Sociology*, **40**(3): 439–519

Walter, A. (1990) *Funerals and How to Improve Them*, London, Hodder & Stoughton

Walter, A. (1994) *The Revival of Death*, London, Routledge

Walter, A. (1996) *The Eclipse of Eternity*, London, Macmillan

Walter, A. and Davie, G. (1998) 'The religiosity of women in the modern West', *British Journal of Sociology*, **49**(4): 640–60

Walton, A. (1994) *The Revival of Death*, London, Routledge

Walton, A. (1995) *The Eclipse of Eternity*, London, Macmillan

Wartenberg, T.E. (1990) *The Forms of Power: From Domination to Transformation*, Philadelphia, Temple University Press

Waters, M. (1995) *Globalization*, London, Routledge

Watson, J. (ed.) (1977) *Between Two Cultures*, Oxford, Basil Blackwell

Weber, M. (1922/1963) *The Sociology of Religion*, London, Beacon Press

Weber, M. (1948a) 'Class, status and party', in H. Gerth and C. Mills (eds), *From Max Weber: Essays in Sociology*, London, Routledge & Kegan Paul

Weber, M. (1948b) 'The social psychology of the world religions', in H. Gerth and C. Wright Mills, *Essays from Max Weber*, London, Routledge & Kegan Paul

Weber, M. (1948c) *From Max Weber*, in C. Mills (ed.), London, Routledge

Weber, M. (1976) *The Protestant Ethic and the Spirit of Capitalism*, (Talcott Parsons tr.), London, Allen & Unwin

Weber, M. (1978) *Economy and Society. An Outline of Interpretive Sociology*, Berkeley, University of California Press

Weiner, G. (1994) *Feminism in Education: An Introduction*, Buckingham, Open University Press

Weiner, G. *et al.* (1997) 'Is the future female? Success, male disadvantage, and changing gender patterns in education', in A. Halsey, H. Lauder, P. Brown and A. Stuart-Wells (eds) *Education: Culture, Economy, Society*, pp. 620–30, Oxford, Oxford University Press

Weiss, L. (1998) *The Myth of the Powerless State*, Oxford, Polity

Weiss, L. and Hobson, J. (1995) *States and Economic Development*, Oxford, Polity

Westergaard, J. (1995) *Who Gets What? The Hardening of Class Inequality in the Late Twentieth Century*, Cambridge, Polity

Weston, K. (1991) *Families We Choose: Lesbians, Gays, Kinship*, New York, Columbia University Press

Westwood, S. (1984) *All Day Every Day: Factory and Family in Women's Lives*, London, Pluto Press

Westwood, S. and Bhachu, P. (eds) (1988) *Enterprising Women: Ethnicity, Economy and Gender Relations*, London, Routledge

Whelan, C. (1993) 'The role of social support in mediating the psychological consequences of economic stress', *Sociology of Health and Illness*, 15: 86–101

Whitley, R. (1992) *East Asian Business Systems*, London, Sage

Whitley, R. and Kristensen, P. (eds) (1996) *The Changing European Firm*, London, Routledge

Whitley, R. and Kristensen, P. (eds) (1997) *Governance at Work*, Oxford, Oxford University Press

Whitty, G. (1997a) 'Marketisation, the state, and the re-formation of the teaching profession', in A. Halsey, H. Lauder, P. Brown and A. Stuart-Wells (eds) *Education: Culture, Economy, Society*, pp. 299–310, Oxford, Oxford University Press

Whitty, G. (1997b) 'Education policy and the sociology of education', *International Studies in Sociology of Education*, 7(2): 121–35

Willaime, J.-P. (1995) *Sociologie des Religions*, Paris, Presses Universitaires de France

Williams, G. (1984) 'The genesis of chronic illness: narrative reconstruction', *Sociology of Health and Illness* 6: 175–200

Williams, D. and House, J. (1991) 'Stress, social support, control and coping: an epidemiological view', in B. Badura and I. Kickbusch, *Health Promotion Research*, Copenhagen, World Health Organisation

Williams, G., Fitzpatrick, R., MacGregor, A. and Rigby, A. (1996) 'Rheumatoid arthritis', in B. Dave and C. Seale (eds), *Experiencing and Explaining Disease*, Buckingham, Open University Press

Williams, S. (1993) *Chronic Respiratory Disorder*, London, Routledge

Williams, S. and Calnan, M. (1996) 'The "limits" of demedicalisation: modern medicine and the lay populace in "late" modernity', *Social Science and Medicine*, 42: 1609–20

Willis, P. (1977) *Learning to Labour*, London, Sage

Wilson, B. (1982) *Religion in Sociological Perspective*, Oxford, Oxford University Press

Wilson, H. (1980) 'Parental supervision: a neglected aspect of delinquency', *British Journal of Criminology*, 20: 203–35

Wilson, H. and Herbert, G. (1978) *Parents, Children and the Inner City*, London, Routledge & Kegan Paul

Wilson, J. (1975) *Thinking About Crime*, New York, Vintage

Wilson, J. (1987) *The Truly Disadvantaged*, Chicago, University of Chicago Press

Wilson, J. (1993) *The Ghetto Underclass*, London, Sage

Wilson, J. and Kelling, G. (1982) 'Broken windows', *The Atlantic Monthly*, March, 29–38

Wilson, W. (1996) *When Work Disappears*, New York, Knopf

Witz, A. (1997) 'Women at work', in D. Richardson and V. Robinson (eds), *Introducing Women's Studies*, 2nd edn, London, Macmillan

Wolffe, J. (1993) 'The religions of the silent majority', in G. Parsons (ed.), *The Growth of Religious Diversity*, Vol. 1, *Traditions*, London, Routledge

World Bank (1996) *World Development Report*, Oxford, Oxford University Press

World Resources Institute (1994) *World Resources 1992–93: A Guide to the Global Environment*, New York, Oxford University Press

Wright, C. (1986) 'School processes: an ethnographic study', in J. Eggleston, D. Dunn and M. Anjali (eds) *Education for Some*, Stoke-on-Trent, Trentham Books

Wright, C. (1992) 'Early education: multi-racial primary school classrooms', in D. Gill, B. Mayor and M. Blair (eds) *Racism and Education*, London, Sage

Wright, E. (1976) 'Class boundaries in advanced capitalist societies', *New Left Review*, **98**

Wright, E. (1980) 'Class and occupation', *Theory and Society*, **9**(1): 177–214

Wright, E. (1985) *Classes*, London, Verso

Wright, E. (ed.) (1989) *The Debate on Classes*, London, Verso

Wright, E. (1997) *Class Counts*, Cambridge, Cambridge University Press

Wrong, D. (1988) *Power. Its Forms, Bases and Uses*, 2nd edn, Chicago, University of Chicago Press

Yearley, S. (1996) *Sociology, Environmentalism, Globalization: Reinventing the Globe*, London, Sage

Young, M. and Wilmott, P. (1962) *Family and Kinship in East London*, Harmondsworth, Penguin

Young, M. (ed.) (1971) *Knowledge and Control*, London, Collier Macmillan

Young, M. and Wilmott, P. (1973) *The Symmetrical Family*, Harmondsworth, Penguin

Zaretsky, E. (1976) *Capitalism, The Family and Personal Life*, London, Pluto Press

Zelizer, V. (1994) *The Social Meaning of Money*, New York, Basic Books

Index